What Educators and Parents Are Saying About The Spalding

"The strength of The Spalding Method is that children quickly learn the skills of reading, enabling them to understand and enjoy good literature at an early age. Spalding is effective because the principles and methods of instruction are well grounded in reading research, as appropriate for individuals with dyslexia and other language-based reading disorders as for students in regular classrooms."

> Sylvia Richardson, MD, LittD (Honorary)
> Distinguished Professor of Communication Sciences and Disorders,
>   Clinical Professor of Pediatrics, Emerita
> University of South Florida, Tampa, Florida

"Working with a multidisciplinary team, I use The Spalding Method to help children struggling to read because of specific learning disabilities or inadequate instruction. *The Writing Road to Reading* is a powerful tool for professionals because it is based on knowledge of how the brain works, coupled with sound educational principles. The Spalding Method changes lives: not only do students gain in literacy and self-confidence, but success with literacy is linked to good social and emotional adjustment and strong vocational outcomes."

> Carol Margeson, PhD
> Clinical Psychologist
> Sydney, Australia

"Romalda Spalding's *The Writing Road to Reading* is a total language arts method that captures all the richness and variety of the English language. For over fifty years classroom teachers across America have found that it works with all students. . . . I enthusiastically endorse The Spalding Method because I know that if it were taught in every classroom, illiteracy would vanish."

> Robert Sweet
> Former professional staff member, Committee on Education and the Workforce
> United States Congress

"Despite having a master's degree in learning disabilities, I was not successful in teaching my special education students (many of whom were dyslexic) what they most wanted to learn—how to read—until I took my first Spalding course in 1985. Since that time, I have seen many angry, withdrawn, or depressed students become eager, participating learners because they finally understand how English works. As I continue to teach students who are falling through the cracks of our educational system, I know that I will never stop using this wonderful method."

> Eileen Oliver
> Retired special education teacher
> Birmingham, Alabama

"*The Writing Road to Reading* program provides language instruction at the sound, word, sentence, and paragraph levels. The program's multisensory instructional delivery system develops both visual-motor and auditory processing skills required for success with language in print. Students who are instructed with this program become confident, effective readers and communicators."

Ann Remond, PhD
Cognitive scientist
Sydney, Australia

"The language arts are considered foundational and paramount to all of the many academic skills taught at Fort Caspar Academy. The Spalding Method is a structured, thorough, and consistent way for students to learn all the language skills. As a result, student proficiency in reading, writing, spelling, and comprehension is outstanding. Parents are excited about the growth they see in their children's reading skills, and teachers are appreciative of the precise training available through Spalding Education International."

Randall Larson, Principal
Fort Caspar Academy
Casper, Wyoming

"During my thirty-five-year educational career, I have not experienced an English language arts program that is better researched or more successful than the Spalding program, which we have used for the last sixteen years. As I experienced the Spalding training with my staff, no one imagined the success our students would eventually experience. Prior to the National Blue Ribbon Award that was earned by Village Christian Schools in 2003 and prior to our becoming a Spalding Accredited School, my staff and I began to see tremendous gains in our students' progress in the areas of spelling, reading, and writing. As we tracked the success of the Spalding program through the years, we realized that our students consistently scored within the 80th to 90th percentile nationally. The objective-measured successes of our students are significant, but what we did not anticipate were those aspects of higher-order thinking—application, analysis, evaluation, synthesis—that our students gained as a result of Spalding. These increased levels of students' critical thinking extend to other areas of the curriculum as well! I remember a comment a father made to me when visiting our kindergarten program: "It feels like our son will be enrolling in Kindergarten University!" When surveying the English language arts landscape today, we have yet to encounter a better multisensory, comprehensive, total language program than Spalding!"

David Vegas, Principal
Village Christian School
Sun Valley, California

"After successfully teaching bilingual students for fourteen years in Tampa, Florida, using The Spalding Method, I retired to Dallas, Texas, to be with my granddaughters. Being a "doubting Thomas," I was skeptical when I started using Spalding to formally teach my three-and-a-half-year-old granddaughter and her four-year-old friend in January 2008. My doubts soon evaporated. I followed the kindergarten teaching guide religiously, and after thirty-three thirty-minute lessons, these little girls were reading. They are now in first grade, spelling as well as reading, on a fifth-grade level. I used the same process with my soon-to-be four-year-old second granddaughter, with the same success. She is very proud of her pink notebook! These little "Spalding Einsteins" are my best advertisement. We underestimate children. With the right program, they can learn at an early age. My twenty-month-old granddaughter is on her way. With The Spalding Method, all children can learn."

Bertha Zapata
Retired ELL teacher, proud *abuela* of three
Dallas, Texas

"Spalding opened the doors of reading to my daughter Olivia. After seven years in the public school system, Olivia showed no progress. Her tutor exposed her to The Spalding Method in intensive summer tutoring, and Olivia's reading level rose by three grades! I am very thankful for the Spalding program and to the dedicated Spalding tutor for improvement in Olivia's reading abilities."

Wendy Calel, parent
Birmingham, Alabama

"When Gallego Basic Elementary opened in 1983, Spalding's *Writing Road to Reading* was selected for incorporation into reading instruction at all grade levels. Gallego is located on the south side of Tucson, Arizona, where we serve a high minority population. Eighty-nine percent of Gallego's students are Hispanic and 20 percent of this population are identified as English Language Learners (ELL). Because we are a magnet school, parents know our expectations when they come to Gallego and they want to be active partners in their children's learning. Having everyone working together as a team has assisted Gallego throughout the years to raise our students' achievement.

"At Gallego we believe that it is our responsibility to set high expectations for our students and that their success is a reflection of this belief. The majority of our students enter middle school reading at or above grade level.

"It has always been a priority of the school's leadership and teachers to implement The Spalding Method within a highly structured environment that encourages learning, personal responsibility, and student accountability. When Spalding entered into a research study to evaluate its program, Gallego jumped at the chance to participate. This provided the staff with the opportunity to reflect on daily practices and reaffirm what each of us needed to do to maintain fidelity with the Spalding process. As a result, good teachers got better at delivering consistent quality instruction within all Gallego classrooms."

Debra Bergman, EdD, Principal
Gallego Basic Elementary School
Tucson, Arizona

"We have implemented The Spalding Method since 1983 at Alhambra Traditional School (ATS) and consider this approach to teaching reading and language arts the secret to our students' success. Success at ATS means more than beating national and state averages on standardized tests. Alhambra Traditional School consistently claims some of the highest scores in Arizona on standardized tests in reading, writing, and math.

"This remarkable student achievement is rooted in the professional development and ongoing support provided by Spalding Education International (SEI). In partnership with SEI, Alhambra Traditional School has attained Spalding accreditation, a rigorous process that ensures elevated levels of teacher training and instructional leadership in the delivery of The Spalding Method. The accreditation process was challenging and required our teachers to grow dramatically, but the results of the collaboration speak for themselves.

"As we welcome the third generation of students to Alhambra Traditional School, we know that using The Spalding Method ensures our students will be exceptional readers, writers, and thinkers. For the uncertain future they may face, we can do them no greater service."

> Tracey Lopeman, EdD, Principal
> Alhambra Traditional School
> Phoenix, Arizona

"The Spalding Method has been the language arts program of choice in the Chandler Traditional Academies in the Chandler Unified School District since 2002, when CTA-Liberty opened. Eight years later, the district is proud to offer this exceptional program to students in six elementary schools and one junior high school, confident that students will continue to excel in reading, writing, grammar, speech, and handwriting. At CTA-Liberty, we have been consistently pleased with the literacy progress that our kindergarten through sixth-grade students demonstrate as well as the enthusiasm and enjoyment with which they embrace reading and writing. As a Spalding Accredited School, we are proud of the exceptionally high standards of excellence in language arts teaching to which our faculty is committed. Using The Spalding Method at CTA-Liberty, our teachers have been able to plan and deliver rich, vibrant lessons following the grade level Teacher's Guides, which provide meaningful objectives and engaging activities for the students. We are thrilled to see our students experience solid gains in reading achievement on classroom tests, district benchmarks, and the standardized state assessments. The Spalding Method has enabled our faculty, students, and families to more fully participate in the journey of literacy development that truly enriches the lives of lifelong learners of all ages."

> Beth Ann Bader, EdD, Principal of Chandler Traditional Academy–Liberty campus
> Chandler Unified School District
> Chandler, Arizona

"The Spalding Method has been an effective approach to teaching our elementary children in their public school. We feel we have many opportunities at home to further their school education, owing to the obvious connections between reading, writing, and spelling. Our children's advancement beyond their peers who attend schools where The Spalding Method is not used is clearly evident."

> Laurie and Kevin Moeckly
> Chandler Traditional Academy–Independence campus
> Chandler Unified School District
> Chandler, Arizona

THE WRITING ROAD
TO READING

THE *Writing* ROAD TO READING

The Spalding Method® for Teaching Speech,
Spelling, Writing, and Reading

SIXTH REVISED EDITION

Romalda Bishop Spalding

Mary E. North, PhD, Editor

COLLINS REFERENCE
An Imprint of HarperCollins *Publishers*
www.harpercollins.com

HarperCollins books may be purchased for educational, business, or sales promotional use. For information please write: Special Markets Department, HarperCollins Publishers, 10 East 53rd Street, New York, NY 10022.

SIXTH EDITION

The Library of Congress has cataloged a previous edition as follows:
Spalding, Romalda Bishop.
The writing road to reading : the Spalding method for teaching speech, spelling, writing, and reading / Romalda Bishop Spalding ; Mary E. North, editor.—5th rev. ed.
p.   cm.
Includes bibliographical references (p.) and index.
ISBN 0-06-052010-8
1. Reading—Phonetic method.   2. Language arts (Elementary)
3. English language—Study and teaching (Elementary)—United States.
I. North, Mary E. (Mary Elizabeth)   II. Title.
LB1573.3 .S6 2003
372.46'5—dc21   2002068465

ISBN 978-0-06-208393-7

12 13 14 15 16 WBC/QGD 10 9 8 7 6 5 4 3 2

Contents

Foreword

by S. Farnham-Diggory

Teach the child what is of use to a child, Rousseau said, and you will find that it takes all his time.

What is of use to a child interested in reading is explicit instruction in how the written language works—how it represents the sounds of speech, how it is produced with tools like pencils and chalk, how it signifies words and ideas. A program that provides such instruction—specifically, the Spalding program—absorbs children to an astonishing degree. It does indeed take all their time, or as much of it as teachers will allow.

This is perhaps the most impressive aspect of the Spalding program: its motivating power. This tells a psychologist like myself that Spalding has fully engaged the natural learning dispositions of the mind. We see this routinely in the child's devotion to the task of learning to talk. Learning to read by The Spalding Method inspires similar devotion.

Reading ability is not, however, neurologically prewired the way spoken language ability is. A pervasive error in reading instructional theory is that children will inductively discover the rules of the written language if they are immersed in a written language environment (Goodman and Goodman, 1979; F. Smith, 1971). Children do, of course, discover the rules of their spoken language through simple immersion—but that is because their brains are prewired for speech. Their brains are not prewired for reading.

Left to their own inductive devices, the vast majority of children will not discover how the written language works. What they discover is that they do not understand how it works. And, of course, they think this is their own fault.

One of the most heartbreaking sights in American schools today is that of children—once so eager to read—discovering that they are not learning how. There comes over those sparkling eyes a glaze of listless despair. We are not talking here about a few children and scattered schools. We are talking about millions of children and every school in the nation. And the toll in young spirits is the least of it. The toll in the learning and thinking potential of our citizenry is beyond measure. The reason for this catastrophe is straightforward: American citizens are not learning to read because they are not being taught how to read. The research evidence on this point is unequivocal.

Dr. S. Farnham-Diggory is the former H. Rodney Sharp Professor of Educational Studies and Psychology, and Director of the Reading Study Center and of the Academic Study and Assistance Program, University of Delaware.

Fundamentally, the instructional disaster must be laid at the feet of the basal reader establishment, a billion-dollar industry that supplies every teacher and every pupil with a scheduled sequence of reading materials and lessons. The per pupil costs and profits are astronomical. As in the case of many industries, profits are tied not to healthful outcomes but to sales, and to anything legal that promotes sales. The fact that most people are not learning how to read does not deter basal sales. School systems simply switch basals, even on a statewide basis, making the sales game pretty exciting. But few systems have dared face the fact that none of the basals is effective.

This is not the place to present a detailed critique of the basals, but in summary, the problem is that they have lost touch (1) with the basic principles of skill acquisition and (2) with the nature of the reading process. A pervasive problem, for example, is that basal programs do not provide sufficient practice. A reading assignment may not even incorporate a rule that was just taught. If you understand how skill development works, and how reading works, you can easily see where the basals go wrong and where the Spalding program does not. Let me explain what I mean.

Reading and Spelling Processes

Reading is now recognized as a *complex* skill—which means that it requires coordination of a number of subskills, just as piano playing or basketball does. The core reading subskill is forming connections between speech and print. More technically, this comes down to connections between specific speech units called phonemes and specific letters that represent them. For example, the letter *p* represents the phoneme /p/. Spoken words are sequences of phonemes. Different words are made up of different sequences of phonemes. Since letters represent phonemes, a different sequence of phonemes will be represented by a different sequence of letters. That is the fundamental literary principle in all languages that use alphabetic systems, and it has to be thoroughly mastered.

However, a serious theoretical error continues to pervade many systems of reading instruction. It is that phoneme-letter correspondences cannot be or should not be taught in isolation, because they do not exist in isolation. Phonemes change slightly from word to word. The phoneme /p/ as pronounced in the word *pot* will have more air behind it than the same phoneme as pronounced in the word *spot* or *top*. The phonemes would look different on a spectrograph. From this fact, an incorrect conclusion was drawn: that isolated phonemes should not be taught as such, because they do not exist in "pure" form.

As a result, many reading programs tell children something like this: "This letter *b* is the first sound in the word *boy.*" The teacher is instructed never to pronounce that phoneme in isolation. The results have been disastrous. It is simply not clear to most children what they are supposed to be learning. They do not know exactly what that letter *b* stands for, and the confusion increases as more and more phonemes are taught by this *implicit* (as it is called) method.

The children's confusion has given rise to a second theoretical error: the belief that children cannot hear phonemes in words—that they cannot analyze the sound pattern of a word. Of course they can if they know what they are supposed to be listening *for*.

Analogous theoretical errors would arise if we never taught colors in isolation, reasoning that colors never exist in isolation but are always a property of some object, and are slightly different in each case. You could point to the sky and say, "That is blue" and "Blue is what the rug is" and "Blue is what your mother's eyes are," and so on. You would soon have a thoroughly confused child, and you might well come to the erroneous conclusion that some children cannot *see* blue—that they cannot analyze colors of objects.

In fact, it takes a child only a minute or so to learn from a color chip what color is called *blue*. He can then easily categorize objects as blue, even though he never again sees any blue as pure as the color chip, or, indeed, never sees any two blues that are exactly the same.

Similarly, children can easily learn isolated phonemes, and once they have learned these, they can easily identify them in words. Once they understand what they are supposed to be listening *for*, they can readily categorize a wide range of /p/ sounds as all being represented by the same letter *p*. The research evidence on this point is absolutely beyond dispute (Groff, 1977; Hohn and Ehri, 1983; C. L. Smith and Tager-Flusberg, 1982; Treiman, 1985; Treiman and Baron, 1983).

The fact is that human brains are prewired for categorizing sensory inputs. A sound does not have to be exactly like another sound for a child to recognize that the same symbol stands for both. We could not function on this planet if our brains did not have the ability to categorize a range of sensory inputs, and thus recognize that the same rule applies to them. Once you have heard one saber-toothed tiger growl, you had better believe you have heard them all.

This, then, is the core reading subskill. You have to learn which letters represent which phonemes in English. You do not have to learn every single letter-sound unit, but you need a substantial "working set." In every complex skill, there is a similar working set of basic units that have to be learned—foot positions in ballet, for example—out of which higher-order units can then be constructed. We can call the working set of letter-phoneme units the *first-order skills* of literacy.

The term *second-order skills* refers to the fact that words are not random collections of phoneme-letter units. Some units are strongly associated with others; some units preclude the appearance of others; and so on. The skilled reader and speller knows these rules. A good instructor will teach them explicitly. It is true that second-order rules are implicit in words, and that if you simply memorized many words you would ingest some second-order rules as well. But you will not have control of them.

One of the golden oldies of learning psychology is that rules are applied most extensively and efficiently if they are verbalizable. Once you can say what a rule is, you have maximally flexible use of it. The well-instructed literate will be able to articulate both first-order and second-order rules, as well as express them in behavior.

One interesting neurologically based difference between reading and spelling, however, is that the second-order skills of spelling are different in *format* from those of reading. When you spell, you activate your rule knowledge sequentially. When you read, you activate it holistically—you see a whole group of letters at once.

This means we want second-order rule knowledge to be represented in both ways in the minds of students: we want them to know that certain sounds (and the associated letters) follow others, or are influenced by others, sequentially; and we also want them to know that certain letters (and the associated sounds) are grouped simultaneously with certain other letters. You will see how cleverly Spalding has charted a path through this instructional thicket.

There are also what we can call *third-order skills* of literacy—involvement of learning and thinking processes. But these third-order skills belong to a different stage of reading instruction, as will shortly be explained. The summary point at the moment is that the complex skills of reading and spelling require the coordination of a number of subskills, the most important being first-order subskills of pairing letters with phonemes, second-order subskills of grouping letter-phoneme units lawfully, and third-order subskills of thinking and learning.

Stages of Reading Acquisition

A helpful framework for organizing an instructional sequence for reading was provided by Dr. Jeanne Chall (1983a, 1983b), while she was director of the Reading Laboratory at Harvard University. According to Chall, we progress through six stages of reading skill development. Stage 0 is a prereading stage. Children are essentially discovering the world of print from billboards, cereal boxes, and the like. Stage 1 is the first stage of reading, and is characterized by recognition of the alphabetic principle—namely, that letters represent speech sounds or phonemes. Stage 2 is the expansion and consolidation of this principle, mastery, to the point of automaticity, of the orthographic rules of the language. Stage 3 is the beginning of higher-order learning and acquisition of thinking skills. As the saying goes, you are no longer learning to read; you are reading to learn. Essentially, you can now develop and embed comprehension subskills in the overall reading process. You can, for example, "flag" key concepts as important to remember while you're reading along. Stages 4 and 5 involve higher types of analytical and synthetic reasoning, as when you compare points of view or use new information to modify a personal theory—all during the ongoing process of reading.

Chall provided convincing evidence that reading skill acquisition does progress through these stages, in the order described.

Strategy Training Needs

A large number of college students lack Stage 3 skills, not to mention the higher-order Stage 4 and Stage 5 skills that college is really about. In part, the deficiencies arise from the fact that the skills were never explicitly taught. It is a depressing fact, for example, that a youngster can go all the way through a biology course in high school without ever having once discussed the text material in class. Assignments are made, and students are expected to read them and comprehend them, as demonstrated by performance on so-called comprehension tests, but not once will there have been a moment's training in the skills of understanding scientific text.

This is very serious, and I want to make clear that my current emphasis on Stage 1 and Stage 2 training doesn't mean that I think comprehension training is unimportant. The problem is that it cannot *begin* until Stage 2 decoding is automated, simply because a reader does not have available attentional capacity. The mind "frees up" for comprehension operations only after decoding operations become automatic. If you try to teach comprehension skills before then, you will generate a cycle of confusion: the attentional capacity necessary for mastering decoding will be drained by attempts to "remember the main idea," and capacity for comprehending will be simultaneously drained by decoding efforts. So neither Stage 2 nor Stage 3 mastery is achieved.

It is simply imperative to first consolidate and automate the Stage 2 decoding skills, which is what the Spalding program does, so that you can then go on to provide explicit instruction in higher-order reading routines. We turn now to the details of the Spalding system.

Why the Spalding Program Works

The program begins by teaching a set of phoneme-letter units that Spalding calls phonograms. There are seventy of these: the letters of the alphabet plus some multiple-letter units like *ea* and *ng*. These particular phonograms were selected by Anna Gillingham for the famous neurologist Samuel Orton, who later also asked her to develop a method for teaching reading to dyslexics. Spalding, after teaching a child for two and a half years under Orton's guidance, developed her own method for classroom teaching to prevent or remediate writing and reading problems. (Her method is also, in my judgment, far better for dyslexics than the Orton-Gillingham method.)

An important point about the Spalding phonograms is that they are correct by modern linguistic standards. That is, the letters represent minimal speech units (phonemes), *not* blends. In many of the basals, or in other collections of so-called phonics units, children have to learn excessive numbers of essentially arbitrary letter-sound units. This misses the point of the alphabetic system: letters are supposed to represent the minimal sound units of the language, not larger units. If you specify larger units, you lose the very flexibility and parsimony that the alphabetic system optimizes.

Learning the phonograms is a straightforward paired-associates task that forms tight neural links between particular phonemes, particular letters, and particular motor (writing) movements. When you master the set, you have, in effect, stocked your long-term memory with a working sample of the orthographic units of English. You can access members of this set easily and flexibly, and you can output them in written or spoken form. Learning to do this is, amazingly, great fun for students of all ages. It does absolute wonders for the self-esteem of those wounded souls suffering from years of reading failure.

After the phonograms have been learned, instruction in spelling begins. Spalding uses a list of words compiled by frequency. Eight standardized tests that sample from this list are administered, and instruction is keyed to the threshold of a child's ability. This is strongly motivating. Easy words are boring; excessively difficult words are discouraging. Words that you can almost but not quite spell are fascinating, and discovering that you can actually figure out how to spell them is fair cause for jubilation—especially for a child with a history of spelling failure.

The spelling lesson "script" is exact. The teacher says a word and calls on the children to say the first syllable (or the first sound of a one-syllable word). The children write it, then dictate it back as the teacher writes it on the board. The child progresses systematically through the word. If there is any difficulty, the class discusses the rule involved.

Over the course of spelling, children learn by example twenty-nine second-order rules, such as the five reasons why a silent *e* is attached to the end of a word. Given seventy phonograms and twenty-nine rules, you can spell about 80 percent of English words, and a higher percentage of the most frequent ones. The spelling words are written in notebooks. After second grade, some of the rules will be, too, and again with examples. Each child thus accumulates a personal list of hundreds of words for which the spelling has been worked out and repeatedly practiced. First-graders and many kindergartners go at a pace of thirty words a week.

The personal spelling book has a remarkable psychological impact on children (not to mention parents). Most of their schoolwork disappears into teachers' files somewhere. The typical schoolchild never sees a cumulative record of daily accomplishments. A spelling book with hundreds and hundreds of correctly spelled words in it (words in the spelling book are checked to make sure all are spelled correctly) is a mighty impressive achievement. In addition, of course, the spelling book is a reference book, and children religiously use it as such. Thus the spelling book serves as a practice, motivational, and reference device all at the same time.

In conjunction with the spelling, a simple marking system is taught. For example, both letters of a two-letter phonogram are underlined. This shows that they go together to form a unit. As another example, little numbers are used to indicate which sound is being used, if there is more than one. Thus, *mother* is marked as:

mo$\underline{th}^{2}$ $\underline{er}$

This shows that *th* and *er* are units, and that the second (in order of frequency) *th* sound is active. There are about five of these marking conventions. As soon as the class learns them (which is almost immediately), the students mark the word they have just produced. In this way, the process of spelling and marking works like a problem-solving seminar, with the students deeply absorbed in doing some of the best analytical thinking of their lives.

Now you see how Spalding deals with the problem of representing second-order grouping rules both sequentially and holistically. Once the phoneme-letter sequences have been produced (spelling), they are graphically coded. What goes into your visual memory, then, is a holistic, graphic pattern that depicts lawful organizations of the first-order units.

When you see the word again (unmarked), it is this visual pattern, *not the sequence of sounds,* that will be activated. Thus Spalding minimizes the risk of setting up "sounding-out" habits that interfere with holistic word perception. Words are not sounded out during reading except rarely, when a difficult one is encountered, because they do not have to be. Structural analysis is not taught during reading; it is taught during spelling, when you have to do that sort of analysis anyway. The output of the analysis is then marked graphically, so the structure can be retrieved as a visual whole, and will not have to be sounded out again.

When about thirty phonograms are learned, reading begins. A major shock for new Spalding teachers is that reading is never *taught.* It just begins. After hours of phonogram learning, sequential word analysis, and graphic marking, children can read. They simply pick up a book and start reading. (It is, of course, a pretty exciting day.) They start right in thinking and reasoning about content. From the very first day of reading, the emphasis can be on ideas, information, forming inferences, tracing implications, and the like, because the emphasis doesn't have to be on word-attack. Stage 2 skills have been mastered. Attention is now available for mastering comprehension skills. In Chapter 1 Spalding provides an overview of her approach to Stage 3 training.

By grade two, the children are reading such treasures as Thurber's *Many Moons* and Williams's *The Velveteen Rabbit*. Third-graders polish off *Charlotte's Web* with aplomb. These are their *readers*, you understand. The children move quickly and deeply into the very best literature, and also into biography, poetry, and science. A list of fine writing is given for beginners through grade six in Part Two, "Instructional Materials" (see pages 202–205).

But that is not the end of it. Children work on integrated language arts lessons about two hours every day. In the Spalding system, children write stories, plays, poems, and research reports as intensively as they read.

It is very important to understand this, and not to make the mistake of thinking that the richness of language arts is missing from the Spalding system. On the contrary, the richness far exceeds that found in the basal programs, because the children have the skills to participate fully in the literature culture and to pursue what interests them as fast and as far as they want to go.

When The Spalding Method is used in a remedial program, the leaps that children make can be downright alarming. Putting a logical system into the hands of intelligent children who have searched desperately for just such a system may enable them to run farther and faster with it than you dared to imagine. We have had children, who were years below standard, reading at grade level in a matter of months (see page 190).

Whatever the true success rate, it comes about because the Spalding system capitalizes on a body of psychological principles that are dead right in contemporary theoretical terms. Mrs. Spalding obviously had no way of anticipating that. Her own theoretical guidelines came from the teachings of William McCall at Columbia Teachers College, Orton's views of how the brain works, and the linguistics of the period. These theories have all been superseded in their respective fields, but the Spalding system can be recast in current theoretical frameworks because it was really derived from an intensive study of how children learn. (The same can be said of Montessori.) Of course other good reading teachers have emphasized some of the same principles. In my collection of early readers is one published in 1855. It starts out with a list of phonograms, and includes a simple marking system. These ideas have been around for a long time, but it remained for Spalding to combine them and forge them into a system of stunning efficiency.

Preface

by Mary E. North, PhD

Since the previous edition of *The Writing Road to Reading*, important advances have occurred in reading research and at Spalding Education International (SEI). SEI, a nonprofit 501(c)(3) corporation, was founded in 1986 by Romalda Bishop Spalding to perpetuate her method beyond her lifetime.

For over forty years, Mrs. Spalding inspired teachers and parents with her love of literature and her desire to help all children learn to speak precisely, spell accurately, write proficiently, and read fluently with comprehension. She often said that her dream was to prepare *all* children to become "lifelong learners," including those who need challenge and those who require more help. The Spalding Method is a diagnostic approach that requires continuous monitoring of students' progress and adjustment of instruction to meet students' needs. Those familiar with earlier versions will find that the text has been reorganized in accordance with her desire to make learning the language easy and enjoyable and to incorporate the latest research findings.

Book Organization and Features

The book is divided into two parts: "Lessons, Procedures, and Why This Method Works," which describes the content and methodology of the program; and "Instructional Materials," for use in lesson planning and instruction. Following a foreword and a preface, Part One consists of an introduction and six chapters. Dr. Sylvia Farnham-Diggory provides an overview of *The Writing Road to Reading* in the Foreword. The Preface explains the reason for the sixth edition and acknowledges those who made it possible. The Introduction sets forth essential instructional components, and the educational philosophy and methodology that define The Spalding Method. Chapter 1, "Planning Integrated Language Arts Lessons," describes what to teach. Chapter 2, "Delivering Integrated Language Arts Instruction," explains how to teach the content using procedures that have been tested and refined over the fifty years since Mrs. Spalding originally developed her method. Chapter 3, "Assessing Skills Mastery," explains the Spalding pretesting process for first-grade and older students to determine where to begin instruction, and then provides daily, weekly, and monthly assessments for measuring students' progress. Chapter 4, "Evaluating Skills Mastery," explains how to use the information from the spelling, writing, and reading assessments to improve initial teaching and differentiate instruction to meet individual student needs. Chapter 5, "Why *The Writing Road to Reading* Works," summarizes current research and explains how evidence-based components are taught in The Spalding Method. Chapter 6, "Advancing Literacy," presents the SEI mission, historical evidence of the method's effectiveness, and services.

Each chapter in Part One begins with an overview, a visual layout of major sections. The body of the chapter consists of three to five main sections and a number of subsections. Each chapter concludes with a summary, including key points and a few comments. New features in the Sixth Edition are example dialogues for teaching complex sentences and five mental actions designed to help teachers and parents implement the lessons.

Part Two, "Instructional Materials," includes the essentials from the previous edition: an updated list of recommended children's literature, the seventy common phonograms, the language rules, and a revised and renamed Spalding Spelling/Vocabulary Word List in order of introduction and in alphabetical order. New features include a list of Spalding Series 1 and 2 leveled readers; a list of seventeen additional phonograms; a new section on morphology; an updated recommended language arts scope and sequence; and "Resources," an updated list of teacher materials, including *Kindergarten Through Sixth-Grade Teacher Guides*.

Part One

LESSONS, PROCEDURES, AND WHY THIS METHOD WORKS

INTRODUCTION

ENGLISH has become an international means of communication. Scholars estimate that more than 1 billion people speak English. It is a required study in the schools of most countries, and its use is expanding rapidly in scientific and technological fields; e.g., its use is mandatory in international aviation communications. Expansion is basically because English has the richest and largest vocabulary, simple inflections, and no genders, and is, except for its spelling, perhaps the easiest language to learn. The ability to convey and receive information through this rich medium takes on added importance in democratic nations whose preservation depends on a literate people. Civilization is not inherited; its advance is contingent on the ability of each generation to fully communicate and teach its children the recorded wisdom of past ages.

Romalda Bishop Spalding wanted all children to benefit from the most effective method that could be devised for teaching the basic skills of writing and reading. Without these skills, futures are stunted and dreams are unfulfilled. With that in mind, she developed and used her method exclusively over forty years of teaching in all elementary grades, in tutoring hundreds of individuals, and in presenting her course to thousands of teachers. Mrs. Spalding constantly sought ways to make her method easier to teach and learn. This Sixth Revised Edition of *The Writing Road to Reading* carries that process forward.

Children are directly taught all elements of the language beginning in prekindergarten, kindergarten, or first grade. They spell a word by writing its sounds and reading aloud their own writing: thus the title of this book, *The Writing Road to Reading.* Spalding manuscript writing is almost identical to the letters children see on the printed page. Inattention, even from the first day, is seldom a problem, because they are actively engaged in speaking and writing. In spelling, writing, and reading, children apply their minds and their knowledge of phonics instead of memorizing by rote.

The Writing Road to Reading and the corresponding *Grade-Level Teacher Guides* outline the content and methodology for rapidly teaching children, or adults, accurate speech, writing, spelling, and reading. The method is organized so that children first learn letters and letter combinations (phonograms) and use them to construct high-frequency words on paper. Children find this far more interesting and instructive than workbooks and worksheets. Adults tend to greatly underestimate the mental abilities of children. Experience shows that any child entering school at the age of five or six is able, willing, and eager to write and read if taught by this logical approach to language.

Essential Elements

The Writing Road to Reading program integrates four essential elements: comprehensive spelling, writing, and reading curricula, and The Spalding Method. After the publication of *The Report of the National Reading Panel* (2000), most publishers incorporated the research-based components identified in that report: phonemic awareness, phonics, vocabulary, fluency, and comprehension. *The Writing Road to Reading* also includes these critical components, but it is the *way* these components are taught that makes Spalding unique. Therefore, the method will be described first.

The Spalding Method

Spalding combines an educational philosophy with a methodology consisting of time-tested principles of learning and instruction that are applied across the curricula.

Philosophy

Child-Centered Approach

The physical and mental well-being of students is primary. Before any instruction begins, ensuring that children sit and write comfortably permits them to concentrate fully on learning. Providing all students the opportunity to succeed every day, to be respected and appreciated, ensures that their emotional needs are being met. Children need and desire strong guidance, leadership, and reasoned discipline from their teachers.

High Expectations

Underlying the philosophy is Mrs. Spalding's conviction that *all* children can learn. When teachers have high expectations, children are more likely to set high standards for their own work. Students of all ability levels should be challenged to produce work that fully develops their intellect.

Teacher Improvement

Teachers must be objective about their abilities and efforts and assume responsibility for improving. At its best, teaching is a creative activity, and creative people are open to constructive criticism, always striving to perfect their skills. Dr. Samuel T. Orton, the eminent neurologist and brain specialist, once told Romalda Spalding to put her feelings in her pocket so she could improve her teaching. Teachers who continue to grow professionally, who put forth the effort to expand their knowledge, to analyze their lessons, and to refine their technique, can expect to see children learn and grow.

Methodology

Explicit, Interactive, Diagnostic Instruction

When teachers explain the purpose of each new task and how students will be able to use their new skills, attention and motivation are enhanced. *Explicit instruction* means that every *new* skill, procedure, or concept is modeled, i.e., explained and demonstrated.

Interactive instruction means that teachers continually engage students in dialogues and activities and ensure that all students participate. After providing explicit instruction, teachers ask questions that check not only students' knowledge and understanding but also their ability to use higher-level thinking (e.g., applying, reasoning, analyzing, and evaluating). Teachers guide and prompt (coach) as students attempt each task. Teachers continue to provide support (*scaffold*) as needed and withdraw support (*fade*) when students can independently perform the task. As students articulate what they have learned, reflect on their performance, and then perform each task independently after achieving mastery, they develop habits of mind that serve them well throughout their education and their lives. Activities that are relevant to the objective and advance students' learning develop mastery.

Diagnostic instruction means that during this daily interaction, teachers carefully observe each student's progress and differentiate instruction to meet individual needs. They identify children who understand the model, those who will need extra help in small groups, and those who will need challenge. Teachers do not stop teaching and then diagnose, because diagnosing is built into daily instruction just as asking higher-level questions is part of checking students' understanding.

Sequential, Multisensory Instruction

Romalda Spalding learned from Dr. Orton to divide each task into its component parts, teach them sequentially, and *talk about* each part. *Sequential instruction* is structured to proceed from the simple to the complex and is cumulative across all grade levels. *Multisensory instruction* means that students see, hear, say, and write using all channels to the brain, the stronger channels reinforcing the weaker. Using all four sensory channels reduces the amount of practice required for mastery and helps prevent or overcome learning difficulties. The success of The Spalding Method, even with children who have severe language problems, is in large part due to the multisensory nature of the method.

Integrated Instruction

Integrated instruction means that the connection between speaking, writing, and reading is constantly taught and reinforced. High-frequency words analyzed for pronunciation and spelling rules in the spelling lesson are studied for meaning, usage, morphology, and parts of speech in the writing lesson. Learning is enhanced when students apply language arts skills in other subjects. In short, the components of the Spalding methodology are not taught as discrete entities. They are part of a cohesive whole, each part working in concert with the rest.

Integrating a sound educational philosophy with these principles of learning and instruction provides consistency in teachers' decision making, lesson planning, and teaching.

Motivation to learn and retention of content are enhanced when teachers adhere to the philosophy and apply these principles during lesson planning and delivery of instruction.

The Spelling Lesson

English is a phonetic language. In the spelling lesson, phonemic awareness, systematic phonics instruction with handwriting, analysis of sounds, and construction of high-frequency vocabulary words are taught. The *core* of the method is having children understand the alphabetic principle, that alphabet letters and letter combinations represent speech sounds. This connection is made clear by having children say the sounds for familiar spoken words. Thus spelling is taught from the spoken word to the written form. A unique feature of *The Writing Road to Reading* is that children and older struggling readers are taught all common sounds represented by a single letter or letter combination (phonogram). Knowledge that phonograms may represent more than one sound enables beginners to sound out high-frequency words such as the pronoun *me* and the verb *do*.

Another unique feature is that the sounds represented by phonograms are taught with handwriting. Precise techniques for good, easy handwriting and for accurate pronunciation are taught from the beginning. Students learn phonograms not by copying them but by writing them after hearing and saying them. Soon they learn to combine these sounds to pronounce high-frequency words and write them from dictation in a spelling notebook—another distinguishing feature. Learning to spell high-frequency words by writing them connects the spoken sounds to the written symbols quickly and efficiently. Students can pronounce and spell high-frequency words because of the Spalding Marking System, which helps them to connect speech to print—another unique feature (see Chapter 2, page 59). High-frequency words are taught so children can quickly become independent readers. These are only a small number of the words students will need to know and use, but they do include practically every pattern of English spelling and speaking.

After spelling dictation, the structure of words written that day is discussed. Some words may have difficult phonograms, or rules that govern their pronunciation or spelling, or prefixes or suffixes. The logic of the language is clearly revealed. It is logic so basic that the teacher can instruct the entire class or a single student.

The Writing Lesson

Writing instruction begins in kindergarten and first grade by teaching children to use spelling words in oral sentences. Learning to construct oral sentences prepares children for writing and reinforces the meaning and usage of unfamiliar spelling/vocabulary words. After a sufficient number of high-frequency words are written in the spelling/vocabulary notebook, children use them to compose and write two or three sentences daily. An additional unique feature is that children are explicitly taught the meaning, usage, parts of speech, and structure of the words most needed for speech, writing, and reading. Language rules are taught just before they are needed to write declarative sentences. Children begin reading from their original sentences. *Composing original sentences is the activity that most fully requires the mind to apply all previously learned skills.* Soon students are taught to use the writing process to compose single paragraphs, then compositions, and then poetry.

The Reading Lesson

At every grade level, literary appreciation and comprehension are taught from the first day of class as children listen and respond to stories read aloud by the teacher. Children enjoy the stories, enlarge their vocabularies, and expand their understanding of people and the world.

Kindergarten and first-grade children are explicitly taught three basic types of text structure while listening to the teacher read *Spalding Series 1* or *Series 2 Leveled Readers*: narrative, informative, and a combination we call informative-narrative. When sufficient high-frequency words have been studied and written in the spelling lessons (about two months of instruction), beginners are ready to read *Spalding Series 1 Leveled Readers*. *Series 1* and *2 Readers* are leveled to provide practice of phonograms as they are taught in the spelling lessons. In Spalding schools, *Series 1* and *2 Readers* are used in kindergarten and first grade, but they may be used for older beginning readers. *Series 1* and *2 Readers* are listed along with recommended books for grades two through six in Part Two, "Instructional Materials," starting on page 200. Additional fine literature that may be read for enjoyment or to provide more practice is listed by grade levels on the Spalding Web site. Spalding students quickly progress to reading *well-written* books because they have been taught phonics and understand how words and sentences are constructed. *They are not dependent on reading words that contain only the first (most frequent) sound of the vowels and consonants, as is common in other methods.* They can read high-frequency words like *me, do, go, so,* and *is* from the beginning. By first listening to and then reading fine literature, children develop a love of reading and a taste for good writing from the beginning of instruction.

A final unique feature of *The Writing Road to Reading* is that children are explicitly taught to think and talk about their thinking (metacognition). They learn to consciously use five comprehension strategies that are mental actions needed for skilled reading. These six unique features of *The Writing Road to Reading* help students excel at spelling, writing, and reading.

The Teacher's Role

This book is written for professional teachers and home educators who want the most efficient and effective way for their students to learn to spell, write, and read. When children enter school, regardless of home training or lack of it, they expect the teacher to teach them and to command their attention. Most already have a few thousand words in their speaking vocabulary, and they find it exciting to learn to write the letters that represent the sounds they use in speaking. When they are taught to write the sounds they speak, the whole world of print becomes understandable and logical, and learning to read and write becomes a pleasure. That pleasure is their reward for the effort they put forth; they need no other. Similarly, teachers experience great satisfaction when their competent teaching leads to students' success.

The Writing Road to Reading proceeds at a much faster pace than most programs. It is important that teachers maintain appropriate pacing during whole-group instruction so the progress of the more able learners is not slowed. It is a mistake to delay learning to read for any student. Providing small-group instruction for students who need more practice and independent activities for more able learners meets the needs of all students. See *Spalding Kindergarten Through Sixth-Grade Teacher Guides* for recommendations.

At all times, the teacher should be a model of precision, appropriate expression, and dignity. Oral and written communication is concise, descriptive, and coherent. When teachers consistently model these characteristics, students progress more rapidly. The interest and attention of all children are captured when they participate in every lesson. Teachers need 90 to 120 minutes each day for teaching the important skills in spelling, writing, and reading.

It is important to understand the Spalding philosophy and methodology before beginning instruction. The teacher must be familiar with this book and the appropriate *Kindergarten Through Sixth-Grade Teacher Guide*, know where to find topics, and be able to follow detailed teaching directions. The book provides accurate and practical ways to teach and is written without technical terms. It is, therefore, valuable to teachers, parents, tutors, and clinicians for improving any individual's spelling, writing, and reading skills.

The introduction of phonograms and the rule page instructions provided in *The Writing Road to Reading* are necessarily written for beginners, whether in kindergarten or in first grade. Older students beginning with this method, regardless of their other training in lower grades, need the same teaching and practice as children just entering school; but they are pretested to determine where to begin instruction, and they proceed at a faster pace. Thirty-two weeks of daily/weekly lesson plans are provided in each of the *Kindergarten Through Sixth-Grade Teacher Guides*.

The Reading Debate

Many schools are attempting to implement the research-based components identified in the last ten years; however, these components are frequently not integrated, and therefore are less effective. Today, numerous phonics approaches are available to teachers and home educators, and they require a brief comment. Most are expensive. Most phonics methods teach the phonograms from printed words, and the words, therefore, are taught in categories that illustrate the particular phonogram being learned, but this is not the way words occur in literate English sentences. The failings of these methods are that they neglect spelling and do not teach children to say the sounds and write the symbols before the children try to read.

It can no longer be said that the knowledge needed to provide successful instruction is lacking. What is lacking is its classroom implementation. Most colleges of education do not teach the science of reading. Many still teach reading by the "eclectic" approach—that is, by combining methods—on the theory that some children learn best by one method and some by another. There are, in fact, only two methods: phonic analysis and the "look-say," whole-word, or whole-language method.

More recently, whole language has assumed the protective coloration of "balanced reading." In actual practice, this is the whole-word method with some phonics added sporadically over time. The phonics provided is likely to be incomplete at best because very few teachers have been taught the importance of teaching it directly and systematically. Even if a teacher has the necessary training and the time to teach both methods, children often find the mixture confusing because the methods are based on opposing premises. (The whole-word method encourages children to guess because it is based on memorizing the visual form. Systematic phonics methods emphasize attention to sounds and the letters that represent the sounds.)

Misguided instruction and instructional confusion have resulted in such a high percentage of reading failures that Dr. Reid Lyon and colleagues observed:

> The often-heard statement that many children identified as LD are actually "teaching-disabled" is unfortunately accurate in many cases. Our research has taught us that almost all children can learn to read if taught by appropriate methods, but clearly many students are not receiving appropriate instruction for their reading needs. Is this the teacher's fault? We don't think so. In our experience, people become teachers in order to help make significant positive changes in students' lives and teaching children to read is certainly one of those goals. Teachers, however, like the rest of us, frequently teach what they have been taught.
>
> We doubt that the colleges of education will change their current preparation practices in the near future. What is clear is that teachers must be provided the critical academic content, pedagogical principles, and knowledge of learner characteristics that they need in order to impart systematic and informed instruction to their students. (Lyon et al., 2001, 280–281)

The Writing Road to Reading is designed to do just that. See Chapter 5 to learn why *The Writing Road to Reading* works.

PLANNING INTEGRATED LANGUAGE ARTS LESSONS

ROMALDA SPALDING believed that teaching is a constant stream of professional decisions made before, during, and after interaction with students. She wanted teachers to be *decision makers*. Teaching decisions fall into three categories: what content will be taught, what teachers will do to facilitate acquisition of the content, and what students will do to learn and to demonstrate that learning has occurred. Student achievement is enhanced when teachers' professional decisions are based on a thorough understanding of the content, sound principles of learning and instruction, and sensitivity to the student and the situation. Empowered with this knowledge and philosophy, teachers can design lessons that meet the needs of average students, of gifted students who need extra challenge, of English Language Learners, and of students with dyslexia or related disabilities who need additional help.

The Spalding Method is a *diagnostic* teaching method. This means that teachers continuously observe and informally and formally evaluate students' performance and behavior to plan the most effective instruction. They compare students' achievement with the grade-level curricula, determine students' instructional levels, and plan appropriate lessons with sufficient practice activities. The Spalding curricula are designed to integrate spelling, writing, and reading lessons within a 90-minute to 120-minute block per day. (Lessons may be divided into segments that allow for breaks such as recess.) The time allotted to each lesson varies depending on the grade and skill level of students. Lessons are organized around this Spalding language arts circle, with the Spalding educational philosophy and methodology being implemented throughout all lessons.

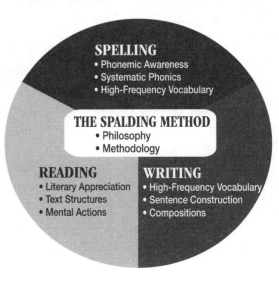

The primary emphasis (the most instructional time) in kindergarten through second grade is given to the spelling lesson because essential subskills of reading are taught there. The primary emphasis shifts from spelling to reading and writing when children have automated their performance on the basic skills. For many Spalding children, this transition occurs in the second grade. At that point, each day's spelling lesson should average thirty minutes, with the remaining time divided between reading and writing lessons. Upper-grade allotments are adjusted according to student needs and school schedules. (See the "Planning" section of the *Kindergarten Through Sixth-Grade Teacher Guides* for details.)

This integrated language arts lesson plan is also effective in special education resource rooms or tutorial settings. Assuming a one-hour resource or tutorial session, approximately thirty minutes are allowed for the spelling lesson because it is the foundation for reading and writing. About fifteen minutes are provided for vocabulary development and oral sentence construction to reinforce the skills learned in spelling. The remaining time is devoted to literary appreciation. An enjoyable poem or short story can be read aloud so students see that the goal is pleasurable experiences with books. As soon as these students have automated performance on the basic skills, more time is devoted to the writing and reading lessons.

The first step in planning effective lessons is organizing an environment that is conducive to learning.

An Environment Conducive to Learning

The Spalding Method is grounded in the educational philosophy that each student's physical and mental well-being is a primary concern of Spalding teachers.

Physical Well-Being

Physical well-being means that students can learn without experiencing discomfort.

Providing Physical Well-Being

1. Plan a quiet, orderly classroom, free from clutter and from distracting visual stimuli. Include a centralized, convenient location for classroom materials.
2. Plan to seat all students facing the front for explicit instruction in spelling, writing, and reading lessons. This seating arrangement focuses students' attention on the lesson content. (Provide alternative seating arrangements conducive to individual, small-group, and cooperative learning activities.)
3. Plan seating assignments that consider individual needs (e.g., seat students who have difficulty up front where you can monitor their progress, and seat left-handed writers where they have an unobstructed view of you and the board.)

Mental Well-Being

Mental well-being involves feeling accepted and successful. The goal is for all students to achieve their potential in an atmosphere of mutual respect.

Facilitating Mental Well-Being

1. Plan class rules, expectations, and consequences that require all students to be treated with respect. Expect students to respect their own and others' property, work areas, and individual differences.
2. Plan a predictable daily schedule, allowing for flexibility as appropriate. (Provide copies of the schedule for students as needed.)
3. Plan daily routines that provide a sense of order and stability.
4. Plan to use visual materials, such as graphic organizers (e.g., Spalding posters) or illustrations to make abstract concepts more concrete. (See Chapter 4, "Evaluating Skills Mastery").
5. For students having difficulty learning, plan to break tasks into smaller parts, explain each part, and provide more practice. Be prepared to repeat directions or steps. These students may not generalize easily.
6. Plan appropriate, meaningful, clearly defined assignments that consider individual differences (e.g., allow students having difficulty writing to give sentences orally; provide challenging extensions for able learners).
7. Plan to emphasize each student's progress and strengths, not weaknesses (e.g., record the number of correct responses rather than the incorrect number on assignments and quizzes).

Lesson planning that provides for students' physical and mental well-being sets the stage for learning. Matching instruction to individual differences maximizes students' interest and confidence.

The next step in planning an effective lesson is knowing what to teach in spelling, writing, and reading lessons. Lesson content is found in the following pages of this chapter. Grade-level and lesson objectives are found in the "Planning" section of the *Kindergarten Through Sixth-Grade Teacher Guides.*

Spelling: What to Teach

Historically, every phonetic language has developed from speech to letters that represent speech sounds and then to words and sentences. *The Writing Road to Reading* follows that plan: it starts with children's oral language; then explicitly and systematically teaches the letters and letter combinations (phonograms) that represent speech sounds; then teaches how to use the phonograms to say, write, and read high-frequency words. Spelling instruction is divided into three main strands: phonemic awareness, systematic phonics, and high-frequency vocabulary. These are the first three research-based components identified by the *Report of the National Reading Panel* (2000). Explicit instruction begins with the first research-based component.

Phonemic Awareness Instruction

The basic concept all beginners, and older students who are having difficulty, need to understand is that spoken words consist of sequences of sounds (phonemes). Failure to understand this is a primary cause of reading difficulties. In normal speech, the teacher pronounces a familiar, high-frequency word such as *me*. Children hear the word and see the teacher hold up two fingers and say /m/ /ē/ while pointing to each finger.

Children say the sounds. The teacher makes sure each child hears and says the individual sounds in each word, then blends the sounds to say the word. Each day children sound out new high-frequency words. (See pages 5–6 in the "Delivering" section of the *Kindergarten Through Sixth-Grade Teacher Guides*.) Kindergartners are eager to learn the connection between sounds and letters, and research has shown that phonemic awareness training is more effective when followed quickly by systematic phonics instruction.

Systematic Phonics Instruction

Spalding phonics instruction includes explicit, systematic, and sequential presentation of letters and letter combinations with handwriting and English rules that govern phonogram pronunciation and placement. Beginners, and older struggling readers, must understand that speech sounds (phonemes) are represented by alphabet letters and letter combinations (graphemes). They must also learn that letters and letter combinations occur in patterns within words, and that their use in spelling and reading may be governed by rules.

Phonograms with Handwriting

The term *phonogram* is derived from the Greek words *phono* (sound) and *gram* (writing); thus, a Spalding phonogram is a single letter, or a fixed combination of two, three, or four letters, that is the symbol for one sound in a given word. Students are taught all common sounds represented by a single phonogram. Knowing that phonograms may represent more than one sound enables beginners to sound out high-frequency words such as the article *the* and the pronoun *you*.

Phonogram sounds are taught along with letter formation (handwriting). The child hears, sees, writes, and reads the phonograms. Four sensory pathways are activated: auditory, visual, kinesthetic, and tactile. The title of this book, *The Writing Road to Reading*, is not just a play on words. Teaching handwriting and written spelling before reading from books is fundamental. While kindergartners are developing fine motor control, they read (say sounds) and write the phonograms in the air or in sand or another medium. The techniques of easy, legible, and neat handwriting are taught using the phonograms for daily handwriting practice.

Manuscript writing is used at first, whatever the age of the student, because it provides the needed visible link between handwriting and all printed matter, and it is commonly used for lettering drawings, maps, and diagrams. See instructional strategies and procedures for teaching phonograms with manuscript handwriting on pages 43–55 in Chapter 2 and cursive writing for students in grade two and above on pages 66–73.

The seventy phonograms, which were identified many years ago, have stood the test of almost six decades of use because they simplify English spelling. The fixed combinations absorb most of the silent letters (e.g., *igh* says /ī/), except the final *e*'s. The latter are easily taught by explaining reasons for most of them. (See pages 79–80 in Chapter 2.)

English Spelling, Pronunciation, and Language Rules

The spelling of English words is a major obstacle to easy writing and accurate reading. However, learning to spell words by applying phonograms and rules avoids that problem by uniting the spoken sounds of English words to their written forms. English spelling may seem inconsistent; in fact (with few exceptions), it follows certain patterns and rules. Twenty-nine rules that govern pronunciation, spelling, and language use are explicitly taught. See Part Two, "Instructional Materials," pages 221–223. Rules are never memorized by rote; rather, those that apply to pronunciation and placement of phonograms within words are taught and practiced during daily phonogram reviews. Rules that govern capitalization, tenses, and affixes are taught as facts about the language just before they are needed to spell a word. Thus rules are learned from applications rather than as isolated facts. It should be made clear to students that although no rule is absolute, rules hold true often enough to be very helpful.

Word Fluency (Automatic Word Recognition)

Word fluency, often referred to as *automatic word recognition*, is another crucial component taught in *The Writing Road to Reading*. As the last step in spelling dictation and at other convenient times, the spelling/vocabulary words are read two ways: for spelling and for reading. When reading words for spelling, students say one-syllable words by sounds and multisyllable words by syllables so they process the sounds or the syllables *sequentially* as needed for spelling, writing, and decoding unfamiliar words. When reading words for reading, students pronounce the words in normal speech, thus building automatic word recognition—a prerequisite for *text* fluency. By reading two ways, students quickly learn both the spelling and the pronunciation of words without using the schwa. Soon, high-frequency words are recognized as representing ideas without the need to separate their component phonograms.

High-Frequency Vocabulary Instruction

Vocabulary instruction is the third research-based component taught in *The Writing Road to Reading*. Vocabulary development begins with preschoolers' spoken vocabulary and progresses to words most frequently used in writing and reading. In the first few years of life, children learn to use or understand more than 3,000 words. Spalding's Spelling/Vocabulary Word List is based on the 1,000 most frequently used words compiled by the late Dr. Leonard P. Ayres. Of these words, 700 are in the oral vocabulary of most five- and six-year old children. In addition, these 1,000 words account for 85 percent of words used in speaking, writing, and reading. The first 100 words in the Spelling/Vocabulary Word List include the 10 English words most often spoken and a majority of the words most often used in reading and writing.

A computer comparison of the original list with other high-frequency lists and the Collins COBUILD English Dictionary (1996) shows that the original list is remarkably stable. The COBUILD dictionary includes The Bank of English, 200 million words covering a vast range of current British and American English. Words are ranked by frequency. The highest-frequency words are considered part of the essential core vocabulary of the language. Over the years, Romalda Spalding and Spalding Certified Teacher Instructors added grade-level words drawn from science, social studies, and math texts. Of the more than 2,300 words in the current Spalding Spelling/Vocabulary Word List, all either are in the core vocabulary or provide practice with phonograms or spelling rules. The Spelling/Vocabulary Word List for students in kindergarten through sixth grade is found in Part Two, "Instructional Materials," starting on page 254.

The Spalding Marking System helps students of any age connect speech sounds to the written symbols in words used in daily speaking, writing, and reading. Five simple conventions enable kindergartners to read high-frequency words such as *me, do, go,* and *is* rather than be limited to words that use only the first, most common, vowel or consonant sound: (1) Vowels are underlined at the end of a syllable when they say their second sound (name), e.g., *me* and *go*. (2) Multiletter phonograms are underlined to show they represent one sound, e.g., *she*. (3) Silent letters and phonograms that represent a sound not given on the phonogram card are underlined twice, e.g., *half, friend*. (4) Numbers are placed above a phonogram when its sound is not the first sound, e.g., *do*. (5) Some words are bracketed together to indicate a relationship, e.g., (*coming/come*). Use of underlines, numbers, and brackets requires students to think and helps them analyze the spelling and pronunciation of words.

Students always learn new words by studying the phonetic sounds of the spoken word. Students of any age write, from dictation, the high-frequency spelling/vocabulary words in primary (kindergarten–grade two) or intermediate (grade three and above) notebooks. They *hear* the teacher say the word. Then they *say* each sound and say each sound again *just before* they *write* it. They *see* what they have written as they *read* it. Learning to spell and read words by writing them from dictation connects the spoken sounds to their written symbols. *All* students can learn because every avenue to the mind is used. This multisensory method facilitates long-term retention of the words they write and read. Construction of the notebook teaches students to analyze the *written* spelling of words so they can spell, write, and read words that will be most useful to them. The more words students analyze and read from their notebooks, the more familiar they become with language and spelling rules.

The primary, or the intermediate, notebooks become students' prized spelling books to which they constantly refer. Construction of the notebooks is the heart of *The Writing Road to Reading*, the foundation for language arts instruction, and the critical activity for student achievement. It not only provides multisensory instruction of high-frequency spelling words, but also integrates vocabulary instruction with rules of the language.

Spalding students learn to pronounce, write, spell, and read high-frequency words in the spelling lesson. In the writing lesson, they learn the meaning, usage, and parts of speech of the same words. This progression of moving from speech sounds to written phonograms to words enables students to speak, spell, write, and read fluently. These skills are basic to our culture, and writing is the one that does most to unite and reinforce the others.

Writing: What to Teach

To plan effective writing lessons, teachers need to know a great deal about the English language. In speech, our tone of voice, inflection, facial expressions, and gestures help to communicate what we intend. Writing, however, is a solitary, not a social, activity. Writing requires logical thinking, precise selection, and correct ordering of words to convey meaning. Anyone who has ever attempted to put thoughts on paper in a coherent manner, or to describe or persuade in print, will have begun to develop what teachers call "literary appreciation." That is, he or she will have some insight into the complexities of writing and an inkling of the elements that make up good writing.

Spalding writing lessons are divided into three main strands: high-frequency vocabulary, sentence construction, and composition. All strands are taught throughout the grades. With students of any age, the writing lesson begins by integrating vocabulary development with sentence construction. A common frustration voiced by teachers is that students may spell words correctly on weekly tests, but misspell the same words when writing stories or other assignments. When students write compositions, incorrect spelling indicates that they are relying solely on visual memory rather than applying spelling and language rules. Learning the meaning and usage of the spelling/vocabulary words by writing sentences reinforces correct spelling of words in context.

High-Frequency Vocabulary

At any grade level, students need an expanded vocabulary to write proficiently. For students to achieve mastery of unfamiliar words, all aspects must be taught. In the spelling lesson, students learn to pronounce, spell, and legibly write grade-level words in their spelling/vocabulary notebooks. Precise pronunciation, legible handwriting, and accurate spelling are stressed in this lesson.

In the writing lesson, the emphasis shifts to precision in the selection and use of words. Each day, students work with the high-frequency words that were introduced during spelling dictation. As the words become more difficult, the concepts of base words, word roots, prefixes, and suffixes are included in the objectives.

Spalding's emphasis on fine literature in the reading lesson provides students with an expanded vocabulary and good models for developing skillful writing. However, good models alone will not develop ownership of a rich vocabulary. Students are explicitly taught the structure of language (morphology, grammar, and syntax) and provided daily opportunities to practice what they have learned by writing simple, compound, and complex sentences, and compositions.

Sentence Construction with High-Frequency Vocabulary

Fine writers have an excellent command of the English language. They vary simple, compound, and complex sentences, using precise language in artful, descriptive phrases to achieve the exact effect they want. Competent writing requires facility with all aspects of spoken and written language: sentence construction, grammar, and syntax. Because many language texts teach each of these in isolation (a chapter on sentence construction and separate chapters on each part of speech), students often have a hard time seeing the relationship and applying that knowledge to their own writing. In *The Writing Road to Reading*, word usage (grammar) and order (syntax) are integrated into instruction in the attributes of simple, compound, and complex sentences. Students thus grasp language as a unified whole and are better able to apply what they learn.

Students of any age begin by learning or reviewing the attributes of simple sentences. Initially, in sections A–G of the Spelling/Vocabulary Word List, more time is spent on correct usage because the majority of these words are in the spoken vocabulary of most kindergarten and first-grade children. For example, the first ten spelling/vocabulary words include the pronouns *me, it, she*; the verbs *do, go;* the linking/helping verb *is*; the conjunction *and*; prepositions *at, on*; and the adjective (article) *a*. Some beginners who have had good sentence construction modeled at home are able to use these words appropriately. However, many, if not most, children need explicit instruction in word usage. With each successive lesson, teachers reinforce correct sentence construction.

Kindergarten and first-grade children *write* and read their own sentences after they have written and read about 100 words in their primary notebooks. These daily, integrated spelling and writing lessons reinforce automatic word recognition, meaning, rule application, and sentence structure (grammar and syntax). Children apply language rules more quickly because teachers explain the purpose of each rule and provide integrated, meaningful practice. Knowledge of sentence structure expands as children are introduced to increasingly difficult concepts throughout the grades.

Daily practice using sections A–G words in oral sentences enables kindergarten and first-grade children to make a smooth transition to writing four types of simple sentences, followed by easy compound and complex sentences. The focus of writing lessons in sections H–K is on teaching beginners of any age the attributes of simple, compound, and easy complex sentences. Children develop mastery of these basic tools of composition by daily practice, composing different types of sentences orally; and then by independently writing sentences of each type. Upper-grade teachers use simple diagnostic techniques to determine where to begin language instruction for older students. (See the "Assessing" section of the *First Through Sixth-Grade Teacher Guides* for pretesting procedures.) Another tool for preparing students to write compositions is teaching them to think about and discuss the structure of language.

Primary-grade children learn the names of the parts of speech after they have learned how words are used in constructing oral sentences. Beginners are familiar with, and enjoy, categorizing different kinds of animals, colors, and objects. They extend that ability in the integrated writing lesson. They are taught to categorize different kinds of *words* according to the jobs these words perform. Words in sections A–G are used for beginners of any age because the students can spell and read these words, and because the words include seven of the eight parts of speech. Being able to name, define, and explain characteristics of a category requires higher-level thinking. It enables students to understand why words behave differently from each other and why position in a sentence affects meaning and sometimes punctuation. Interactive dialogue in the whole group improves retention because children learn to explain the purpose of each part of speech and participate in meaningful language practice. The order of instruction of the parts of speech is outlined in lesson plans in the "Planning" section of the *Teacher Guides*. Nouns are introduced first, followed by action verbs, and subject and object pronouns, because they form the foundation for writing simple sentences.

Integrating listening, speaking, reading, and writing in every lesson not only facilitates students' understanding, but also enhances their retention of complex language concepts. According to Farnham-Diggory (1990), this concept of integrated language arts instruction can be traced to the Greeks and Romans. In the Roman system, children first listened as the teacher spoke or read aloud; the children then spoke in response, then wrote, and finally read aloud what they had written. The Romans explained that sight, sound, and sense were to be constantly interrelated.

Composition

For primary-grade children, composition instruction begins after the attributes of written sentences are learned. Within a few weeks, they learn to compose two or three sentences about a single topic and explain the concept of related thoughts. While they are still practicing related sentences, teachers explain and demonstrate how to use the writing process to compose different types of writing. Composition begins with familiar topics, such as pets. For older students who have mastered the previous year's objectives, review of sentence construction and composition instruction may begin simultaneously.

During preparation for writing (prewriting), students of any age learn to gather information and plan their writing for different audiences and purposes. After committing their thoughts to paper (composing), they learn to revise for precise language, sentence order, clarity, and meaning. Once they have revised content, they learn to edit their work for capitalization, punctuation, grammar, and spelling. Finally, they publish different types of writing that communicate effectively and reflect their knowledge of standard English structure and conventions.

Students' compositions are only as good as the individual sentences that make up their paragraphs. Knowledge of the parts of speech provides a vocabulary for discussing how to improve their writing. Categorizing parts of speech and writing sample sentences in the whole group help students use words appropriately when independently writing simple, compound, and complex sentences. During integrated writing lessons, students are introduced to and practice increasingly difficult language concepts. Therefore, students in every grade practice sentence and paragraph construction all year long.

Reading: What to Teach

Reading, like writing, is a complex process, composed of many subskills. Students who have not mastered the subskills do not find pleasure in reading, and they suffer academically and emotionally. Reading instruction in *The Writing Word to Reading* is divided into three strands: literary appreciation using fine literature, text structure, and mental actions essential for skilled comprehension. Text fluency and expressive reading are developed while reading aloud. Text fluency and comprehension are the last two research-based components identified in the *Report of the National Reading Panel*. All three strands are taught throughout the grades using increasingly challenging materials.

Literary Appreciation

The ability, along with the desire, to read well-written books is one, if not the major, goal of Spalding language teaching. The *ability* to read is taught in the spelling lesson. The *desire* is fostered in *literary appreciation* lessons that begin on day one in every grade. During literary appreciation lessons, teachers focus on attributes of fine literature, expanding students' understanding of narrative elements, and fostering fluent and expressive reading.

Attributes of Fine Literature

Rebecca Lukens (2003, 29) notes, "Classics are books that have worn well, attracting readers from one generation to the next. They cross all genre lines." Despite changes in society, classics are relevant to new readers. To foster appreciation for fine writing, five attributes of fine literature are explicitly taught: *precise language, emotional appeal, content, insight into people and life,* and *universality*. In addition to the attributes, Spalding also teaches the terms that describe some of the devices of style used by authors (see Part Two, "Instructional Materials," page 197).

The storyteller has been with us for as long as the human race has memories. Stories can be told in prose or in poetry. Fine books teach the beauty of well-chosen words (*precise language*). Such books also have the power to touch the heart (*emotional appeal*). They provide diverse knowledge and supply a storehouse of practical wisdom with which to confront unforeseen difficulties (*content*). Dialogue and situations enable readers to discern implied main ideas, a character's motives and desires, and rewards or consequences of different kinds of behavior (*insight*). Good books also share common traits and experiences that are enjoyed by readers across time and cultures (*universality*). In short, fine literature deals with all of human experience, deepening understanding and stimulating imagination and reflection. Finally, and perhaps most important of all, it helps us understand ourselves.

Expanding Understanding of Narrative Elements

During literary appreciation lessons, students expand their understanding of narrative elements. They have heard narratives since their preschool years. Now, they learn that some settings are important and some are not and that characters develop during the sequence of events we call the plot. They also learn about the author's point of view and main idea/theme. Older students learn about the author's tone and style.

Fluent and Expressive Reading

Text fluency is another research-based component of reading. As primary-grade children listen to teachers read aloud, they learn that fluent and expressive reading enhances their pleasure and understanding. Although beginning readers cannot start out by reading fine literature, they can begin to practice fluent reading after only thirty phonograms have been learned. Kindergartners can read Book 1, a narrative, in *Learning to Read and Loving It*, in *Spalding's Series 1 Leveled Readers*. To develop fluent and expressive reading, each day children read a few sentences chorally at first, then individually. *Series 1 Readers*, consisting of twenty books, provide practice with newly introduced phonograms while reinforcing the differences between narrative, informative, and informative-narrative writing. Twenty-four *Series 2 Leveled Readers, Reading and Loving It*, provide practice with seventy phonograms and reinforce understanding of three types of writing and first- and third-person point of view. See the recommended list of books in Part Two, "Instructional Materials," and in the Introduction to the *Kindergarten Through Sixth-Grade Teacher Guides*. Additional grade-level recommendations are listed on the Spalding Web site: www.spalding.org. Recreational reading should also be encouraged. Students at every grade level should have a library book to read whenever time permits.

Students must be able to read text fluently so they can concentrate on deriving meaning. Reading aloud motivates students to practice their reading; in fact, the students don't realize they are practicing fluency. They are just enjoying the stories because they can read and understand them. Through reading aloud, students also learn to speak and write well.

Text Structure

Another prerequisite skill for comprehension is discerning the type of text being read. During *text structure* lessons, students are taught that authors organize their writing differently depending on their purpose for writing. Even beginners can learn the distinguishing characteristics of three *basic* types of writing: narrative, informative (expository), and a combination that we call informative-narrative. *Series 1 Leveled Readers* are used to teach elements of narrative, then informative (expository), and finally informative-narrative writing. Knowing how the three types of writing differ enables students to immediately focus attention on the pertinent elements, i.e., what's most important in each type of text. Primary and intermediate comprehension booklets that have short, interesting narrative, informative, and informative-narrative passages are used to teach and test students' understanding of text structure. See the Introduction to the *Kindergarten Through Sixth-Grade Teacher Guides.*

Narrative Writing

Narrative writing tells a story. Narratives are introduced first because they are easier for children to understand. Parents and kindergarten teachers usually read aloud from nursery rhymes, fairy tales, and stories. In text structure lessons, students are taught to identify and name the *basic* elements of narratives. Coordinating lessons in text structure with literary appreciation helps students expand this basic knowledge. Basic literary terms introduced in kindergarten and first grade form the foundation for analysis of increasingly difficult narratives as students progress through the grades. Specific instructional practices and example dialogues for teaching these and other literary analysis skills are explained and demonstrated on pages 131–138 in Chapter 2.

After students have been taught first- and third-person points of view in the writing lesson, they learn to identify the author's point of view in short narratives. After they can consistently identify the author's purpose, point of view, and elements of narratives, they are ready to learn the characteristics of informative paragraphs.

Informative (Expository) Writing

Students learn that informative (expository) writing sets forth a series of facts, propositions, or arguments in a logical order. They learn that informative writing is organized around a topic and contains factual information about that topic. Sample dialogues for teaching informative elements are found on pages 138–140 in Chapter 2. After students have learned to write topic sentences in *composition* lessons, they identify topic sentences in paragraphs in the comprehension booklets.

Informative-Narrative Writing

When students can easily distinguish between narrative and informative writing, they are ready to learn that authors sometimes combine the elements of both. A sample dialogue that introduces the author's purpose and a few elements of informative-narrative writing is found on pages 140–141 in Chapter 2.

When students can easily distinguish between the three types of writing, they are ready to learn to consciously use the five mental actions necessary for skilled comprehension.

Mental Actions

Metacognition (thinking about your thinking) and five mental actions (comprehension strategies) used to comprehend text are explicitly taught. Instruction begins in kindergarten as children listen to the teacher read aloud. Students are taught to be active listeners and readers by *monitoring their comprehension*. Skilled comprehenders are engaged—they know they need to ask questions or reread when something no longer makes sense. But poor comprehenders don't know how to check their understanding—they just limp along. To enrich their understanding, all students are also taught to *make connections* between their prior knowledge and information in the text. Using their knowledge about text structure, they can *predict* the author's purpose and type of writing. When students can *consciously* use the first three mental actions, they are taught to *predict* a topic and a main idea. Next, they learn to *reformat* (categorize) information into essential and additional information. Finally, they are taught to use essential information to identify stated or derive implied topics and main ideas (*mentally summarize*).

These actions are not used in any particular order. Rather, they are used as needed—simultaneously or in parallel. Many students automatically engage in these mental actions while listening and reading. However, we now know that conscious use enhances all students' comprehension. The actions are specific strategies students can use to clarify meaning when comprehension breaks down. Students who are able to analyze their own thinking while listening and reading (metacognition) increase their comprehension; and increased comprehension, in turn, significantly improves their school performance. Sample dialogues are found on pages 140–148 in Chapter 2.

Four Steps to Effective Lesson Planning

After teachers understand the content to be taught in integrated spelling, writing, and reading lessons, a routine for planning the daily and weekly lessons should be established. A successful routine includes four steps: (1) selecting instructional objectives at the correct level of difficulty; (2) selecting instructional delivery levels for each objective; (3) aligning information, questions, responses, and activities to each lesson objective; and (4) preparing the introduction and conclusion.

Step 1: Selecting Instructional Objectives at the Correct Level of Difficulty

Teaching at the correct level enhances learning because students are neither bored by material they already know nor frustrated by tasks that are too difficult. Determining the correct level of difficulty involves (1) analyzing the grade-level curricula and (2) analyzing student achievement.

Analyzing the Curricula

Spalding language arts curricula contain research-based components that are set forth as *instructional objectives*. An *instructional objective* is a clear statement of what teachers want students to know and be able to do at the completion of a learning task. Spalding instructional objectives are of two types: grade-level (end of year) objectives and lesson objectives. *Grade-level* objectives state what each student should know (general content) and be able to do (observable, measurable behavior) by the end of the year.

Phonemic Awareness Grade-Level Objectives: Examples

The student will . . .

- segment spoken words into sounds and syllables (phonemic awareness).
- blend spoken sounds into words (phonemic awareness).

In the initial grade-level objective listed in the first box, primary-grade children are to master *the sounds in spoken words* (content). The observable, measurable student behavior is the ability to *segment*. Kindergarten–Sixth Grade-Level Objectives are found in "Recommended Language Arts Scope and Sequence" in Part Two, "Instructional Materials."

Lesson objectives state what each student should know (specific content) and be able to do at the conclusion of a lesson. In the first-grade example listed in the next box, the *observable, measurable behavior* part of the objective remains the same, but the *specific content* (difficulty and number of words) varies according to grade level.

Phonemic Awareness First-Grade Day 1 Lesson Objectives: Examples

The student will . . .

- segment the spoken words *me, do, and, go,* and *at* into individual sounds.
- blend individual sounds into the spoken words *me, do, and, go,* and *at.*

Both grade-level and lesson objectives consist of these two parts: the *content* to be learned (knowledge) and the *observable* and *measurable* student behavior that demonstrates performance. Both are sequenced from easiest to hardest and from most concrete to abstract. Thirty-two weeks of grade-appropriate lesson objectives are found in the "Planning" section of the *Kindergarten Through Sixth-Grade Teacher Guides.*

Analyzing Student Achievement

Analyzing and understanding the curricula are important, but not sufficient. Planning objectives at the correct level of difficulty also requires recognizing able learners who need challenge, students who are experiencing difficulties, and students with language disabilities. In addition to whole-group instruction, some students having difficulty may need preteaching and/or reteaching. Students with a *specific learning disability* or *attention deficit disorder* require considerably more help. Specific instructional strategies and procedures for differentiating instruction are found in Chapters 2 and 4 of this text and in the "Evaluating" section of *Kindergarten Through Sixth-Grade Teacher Guides.*

The work of creating grade-level and lesson objectives has been done. The teacher's task is to plan differentiated instruction that implements the objectives set forth in the grade-level *Teacher Guides.*

Step 2: Selecting Instructional Delivery Levels for the Objectives

Step 2 in planning each lesson is determining the appropriate instructional delivery level. If it is new learning, teachers explain and demonstrate the expected performance (*model*). If the content or procedure is being reviewed, teachers guide and prompt (*coach*) as students attempt the task. As students begin to master the performance, teachers support only when needed (*scaffold*) and withdraw support (*fade*) when students can perform independently. *Continuing support when students no longer require it is as serious an error as failing to provide help when it is needed.* See detailed descriptions on pages 1–3 in Chapter 2 and pages 1–2 in the "Delivering" section of the *Kindergarten Through Sixth-Grade Teacher Guides.*

Implementing the correct instructional delivery level for each objective helps students become self-sufficient more quickly. As students become adept at basic skills, teachers will adjust the instructional level *multiple* times within each integrated spelling, writing, and reading time frame.

Step 3: Aligning Information, Questions, Responses, and Activities to Each Lesson Objective

The next step in planning effective lessons is to read each objective and consider the *information* students need to understand the skill or concept, the *questions* that check students' understanding, the *responses* to students' questions or comments, and the *practice activities* that ensure students' mastery of the objective. This means that the content presented, the teacher's actions that facilitate students' understanding, and the activities are *focused* on the lesson objective.

Aligning Information to Each Objective

Information is the foundation for thinking and learning. It is impossible to comprehend, write, solve problems, or be creative without information. Since teachers have so much information to share, the following procedure helps design aligned lesson content.

Aligning Information to Each Objective

1. Identify the information that is essential for achieving the objective (need to know).
2. Organize the information so students will see the relationship of each part to other parts and to the whole, and use simple and direct vocabulary that precisely describes distinguishing features, rules, or concepts to be taught.
3. Prepare examples that are accurate and unambiguous, and highlight the distinguishing feature or features or the essence of the concept or generalization to be taught. (Don't wait until you are in the midst of a lesson to think of an example.)

To assist teachers in planning aligned information, spelling, writing, and reading examples are provided.

Aligning Information to Each Objective: Examples

Spelling Lesson

- If the objective is "Say and write phonograms *a*, *c*, *d*, and *f*," the relevant information is the features and sounds of each phonogram. Chapter 2, pages 45–47, provides precise dialogue containing the relevant information for introducing phonograms. The sounds the teacher says and the letters written on the board are clear examples. (Telling children what words they can form with those phonograms is not aligned to this objective. Save that information for the writing lesson.)

Writing Lesson

- If the objective is "Write simple sentences," the relevant information is a capital letter to signal the beginning of the thought about a person, place, or thing; a verb to express the action; and a period (full stop) to signal the end of the thought. For this objective, one or more example sentences are needed to clearly demonstrate all the attributes of simple sentences.

Reading Lesson

- If the objective is "Identify precise language in a story read aloud," the characteristics of precise language are relevant. (See page 131 in Chapter 2.) Preselect clear examples from the story to be read aloud.

Every class is different, as is every student. To plan the correct level of difficulty, teachers tailor the amount of information needed and the examples.

Aligning Questions and Responses to Each Objective

After planning aligned information, the next step is planning questions that check students' understanding and responses that reinforce students' learning. To maintain students' attention on the new learning, questions that check students' understanding and the teacher's responses to their answers or comments must also be aligned.

Preparing Aligned Questions and Responses

1. Plan questions that require students to (1) make discriminations based on the presence or absence of the critical attributes that have been taught, (2) explain application of a rule, or (3) explain the essence of a concept.
2. Plan responses to students' answers that (1) reinforce the correct information; (2) dignify their response, then correct a wrong or incomplete answer; or (3) redirect attention to the objective.

The following examples of aligned questions and anticipated responses assist teachers in planning their own questions and responses.

Aligning Questions and Responses to Each Objective: Examples

- To check students' understanding, ask, "What features do we use to form the letter *a*?"
- To reinforce correct responses, plan to reinforce critical attributes. For example, if a student answers, "The letter *a* is formed with a circle that begins at 2 on the clock and a short line," an aligned response is, "Yes, *a* has two features, a circle that begins at 2 on the clock and a short line."
- If a student's answer is incomplete, "The letter *a* is formed with a circle that begins at 2 on the clock," an aligned response is, "The letter *a* is formed with a circle that begins at 2 on the clock and a short line."
- If students' questions or comments are not relevant to the objective, a standard response is, "That is a great question (or comment). We will discuss that in our writing (or reading, science, social studies) lesson." Then remember to do so.

Aligning Practice Activities to Each Lesson Objective

Well-planned lesson activities are aligned to the objective and incorporate the principles of skill learning: task analysis, practice, and attention management (see Chapter 5). Each activity should provide opportunities for students to analyze the task, to practice it until mastery is achieved, and to manage their attention. Since attention can be focused on only one task at a time, having all students participate develops attention control.

Preparing Aligned Practice Activities

Task Analysis

Plan practice activities that require students to . . .

- articulate distinguishing features and attributes.
- analyze and explain steps of a procedure or process.
- analyze and explain application of a rule or the essence of a concept.

Practice

- For new learning, plan short and frequent practice.
- After students accurately perform a skill, explain the application of a rule, or explain a concept; plan to distribute practice over time to ensure that it is retained in long-term memory.

continued

Attention Management

- Plan to have all students actively participate to maintain attention on the task.
- Plan to monitor students' participation daily (e.g., move about the room, assisting as needed, to ensure that students are on task).
- For questions that check for understanding and that require reflection, plan "think time" and some type of visible student responses that ensures active participation.
- Plan signals for students to switch attention as needed to accomplish the task; e.g., cover a phonogram card when a sound is mispronounced.

Practice activities can enhance students' learning or detract from it. The following aligned practice examples enhance learning.

Planning Analytical Practice Activities: Examples

Spelling Lesson—Task Analysis

- If the objective is "Say and write phonograms *a, c, d, f*," plan to have students articulate the distinguishing features of each letter.
- If the objective is "Say, write, and read *me* through *she*," plan to have students analyze (segment) the sounds in *me*, say and write the phonograms that represent those sounds, then read the word. Caution: when analyzing sounds in a particular word (e.g., *me*), do not talk about the other sound of phonogram *e*. That diverts attention from the objective ("Say, write, and read the word *me*").

Writing Lesson—Task Analysis

- If the objective is "Identify attributes of a simple sentence," plan time for students to identify the word to capitalize, the subject noun or pronoun, the action word, and the end punctuation of one or more example sentences.
- If the objective is "Compose an informative narrative," plan time for students to analyze decisions to be made during each stage of the writing process.

Reading Lesson—Task Analysis

- If the objective is "Identify precise language," preselect words for students to analyze and explain why the author chose those words.

Examples of massed and distributed practice activities are patterns that enable teachers to check their own practice activities.

Planning Massed and Distributed Practice Activities: Examples

Spelling Lesson—Massed Practice and Distributed Practice

- After introducing the first four phonograms to kindergartners and first-graders, plan two-minute oral phonogram reviews four times a day, rather than one eight-minute review once a day. As more phonograms are introduced and students become more proficient, plan to review twenty to thirty phonograms in five to eight minutes once a day prior to spelling dictation.
- Remove single-letter phonograms from the daily review pile as soon as students say and write them accurately. Review these once a week, then once a month. Include difficult phonograms each time they occur in the week's spelling dictation lessons until mastery is achieved.

Writing Lesson—Massed Practice and Distributed Practice

- After sections A–G have been written in the notebook, plan to have students write two or three simple sentences daily until most students consistently include all attributes of simple sentences.
- Plan to reinforce attributes of simple sentences throughout the year by having students write and edit three types of compositions.

Reading Lesson—Massed Practice and Distributed Practice

- Plan time to have students identify precise language until they can accurately identify precise language in new stories.
- Plan to review narrative structure on a regular basis after introducing informatives.

Finally, aligned practice activities should also provide students with opportunities to manage their attention so new learning can be mastered quickly. Through daily practice, students learn to maintain and switch attention as needed to accomplish a task.

Planning Practice Activities That Develop Attention Management: Examples

Spelling Lesson—Maintaining Attention

- Plan choral rather than individual responses during oral and written phonogram reviews and spelling dictation.

continued

Spelling Lesson—Switching Attention

- Provide time for reading spelling/vocabulary words two ways: reading for spelling practices processing sounds sequentially; reading the whole word develops fluency. Explain to students that daily practice in switching attention prepares them for using this strategy when they are reading books.

Writing Lesson—Maintaining Attention

- Plan to have students individually mark the subject noun or pronoun in a sentence. Have them check with a partner before whole-group discussion.

Writing Lesson—Switching Attention

- Plan opportunities for students to revise sentences written on the board for word choice, then switch attention to editing for English conventions. Explain that this prepares them for the same process in writing compositions.

Reading Lesson—Maintaining Attention

- After presenting questions for reflection or to check for understanding, ask all students to think about the questions and then to write responses on think pads or individual slates or respond by raising their hands. Then call on one or more individuals.

Reading Lesson—Switching Attention

- When students stumble over an unfamiliar word, repeat the last word read correctly (signal), then coach as they decode the unfamiliar word. Have them reread the entire sentence to regain comprehension. Have students use the same process when reading silently.

Aligning information, questions and responses, and practice activities to each objective facilitates retention of skills and concepts, thereby enhancing students' learning.

Step 4: Preparing the Introduction and Conclusion

Last, teachers design an introduction and conclusion that are also aligned to the objective.

Introducing the Lesson

Students usually expend more effort and consequently increase their learning if they know *what* they will be learning and *why* it is important (the purpose of learning).

Designing Lesson Introductions

1. Plan an introduction that focuses attention on the new lesson content and connects to students' prior learning.
2. Plan active participation by all students.

The following examples make an abstract concept concrete.

Planning Lesson Introductions: Examples

Spelling Lesson

TEACHER: "Yesterday you practiced saying and writing four phonograms. Let's review those sounds."

STUDENTS: "/ă/ /ā/ /ah/ /k/ /s/ /d/ /f/"

TEACHER: "You remembered the sounds of the first four very well. Today you will learn to say and write four new phonograms: *g*, *o*, *qu*, and *s*."

Writing Lesson

TEACHER: "You have been composing oral sentences using sections A–G words. Tell me what you included in those sentences."

STUDENTS: "We included who the sentence was about and what was happening."

TEACHER: "Yes. A good oral sentence tells who the sentence is about and what is happening to a person or animal. Today, I will explain what else you must include when you write sentences."

Reading Lesson

TEACHER: "You have identified precise language in stories I have read aloud. Think about some of the precise language we've talked about, then tell me what precise words are and why authors select words carefully."

STUDENTS: "Precise language paints a picture of the characters and the setting. This makes you feel as if you know the characters. You can imagine where they are and what they are doing."

TEACHER: "Yes. When the author clearly describes the characters, the setting, and the action, the story becomes real. Today, I will teach you that authors also appeal to our emotions by the words they choose."

These sample introductions direct students' attention to the new objective; they connect with students' prior knowledge; and they require active participation.

Closing the Lesson

An effective closing of the lesson requires all students to summarize their learning. It also includes a transition to the new objective that makes clear the relationships within and between language arts subjects.

Designing Lesson Closures

1. Plan active participation by all students: Prepare questions that require students to mentally summarize what they learned about critical aspects of the lesson objective; provide wait time for each student to think, then ask individual students to share; and hold all students accountable by calling on different students (nonvolunteers) in successive lessons.
2. Plan smooth transitions from one objective within a lesson to another and between spelling, writing, and reading lessons.

Examples of effective closures follow.

Planning Lesson Closings: Examples

Transitions Within Lessons

TEACHER: "We just finished reviewing two-letter phonograms that have different pronunciations or different spellings depending on their locations within a word. Tell me how that helps you spell and read."

STUDENTS: "Knowing that we use *ay* to say /ā/ at the end of English words helps to improve our spelling. Knowing that the letter *a* usually says /ā/ at the end of a syllable helps us read words more quickly."

TEACHER: "Yes. You can read these phonograms automatically, so you will be able to read books fluently. Now we will practice writing them so you can spell accurately."

Transitions Between Lessons

TEACHER: "In the reading lesson today, you read an informative-narrative passage. What were the narrative and the informative elements of the story?"

STUDENTS: (Guide as students identify the elements.)

TEACHER: "Yes. This informative narrative has two characters, a simple setting, and lots of facts. Today, I will teach you to write an informative narrative."

Transitions are made more efficient when the teacher develops daily routines in spelling, writing, and reading lessons. Well-developed routines free students' working memory for concentration on the new information to be presented (see Chapter 5, page 180).

It is often said that preparation is 90 percent of any task. Providing a suitable climate and preparing well-designed lessons ensure that most language arts lessons will be successful for most students.

Chapter Summary

Successful practitioners of *The Writing Road to Reading* program must plan an environment conducive to learning and must know the content to be taught, the most effective way to teach it (Chapter 2), and the principles of learning and instruction (Chapter 5). Integrating content, principles, and procedures empowers teachers to be successful decision makers, equipping them with the ability to help *all* students learn to read and write. Chapter 2 will provide explicit instructional strategies, procedures, and sample dialogues for teaching integrated spelling, writing, and reading lessons.

Chapter 2

DELIVERING INTEGRATED LANGUAGE ARTS INSTRUCTION

CHAPTER OVERVIEW

Explicit, Interactive, Diagnostic Instruction

Delivering Integrated Spelling Instruction

Delivering Integrated Writing Instruction

Delivering Integrated Reading Instruction

Explicit, Interactive, Diagnostic Instruction

CHAPTER 1 focused on *what* spelling, writing, and reading components to teach. Chapter 2 focuses on *how* to teach those components. Romalda Spalding's study under the neuropsychologist Dr. Samuel Orton, her experience at Harvard's Children's Hospital, and over twenty years of teaching students from varied backgrounds enabled her to incorporate time-tested principles of learning and instruction in her method. Students learn most efficiently if the instruction is explicit. Continuous teacher-student interaction enables teachers to evaluate their instruction, identify students who need challenge and those who need additional help, and differentiate instruction accordingly.

Modeling

When *modeling,* the teacher carries out each task while the student observes and builds a conceptual model of the processes that are required to accomplish the task. Although many tasks are concrete and observable, this is not the case with cognitive tasks such as reasoning, problem solving, knowledge retrieval, and decision making. Therefore, the teacher makes these tasks visible by thinking out loud while describing the reasoning process.

Spalding teachers provide clear, concise models for each new spelling, writing, or reading task. These tasks range from modeling precise pronunciation of phonemes in spelling to modeling the writing process for composing narrative and informative passages to modeling the five mental actions that enhance reading comprehension.

Coaching

When coaching, the teacher guides, prompts, and provides feedback as the student performs a task, or part of a task. The goal is to bring the performance of the novice closer to that of the expert. During the coaching phase, the teacher prompts a component of the working memory system. The teacher guides and supervises practice until automaticity is achieved.

Spalding coaching begins after the teacher has provided one or more clear, specific models and has checked students' understanding of each new spelling, writing, and reading skill.

Scaffolding and Fading

In instructional terms, a *scaffold* is a support system. When *scaffolding*, the teacher provides support because novice learners are not yet able to perform a task independently. The difference between coaching and scaffolding is in degree. During the coaching phase, the new skill is not yet in long-term memory, so *most* students need help *most* of the time. In scaffolding, help is more sparing, given only as need is demonstrated. *Fading* occurs when the majority of students know the content and can apply their knowledge independently. Continuous careful observation of all students actively participating enables the teacher to monitor and adjust the level of support and the amount of practice needed by each student.

For example, Spalding teachers can usually fade quickly on single-sound consonants, easy multiletter phonograms, attributes of *simple sentences*, and elements of narratives. However, they need to scaffold longer on difficult multiletter phonograms, complex sentences, multiparagraph passages, and the use of five mental actions to derive implied main ideas. During this process of modeling, coaching, scaffolding, and fading, students' participation helps them become independent learners.

Articulation

The teacher requires *students* to verbalize the principles, rules, or situations underlying knowledge use. This process can take place through questions that check understanding, dialogues, critiques, or summaries. It is well known in learning theory that verbalizing aids transfer to new situations. As students put their understanding into words, they learn to generalize more efficiently and to discover aspects of the principles they did not understand before.

Spalding students explain letter formation and placement within words; rule applications; differences between simple, compound, and complex sentences; and attributes of narrative and informative text.

Reflection

Reflection occurs when students evaluate their performance of motor tasks, their problem-solving skills, and their thinking processes. During the process of reflection, teachers have students compare their performance with expert performance to determine progress toward proficiency. Teachers may show videos of proficient students implementing spelling, writing, and reading tasks. Spalding students compare their letter formation today with that of yesterday, and their handwriting in new notebook sections with previous sections, and reflect on how knowing the rules has improved their spelling and reading. They reflect on their daily performance composing written sentences and then paragraphs. In reading, they reflect on books they have read and explain how mental actions and knowledge of text structure assist their comprehension.

Exploration

During exploration, students are encouraged to apply skills to new situations; they figure out how and when each skill is relevant; and they take complete responsibility for their performance. Spalding students apply their decoding skills to reading independently. They apply their knowledge of phonograms, spelling rules, and attributes of sentences to compose simple, compound, and complex sentences and later to compose informative-narrative, informative, and narrative paragraphs. They use their knowledge of five mental actions to comprehend library books and content-area texts read independently. Dr. Sylvia Farnham-Diggory, former H. Rodney Sharp Professor of Educational Studies and Psychology and director of the Reading Study Center, University of Delaware, had this to say after analyzing The Spalding Method:

> Instructionally, a Spalding teacher has been trained to *model* her own analytical processes; she is trained to *coach* rather than didactically preach; and she is trained in techniques of *scaffolding*. The whole curriculum is, in effect, a giant scaffold. It provides a supporting structure for dealing with print. *Articulation* of principles is consistently demanded of students. They must always explain and justify their reasoning. *Reflection* is embodied in the marking system—the simple but very effective system for annotating parts of words that exemplify rules. . . . *Exploration* is assured through the program's emphasis on literature. Both teacher and students plunge into new realms together, and many is the time I've heard *teachers* express surprise and relief to discover that the principles they've been teaching really do come to their rescue in literature that was never written with those principles in mind. (1987, 13–14)

Delivering Integrated Spelling Instruction

Spelling lessons include explicit, interactive, diagnostic instruction in phonemic awareness, systematic phonics, and automatic word recognition of high-frequency vocabulary, frequently referred to as *word fluency*.

Phonemic Awareness

Beginners at any grade level and adult nonreaders need to understand that spoken words consist of sequences of sounds (phonemes). Many adult nonreaders are surprised to discover that English makes sense if they understand this principle.

Grade-Level Sequence

To teach phonemic awareness informally to preschool children, the teacher can say short words, such as *me*, then say the word by sounds: /m/ /ē/. Counting and then blending the sounds will also make children aware that words are made up of individual sounds. Teaching the alphabet song and alphabet names, reading poems that rhyme, and drawing children's attention to the ending sounds also develop phonemic awareness. Young children love to play these and other word games. Explicit, systematic phonemic awareness instruction begins on the first academic day of school. Primary-grade teachers model segmenting spoken words into individual sounds, counting the sounds, and then blending them into words. Teachers in third grade and above review phonemic awareness. See lesson objectives for academic day one in the "Planning" section of the *Kindergarten Through Sixth-Grade Teacher Guides*.

Segmenting spoken words into individual sounds is the first step in spelling dictation. Blending those sounds into words is the last step, so isolated phonemic awareness activities are phased out when spelling dictation begins. Detailed instructional strategies for phonemic awareness activities are found in the "Delivering" section of the *Kindergarten Through Third-Grade Teacher Guides*.

Systematic Phonics

In Spalding phonics instruction, the sounds represented by alphabet letters and fixed letter combinations (phonograms) are taught with handwriting.

Preparing Students for Seeing, Saying, and Writing Phonograms

Teaching handwriting with phonograms uses four channels to the mind—seeing, hearing, saying, and writing. Primary-grade children, and older students having difficulty, are taught that the mind directs the hand to write accurately. Writing letters and numbers correctly requires a thorough knowledge of how each letter and number is formed. If letters are formed incorrectly, they are visualized incorrectly. Then, students will not form the correct symbols for the sounds; and motor patterns, once established, are difficult to correct. This can be a cause of serious *reading* difficulties because beginners do not then recognize the letters when they appear in print. Saying the sounds and writing the phonograms will prevent or overcome confusion and awkward and reversed letter formation.

Many teachers and parents fail to realize the importance of teaching the correct formation of letters from the start of teaching the written language. In The Spalding Method, the techniques of easy, legible, and neat handwriting are taught from the beginning, so handwriting can be an accurate and easy tool for learning. Students who are denied explicit and sustained handwriting instruction will be hampered and frustrated when learning to compose sentences and paragraphs (see Chapter 5, "Why *The Writing Road to Reading* Works").

Grade-Level Sequence

Beginning on academic day one, teachers explain that a phonogram is a single letter, or a fixed combination of two, three, or four letters, representing one sound in a given word. They explain that knowing the phonogram sounds will help students read. Knowing the purpose of each task enhances motivation to learn. Many schools schedule a course called "Parent Introduction to Spalding" so parents can help their children at home. This course is especially valuable for parents of students who need extra help.

Beginning on academic day two, kindergartners are taught to recognize and say the sound or sounds for one new phonogram each day, beginning with the vowel *o* because it has only one feature—a circle. While kindergartners are learning the sounds of the first twenty-six phonograms, teachers prepare them for writing the phonograms. Each day, the students practice saying and forming letters in the air, in sand, or in another suitable medium. Prewriting activities such as stringing beads, cutting, gluing, and coloring help students develop sufficient motor control to begin writing phonograms on 5/8-inch (1.6-cm) lined paper (about week four). In about three months, they are ready to write in their spelling/vocabulary notebooks, and the teacher dictates the high-frequency words they segmented and blended earlier.

First-grade to sixth-grade students say and write new phonograms each day until all seventy phonograms have been introduced. See the grade-appropriate sequence in the "Planning" section of the *Kindergarten Through Sixth-Grade Teacher Guides* and the instructional strategies and procedures for oral and written phonogram reviews in the "Delivering" section.

Instructional Strategies

Clear and easy handwriting takes *patient* supervision and consistent feedback from the teacher each day, as well as personal evaluation from students, to develop a sense of pride and accomplishment. *Success in these handwriting skills gives students of any age great pride and interest in learning each day's lesson and builds self-confidence.*

1. Check that chairs and desks or tables are the right height to ensure students' comfort. Students' feet should touch the floor, and their arms should rest comfortably on the desks. Clear the desk of books and materials not needed.
   - Seat *left-handed students* on the side of the room to the teacher's right so they can easily face the teacher as they look up from their writing.
2. Teach comfortable sitting and arm positions and techniques for both left- and right-handed students.
   - Sit with *hips against the back* of the chair, *feet flat* on the floor, and *back straight*, with *head high*. The straight spinal column supports the head.
   - Keep two inches between the body and the desk. Lean forward just enough to see the paper clearly, but *keep the head high*. Let the chair support the weight of the body. Do not let the head fall forward, because the neck and back muscles would then carry its heavy weight.
   - Place both *forearms on the desk* with the *elbows just off the front edge* and *comfortably close* to the body. The *elbow* on the writing arm should be *stationary* so the student learns to write with the hand, not the entire arm.
3. Model (explain and demonstrate) a comfortable pencil grip, correct paper position, and techniques for both left- and right-handed students.
   - Explain that in writing letters, the parts of the body actively engaged are the *mind*; the *mouth*, which quietly says (aloud at first) the detailed steps necessary to write each letter; the *hand* holding the pencil to write; and the other *hand*, which holds and moves the paper.
   - Explain that a *six-sided* common *wood pencil* is used for beginners of every age because it can be controlled more easily than a round one.
     - ➤ Explain and demonstrate that a pencil held across the palm of your hand weighs so little that minimal pressure from the hand is required to hold and move it. (Hold a primary-grade child's elbow in one of your hands and the child's hand in

the other to show that no weight is felt in the arm and hand. There should be no pressure in the arm or fingers.)

➤ Teach students that the *middle* finger and *thumb* form a vise for holding the pencil. The index, or *pointing*, finger rests between the middle finger and the thumb. The *pointing* finger curves, and the end of the nail sits on the pencil where the paint ends, about an inch from the point. All *knuckles* including the thumb, should be *bent*, and the fingers and thumb should be *rounded* to the same degree (liken this to the way a cat's claws are rounded). The pencil should rest forward of the main knuckle. Let a little light show through under the big knuckle of the little finger so that the writing hand can move easily.

➤ Explain that you write with the *point* of the pencil. The other hand moves the paper enough so that the pencil point remains in a small area just forward of the center of the body.

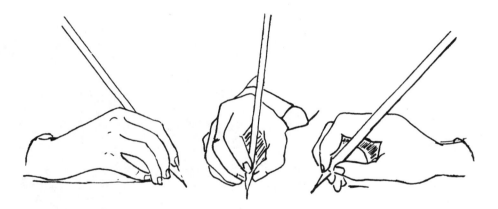

These sketches show how the pencil is held in the right hand.

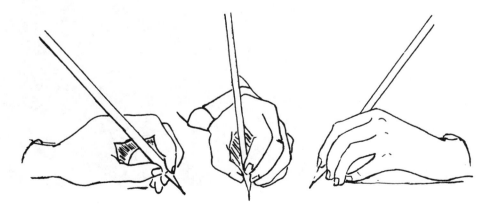

The pencil is held this way in the left hand.

- Teach students the following paper, hand, and arm positions for writing.
  - ➤ Place the hand that does not hold the pencil across the top edge of the paper, to hold the paper steady or move it back and forth and up and down as needed.
  - ➤ Use one hand for holding the pencil and writing. The *wrist* should be *straight*, and the whole hand and arm should be *below the baseline* on which they write. (Never use the writing hand to hold the paper.)
  - ➤ Keep the *side edge* of the *paper* and the *arm* of the hand that holds the pencil *parallel*, like the two rails of a railroad track.
  - ➤ Left-handed students should keep the paper *parallel* to the *writing (left)* arm. Place a strip of tape near the top of the desk to show the correct slant for the top edge of the paper. Explain that this keeps the paper from being turned like that of right-handed students.

Correct writing position
for left-handed student

Correct writing position
for right-handed student

4. Provide appropriate paper for handwriting.
   - For beginners through second grade, use paper with ⅝-inch (1.6-cm) spacing between lines. Wider spacing forces children to draw letters instead of writing. (Paper with a dotted midline is *not* used, because it is hard for children to touch the baseline *and* the midline. Instead, teach the concept of "halfway between lines" (midpoint) because it is essential for understanding the size relationship between tall and short letters. (See Instructional Strategies in the "Delivering" section of the *Kindergarten Through Third-Grade Teacher Guides.*)
   - For third grade and above, use paper with standard ⅜-inch (1.0-cm) spacing.
   - From the beginning, teach students to follow directions, to articulate the purpose of legible handwriting, and to describe the steps involved.
5. Explain and demonstrate features and reference points.
   - Manuscript letters are made of a circle, or parts of it, and straight lines.
   - The *clock face* is the reference point for forming a circle and letters or parts of letters that begin at 2 on the clock.

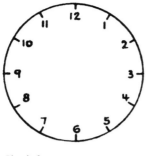

Clock face

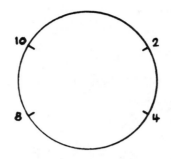

These are the four
points used most often.

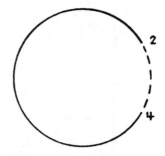

This shows how the clock
is used to write *c* (from 2 to 4).

- The *midpoint* is the reference point for *halfway* between the top line and the baseline. (See the "Delivering" section of the *Kindergarten Through Second-Grade Teacher Guides.*)
6. Model feature formation.
   - During direct instruction, seat students who have difficulty learning nearby; during the day, make time to provide the *extra* practice they need in a small group.
   - Explain and demonstrate correct formation of the following six features that are used to form all alphabet letters. For primary-grade children, use the Spalding Feature Formation poster (available in individual or classroom size) to provide a visual image.
     ➤ A circle that begins just below the midpoint at 2 and goes up and around the clock to 2
     ➤ A short line that begins at the midpoint and sits on the baseline
     ➤ A tall line that begins just below the line above and sits on the baseline
     ➤ A straight line that begins at the midpoint and extends the same distance below the baseline
     ➤ A line that begins at the midpoint and slants to the baseline in the direction we write
     ➤ A short horizontal line in the direction we write

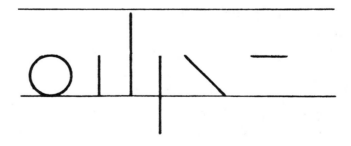

Do not let students retrace the horizontal line backward before lifting the pencil, because this habit reverses the correct directionality that helps them write and read accurately.

- Coach students as they practice identifying 2 on the clock and the hand and arm movement involved in making a circle beginning at 2 on the clock (see page 42).
- Coach students as they practice forming the six features. Monitor them while they practice making circles that begin at 2 on the clock just below the midpoint, short lines that begin at the midpoint, and tall lines that begin just below the line above.
- For students with severe motor or memory problems, see Chapter 4, "Evaluating Skills Mastery," page 158.

Introducing Phonograms 1–8 with Handwriting

Mrs. Spalding gave a great deal of study to the techniques of teaching good and easy handwriting. *The prime reason is that it is the simplest, most direct means of connecting sounds of English to their letter forms.* Few, if any, books on handwriting connect the *sounds* of the letters with our written language. Yet what meaning can the form of a letter have unless it conveys its sound as the student learns to write it? This is one of the reasons why *writing* is the logical road to *reading*. Manuscript writing is used at first, whatever the age of the student, because it makes the needed visible link between handwriting and all printed matter. Even in the computer age, manuscript is needed for lettering maps, diagrams, and drawings.

Grade-Level Sequence

Kindergartners begin writing one new phonogram per day after they have developed fine motor control, typically after four weeks. First-graders learn or review four new phonograms with handwriting each day; second-graders learn or review the alphabet in two days; third-graders, and older students, learn or review all seventy phonograms in four days. (See the weekly sequence in grade-level lesson objectives in the "Planning" section of the *Kindergarten Through Sixth-Grade Teacher Guides*.)

Instructional Strategies

1. Follow these procedures when giving instruction on a board or easel.
   - Stand to the left of what is to be read and place your index finger before the center of the first letter when pointing to anything on a board or when pointing to words on paper or in a book.
   - Slide your finger over what is read so that your index finger is always at the place where the reading is taking place. (This is very helpful for those students who tend to confuse the proper direction of text.)
2. Explain that the purpose of writing phonograms is to link the sounds of the language to the printed symbols. Then explain general rules for manuscript handwriting.
   - All letters sit on a baseline.
   - For letters that begin at 2 on the clock, rounding conforms to the curve of the circle. Every round letter should fit on the same-size clock.
   - Lines begin at the top and are straight and parallel. All letters that go below the baseline go the same distance below the baseline as above it.

- Letters or parts of letters are of two sizes. They are either tall or short. Tall letters or tall parts approach but do not touch the line above. Short letters or short parts are half as high as tall letters. They begin at the *midpoint* between the height of a tall letter and the baseline.
- Dots and crossbars are tiny, formed just above the *midpoint*; crossbars are formed in the direction in which we write.

3. Ask questions to check students' understanding: e.g., "Where do all letters sit?" or "What are two types of letters?" Questions such as these enhance understanding and application.

4. Model (explain and demonstrate) precisely how each manuscript letter that begins at 2 on the clock should be formed and placed.
   - Show the clock face and explain that it is used as a reference to form the clock letters.

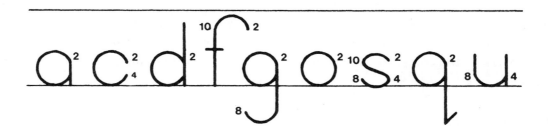

- Show each phonogram card and say the sound or sounds precisely—*not* letter names, because the names of only five letters (the vowels *a*, *e*, *i*, *o*, and *u*) are sounds, and their names are not their most common sounds.
  - ➤ Standardize descriptive phrases; e.g., say consistently, from the beginning, "Letters that begin at 2 on the clock *go up and around* the clock," and say "*the direction in which we write*," rather than the words *left* or *right*.
  - ➤ Point out any differences between the print on the Spalding phonogram cards and the manuscript letters in text, to familiarize primary-grade children with both the printed form and the written manuscript form of these letters, thus eliminating confusion when they begin to read from books. (The letters *a* and *g* may have forms in print quite different from those in manuscript.)
- After introducing each phonogram, ask one or two questions to check students' understanding of the letter features before they write the phonogram. Questions, such as "Where does this phonogram start?" and "What two features are used to write this phonogram?" give students an opportunity to articulate the formation of letters.

5. Model precisely, saying the sound or sounds and forming manuscript letters that begin at 2 on the clock: *a, c, d, f, g, o, s, qu*. Follow the procedures with precise dialogue (see the next page) and the sequence in the "Planning" section of the *Kindergarten Through Sixth-Grade Teacher Guides*.

Procedures for Introducing Phonograms 1–8 with Precise Dialogue

"I will show you how each letter is written."

Show card 1 and say its three sounds: /ă/ /ā/ /ah/. Students repeat the sounds.

"This is a short letter. Short letters fill the space between the *midpoint* and the baseline. Form the letter without lifting the pencil. Start far enough in from the edge of your paper to make a clock face. *Start at 2 and go up and around the clock, touching the baseline and stopping at 2. Pull a straight line down to the baseline.*"

Coach and monitor students as they say the sounds and repeat the directions (italicized) softly as they write the letter on their paper.

Show card 2 and say two sounds: /k/ /s/. Students repeat the sounds.

"This is a short letter. It starts just far enough from *a* to make the clock face. *Start at 2 and go up and around the clock, touching the baseline and stopping at 4.*"

Coach and monitor students as they say the sounds and repeat the directions (italicized) softly as they write the letter on their paper.

Show card 3 and say the sound: /d/. Students repeat the sound.

"This is a short letter with a tall part. Form the letter without lifting the pencil." Put your finger before the round part to show that the round part comes first. Draw attention to the feel of the upturned tongue where it touches the upper ridge behind the teeth as the letter *d* is sounded. Say, "*Start at 2 and go up and around the clock, touching the baseline and closing the circle at 2. Continue straight up toward the line above but do not touch it. Without lifting the pencil, come straight down to the baseline (retrace).*"

Coach and monitor students as they say the sound and repeat the directions (italicized) softly as they write the letter on their paper. Make sure that the tall part is twice the height of the short part.

continued

Show card 4 and say the sound: /f/. Students repeat the sound. (Demonstrate on a clock where this letter begins and that it conforms to the width of a clock. Emphasize that the crossbar is formed in the direction in which we write.)

"This is a tall letter. *Start at 2 just below the line above. Without touching the top line, go up and around to 10 and pull a straight line down to the baseline. Lift the pencil. Form a tiny crossbar just above the midpoint.*"

Coach and monitor students as they say the sound and repeat the directions (italicized) softly as they write the letter on their paper.

Monitor students to ensure that they begin at 2. Make sure each student writes the letter *f* before making the crossbar in the direction we write. Check that students do not retrace the crossbar backward.

Show card 5 and say the two sounds: /g/ /j/. Students repeat the two sounds.

"This is a short letter. *Start at 2 and go up and around the clock, touching the baseline and stopping at 2. Pull a straight line down the same distance below the baseline and around from 4 to 8.*"

Coach and monitor students as they say the sounds and repeat the directions (italicized) softly as they write the letter on their paper. Make sure that the width below the line matches the round part above and that a short letter could sit on the baseline beneath *g* without touching *g*.

Show card 6 and say the three sounds: /ŏ/ /ō/ /o͞o/. Students repeat the sounds.

"This is a short letter. *Start at 2 and go up and around the clock, touching the baseline and stopping at 2.*"

Coach and monitor students as they say the sounds and repeat the directions (italicized) softly as they write the letter on their paper.

Show card 7 and say the two sounds: /s/ /z/. Students repeat the two sounds.

"This is a short letter. *Start at 2, go up and around to 10, and slide across to 4 (directly below 2). Curve down, touching the baseline and curving up to 8 (directly below 10).*"

Coach and monitor students as they say the sounds and repeat the directions (italicized) softly as they write the letter on their paper. Make sure each student begins at 2 and goes up, then finishes at 8 on the clock.

Show card 8 and say the sound: /kw/. Students repeat the sound.

"It takes two letters to say /kw/. Both are short letters. Each is formed without lifting the pencil. The tiny flag is formed in the direction in which we write. The second letter sits close. *Start the first letter at 2 and go up and around the clock, touching the baseline and stopping at 2. Pull a straight line down the same distance below the baseline, and make a tiny flag in the direction we write. Start the second letter at the midpoint with a short down line to 8, round from 8 to 4 touching the baseline, continue up to the midpoint, and retrace the straight line down to the baseline.*"

Coach and monitor students as they say the sound and repeat the directions (italicized) softly as they write the letter on their paper.

Instructional Strategies (Continued)

6. Observe students' writing daily and listen as they explain the concepts and procedures; then provide further instruction or refinements in small groups as needed (see Chapter 4).

   • Each day after introducing the number of phonograms appropriate for your grade level, have primary-grade children practice saying and writing the phonograms across the page to develop ease of formation and correct spacing between the clock letters. See written phonogram review procedures in the "Delivering" section of the *Kindergarten Through Sixth-Grade Teacher Guides*. Their papers should look like this. Note that each letter is written once.

   • Have beginners practice writing at least three different single-letter phonograms at a time (e.g., *a c d*), rather than a row of each letter. This requires them to use their minds while practicing letter formation.

   • Have primary-grade children also practice on the board or easel.

     ➢ Draw lines about three inches (7.5 cm) apart on the board; the top line should be no higher than the tallest student.

     ➢ Model position at the board and correct chalk or marker grip.

     ➢ Each student should stand comfortably close to the board and write no higher than the top of his or her head.

➤ Have each student hold the chalk or marker with four fingers along its length and the thumb on the opposite side.

➤ Have each student write with the side of the point—not with the point itself— to eliminate squeaking and slipping.

- Model erasing at the board and at the desk.
  - ➤ When erasing, start where the writing began.
  - ➤ Begin from the top and go down, then up and down across the board in the direction we read and write.
  - ➤ Have small groups take turns writing at the board.
- Send one row of students at a time to the board to review each day's lesson.
- Make sure each student holds the marker properly, says the sounds and writes each letter correctly, and then erases correctly. Errors in writing can thus be readily caught and corrected.

Introducing Phonograms 9–26 with Handwriting

After students can consistently say and write phonograms 1 through 8, introduce phonograms that begin with a line.

Instructional Strategies

1. Teach line letters as soon as students are adept at starting clock letters far enough from the preceding letter to make the circle and are able to begin each letter at 2 and *go up and around* the clock. (See *Kindergarten Through Second-Grade Teacher Guides* for appropriate pacing.)

2. Model *forming* line letters close to the preceding letter. Do not lift the pencil off the paper to complete any of the lowercase letters except in making the second part of *k*, crossbars, and dots. Show how the numbers on the clock face are used to write line letters with clock parts.

3. Ask questions to check for understanding before children write the letters that begin with a line, such as "Is this phonogram tall or short?" or "Where do we start this phonogram?" Follow the procedure with precise dialogue below. See the illustration.

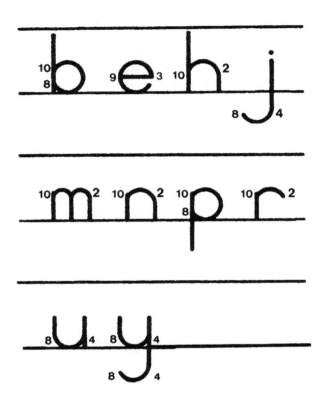

Procedures for Introducing Phonograms 9–26 with Precise Dialogue

Show card 9 and say the sound: /b/. Students repeat the sound.

"This is a tall letter with a short part. The lips form a line in saying /b/. This helps you remember to start with a line when writing this phonogram. Form the letter without lifting the pencil. *Start at the top just below the line above; pull the pencil down to the baseline. Retrace to 10; curve around the clock to 2, touching the baseline and curving up to 8.*"

Have all students feel the line their lips make when they say /b/. (The kinesthetic feel of the two letters *b* and *d* can keep students from reversing them. Do not teach these two letters together, however.)

Coach and monitor students as they say the sound and repeat the directions (italicized) softly as they write the letter on their paper.

continued

Show card 10 and say the two sounds: /ĕ/ /ē/. Students repeat the sounds. (Put 9 and 3 on a clock face to show letter formation.)

"This letter is short. Form it without lifting the pencil. *Start midway between the height of a short letter and the baseline. Make a straight line from 9 to 3 on a clock. Form a corner by continuing up and around the clock, touching the baseline and stopping at 4.*"

Coach and monitor students as they say the sounds and repeat the directions (italicized) softly as they write the letter on their paper. See the model on page 49. Note that *e* is the only letter for which a line is made in reference to the clock face.

Show card 11 and say the sound: /h/. Students repeat the sound.

"This is a tall letter with a short part. Form it without lifting the pencil. *Start at the top just below the line above; pull a straight line down to the baseline. Retrace to 10, round from 10 to 2, and pull a straight line to the baseline.*"

Coach and monitor students as they say the sound and repeat the directions (italicized) softly as they write the letter on their paper.

Show card 12 and say the two sounds: /ĭ/ /ī/. Students repeat the two sounds.

"This is a short letter. *Start at the midpoint and pull a straight line to the baseline. Make a small dot by pressing the pencil just above the letter and lifting it.*"

Coach and monitor students as they say the sounds and repeat the directions (italicized) softly as they write the letter on their paper.

Show card 13 and say the sound: /j/. Students repeat the sound.

"This is a short letter that goes below the baseline. *Start at the midpoint, pull a straight line down the same distance below the baseline, and round from 4 to 8. Make a small dot by pressing the pencil just above the letter and lifting it.*"

Coach and monitor students as they say the sound and repeat the directions (italicized) softly as they write the letter on their paper.

Show card 14 and say the sound: /k/. Students repeat the sound.

"This is a tall letter with a short part. *Start at the top and pull a straight line to the baseline. Start the short part at the midpoint, slant down and in to the tall line, and then slant down and out to the baseline.*"

Coach and monitor students as they say the sound and repeat the directions (italicized) softly as they write the letter on their paper. Make sure the second part starts at the midpoint, slants down and in to the tall line, then slants down and out to the baseline.

Show card 15 and say the sound: /l/. Students repeat the sound.

"This is a tall letter. *Start at the top and pull a straight line to the baseline.*"

Coach and monitor students as they say the sound and repeat the directions (italicized) softly as they write the letter on their paper.

Show card 16 and say the sound: /m/. Students repeat the sound.

"This is a short letter. *Start at the midpoint and pull a straight line down to the baseline, retrace to 10, round from 10 to 2, and pull a straight line to the baseline. Retrace to 10, round from 10 to 2, and pull a straight line to the baseline.*"

Coach and monitor students as they say the sound and repeat the directions (italicized) softly as they write the letter on their paper.

Show card 17 and say the sound: /n/. Students repeat the sound.

"This is a short letter. *Start at the midpoint and pull a straight line down to the baseline, retrace to 10, round from 10 to 2, and pull a straight line to the baseline.*"

Coach and monitor students as they say the sound and repeat the directions (italicized) softly as they write the letter on their paper.

Show card 18 and say the sound: /p/. Students repeat the sound.

"This is a short letter that goes below the baseline. *Start at the midpoint, pull a straight line down the same distance below the baseline, retrace to 10, and curve around the clock, touching the baseline and curving up to 8.*"

Coach and monitor students as they say the sound and repeat the directions (italicized) softly as they write the letter on their paper.

Show card 19 and say the sound: /r/. Students repeat the sound.

"This is a short letter." *Start at the midpoint, pull a straight line to the baseline, retrace to 10, and round from 10 to 2.*" Demonstrate that it conforms to the width of a clock face.

Coach and monitor students as they say the sound and repeat the directions (italicized) softly as they write the letter on their paper. Make sure that each student rounds the curved part over to 2 on the clock.

continued

Show card 20 and say the sound: /t/. Students repeat the sound.

"This is a tall letter. *Start at the top, and pull a straight line to the baseline. Lift the pencil. Draw a tiny crossbar just above the midpoint in the direction we write.*"

Coach and monitor students as they say the sound and repeat the directions (italicized) softly as they write the letter on their paper. Check that students do not retrace the crossbar backward.

Show card 21 and say the three sounds: /ŭ/ /ū/ /o͝o/. Students repeat the three sounds.

"This is a short letter. *Start at the midpoint with a short down line to 8, round from 8 to 4 touching the baseline, continue up with a straight line to the midpoint, and retrace a straight line down to the baseline.*"

Coach and monitor students as they say the sounds and repeat the directions (italicized) softly as they write the letter on their paper.

Show card 22 and say the sound: /v/. Students repeat the sound.

"This is a short letter. Form it without lifting the pencil and slant lines in the direction in which we write. *Start at the midpoint, slant a straight line down to the baseline in the direction in which we write. Slant a straight line up to the midpoint.*"

Coach and monitor students as they say the sound and repeat the directions (italicized) softly as they write the letter on their paper.

Show card 23 and say the sound: /w/. Students repeat the sound.

"This is a short letter. Form it without lifting the pencil and slant lines in the direction in which we write. *Start at the midpoint and slant a straight line down to the baseline. Slant a straight line up to the midpoint, slant a straight line down to the baseline, then slant a straight line up to the midpoint.*"

Coach and monitor students as they say the sound and repeat the directions (italicized) softly as they write the letter on their paper.

Show card 24 and say the sound: /ks/. Students repeat the sound.

"This is a short letter. *Slant the first line in the direction in which we write. Start at the midpoint and slant a straight line down to the baseline. Lift the pencil and start at the midpoint. Slant a straight line through the middle of the letter down to the baseline.*"

Coach and monitor students as they say the sound and repeat the directions (italicized) softly as they write the letter on their paper. Check that students do not retrace.

Show card 25 and say the three sounds: /y/ /ĭ/ /ī/. Students repeat the sounds.

"This is a short letter that goes below the baseline. Form it without lifting the pencil. *Start at the midpoint with a short down line to 8, round from 8 to 4 touching the baseline, and continue up to the midpoint. Pull a straight line down the same distance below the baseline, and round from 4 to 8.*"

Coach and monitor students as they say the sounds and repeat the directions (italicized) softly as they write the letter on their paper. Make sure the width below the line matches the round part above.

Show card 26 and say the sound: /z/. Students repeat the sound.

"This is a short letter. Form the letter without lifting the pencil. *Start at the midpoint and make a straight horizontal line in the direction in which we write. Slant a straight line down to the baseline below the starting point of the top line. Make a straight line in the direction in which we write.* The top and bottom lines should be parallel."

Coach and monitor students as they say the sound and repeat the directions (italicized) softly as they write the letter on their paper.

Instructional Strategies (Continued)

4. As with clock letters, have students practice writing line letters across the page to develop ease of formation and correct spacing between letters. The papers should look like this.

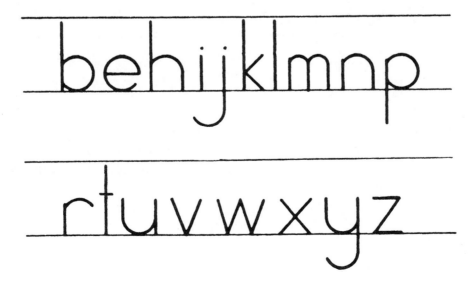

Practicing Manuscript Letters 1–26

After letters that begin at 2 on the clock and those that begin with a line have been taught, teach the spacing of both kinds of letters by dictating the alphabet, saying only each letter's sound or sounds.

Instructional Strategies

1. Have students say the sounds and write the letters across the page. The first letter written on a page should be written carefully because every letter that follows should be of the same relative size. The papers should look like this.

Introducing Phonograms 27–70 with Handwriting

After students can easily say and write phonograms 1 through 26, teach them phonograms 27 through 70 following the sequence in the grade-level lesson plans in the "Planning" section of the *Kindergarten Through Sixth-Grade Teacher Guides*.

Instructional Strategies

1. Introduce phonograms 27 though 70 in the same manner as the single letters.
   - Continue to emphasize correct formation and spacing while writing two-, three-, and four-letter phonograms.
   - Check students' understanding of multiletter phonograms by asking, "Where does the next letter start?" This question should bring one of two responses: "At 2 on the clock. Start just far enough away to make a clock," *or*, "It begins with a *line*, which *sits close* to the last letter. A line starts at the top."
2. Model (explain and demonstrate) the spacing of letters within a word and spacing between sentences.
   - A space the size of one round letter is left between words.
   - A space of two letters is left between sentences.
3. Provide practice of the phonograms and all their common sounds daily until the students see each in a printed word as standing out as a *sound,* not merely as letters.
   - Provide oral phonogram review (OPR) daily. During OPR, the students read the sounds from the cards.
   - Provide written phonogram review (WPR) daily. During WPR, the teacher dictates the sounds of the phonograms for the students to write; and students write single and multiletter phonograms in columns down the page rather than across the page.
   - Establish a consistent routine that makes daily OPR and WPR efficient. (See the detailed, grade-appropriate instructional strategies and procedures for these daily reviews in *Kindergarten Through Sixth-Grade Teacher Guides*.)

Introducing Manuscript Capital Letters

Grade-Level Sequence

After kindergartners can write the lowercase letters correctly, introduce the capitals needed to write their names. Be sure to introduce the capital letters *A* and *G* before dictating sections A–G words to be written in their primary notebooks. (See *Kindergarten Teacher Guides*.) Students in grades one and above are taught to form the capital letters after the lowercase letters are well learned. (See *First Through Sixth-Grade Teacher Guides*.)

Instructional Strategies

1. Teach the formation and use of capital letters and require beginners of any age to state the reason each time they use a capital. When students learn that a capital is used *only* where the rules of English require it, they will not insert capitals indiscriminately. (See *Kindergarten Through Sixth-Grade Teacher Guides*.)
   - All capital letters are *tall.*
   - Capital letters almost fill the space between the baseline and the line above.
   - The rules for *round* lowercase letters also apply to the following capital letters: *C, G, O, Q, S*. They each start at 2 on the clock and *go up*. Since these are tall letters,

the round parts are somewhat elongated vertically. The crossbar on the *Q* starts inside the bottom of the circle and slants *in the direction in which we write*, ending *just below* the baseline.

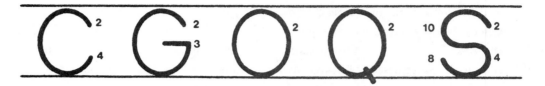

- In writing capital letters beginning with lines, make the vertical line first, starting at the top. The horizontal lines of *A*, *E*, *F*, *H*, *I*, *J*, and *T* are made in the direction in which we write. Where there is more than one horizontal line, make the top line first (*E*, *F*, *I*). Lift the pencil before making the second lines of *A*, *B*, *D*, *E*, *F*, *H*, *I*, *J*, *K*, *M*, *N*, *P*, *R*, and *T*, and they also begin at the top. *Y* is the only capital that is finished below the baseline.

2. Say the sound or sounds of each capital letter before demonstrating how to write it, and have students repeat the sounds before they write each letter.
3. Teach students that the capital letters *V*, *W*, *X*, and *Z* are made just like their lower-case letters.
   - Start at the top and make the line that slants in the direction in which we write.
   - Form *V* and *W* without lifting the pencil.
   - Start the second line of *X* at the top.
   - Write the top line of *Z* in the direction in which we write and finish without taking the pencil off the paper.

Introducing Numbers

Grade-Level Sequence

Kindergarten children learn the numbers as needed. First-grade and older students review numbers after they have learned or reviewed all manuscript capitals. See the sequence of introduction and review in *Kindergarten Through Sixth-Grade Teacher Guides.*

Instructional Strategies

1. Demonstrate and explain the following rules for forming numbers.
    *   All numbers should be made halfway between the size of a short and a tall letter so that the number 1 will not be confused with the letter *l* and the number 0 will not be confused with a capital O.
    *   The numbers 8, 9, and 0 begin at 2 on the clock. Since they are taller than short letters, elongate them somewhat vertically.
    *   The spacing of numbers that begin at 2 on the clock is the same as for manuscript letters. Start just far enough away to begin a new number at 2 on the clock.

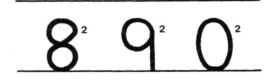

    *   The numbers 1, 4, 5, 6, and 7 begin with a line, and all lines start at the top. The left-hand vertical line of 4 is formed first. The horizontal line of the 5 is short and is drawn last *in the direction in which we write.* The bottom of 6 ends on the baseline so it never looks like 0. The number 7 begins with a line drawn *in the direction in which we write.* The numbers 1, 4, 5, and 6 sit very close to the preceding number.

    *   Numbers 2 and 3 begin at 10 on the clock and sit very close to the preceding number. Note that no lowercase letter starts at 10, so these two numbers should be thoroughly understood by students who seem confused about direction. Before the students write 2 and 3, ask where these two numbers start until every student knows they begin at 10 on the clock. This is very important, to prevent reversing.

2. Have students write all the numbers on a line showing the proper spacing.

High-Frequency Vocabulary

Constructing a Spelling/Vocabulary Notebook

In *The Writing Road to Reading*, students learn to read by writing high-frequency words from the Spalding Spelling/Vocabulary Word List in *primary* or *intermediate spelling/vocabulary notebooks*. Constructing a notebook teaches students to analyze the *written* spelling of words so they can spell, write, and read words encountered in books. The more words students analyze and read from their notebooks, the more familiar they become with written language. They expect the words they write and read to make sense because nonsense words (*pif, rif*) are never taught. The notebook is the foundation for language arts instruction; therefore, construction of the notebook is a critical activity for student achievement in *The Writing Road to Reading*.

The primary notebook is a *sewn*, stiff-cover composition book, 8½ by 6¾ inches (21.6 × 17.1 cm), with thirty-four leaves, each having twelve lines with ⅝-inch (1.6-cm) spacing. (A thicker book raises a primary-grade child's arm too high to write comfortably.)

The intermediate notebook is a *sewn*, hardcover composition book, 9¾ by 7½ inches (24.8 × 19.0 cm), with fifty leaves, each having twenty-three lines with ⅜-inch (1.0-cm) spacing. The intermediate notebook has two parts: rule pages and the Spalding Spelling/Vocabulary Word List. The pages designated as *rule pages* include phonograms and example words for the first sixteen rules. Lists of multiletter phonograms and additional, less common, phonograms are included for your convenience. (See Part Two, "Instructional Materials," pages 248–251.)

Grade-Level Sequence

Children in kindergarten through grade two begin writing high-frequency words from the Spalding Spelling/Vocabulary Word List on page 1 in their primary notebooks after they have learned to say and write forty-five phonograms and have written all the numbers. (See the *Kindergarten Through Second-Grade Teacher Guides* for specific lesson objectives.)

Students in grades three and above begin writing in their intermediate notebooks after they have learned to say and write all seventy phonograms in manuscript and have written all the numbers. These students begin writing words in the middle of the notebook, where the stitching makes it open easily. Pages are folded, forming a crease, so two columns can be written.

Instructional Strategies

While beginners of any age are mastering the first forty-five phonograms, emphasize the importance of precise handwriting and preteach the following terms, the Spalding Marking System, and rules needed to begin dictation in the notebook.

1. Explain the following terms.
   - A *syllable* is a single word or the part of a word that is pronounced by a single impulse of the voice. (This is the basic phonological unit of speech in all languages.)
   - *Vowels* are the alphabet letters *a, e, i, o,* and *u.* The letter *y* is considered a vowel when it says /ĭ/ or /ī/. Every syllable must have at least one vowel.
   - *Consonants* are all the alphabet letters that are not vowels.
2. Model identifying syllables by tapping the palm to demonstrate the meaning of *impulse* or *beat* (e.g., *me, do, lit tle*); coach and monitor as beginners tap their palms as you say simple single and multisyllabic words.
3. Model identifying vowels and consonants in words written on the board; then, coach and monitor students as they identify vowels and consonants from words written on the board.
4. Explain the purpose of the unique Spalding Marking System and demonstrate its use.
   - The marking system facilitates automatic word recognition by helping beginners of any age connect speech sounds to the written symbols that represent those sounds. Use of underlines, numbers, and brackets requires students to think as they analyze the spelling and pronunciation of words.
   - The following conventions explain the simple markings used to teach students how the rules and phonograms actually work.

Marking Conventions

➤ A vowel at the end of a syllable when it says /ā/, /ē/, /ō/, or /ū/ is *underlined in the direction we write*.

   me̲   o̲ pen   Ju̲ ly̲

An underline is drawn *just under the baseline* but far enough below to clearly distinguish it. There should be a small white space between the baseline and the underline.

➤ Phonograms of two, three, or four letters are underlined in the direction we write to unite these letters as the symbol for a single sound in a given word.

   t̲h̲in   bridge̲   eight̲

➤ Silent letters, phonogram sounds that are not given on the phonogram cards, and four of the five kinds of silent final *e*'s are underlined twice: ha̲l̲f (We say *"haf"* but write *half*); fri<u>e</u>nd (/ĕ/ is not a common sound of *ie*). The five kinds of silent final *e*'s are distinguished by the jobs they do. The first kind of silent final *e* lets the vowel say its second sound; thus the vowel, the consonant or consonants, and *e* are underlined once. The second kind is needed because English words do not end in *v* or *u*. The third is needed to let the *c* and *g* say their second sound. The fourth is needed because every syllable must have a vowel. The fifth silent final *e* is left from Old English. It does not have a job. Each except the first has a small number beside the double underline to show which kind it is.

<u>t</u>i<u>me</u>
ha<u>v</u><u>e</u>$_2$ bl<u>u</u><u>e</u>$_2$
<u>c</u>han<u>c</u><u>e</u>$_3$ <u>c</u>har<u>g</u><u>e</u>$_3$
lit tl<u>e</u>$_4$
<u>are</u>$_5$

➤ Numbers are placed above a phonogram when its sound is not the first sound. A small number is placed just above (not touching) the middle of the letter in a single-letter phonogram that has more than one sound. For a multiletter phonogram, the number is written just above and between the letters to indicate the sound. When no number is written above, this signifies that the first sound is the one used in the word. Silent final *e*'s are also numbered as shown above.

d$\overset{3}{o}$ l$\overset{2}{\underline{ow}}$
w$\overset{3}{a}$$\overset{2}{s}$ y$\overset{3}{\underline{ou}}$
p$\overset{3}{u}$t   c$\overset{4}{\underline{ou}}$n try
th$\overset{5}{\underline{ough}}$t
dr$\overset{6}{\underline{ough}}$t

➤ Some words are bracketed together for comparison.
  * A derived word with a base word (*coming/come*)
  * Words with the same spelling pattern (*catch, catcher, kitchen*)
  * Words that sound the same but use different phonograms to denote meaning (*meet/meat*)
  * Two words that might easily be confused (*form/from*). Bracketing words connects spelling and language and alerts the teacher to relationships that need to be taught in the integrated spelling and writing lesson.
5. Model the Spalding Marking System using sample spelling/vocabulary words.
  • Explain that underlines, numbers, and brackets must be formed carefully and accurately if they are to serve as visual signals, as explained below.
  • Using the word *me*, demonstrate *underlining* the exact width of the *e*. Using the word *she*, demonstrate underlining the exact width of the /sh/ by starting at the beginning of the phonogram, going to the end of the phonogram, and *lifting the pencil*. The underline signals that those two letters represent one sound. Coach and monitor students as they use a separate piece of lined paper to practice writing words and underlining phonograms.

- Using the word *do*, demonstrate placing a small number 3 neatly just above the *o* to show that the third sound of *o* is used. Using the word *the*, demonstrate that the number 2 is written neatly between the *t* and the *h* to say /th/. Coach and monitor students as they use a separate piece of lined paper to practice writing words and numbering phonograms.
- Using the two words *your* and *you*, demonstrate that a bracket begins with a tiny horizontal line halfway between the top and the baseline (at midpoint), continues with a straight vertical line down to just below the baseline under the last words of the set, and ends with a tiny horizontal line in the direction we write. The bracket must be clearly separate from the first letter of each word so the word is easy to read. Coach and monitor students as they use a separate piece of paper to practice writing these words and forming brackets precisely.

6. Preteach selected rules prior to dictating words for the notebook.
   - Teach each rule before it is needed to spell a word. The first word, *me*, illustrates rule 4: "Vowels *a, e, o,* and *u* usually say /ā/, /ē/, /ō/, or /ū/ at the end of a syllable." The whole rule is not *directly* taught (or memorized). Rather, teach the part of the rule that explains the spelling of individual words. Students soon learn that rule 4 applies to vowels *a, e, o,* and *u.*
   - Model marking rule numbers in the notebook beginning with rule 4, which explains the pronunciation of the first word, *me.* ("In *me,* the *e* says /ē/ at the end of the syllable.") Teach only the part of the rule that explains the spelling of the individual word.

➤ For the word *me*, hold up two fingers of one hand, and with the other hand point to the finger representing the sound /m/, then the finger representing the sound /ē/. Make certain the orientation is in the direction students read. Explain that the *e* is underlined to remind them that *e* says /ē/ at the end of a syllable.

➤ Explain the term *abbreviation*. Demonstrate writing r. as the abbreviation for rule and the number 4 one inch (2.5 cm) from the word *me*.

➤ Using the words *go, a, she, so, no*, demonstrate that rule 4 also helps us know how to pronounce vowels *a, e,* and *o* at the end of a syllable.

➤ Have students explain why the vowel is underlined in these words. Their response should be something like this: "In *go* (or *no*), the *o* says /ō/ because it is at the end of a syllable (or one-syllable word)."

• Explain that students will continue to mark rule numbers in their notebooks until they can explain and consistently apply rules while reading and writing.

7. Distribute the primary (or intermediate) notebooks.

• Explain to students of any age that the purpose of writing the notebook is to understand how the English language works. Also explain that the notebook pages will be numbered for quick reference, so their notebooks will be alike, and so they can use the notebooks for reading words two ways: for spelling and for reading.

➤ Number the notebooks for kindergartners beginning on page 1. (See Part Two, page 229.)

➤ Have first- and second-grade children begin numbering on page 1.

➤ Explain to students in grades three and above that their notebooks have two parts: rule pages (see samples starting on page 237 and the grade-appropriate spelling/vocabulary words). Coach and monitor as students number rule pages 1–8 in the upper right-hand corners; number spelling page 1 on the upper right corner at the middle of the notebook, where the stitching makes it open easily; continue numbering in the upper left and right corners.

8. Preteach multisyllabic word dictation procedures before they are needed for writing the first multisyllabic word.

• Explain to students of any age that writing words by syllables trains the brain to spell and sound out (decode) unfamiliar multisyllabic words by breaking them into syllables. Even beginners can learn to spell large words when they understand this principle.

• For all students, use the right hand to demonstrate the first syllable of multisyllabic words; use the left hand to represent the second syllable; then cross the right arm over the left to represent succeeding syllables. This kinesthetic effect has proved helpful to many students, regardless of age. (Do *not* confuse the presentation by calling the hands left and right.)

• For beginners, the first two-syllable word is *little* and the second is *ago*.

➤ Holding up three fingers of your right hand, say *lit* and have the students write it. Then hold up three fingers of your left hand and say *tle*.

> ➤ Model writing *lit tle* on the board or easel, leaving the space of one clock letter between syllables (*lit tle*).
> ➤ Coach and monitor beginners as they practice writing sample words (e.g. *little*, *ago*, *into*) on a separate piece of paper.
- Model applying common syllable structures when multisyllabic words are encountered in the Spalding Spelling/Vocabulary Word List; coach and monitor students as they apply these structures. (These structures are explained under the heading "Syllable Division Patterns," in "Morphology," page 225).
- Have students *stress* the vowel sound to agree with the spelling when pronouncing each syllable before writing it (*be come*, not *be cum*). The dictionary states that a monosyllable such as the word *do*, when pronounced alone, always stresses the vowel. Stressing vowel sounds makes spelling more phonetic and easy to learn. Dictionaries explain the variations in pronouncing words in different contexts and uses.

9. Follow grade-appropriate instructional strategies and the spelling dictation procedure in the *Kindergarten Through Sixth-Grade Teacher Guides*. While students are learning the procedure, the process takes a little longer; as soon as the procedure becomes routine, spelling dictation should average about one word per minute.

Spelling Dictation

The primary focus of the *first* dictation lesson is learning the procedure. Students have been pretaught rule 4; the terms *syllable*, *underline*, and *number*; and formation of the capitals *A* and *G*, to be used in writing the heading for sections A–G. Students have practiced underlining and numbering on separate pieces of paper. The teacher does most of the talking because she is modeling each step of the procedures (see the "Delivering" section of the *Kindergarten Through Sixth-Grade Teacher Guides*). The following is a sample dialogue for kindergarten or first-grade children. Although this dialogue is presented for beginners, the basic procedure is the same for students of any age.

Spelling Dictation: Example Dialogue (see page 229)

TEACHER:	"You have been eager to write spelling words in your notebooks. You are doing well with underlining and numbering. Today, we begin the notebook. Center the heading A–G on the first line of column 1." (Demonstrates.)
STUDENTS:	(Write the title A–G in capitals on the top line as the teacher monitors them.)
TEACHER:	"This is the procedure we will follow. I will say the word in normal speech and use it in a sentence. Then, you will say each sound precisely as I use my fingers to represent the sounds. Next, you will say sounds again softly just before you write them. Last, look up at my face to show that you are ready for the next step. Listen carefully as I say the word: '*me*. Give the book to *me*.' Say the sounds as I say them."
STUDENTS:	In unison, say, "/m/ /ē/."
TEACHER:	"Now I will say each sound softly just before I write it." (Teacher sounds, then writes *me* on board or easel.) "Now it is your turn. Say the sounds just before you write."
STUDENTS:	(Say sounds softly. Write *me* in notebook. Look up at teacher.)
TEACHER:	"We have talked about the rule that tells us that the phonogram *e* usually says /ē/ when it comes at the end of a syllable. I will think out loud as I decide how to mark this word. The word *me* is one syllable. To show that *e* says /ē/, I will underline it." (Teacher writes r. 4.) "Now it is your turn."
STUDENTS:	(Underline *e* in *me*. Look up at teacher.)
TEACHER:	"Now I will read the word: *me*. Your turn."
STUDENTS:	In unison, read "*me*."
TEACHER:	"Next, I will write 'r. 4' one inch away from the word to remind me that *e* usually says /ē/ at the end of a syllable." (Teacher writes r. 4.) "Your turn."
STUDENTS:	(Write "r. 4" one inch from the word as teacher monitors them.)
TEACHER:	"Let's try the word *do*. 'Do your work carefully.' Say each sound when I say it."

STUDENTS:	In unison, say, "/d/ /oo/."
TEACHER:	"We use the phonogram that says /ŏ/ /ō/ /o͞o/. I will say each sound of the word just before I write it." (Teacher says, "/d/ /o͞o/" and writes *do*.) "Your turn. Say the sounds softly just before you write."
STUDENTS:	(Say sounds softly. Write *do* in notebook. Look at teacher.)
TEACHER:	"Now I will write a tiny three above the /o͞o/ to show that it says its third sound. Your turn. Write a tiny 3 just above /o͞o/."
STUDENTS:	(Write a 3 above the /o͞o/. Look at teacher.)
TEACHER:	"Now I will read the whole word: *do*. Your turn."
STUDENTS:	In unison, read "*do*."
TEACHER:	(Continues dictating the next three words.)
TEACHER:	"Tomorrow, I will not write before you write. You will do it on your own and then, you will be the teacher and dictate the sounds as soon as you see I'm ready to write on the board. Then say only the sound I should underline, read the word, and tell me what rule if there is one."

Introducing Punctuation Marks

Explicit teaching of the purpose of punctuation marks keeps students from putting periods (full stops) and commas just anyplace and helps them notice commas and periods on the printed page. Explicit teaching of the formation provides a precise kinesthetic feel.

Grade-Level Sequence

The purpose and formation of punctuation marks are taught just before students begin writing sentences (week six in kindergarten). See the grade-level objectives for introducing and reviewing punctuation in the *Kindergarten Through Sixth-Grade Teacher Guides*.

Instructional Strategies

1. Model (demonstrate and explain) formation of periods and commas.
   - Demonstrate and say, "A period (full stop) is made by pressing the pencil on the line close to the letter it follows and lifting the pencil."
   - Demonstrate and say, "A comma is a *tiny* half-clock. It starts on the baseline close to the letter it follows and goes below the line, rounding clockwise from 12 to 6."
2. Model (demonstrate and explain) that parentheses, question marks, exclamation marks, quotation marks, and apostrophes are started at the same height as numbers and are curved like commas.

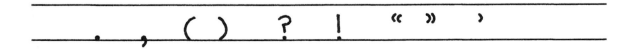

Introducing Cursive Lowercase Handwriting

The computer has not eliminated the need for cursive writing. Because learning cursive writing calls upon many areas of the brain, this skill fosters neural connections between the right and left hemispheres. (See Chapter 5, page 171). If children aren't taught it properly, they make it up as they go along and their handwriting never becomes fluid but becomes instead a barrier to written expression. Cursive writing is learned from *correct* manuscript writing.

Grade-Level Sequence

Cursive handwriting is explicitly taught to students in second grade and above. The second-grade lesson objectives introduce cursive writing after students have perfected basic manuscript writing. Once the rules for cursive handwriting have been introduced, students are immersed in cursive by writing phonograms, then words, and then short sentences. (Following this plan enables second-graders to make the transition quickly, and their quality of writing is remarkably good after about three weeks of instruction.) Cursive handwriting is thoroughly reviewed at the beginning of third grade for teachers who wish to introduce handwriting then and briefly reviewed in grades four through six. For grade-level lesson objectives relating to cursive handwriting, see the "Planning" section in the *Second Through Sixth-Grade Teacher Guides*.

Instructional Strategies

1. Explain that the purpose of cursive writing is to develop fluency: connecting letters increases the speed of writing, improves the attention span, and fosters academic performance. Mastery of cursive writing enables students to more quickly complete daily assignments such as note taking, exam essays, and tasks that require personal communication. (Students feel successful as they develop ease with handwriting.)
2. Model (explain and demonstrate) the general rules for cursive handwriting and ask questions to check understanding.
   - All letters sit on the baseline.
   - All letters or parts of letters are of two sizes: tall or short. Short letters are half the size of tall letters.
   - All vertical (down) lines start at the top and are straight and parallel; they may slant slightly *forward* for the right-handed student or slightly *backward* for the left-handed student.
   - All upswings for lowercase letters are *forward*.
   - All lowercase letters, except *b*, *o*, *v* and *w*, end with a tiny *forward* upswing from the baseline.
   - All letters within a word are connected; if a letter ends at the *midpoint*, use a dip to connect it to the next letter.
3. Model (explain and demonstrate) cursive writing features and connecting lines.

Cursive Writing Features and Connecting Lines Between Letters

— a short upswing from the baseline to the midpoint

— a tall upswing from the baseline to just below the top line

— a short upswing that curves over to 2 on the clock

— a dip kept at the height of a short letter across to the start of the next letter, or as a tiny ending on the letters *b, o, v,* and *w*

— a dip that curves over to 2 on the clock

4. Model the transition from manuscript to cursive writing.
   - Model writing the manuscript alphabet on the board and emphasize that clear manuscript will facilitate the transition to cursive writing.

abcdefghijklmnopqrstuvwxyz

   - Using a colored chalk or marker, form dotted, connecting lines over the manuscript letters as shown below.

abcdefghijklmnopqrstuvwxyz

   - Explain that the solid lines show to what extent the letters are alike, and the colored, dotted lines show most of the differences between manuscript and cursive writing.
   - Identify similarities and differences between manuscript and cursive writing; have students articulate the differences between the two types.

5. Model precisely saying the sound or sounds and forming cursive letters that begin at 2 on the clock: *a, c, d, g, o, q.* Follow the procedures with the precise dialogue below.

Procedures for Introducing Cursive Letters That Begin at 2 on the Clock

"I will say the sounds and show you how each cursive letter that begins at 2 on the clock is written. Then I will listen and observe as you say the sounds and form each letter without lifting the pencil."

Show card 1.
  Say sounds, then say, "Start at 2 and go up and around the clock, touching the baseline and stopping at 2; pull *straight down* to the baseline, *finishing with a tiny upswing.*"

a

continued

Show card 2.

Say sounds, then say, "Start at 2 and go up and around the clock, touching the baseline and finishing at 4."

Show card 3.

Say sound, then say, "Start at 2 and go up and around the clock, touching the baseline and closing the circle at 2. Continue straight up toward the line above but do not touch it. Retrace *straight down* to the baseline, *finishing with a tiny upswing*."

Show card 5.

Say sounds, then say, "Start at 2 and go up and around the clock, touching the baseline and stopping at 2; pull *straight down* the same distance below the baseline, and curve sharply backward, forming a narrow loop that crosses at the underside of the baseline, and *finishing with a tiny upswing*."

Show card 6.

Say sounds, then say, "Start at 2 and go up and around the clock, touching the baseline and finishing at 2 *with a tiny dip*."

Show card 8

Say, "We will write only the letter that begins at 2." Say sound, then say, "Start at 2 and go up and around the clock, touching the baseline and stopping at 2. Pull *straight down* the same distance below the baseline, and curve sharply forward, forming a narrow loop that touches the down line at the underside of the baseline, *finishing with a tiny upswing*."

- Provide multiple opportunities for students to practice at the board, followed by specific, immediate feedback on their performance; have them articulate the differences between each manuscript and cursive letter to enhance memory.
- Model evaluating your cursive writing; have students evaluate yours and then their formations daily to measure their progress.
- Model saying sounds and forming simple words that use these letters with the first connecting line: a short upswing over to 2 on the clock (e.g., *ad, add, ago, cad, go, dad,*); coach students as they say and write a few words to practice cursive letters with short upswings over to 2 on the clock.

Words Written with Cursive Connecting Strokes: Example Dialogues

- Say, "Today I'll model writing *ad*, which uses the first connecting stroke: *a short upswing that curves over to 2 on the clock*. Start *ad* at 2 and go up and around to 2; pull *straight down* to the baseline; continue with a *short upswing curving over to 2*; go up and around and then straight up toward the line above, but do not touch it. Retrace, finishing *with a tiny upswing*."
- Say, "Today I'll model writing *go*, which also uses a short upswing that curves over to 2. Start at 2 and go up and around to 2; pull *straight down* the same distance below the baseline; curve sharply backward, forming a narrow loop that crosses at the underside of the baseline. Continue with a short upswing curving over to 2. Go up and around to 2, *finishing with a tiny dip*."

6. Model precisely saying the sound or sounds and forming cursive letters that begin with a short upswing: *e, i, j, p, r, s, u, v, w, y*. Follow the procedures with the precise dialogue below.

Procedures for Introducing Cursive Letters That Begin with Short Upswings

"I will say the sounds and show you how each cursive letter that begins with a short upswing is written. Then I will listen and observe as you say the sounds and form each letter without lifting the pencil."

Show card 10.

Say, "Start with a short upswing and curve back sharply; pull *straight down* to the baseline, *finishing with a tiny upswing*."

Show card 12.

Say, "Start with a short upswing; pull *straight down* to the baseline, *finishing with a tiny upswing*. Form a small dot by pressing the pencil just above the letter and lifting it."

Show card 13.

Say, "Start with a short upswing; pull *straight down* the same distance below the baseline, and curve sharply backward, forming a narrow loop that crosses at the underside of the baseline, *finishing with a tiny upswing*. Form a small dot by pressing the pencil just above the letter and lifting it."

continued

Show card 18.

Say, "Start with a short upswing, pull *straight down* the same distance below the baseline; retrace to 10 and curve around the clock, touching the baseline and curving up to 8; retrace, *finishing with a tiny upswing*."

Show card 19.

Say, "The cursive *r* is very different from the manuscript *r*. Start with a short upswing; slant down slightly, and then pull *straight down* to the baseline, *finishing with a tiny upswing*."

Show card 7.

Say, "The cursive *s* is very different from the manuscript *s*. Start with a short upswing; pull *straight down* to the baseline and curve backward to touch the upswing; retrace, *finishing with a tiny upswing*."

Show card 21.

Say, "Start with a short upswing; pull straight down to the baseline, and round up to the midpoint; pull straight down to the baseline, finishing with a tiny upswing."

Show card 22.

Say, "Start with a short upswing; pull straight down to the baseline, and round up to 12, finishing with a tiny dip."

Show card 23.

Say, "Start with a short upswing; pull straight down to the baseline, and round up to the midpoint. Pull straight down to the baseline, and round up to 12, finishing with a tiny dip."

Show card 25.

Say, "Start with a short upswing; pull straight down to the baseline, and round up to the midpoint. Pull straight down the same distance below the baseline, and curve sharply backward, forming a narrow loop that crosses at the underside of the baseline, finishing with a tiny upswing.

- Provide multiple opportunities for students to practice on the board and on paper; provide immediate feedback; have students evaluate their performance.
- Model saying and writing words that begin with short upswings (e.g., *egg, sad, wed, word,*); coach students as they practice saying and writing these words on the board and on paper.

7. Model precisely saying the sounds and forming cursive letters that begin with a tall upswing: *b, f, h, k, l, t*. Follow the procedures with the precise dialogue below.

Procedures for Introducing Cursive Letters That Begin with Tall Upswings

Show card 9.

Say, "Start with a tall upswing and curve back sharply to form a narrow loop; pull *straight* down to the baseline, and curve around to 12 *at the midpoint, finishing with a tiny dip.*"

Show card 4.

Say, "Start with a tall upswing, and curve back sharply to form a narrow loop; pull *straight down* below the baseline the same distance as a short letter; curve sharply *forward* to form a narrow loop, touching the down line at the *underside* of the baseline, and *finishing with a tiny upswing.*"

Show card 11.

Say, "Start with a tall upswing, and curve back sharply; pull *straight down* to the baseline, then retrace up to the midpoint, and curve around to 2. Pull *straight down* to the baseline, *finishing with a tiny upswing.*"

Show card 14.

Say, "Start with a tall upswing and curve back sharply; pull *straight down* to the baseline, then retrace up to the midpoint, and curve around to touch the down line. Pull out and straight to the baseline, *finishing with a tiny upswing.*"

Show card 15.

Say, "Start with a tall upswing and curve back sharply to form a narrow loop; pull *straight down* to the baseline, *finishing with a tiny upswing.*"

Show card 20.

Say, "Start with a tall upswing; pull *straight down* to the baseline, *finishing with a tiny upswing.* Lift the pencil. Form a tiny crossbar just above the midpoint in the direction we write."

Provide multiple opportunities for students to practice on the board and on paper; provide immediate feedback; have students evaluate their performance.

- Model saying and writing words that begin with tall upswings (e.g., *bat, bog, fat, fog, hat, hog, kit, keg, let, log, tip, top*); coach students as they practice saying and writing words on the board and on paper.
- Provide extra practice writing phonograms *b, o,* and *w* followed by *r* or *s* because the dip replaces the upswing. Notice that the *s* curves over to 8 on the clock and does not touch the dip.

br br   or os   wr ws

8. Model precisely saying the sounds and forming cursive letters that begin at the midpoint when written alone or as the first letter in a word: *m, n, x, z*. Follow the procedures with the precise dialogue below.

Procedures for Introducing Cursive Letters That Begin at the Midpoint	
m	**Show card 16.** Say, "Start at the midpoint and round into a *straight line down* to the baseline; retrace to 10 and round to 2. Pull *straight down* to the baseline; retrace to 10 and round to 2. Pull *straight down* to the baseline, *finishing with a tiny upswing.*"
n	**Show card 17.** Say, "Start at the midpoint and round into a *straight line down* to the baseline; retrace to 10 and round to 2; pull *straight down* to the baseline, *finishing with a tiny upswing.*"
x	**Show card 24.** Say, "Start at 10 and round into a slanted line to the baseline, finishing with a short upswing. Lift the pencil. Start at the midpoint and slant a straight line down through the middle of the letter to the baseline."
z	**Show card 26.** Say, "Start at 10 and round to 2; continue down to 6; curve slightly, and pull *straight down* the same distance below the baseline; curve back sharply to form a narrow loop that crosses at the underside of the baseline, finishing *with a tiny upswing.*"

- Provide multiple opportunities for students to practice on the board and on paper; provide immediate feedback; have students evaluate their performance.
- Model saying and writing words that begin at the midpoint when written alone or as the first letter in a word (e.g., *man, men, nap, nod, zip, zap, zoo*); coach students as they practice saying and writing words on the board and on paper.

9. Model reducing the size of letters in daily lessons; set a cursive handwriting focus for WPR each day; coach second- or third-grade students as they practice reducing their handwriting to prepare for cursive writing using ⅜-inch (1.0-cm) lined paper in place of the ⅝-inch (1.6-cm) lined paper; follow this sequence.
   - Letters that begin at 2 on the clock
   - Letters that begin with a short upswing
   - Letters that begin with a tall upswing
   - Letters that begin at the midpoint
   - Multiletter phonograms
      ➢ Use the single-letter example dialogues as a pattern for modeling multiletter phonogram formation.
      ➢ Plan extra practice for those that use a dip or a dip over to 2 to connect to the next letter because the first letter ends at the *midpoint*. (Make sure students do not return to the baseline. These common connecting errors can be prevented if practice is supervised.)

10. Prepare students for using cursive writing in their notebooks.
   - Prior to dictating each week's spelling words, identify difficult connections as shown above.
   - Include these phonograms in daily WPR. Continue giving precise directions: e.g., "When writing *ou*, remember to use a short dip between *o* and *u*." "When writing *oa*, be sure to dip over to 2 on the clock before forming the *a*."

Introducing Cursive Capital Letters

Grade-Level Sequence

Cursive capital letters are explicitly taught to students in second grade and above after they have mastered cursive lowercase letters. This is at midyear in grade two and at the beginning of the year for grades three and above.

Instructional Strategies

1. Model formation of cursive capital letters; explain how they differ from manuscript capitals; ask questions that check students' understanding of the distinctive features: e.g., "Which capitals start at 2 on the clock?" "Which capitals do not connect to the next letter?"

    • *A, C, E, L, O,* and *Q* begin at 2 on the clock; *O* and *Q* do not connect to the next letter.

    • *B, D, P, R, U,* and *Y* start with a *straight down* line and are completed without lifting the pencil; *D* and *P* do not connect to the next letter.

    • *F* and *T* begin with a dip at the top. *F* does not connect to the next letter.

    • *G* and *S* start with a tall upswing from the baseline.

    • *H* and *K* start at the top and pull straight down to the baseline.

    • *I* and *J* begin at the baseline with a *backward* upswing.

       ➢ For *I*, curve backward to form a narrow loop at the top; pull straight down to the baseline; curve over to 9 on the clock and end with a dip over to the next letter.

       ➢ For *J*, curve backward to form a narrow loop at the top; pull straight down halfway below the baseline; curve *backward* to form a narrow loop, touching the down line at the *underside* of the baseline, *finishing with a tiny upswing.*

    • *M* and *N* begin at the top, rounding into straight down lines and finishing with short upswings to the next letter.

    • *V* and *W* start at the top with slanted down lines, finishing with slanted upswings at the top that do not connect to the next letter.

    • *X* and *Z* begin at 10 on the clock.

       ➢ For *X*, start at 10 and round to 2 into a slanted line to the baseline, finishing with a short upswing to connect with the next letter. Lift the pencil, start just below the top line, and slant a *straight* line *down* through the middle of the letter to the baseline.

       ➢ For *Z*, start at 10, curve around to 2, and continue down to 6; curve slightly, and pull *straight down* halfway below the baseline; curve *back* sharply to form a narrow loop that crosses at the *underside* of the baseline, *finishing with a tiny upswing.*

The Capital Letters in Cursive Writing

Teaching Pronunciation, Spelling, and Language Rule Application
Teachers need to fully understand all the rules so they can correctly explain any word that occurs in speech, writing, and reading. Teachers should allot time for analyzing spelling words and applying rules because these activities help students understand how the language is structured and develop analytical thinking. Teachers need to check application of the rules not only in spelling quizzes, but also when students write sentences and paragraphs. For beginners of any age, rules that apply to phonogram pronunciation and spelling (rules 1–8, 12–20, 23, 25, 27, and 29) are taught and reviewed during oral phonogram review (OPR) and implemented during daily written phonogram review (WPR) and spelling dictation. Language rules (rules 9–11, 21–22, 24, 26, and 28) are introduced in the writing lesson before they are needed to spell words that illustrate the rules. Students practice applying rules when spelling words and when writing assignments.

A parent or teacher who is under the impression that young children lack the ability to learn, understand, and apply pronunciation, spelling, and language rules will be surprised and delighted to see how quickly they do so, and how eager they are to demonstrate this ability to use reasoning in their work.

Grade-Level Sequence

Rules 1–11 are so basic that they are taught to all students. Primary-grade children learn these rules before they are needed to write words in their notebooks. Teachers use the Primary Rule Page posters (see "Resources" in Part Two). Students in grades three and above write words that illustrate rules 1–16 in their intermediate notebooks. Students of all ages apply rules to words in the Spalding Spelling/Vocabulary Word List. Teachers explain that these are facts about the language that will help them write and read words. They should constantly refer to the facts either on the Spalding Primary Rule Page posters or on the rule pages in the intermediate notebook to develop students' understanding and self-confidence in speaking, writing, and reading. (Reproductions of rule pages in the intermediate notebook are in Part Two, pages 237–251.)

Instructional Strategies for Grades Three and Above

1. Coach and monitor students as they number the rule pages as shown in Part Two *before* dictating any words. These pages become their reference for the phonograms and the rules of spelling and pronunciation.
2. Coach and monitor students as they write the rule pages in their notebooks each year. *On each rule page, use the spelling dictation procedure as described in the* Third Through Sixth-Grade Teacher Guides, *including rereading the words for spelling and reading.*
3. Have students use red pencils to underline and number phonograms that illustrate *the rule being taught.* The rule pages are the only place where the red pencil is used.
4. Carefully follow each rule page procedure given below, because completion of these pages helps develop students' analytical thinking. Ensure that students explain how the rule applies to the pronunciation or spelling of words on each rule page.
5. Review, on a *daily* basis, words that use the rules taught on each rule page. (Again, see Part Two, "Instructional Materials," pages 221–223.)

Spelling rules, explanatory notes, miniature reproductions, and rule page instructions for the teacher are given below.

Rule Page 1 (Rules 1–7)

Rule page 1 includes one two-letter consonant (*qu*) and twenty single-letter consonants, the six single-letter vowels (and words to show the common sounds of each vowel), and the five kinds of silent final *e*'s. The first seven rules are applied on rule page 1.

After primary-grade children have learned the first forty-five phonograms (see "Phonograms," pages 208–213), teachers systematically introduce each section of rule page 1 using the Primary Rule Page 1 poster. They provide daily practice of the rules and concepts in each section.

Students in third grade and above write rule page 1 in cursive in the intermediate notebook after they have mastered the first forty-five phonograms and practiced writing all seventy phonograms in manuscript and cursive writing. For third- and fourth-graders or for older students just beginning The Spalding Method, teachers divide the page into separate lessons. Older students who have previously had Spalding instruction may write rule page 1 in one sitting.

Rule Page 1 Procedures with Precise Dialogue

Day 1

1. Explain that the first section of rule page 1 includes the consonants and rules 1, 2, and 3.

2. Dictate the word *consonants* in normal speech. Explain that the title is capitalized and written in syllables. Demonstrate by centering the title on the first line. Have students say the first syllable, *Con*, and then say it again softly to themselves as they write it in the middle of the first line. Next, have them say the syllable *so* and repeat it softly as they write it close to, but not touching, the first syllable. Finally, have students say the last syllable by sounds /n/ /ă/ /n/ /t/ /s/ so they will write it correctly. Have students underline the *o* in black.

3. Say, "On the next line, we will write the single consonants and the two-letter consonant *qu* (/kw/). Say the sound for the first consonant /b/, then write it."

4. With the class, say the sound(s) for each consonant in unison just before writing each. Have students leave the space of a round letter before and after the two-letter consonant *qu* (/kw/).

5. Say, "On the third line, write, '*c* before *e, i,* or *y* says $\overset{2}{\check{c}}$.'" (This is the only time *c* is written with a two above it. Rule 2 explains which sound to use.)

6. Say, "On the fourth line, write, '*g* before *e, i,* or *y* may say $\overset{2}{\check{g}}$.'" (This is the only time where *g* is written with a two above it. Rule 3 explains which sound to use.)

7. Explain that each consonant, except *c, g,* and *s,* has but a single sound. Only *s* when it says /z/ needs a two placed above it.

💡 Model Thinking

Use rules 1, 2, and 3 (see page 221) to explain the pronunciation of words that include phonograms *c, g,* and *qu*. Say, "As I look at the word *queen,* I remember that /kw/ is a two-letter consonant sound, so I pronounce the word /kw/ /ē/ /n/. In the word *cat, c* says /k/ because it is not followed by an *e, i,* or *y*."

✓ Check for Understanding

Ask students to explain why given words are pronounced as they are. Their replies should sound something like this: "In the word *cent,* the *c* says /s/ because it is followed by an *e*." "In the word *gem,* the *g* says /j/ because it is followed by an *e*."

continued

⭐ *Provide Practice*

Have students categorize example words from a textbook paragraph to show that *c* followed by *e, i,* or *y* says /s/ and *g* followed by *e, i,* or *y* may say /j/. This exercise demonstrates that rule 2 is used much more frequently than rule 3.

Day 2

1. Explain that the second section of rule page 1 includes the vowels, words that illustrate the vowel sounds, and rules 4, 5, and 6.

2. Have students skip one space to separate the consonant and vowel sections. Explain that they will center and capitalize the title *Vowels*. Demonstrate in the same manner as on day 1.

3. Have students say and write the title *Vowels* in syllables. Have them underline and number in black.

4. Dictate vowel *a* and have students write it about half an inch from the stitching. Dictate the rest of the vowels to form a column as shown in the illustration.

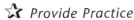

5. Have students draw a vertical line to form a column separating the vowels from the example words as shown in the illustration.

6. Dictate and have students say and write the example words for vowel *a* in three columns. Have them underline and number in black. Proceed to dictate each set in order.

7. Have students brace the words *big* and *gym*, which illustrate the sound /ĭ/.

8. Have students use a *red* pencil to underline the vowels saying their second sounds and to number the third sounds for vowels *a, o,* and *u* as shown in the illustration.

9. After all words in the vowel section have been written, marked, and checked for accuracy, have students read the words for spelling and reading.

💡 *Model Thinking*

Use rules 4, 5, and 6 (see page 221) to explain how to read words that have vowels *a, e, i, o,* and *u* at the end of a syllable. For example, say, "*Navy* must have two syllables because it has two vowels, *a* and *y*. I know that *a usually* says /ā/ at the end of a syllable. I know that *y usually* says /ĭ/ at the end of a syllable. I will read the word, *na vy*."

✔ *Check for Understanding*

Have students explain the pronunciation of other words such as *my*. Their response should sound like this: "In the word *my*, I read /m/ /ī/ because *y* may say /ī/. To spell *my*, I use the phonogram *y* because English words do not end with *i*."

☆ *Provide Practice*

On a separate piece of paper, have students write a few words that illustrate the different vowel sounds. Use words in sections A–G.

Day 3

1. Explain that the last section of rule page 1 includes words that illustrate the five kinds of silent final *e*'s (rule 7).

2. Have students skip one space to separate the sections. Then dictate the word *time*. Explain that the silent *e* lets the vowel *i* say /ī/ in *time*. Explain that single vowels before any single consonant can say /ā/ /ē/ /ī/ /ō/ /ū/ if a silent *e* ends the base word. Have students say the sounds softly as they write this word.

3. Dictate the word *have*. Explain that English words do not end with *v*. A silent *e* is added. Have students say the sounds softly as they write *have*. Dictate the word *blue*. Explain that English words do not end with the single vowel *u*. A silent *e* is added. Have students say the sounds softly as they write *blue* on the same line as *have*.

4. Dictate the word *chance*. Explain that the silent *e* lets the *c* say /s/. Rule 2 explains this. Have students say the sounds softly as they write the word and then underline the phonogram /ch/ in *chance* in black. Dictate the word *charge*. Explain that the silent *e* lets the *g* say /j/. Rule 3 explains this. Have students softly say the sounds as they write the word on the same line as *chance* and then underline the phonograms /ch/ and /ar/ in black.

5. On the next line, dictate the word *little*. Remind students to say and write *little* in syllables. Explain that every syllable must have at least one vowel. (Words in which the second syllable is *ble, cle, dle, fle, gle, kle, ple, sle, tle,* or *zle* have a silent *e* added so each can be a separate syllable. All other syllables in English have a vowel sound.)

6. On the next line, dictate the word *are*. Have students say the sounds softly as they write the word and then underline the phonogram /ar/ in black. The *e* has no job. After the word *are*, have students write *no job e* in parentheses.

continued

7. Have students use a red pencil to underline and number as follows:

In *time,* underline the *i, m,* and *e.* The first job of *e* is not numbered, just as the first phonogram sound is not numbered. Underlining the vowel, consonant, and silent final *e* provides a visual signal that the *e* lets the vowel say its second sound. (Job 1.)

In *have* and *blue,* have students underline the *v* and *u* once and the *e* twice and write small twos beside the double underlining to signal that English words do not end in *v* or *u.* (Job 2.)

In *chance* and *charge,* underline the *c* and *g* once and the *e* twice and write small threes beside each double underlining to signal that the *e* lets the *c* and *g* say their second sounds. (Job 3.)

In *little,* underline the *e* twice and write a small four beside the double underlining to signal that every syllable must have a vowel. (Job 4.)

In *are,* underline the *e* twice and write a tiny five beside the double underlining to signal that this *e* is retained from Old English. (Job 5—no job *e.*)

8. Have students use a black pencil to draw a brace in front of the set of silent final *e* words. Have them write the title *Silent final e's* before the brace as shown.

9. After all words have been written, marked, and checked for accuracy, have students read all the words for spelling and reading.

🔆 *Model Thinking*

Use rule 7 (see page 221) to read and write words with a final silent *e.* Demonstrate on the board and say, "When I see a silent final *e* word like *line,* I will read *līne* because I know the *e* lets the *i* say /ī/. When I want to spell the word *give,* I know I write a silent *e* because English words don't end in *v.*"

✔ *Check for Understanding*

Provide example words and have students mark and explain the jobs of *e.*

☆ *Provide Practice*

Provide a list of silent final *e* words and have students categorize them under one of the five jobs and explain their reasoning.

✍ *Check Application*

In the writing lesson, dictate sentences that include words with a silent final *e* from the spelling lesson. Have students proofread these sentences written on the board or at their desks. Finally, check their application of the rule when they write words independently in sentences and compositions.

Rule Page 2 (Rule 8)

Rule page 2 includes words that illustrate the five spellings for the sound /er/. Rule 8, "The phonogram *or* may say /er/ when it follows *w* (*work*)," is also illustrated on this page. Before primary-grade children write the word *over* in sections A–G, teachers write *over* under *Her* on the nonsense sentence, *Her first nurse works early*, on the Primary Rule Page 2 poster. Under each word, they list the spelling/vocabulary words that illustrate that spelling as it occurs in spelling dictation and words encountered in reading lessons. As words are added, students quickly learn that the spelling *er* is used most often.

Students of all ages should memorize the sentence that lists the *er's*, to enhance retention. For the lesson plan objectives that introduce this rule page, see the "Planning" section of the *Third Through Sixth-Grade Teacher Guides*.

Rule Page 2 Procedures with Precise Dialogue

Day 1

1. Have students measure side 1 of the page to divide it into three equal columns. Have them draw lines between the columns as shown and fold side 2 of rule page 2 in half, providing a total of five columns.

Her	first	nurse₅	works	early.
serve₂	sir	turn	worm	learn
herd	bird	hurt	word	heard
dinner	third	burn	world	search
perfect	girl	church	worth	earn
nerve₂	fir	fur	worthy	earth
berth	birth	purpose₅	worse₄	earnest
western	skirt	surprise	worst	pearl
merge₃	circle₄	hurdle₅	worry	rehearse₅
grocery	firm	Thursday	worship	
perch	thirst	Saturday		
sterling	squirt	further		
verse₄	squirm	disturb		
clerk	chirp	curtain		
certain	confirm	curve₂		

2. Dictate the nonsense sentence *Her first nurse works early*. Demonstrate how to center each word in a separate column on the top line and write the word *early* in syllables. Have students write the sentence and underline and number the silent *e* in *nurse* in black. Then have them underline the five spellings of *er* in red. They do *not* underline the *w* in the word *works*.

3. Have students skip a space. Then dictate the next five words across the columns on the third line. Have students underline and number the *v* and *e* in black. (For third-grade students, writing three rows may be sufficient for day 1.) Have them underline the *er's* in red to focus attention on the five spellings of *er*.

4. After the words have been written, marked, and checked for accuracy, have students read the words in each column for spelling and reading.

continued

✔ *Check for Understanding*

Ask questions about words using these spellings. For example, "Which /er/ is in *church*?" The answer is, "The /er/ of *nurse.*"

☆ *Provide Practice*

Cover the words on the board. Dictate a word using one of the five spellings for *er*. Have students write it on the board or at their desks.

✎ *Check Application*

In the writing lesson, dictate sentences that include these words. Have students proofread their sentences. Finally, check their application of the rule when they write words independently in sentences and compositions.

Day 2

1. Finish dictating words across columns. Have students underline and number other phonograms in black. Then underline the *er*'s in red.
2. After the words have been written, marked, and checked for accuracy, have students read the words down each column for spelling and reading. Reading each column of words helps students remember which phonogram is used in each word.

✔ *Check for Understanding*

Ask students to clarify which /er/ is used in any word on this page.

☆ *Provide Practice*

Provide multiple opportunities to read for spelling and reading. Cover the words on the board. Dictate a word and have students write it on the board or at their desks.

✎ *Check Application*

In the writing lesson, dictate sentences using these words. Have students proofread their sentences. Finally, check their application of the rule when they write words independently in sentences and compositions.

Rule Page 3 (Rules 9 and 10)

Rule page 3 includes words that illustrate how to form derived words by adding suffixes that begin with a vowel to base words. Students in all grades receive instruction and practice in these rules because they are basic to English spelling. Reasoning is required to spell words that follow these rules.

Teachers introduce primary-grade children to rule 9 just before dictating the first derived word in the notebook (*setting* in section K of the Spelling/Vocabulary Word List). "For *one*-syllable words that have *one* vowel and end in *one* consonant (*hop*), write another final consonant (*hop + ped*) before adding endings that begin with a vowel." Rule 9 can be called the *one-one-one* rule. On the left side of the Primary Rule Page 3 poster, base words are listed. On the bottom right, most common endings (e.g., *ing, er, ed*) are listed. Teachers explain how to use the rule to spell derived words. See the explanation below.

Teachers have students in grades three and above write the words on rule page 3 as designated in the "Planning" section in the *Third Through Sixth-Grade Teacher Guides*.

Rule Page 3, Side 1, Procedures with Precise Dialogue

Side 1—Rule 9

1. Side 1 of rule page 3 is already folded in half.
2. Dictate the heading *hop*. Have students center it on the first line in column 1.
3. Have students skip a space. Dictate all base words in column 1. Have students underline and number in black as appropriate.
4. Have students skip three spaces, and then dictate the label *Endings which begin with a vowel*. Demonstrate how to center the label on three lines in column 1.
5. Have students skip one space below the last base word in column 1 and move to column 2. Dictate the endings. Have students write the endings one below the other, underlining, numbering, and bracing pairs in black. Have them use a black pencil to draw a brace in front of the set of endings that begin with a vowel.

 Model Thinking

   Say, "I want to add the ending *ing* to *hop*. This ending begins with a vowel. *Hop* is *one syllable*, ending in *one consonant*, *p*, with *one vowel*, *o*, before it, so I must write another *p* before adding the ending *ing*." Think aloud as you explain that the added consonant preserves the vowel sound in *hop*.

6. Dictate the heading *hopping*. Have students write it in syllables on the first line of the second column and underline *ng* in black. Then have them underline the added *p* twice in red to indicate that the consonant is needed to preserve the vowel sound but is silent when read.

continued

7. Have students skip a space. Dictate each derived word. Have students explain and then apply the rule to each word as they write it in column 2 opposite the base word in column 1 (see "Check for Understanding"). Students underline and number in black as appropriate. Explain that the word *writ* is the archaic past tense of *write*. The word *writ* is still used as a noun in some documents. Writing the base word helps children understand why we write *writ ten*. After dictating *ship,* explain that *shipped* is one syllable because the base word does not end in the sound /d/ or /t/ (see rule 28, page 223).

8. Have students underline the added consonant in each word twice in red to indicate that the consonant is added for spelling but is silent when read.

9. After all words have been written, marked, and checked for accuracy, have students read derived words for spelling and reading.

✓ *Check for Understanding*

Ask, "How do we add *ing* to *set*?" The student replies, "We write a second /t/, since *set* has one syllable, one consonant at the end, and one vowel before the last consonant, and the ending begins with a vowel." Ask, "How do you add the ending *ment* to *ship*?" The answer should be, "We do not add another /p/ to *ship*, because *ment* begins with a consonant, not a vowel." Ask, "How do we add the past tense ending (*ed*) to *talk*?" The reply should be, "We do not write a second /k/, since this base word ends in two consonants, not just one."

☆ *Provide Practice*

The Spalding Word Builder Cards (see "Resources") provide opportunities for guided and independent practice adding endings to base words. Use Word Builders in the whole group or small groups. Have students explain that the purpose of adding a consonant to a base word before adding an ending that begins with a vowel is to preserve the vowel sounds. Also have students explain how the meaning of the ending changes the meaning of the base word. (For example, the ending *er* changes the verb *run* to a noun meaning "one who runs.")

✏ *Check Application*

In the writing lesson, dictate sentences. Have students write them on the board or at their desks and proofread the sentences. Finally, check their application of the rule when they write words independently in sentences and compositions.

Teachers introduce the concept of an accented syllable by saying the word with the accent on the correct and then the incorrect syllable. If students have difficulty, teachers use the word in a sentence, alternating the correct and incorrect accents. After the students can identify which syllable has the accent, teachers introduce rule page 3, side 2 (rule 10): "Words of two syllables (*be gin*) in which the second syllable (*gin*) is *accented* and ends in *one* consonant, with *one* vowel before it, need another final consonant (*be gin + ning*) before adding an ending that begins with a vowel."

Rule Page 3, Side 2, Procedures with Precise Dialogue

Side 2—Rule 10

1. Fold side 2 in half. Explain that on side 2, we will write words that add endings that begin with vowels to two-syllable words.
2. Dictate the heading *begin*. Have students write it in syllables centered on the first line of column 1 of side 2 and then underline *e* in black. They use their red pencils to place the accent on the second syllable.
3. Have students skip one space. Dictate all the base words in column 1.
4. After students write all words in syllables and appropriately underline phonograms in black, have them use a red pencil to mark the accented syllables.

 Model Thinking

Say, "I want to add the ending *ing* to the verb *begin*. The ending *ing* begins with a vowel. The accent is on the second syllable *gin*, and *gin* ends with one consonant, *n*, with one vowel, *i*, before it, so I must add another consonant, *n*, before adding the ending *ing*."

5. Dictate the heading *beginning*. Have students write it in syllables centered on the first line of column 2. Students underline *e* and *ng* in black, then underline the added *n* twice in red to show that it is silent when read.
6. Have students skip a space. Dictate each derived word. Have students explain and apply the rule to each word as they write it in column 2 opposite the base word in column 1, underlining in black (see "Check for Understanding").
7. Have students underline the added consonants in each word twice in red to indicate that the consonant is added for spelling but is silent when read.
8. Have students skip three spaces to separate the sections. Dictate the base words that do not have the accent on the second syllable. Students underline appropriately and mark the accented syllables in black.
9. Dictate the derived words that do not add another consonant. Students underline and number appropriately in black.
10. After all words have been written, marked, and checked for accuracy, have students read the words down and across two columns for spelling and reading.

continued

✓ *Check for Understanding*

Ask, "How do you add the ending *ence* to *occur*?" The students' answer should be, "The ending *ence* begins with a vowel. We add another /r/ to *cur* because the accent is on *cur*, which has one vowel, *u*, followed by one consonant, *r*." Ask, "How do we add the past tense ending (*ed*) to *enter*?" The reply should be, "We do not write a second /r/, since the accent is on the first syllable, *en*."

☆ *Provide Practice*

Use Word Builder Cards in the whole group or small groups. Have students add endings to multisyllabic base words that meet the criteria of rule 10 and those that do not until students can easily apply this rule when they are writing independently.

✍ *Check Application*

In the writing lesson, dictate sentences. Have students write these sentences on the board or at their desks. Have students proofread sentences. Finally, check their application of the rule when they write words independently in sentences and compositions.

Rule Page 4 (Rule 11)

Rule page 4 includes words that illustrate how to form derived words by adding suffixes that begin with a vowel to base words that end in a silent final *e*. "Words ending with a silent final *e* (*come*) are written without the *e* when adding an ending that begins with a vowel."

Teachers introduce primary-grade children to rule 11 just before it is needed to write a word in their notebooks (see the "Planning" section in the *Kindergarten Through Second-Grade Teacher Guides*). On the left side of the Primary Rule Page 4 poster, base words are listed. On the bottom right, most common endings (e.g., *ing, er, ed*) are listed. Teachers explain how to use the rule to spell derived words. See the explanation below.

Teachers have third-grade and older students write the words on rule page 4 in the intermediate notebook after they complete rule page 3 as designated in the "Planning" section in the *Third Through Sixth-Grade Teacher Guides*.

Rule Page 4, Procedures with Precise Dialogue

Side 1—Rule 11

1. Explain that rule page 4 is single-sided. On this page, we will add endings that begin with vowels to words that end in silent final *e*.
2. Dictate the heading *hope*. Have students center it on the first line in the first column. Have them underline the *o*, *p*, and *e* in red.
3. Have students skip a space. Dictate and have students write the base words in the first column, underlining and numbering in black as appropriate. After all words are written, have students use a red pencil to underline and number the silent final *e*'s.
4. Have students skip four spaces. Dictate the label *Endings beginning with a vowel*. Demonstrate how to center the label on three lines in column 1.
5. Have students skip one space below the last base word in column 1 and move to column 2.
6. Dictate the endings. Have students write them in column 2 one below the other, underlining, numbering, and bracing pairs in black (see page 242). Have them use a black pencil to draw a brace in front of the set of endings beginning with a vowel.

Model Thinking

Say, "I want to add the ending *ing* to *hope*. This ending begins with a vowel. In column 2, I'll write *hope* without the *e* and add the ending to form *hoping*." (Demonstrate.)

7. Dictate the heading *hoping*. Have students write the word in syllables on the first line of column 2 and underline *ng* in black.
8. Have students skip a space. Dictate each derived word. Have students explain and apply the rule to each word as they write it in column 2 opposite the base word in column 1 (see "Check for Understanding"). Students underline and number each word appropriately in black.
9. After all words have been written, marked, and checked for accuracy, have students read the words down the columns and across two rows for reading and spelling.

✓ Check for Understanding

Ask, "How do you add the ending *ing* to *come*?" The answer should be, "The ending *ing* begins with a vowel. Write *come* without the *e* before adding the ending *ing*." Have students explain adding endings to words ending with silent final *e*.

continued

☆ *Provide Practice*

Use Word Builder Cards in the whole group or small groups. Have students practice thinking aloud as they add endings to base words that end in silent final *e*. Their responses should sound like this: "I write the base word *desire* without the *e* before adding the ending *able* because *able* begins with a vowel." *Frequently have students identify base words in derived words.*

✍ *Check Application*

In the writing lesson, dictate sentences. Students proofread these sentences written on the board or at their desks. Finally, check their application of the rule when they write words independently in sentences and compositions.

Students must be well taught to see that these endings are added to base words. They must recognize each base word even when the ending forms a separate syllable and the single vowel in the preceding syllable is not marked (*hop ing*).

Rule Page 5 (Rule 12)

Rule page 5 includes words that illustrate rule 12 (see pages 244–245). It is necessary in teaching this rule page to say the names of the letters *ie* and *ei*. Rule 12 tells which phonogram to use: "After *c* we use *ei* (*receive*). If we say /ā/, we use *ei* (*vein*). In the list of exceptions, we use *ei*. In all other words, the phonogram *ie* is used."

This spelling rule is taught to primary-grade children as needed for words in the Spalding Spelling/Vocabulary Word List. For grade two, teachers write the column headings *ie*, *cei*, and *ei says "ā"* on chart paper or on the board. Teachers add words containing these spellings as they are encountered in the Spalding Spelling/Vocabulary Word List, beginning with *field* in section L. Students in third grade or above write the words on rule page 5 as designated in the "Planning" section in the *Third Through Sixth-Grade Teacher Guides*.

Rule Page 5 Procedures with Precise Dialogue

Day 1

1. Have students fold both sides of rule page 5 in half to form four columns.
2. Using the names of the letters, have students center *ie* over column 1, *cei* over column 2, and *ei says "ā"* over column 3. Students underline each phonogram in red.
3. Have students skip a space. Dictate words going across columns 1, 2, and 3 (not down the page) to help students learn when to use *ie* or *ei*. Students underline, number, and brace appropriately in black. For students beginning third grade, five rows may be sufficient for day 1. After these words have been written, have students use a red pencil to underline the *ie* or *ei*.
4. After all words have been written, marked, and checked for accuracy, have students read the words across and down two columns for reading and spelling.

✓ *Check for Understanding*

Ask, "Which spelling is used in *receive*?" The student should say, "I use *ei* because it comes after a *c*"; or if the word is *brief*, "I use *ie* because it comes after *r* and not after *c*, and the sound is not /ā/."

☆ *Provide Practice*

Cover the words on the board. Dictate a word. Have students write it on the board or at their desks.

Day 2

1. Finish dictating columns 1, 2, and 3. Students underline, number, and brace appropriately in black. Note that *the ie* says /ĕ/ in *friend*. Have students underline it twice to indicate that it is an uncommon sound for *ie*. After all words are written, have them underline *ie*'s and *ei*'s in red.

continued

2. In column 4, dictate the title *Exceptions*. Have students write the word in syllables and begin with a capital. Have them underline and number in black.

3. Have students skip a space. Dictate the nonsense sentence *Neither foreign sovereign seized (the) counterfeit (and) forfeited leisure.* Demonstrate how to write it in column 4. Have students write it, underlining and numbering in black.

4. Have students skip a space. Dictate the extra words in column 4. Students write the words, underlining and numbering in black. After all words have been written, have students underline and number the *ei*'s in red.

5. After all words have been written, marked, and checked for accuracy, have students read the words across and down two columns for reading and spelling.

✔ *Check for Understanding*

Cover the words on the board. Ask which spelling, *ie* or *ei*, is used in the listed words. For example, "Which phonogram do we use in the word *vein?*" The student should say something like this: "I use *ei* because I hear the sound /ā/."

☆ *Provide Practice*

Dictate words for students to write at the board or at their desks. Have students explain the spelling. Have students memorize the nonsense sentence in column 4 to help them remember the exceptions.

✍ *Check Application*

In the writing lesson, dictate sentences. Students proofread sentences written on the board or at their desks. Finally, check their application of the rule when they write words independently in sentences and compositions.

Note that the phonogram *eigh* is not considered on this page, because this phonogram says /ā/. It is not *ei* alone. In the word *foreign*, the *ei* says /ĭ/ and the *gn* says /n/. They are not one sound, but *eigh* is one sound.

Rule Page 6 (Rules 13–16)

Rule page 6 contains the usual spellings for the sound /sh/ at the beginning of any syllable after the first one. (See pages 246–247.) These spelling rules are taught to primary-grade children as needed to spell words. Teachers write *ti, si, ci* on chart paper. They add words containing these spellings as they occur, beginning with the word *question* in section N of the Spelling/Vocabulary Word List (see page 309).

Students in third grade or above write the words on rule page 6 as designated in the "Planning" section in the *Third Through Sixth-Grade Teacher Guides*.

Rule Page 6, Procedures with Precise Dialogue

Side 1

1. Explain rule 13: "The phonogram /sh/ is used at the beginning or end of a base word (*she, dish*), at the end of a syllable (*fin ish*), but never at the beginning of a syllable after the first one except for the ending *ship* (*wor ship, friend ship*)."

2. Explain rule 14: "The phonograms *ti, si,* and *ci* are the spellings most frequently used to say /sh/ at the beginning of a second or subsequent syllable in a base word (*na tion, ses sion, fa cial*)."

3. Rule page 6, side 1, is already folded in half. Dictate the headings *ti* and *si*. Have students center the phonograms on the first line of columns 1 and 2. Have them use a red pencil to underline each phonogram.

4. Have students skip the next space. Dictate and have them write the words in column 1, underlining and numbering appropriately in black. After all words are written, have students use their red pencils to underline the phonogram *ti* saying /sh/.

5. Explain rule 15: "The phonogram *si* is used to say /sh/ when the syllable before it ends in an *s* (*ses sion*) or when the base word has an *s* where the base word changes (*tense, ten sion*)."

ti	*si*
na tion	ses sion
col lec tion	com pres sion
po ten tial	dis cus sion
pa tient	de pres sion
am bi tion	ad mis sion
sub stan tial	or
in fec tion	(tense) ten sion
in flu en tial	(manse) man sion
con fi den tial	
im par tial	
su per sti tious	si
tor ren tial	
pa la tial	vi sion
	di vi sion
	oc ca sion
	ex plo sion

 Model Thinking

Say, "I want to write *session*. Since the first syllable, *ses*, ends in *s*, I will use *si* to write *session*."

6. Dictate and have students write the first five words in column 2, underlining and numbering appropriately in black.

7. On the next line, have students center the word *or*.

 Model Thinking

Say, "I want to write *tension*. Since the base word, *tense*, ends in the sound /s/, I will use *si* to write *tension*."

8. Dictate and have students write the word *tense*. Have students put parentheses around *tense* to remind them that there is an *s* where the base word will be changed. Dictate and have students write the word *tension* beside *tense*.

9. Repeat the procedure in step 8 to write the words *manse* and *mansion*.

10. Explain rule 16: "The phonogram *si* may also say /zh/ as in *vi sion*."

continued

11. Skip two spaces. Have students write *si* and center a small two above and between the *s* and the *i*. Have them underline the phonogram in red.

12. Skip a space. Dictate and have students write the next four words, underlining in black as appropriate.

13. After all words in column 2 have been written, have students underline *si* in red. Have them write a small two above and between the *s* and the *i* in words that use *si* to say /zh/.

✔ *Check for Understanding*

Ask questions like, "Which phonogram is used in the word *discussion*?" The student's answer should be, "The phonogram that says /sh/ /zh/ because the syllable before it ends in *s*."

☆ *Provide Practice*

Provide multiple opportunities to read for spelling and reading. Have students identify the phonogram in words given orally. Explain the spelling of words on this page. Continue to give words to students to write independently.

✔ *Check Application*

In the writing lesson, dictate sentences. Have students proofread sentences written on the board or at their desks. Finally, check their application of the rule when they write words independently in sentences and compositions.

Side 2

1. Have students fold side 2 in half, and then dictate the heading *ci*. Have students center the phonogram on the first line of column 1 of side 2. Have them use a red pencil to underline the phonogram.

💡 *Model Thinking*

Say, "I want to write *facial*. Since the base word, *face*, has a *c* where the base word changes, I will use *ci* to write *facial*."

2. Skip a space. Dictate and have students write the base word *face*. Have students put parentheses around *face* to remind them there is a *c* where the base word will be changed. Dictate and have students write the word *facial* beside *face*. Have students underline in black.

3. Dictate and have students write the next two sets of base and derived words, underlining and numbering in black as appropriate.

4. Skip a space. Dictate the base word *music.* Have students put parentheses around *music* to remind them there is a *c* where the base word will be changed. Dictate and have students write *musician* beside *music,* underlining and numbering in black.

5. Dictate and have students write the next two sets of base and derived words, underlining and numbering in black.

6. Skip a space. Dictate and have students write the next seven words, underlining and numbering in black.

7. After all words are written, have students underline *ci* in red.

8. Explain that in some words, no rule governs the choice of *ti, si,* or *ci* for the sound /sh/. The spelling must be memorized, as in *influential.*

9. After all words are written, have students read the words down and across the columns for spelling and for reading.

✓ Check for Understanding

Ask questions like, "Which phonogram is used in the word *spacious*?" The answer should be, "The /sh/ that begins with a short letter because the base word ends in *c.*"

☆ Provide Practice

Provide multiple opportunities to read for spelling and reading. Have students identify the phonogram in words given orally. Explain the spelling of words from rule page 6. Continue to give words to students to write independently.

✍ Check Application

In the writing lesson, dictate sentences. Have students proofread sentences written on the board or at their desks. Finally, check their application of the rule when they write words independently in sentences and compositions.

For spelling and precise speech, it is important that the vowel sounds in each of the last syllables of the words on this page be said accurately. Unless the phonograms are sounded aloud, many rules of spelling do not make sense. It is the failure to combine the sounds with the spelling that makes English seem so difficult to learn and makes so many common words seem to be exceptions to the general rules of spelling. This is another good reason why it is important to teach any new word by writing from its spoken sounds. Saying the sounds of the phonograms enables students to see clearly the relationship between the spoken word, the spelling of the word, and the reading of it. If students, in this way, explain and apply these rules often enough, they will apply them when they write. To teach students to think before they write or speak is an ongoing challenge, but it develops the vital habit of using their minds in what they do and say.

Multiletter Phonograms (Notebook Page 7)

For primary-grade children, teachers write multiletter phonograms on the board or on chart paper when these phonograms are introduced. They have children occasionally read the phonograms from the board as an alternative form of practice. Teachers have children participate in practice activities as described below.

Beginning third-grade and older students write the phonograms on page 7 of their notebooks (see page 248) just before dictation of the Spelling/Vocabulary Word List starts. Older students who have previously had Spalding instruction may write this page in one sitting. (See the "Planning" section in the *Third Through Sixth-Grade Teacher Guides* for specific lesson objectives.)

Notebook Page 7 Procedures

1. Side 1 is already folded in half. Have students fold side 2 in half to form four columns.
2. Dictate and have students write the title *Multiletter Phonograms,* centering it on the first line of side 1.
3. Dictate the multiletter phonograms down each of four columns as shown. For phonograms having more than one sound, dictate the number first and then the sounds.
4. Have students say and write the phonograms, bracing phonograms as shown.
5. Have students participate in practice activities that develop higher-level thinking and enhance retention. Examples follow:

   - Have students read phonograms down each column and explain the distinguishing characteristics of each phonogram. (E.g., "The phonogram *sh* may be used only at the beginning or end of a base word, or at the end of a syllable; the phonogram double *e* is memorized.")
   - Have students use a separate piece of paper to categorize phonograms that have similar characteristics: for example, rule-governed placement (*ay/ai, oy/oi*), same sound (*aw/au*).
   - Have students read or write phonograms that have single sounds (e.g., *sh, ee, ar*) and then read or write those that have two, then three sounds.
   - Have students explain the use of braces in each set of phonograms.
   - Have students explain how phonograms *ow* and *ou* are alike and different. (Both phonograms have the same first two sounds, but *ou* is the only phonogram with four sounds.)

All seventy phonograms are now either on chart paper or on the board (primary grades) or in the notebook (third grade and above).

Additional Phonograms (Notebook Page 8)

Students in grades three and above write additional phonograms on page 8 in their notebooks. These phonograms occur often enough to be useful for older students. Teachers introduce these additional phonograms as needed to spell words in the Spalding Spelling/Vocabulary Word List. (See the "Planning" section in the *Third Through Sixth-Grade Teacher Guides* for specific lesson objectives.) Teachers use the following page to write additional words that have these phonograms.

Notebook Page 8 Procedures

1. Side 1 is already folded in half. Have students fold side 2 in half to form four columns.

2. Dictate and have students write the title *Additional Phonograms,* centering it on the first line of side 1.

3. Skip a space. Dictate each phonogram in column 1 as it is needed to spell an Ayres word using that phonogram.

Additional Phonograms			8
tch	catch	cu	biscuit
eo	people	aigh	straight
eau	beauty	sc	scene
augh	daughter laughter	ge	pigeon
ce	ocean	rh	rhyme
gh	ghost	eu	Europe
gi	region	sci	conscientious
our	journey	pn	pneumonia
di	soldier		

4. In column 2, dictate and have students write the first Ayres word that illustrates the phonogram sound, underlining and numbering in black.

5. Dictate the remainder of the additional phonograms in column 3 and the word that illustrates each phonogram in column 4.

6. Have students participate in practice activities that develop higher-level thinking and enhance retention. Examples follow:

   • Have students read phonograms down each column.
   • Have students use a separate piece of paper to categorize phonograms that have similar characteristics; for example, the same sound (*di/gi/ge, rh/r/wr, pn/kn/gn, gh/gu*).

The teacher or parent who meticulously follows all the procedures and details of teaching required for the students' construction of this notebook will be well rewarded. This textbook is called *The Writing Road to Reading* because writing the notebook develops students' understanding of how the language works. Thus the mastery of the notebook is key to students' success. As students progress through the notebook, teaching becomes easier and a source of pleasure. This is where competent teaching really counts.

Delivering Integrated Writing Instruction

High-frequency words are used to explicitly teach word meanings and usage, parts of speech, and morphology (prefixes, base/root words, and suffixes). The order of introduction is found on pages 422–427 and in the "Planning" section of the *Kindergarten Through Sixth-Grade Teacher Guides*. The grade-appropriate procedure for teaching each of these skills is found in the "Delivering" section of the *Kindergarten Through Sixth-Grade Teacher Guides*.

The Spalding Method is *not* a scripted program. However, sample dialogues that demonstrate the steps in delivering effective instruction of these skills are provided below. Although these dialogues are presented for beginners, the basic language concepts and procedures are the same for students of any age.

Teaching Sentence Construction with Vocabulary Development

Students must have an adequate speaking vocabulary to achieve fine writing at any grade level. The first writing lesson objective at every grade level states: "Compose oral/written sentences that demonstrate usage and meaning of *unfamiliar* words . . ." in the week's spelling/vocabulary lesson.

Word Usage

The focus of *initial* lessons is on teaching primary-grade children to *listen* carefully to how each spelling/vocabulary word is used in sample sentences. Children use words correctly in oral and later in written sentences and explain their uses. Each step in the detailed grade-appropriate procedure for teaching word usage is identified only in the first sample dialogue to ensure that all instructional steps are included. The following dialogue is for the first nine words.

Word Usage in Sections A–G: Example Dialogue

Word 1—Usage

TEACHER: "Class, when I dictated words earlier this morning, I used each word in a sentence. Let's talk about those words now. First, I will compose a sentence using a spelling word. I will explain how the spelling word is used. Then I will ask you to answer questions to show you understand how the word is used. Last, I will ask you to use the spelling word in oral sentences.

me   "The first word in your notebook is *me*. Listen carefully as I compose a sentence using the word *me*.

(Provide a sentence.)	" 'Give the book to *me*.'
(Explain use.)	"*Me* is a little word that takes the place of the speaker's name.
(Model thinking.)	"I could have said, 'Give the book to (my name),' but I would get tired of saying my name over and over. I use the little word *me* to take the place of my name. It takes the place of the speaker's name.
(Check for understanding.)	"What job does the word *me* do?"
STUDENTS:	"The word *me* takes the place of your name."
TEACHER:	"Is it only *my* name?"
STUDENTS:	"No, it is whoever is talking."
TEACHER:	"Yes. You have done a good job of explaining that the word *me* takes the place of my name if I am talking and your name when you are talking.
(Provide practice.)	"Now say this sample sentence: " 'Give the _____ to *me*.' " (Have children give objects to you and each other as they say the sample sentence.)
STUDENTS:	"Give the pencil to *me*." "Give the picture to *me*."
TEACHER:	"Those are good sentences using the word *me*."
(Check application.)	(Make certain children continue to use *me* correctly in successive lessons. Have children independently use *me* when speaking and later in writing.)

Word 2—Usage

TEACHER:	*do*	"Listen to my sentence for the next spelling word, *do*. " 'Bill, *do* your lesson.' "When Bill does his lesson, he is not completely still. He shows action or movement. During spelling, Bill says and writes his phonograms. We say that *do* is an *action* word because it shows that something is happening. Now listen to this sentence. " 'Bill, *do* the dishes.' "Is Bill completely still or moving?"
STUDENTS:		"Moving."
TEACHER:		"Yes. As Bill washes dishes, he shows *action*. Now give me sentences using the spelling word *do*."
STUDENTS:		"*Do* your math." "*Do* your homework."

continued

| TEACHER: | | "Your sentences show that you understand that the spelling word *do* shows action or movement." |
| (Follow procedures.) | | (Make certain children continue to use *do* correctly in successive lessons. Have children independently use *do* when speaking and later in writing.) |

Word 3—Usage

TEACHER:	*and*	"The next spelling word is *and*."
		(Have two girls come forward and join hands.)
		"Listen to this sentence:
		" 'Ann *and* Susie are girls.'
		"The little word *and* connects (joins) the names of two people in that sentence. Now listen to this sentence:
		" 'Bill *and* Bob are boys.'
		"What job does the word *and* have in this sentence?"
STUDENTS:		"The word *and* connects Bill and Bob."
TEACHER:		"Yes. The word *and* connects two people. Now use *and* to connect two people in sentences."
STUDENTS:		"Bill *and* Jim are boys." "Sally *and* Susie play at school."
TEACHER:		"You composed fine sentences to show that the word *and* may be used to connect the names of two people."
		(Next explain that *and* can also connect two things, as in "I have a pencil *and* a pen," and two places, as in, "We go to the cafeteria *and* the library." Demonstrate using objects and places children know. Make certain children continue to use *and* correctly in successive lessons. Have children independently use *and* when speaking and later in writing.)

Word 4—Usage

TEACHER:	*go*	"The next word is *go*. Listen to this sentence:
		" 'John, *go* to my desk.' "
		(Have a child go to your desk.)
		"Notice when John goes to my desk, he moves. *Go* is another *action* word because it tells what is happening. Listen to this sentence:
		" 'Diane, *go* to the pencil sharpener.'

	"Tell me whether Diane is moving or still. Also tell me what kind of word *go* is."
STUDENTS:	"Diane is moving. *Go* is an action word."
TEACHER:	"Yes. It tells what is happening. Now give me sentences using *go*."
	(Make certain children continue to use *go* correctly in successive lessons. Have children independently use *go* when speaking and later in writing.)

Word 5—Usage

TEACHER:	*at*	"The next word is *at*. Listen carefully to this sentence: " 'The children are *at* school.' "*At* shows a relationship between the word that follows it and another word in the sentence. In this sentence, *at* shows a relationship between *school* and *children*. The words *at school* tell where the children are. Listen to this sentence: " 'The children are *at* home.' "Tell me where the children are in this sentence."
STUDENTS:		"At home."
TEACHER:		(Make certain children continue to use *at* correctly in successive lessons. Initially, keep all words in the sentences the same except the noun following *at* so children can focus on the new word *at*. Have children independently use *at* when speaking and later in writing.)

Word 6—Usage

TEACHER:	*on*	"Now we will talk about the word *on*. Listen: " 'The books are *on* the table.' "*On* is another little word that shows a relationship between words, *table* and *books*. The words *on the table* tell where the books are. Listen to this sentence. " 'The books are *on* the desk.' "Tell me where the books are."
STUDENTS:		"The books are *on* the desk."

continued

TEACHER:		"Yes. The little word *on* shows a relationship between *books* and *desk*."

(Make certain children continue to use *on* correctly in successive lessons. Initially, keep all words in the sentences the same except the noun following *on* so children can focus on the new word *on*. Have children independently use *on* when speaking and later in writing.)

Word 7—Usage

TEACHER:	*a*	"The next word is the single letter *a*. It tells us that a person, place, or thing is coming. The word *a* may be used only before a word that begins with a consonant. Listen to this sentence:

" 'Give me *a* ball.'

"The word *a* comes before a *thing* that begins with the consonant *b*. Listen to this sentence:

" 'Give me *a* pencil.'

"Does *a* come before a person, place, or thing and does *pencil* begin with a consonant?"

STUDENTS:		"Yes, *pencil* is a thing. It begins with the consonant *p*."
TEACHER:		"Good job. You identified *pencil* as a thing and you knew that *pencil* begins with a consonant."

(Make certain children continue to use *a* correctly in successive lessons. Be sure each word preceded by *a* begins with a consonant. Have children independently use *a* when speaking and later in writing.

When the other articles *an* and *the* occur in sections A–G, explain that *an* is used with words that begin with vowels, and that *the* is used to mean a *specific one*. Continue checking for understanding, providing practice, and checking application.)

Word 8—Usage

TEACHER:	*it*	"The next word, *it*, takes the place of a *thing*. Listen to these sentences:

		" 'This is my pencil. *It* is red.'
		"The word *it* takes the place of the word *pencil,* which is a thing. I could have repeated the words: '*My pencil* is red.'
		"Listen to these sentences:
		" 'The table is big. *It* is white.'
		"Which word does *it* take the place of? Is it a person or a thing?"
STUDENTS:		"*It* takes the place of *table,* which is a *thing.*"
TEACHER:		"You did a good job of explaining that *it* takes the place of a thing."
		(Have children practice using *it.* Make certain children continue to use *it* correctly in successive lessons. Have children independently use *it* when speaking and later in writing.)

Word 9—Usage

TEACHER:	*is*	"Listen to this sentence using the spelling word *is:*
		" 'Bob *is* a boy.'
		"The word *is* links Bob with *boy.* It tells *who* Bob is. Listen to this sentence, and then tell me what two words are linked by the word *is:*
		" 'Jane *is* my friend.' "
STUDENTS:		"The word *is* links *Jane* and *friend.*"
TEACHER:		'Good thinking. The word *friend* tells *who* Jane is. Now listen to this sentence:
		" 'Bob *is* happy.'
		"The word *is* links *Bob* with *happy.* It tells *how* Bob feels.
		"Listen to this sentence:
		" 'The girl *is* sad.'
		"Think first, then tell me which two words are linked by *is* and whether we know who the girl is or how she feels."
STUDENTS:		"The words *girl* and *sad* are linked by *is.* We know how she feels."
TEACHER:		"Good thinking. The word *sad* tells how the girl feels."
		(Make certain children continue to use *is* correctly in successive lessons. Have children independently use *is* when speaking and later in writing.)

Word Meaning

Since words in sections A–G are in the speaking vocabulary of most kindergarten and first-grade children, few words will need explanation of their meaning. However, as students progress through the Spalding Spelling/Vocabulary Word List, more words need explanation. The detailed grade-appropriate procedure includes unfamiliar words, compounds, homophones (*sea/see*), homographs (*read/read*), homonyms (*pool/pool*), and words that have affixes (*report, planted*). The next dialogue demonstrates teaching meanings of unfamiliar words. It may be modified as needed to teach compounds, homophones, homographs, or words with prefixes and/or suffixes that are derived from base or root words.

Sections A–G Words: Example Dialogue

Word 1—Meaning

TEACHER:	"Class, we have been talking for several days about how words are *used* in sentences. Today, you wrote the word *tan*, which may not be familiar to you. We are going to talk about this word so you will be able to use it correctly in sentences. First, I will compose a sentence that includes words that help you figure out the meaning of *tan*. Next, I will talk about how I decided which words to choose. Then I will ask you to answer questions to show you understand the meaning of *tan*. Last, I will ask you to use *tan* in sentences that show me you understand the meaning. Listen to this sentence:
(Provide a sentence.)	" 'Our desks are *tan,* or light brown.'
(Model thinking.)	"When I composed my sentence, I used the words *or light brown* to help you understand the meaning of *tan*. *Tan* means light brown.
(Check for understanding.)	"Could an orange be called *tan*?"
STUDENTS:	"No, because an orange is not light brown."
TEACHER:	"That is a good explanation of why we would not select the word *tan* to describe an orange.
(Provide practice.)	"Now complete this sentence. " 'The _____ is *tan,* or light brown.' "
STUDENTS:	"The door is *tan,* or light brown." "My shoes are *tan,* or light brown."
TEACHER:	"Good. Your sentences show me you understand the word *tan*."
(Follow procedures.)	(Make certain children continue to use *tan* correctly in successive lessons. Have children independently use *tan* correctly when speaking and later in writing.)

Having all beginners compose *oral* sentences from the start of sections A–G provides *integrated, multisensory* practice that facilitates the transition to *written* sentences.

Language Rules—Sections A–G and Above

To speed spelling dictation, language rules are introduced, practiced, and applied in the writing lesson. Rule application practice begins while students are working on *oral* sentences and continues after they begin *written* sentences.

Written Sentences—Section H and Above

Simple Sentences

Teachers prepare students for *writing* sentences by first writing *simple* sentences on the board. They use words from sections A–G so all students are able to read the sentences. Teachers first demonstrate and explain the attributes of a simple sentence written on the board. A sentence must be one thought, must begin with a capital letter, must end with punctuation, must have logical order, and must have precise language. *For primary-grade students, labels for the parts of speech need not be taught initially.*

Teaching Attributes of Simple Sentences: Example Dialogue

Steps 1 and 2

TEACHER:	"Class, you have been using spelling words in oral sentences for a few weeks. Next week when you begin section H, you will compose *written* sentences using those spelling words.
(Write a sentence.)	"Today, I will write a sentence on the board to show you what to include in your sentences.
(Explain/demonstrate.)	"A simple sentence has one thought about a person, place, or thing. Look at this sentence: " 'The big man runs.' "The words *the man* tell *who* the sentence is about. This sentence is about a person. The word *big* tells *which* man runs. We call *big* a *describing* word (adjective). We call *runs* an *action* word because it shows what is happening. "A *written* sentence must start with a capital letter to show where the author's thought begins. This sentence does begin with a capital. The period (full stop) shows where the thought ends.

continued

"A sentence must have words in the right order to make sense. If I said, 'Runs big the man,' it would not make sense."

Step 3

TEACHER:

"Now I will think out loud as I compose another sentence using spelling words we already know.

(Model thinking.)

"One of our spelling words last week was *boy*. My sentence will be about a *boy*. I must choose an *action* word to tell what the boy is doing. I will choose *play* from our spelling words. I will use a capital with the first word, *the*. I must put an *s* on *play* because I am talking *about* the *boy*. I must put a period (full stop) at the end. Now I will read my sentence.

" 'The boy plays.'

"I forgot to tell which boy, so I will add the word *little* to describe the boy.

" 'The little boy plays.'

"Now I will proofread my sentence to see if I included all the attributes. I started with a capital and ended with a period (full stop). I told which boy and I used the ending *s* on *plays*. My sentence makes sense because the words are in the correct order."

Step 4

(Check for understanding.)

"One word in our dictation today is *hat*. Yesterday, you wrote *mother*. Look at this sentence:

" 'Mother sees a hat.'

"Who is this sentence about and what is the *action* word?"

STUDENTS:

"It is about Mother. The action word is *sees*."

TEACHER:

"Good job of identifying who the sentence is about and what is happening. Think about whether the sentence is about a person, a place, or a thing. Then tell me which one and how you decided."

STUDENTS:

"It is about a person because Mother is a person."

TEACHER:

"Good job. You identified a person and explained how you knew. Now, tell me why I began with a capital."

STUDENTS:

"You began with a capital to show where the author's thought begins."

TEACHER:

"Yes, a capital signals the beginning of a thought. Why did I use a period (full stop) at the end?"

STUDENTS:	"The period (full stop) shows the end of the sentence."
TEACHER:	"Yes. A period (full stop) tells where the thought ends. How do I know that the word order is correct?"
STUDENTS:	"The word order is correct because it makes sense."
TEACHER:	"Could I improve my sentence by adding a word that tells which hat? If so, suggest some words."
STUDENTS:	"Yes. 'Red.' 'Big.' 'Little.' 'Pretty.' "
TEACHER:	"Those are good words to tell which hat Mother sees."

Step 5

| TEACHER: | (Have children use preselected words to compose |
| (Provide practice.) | two or three simple sentences that include all the attributes.) |

Step 6

| TEACHER: | (Each day have children independently compose two or three |
| (Check application.) | simple sentences that include all the attributes.) |

When students compose oral sentences, they often use words that they cannot spell. When students begin writing sentences, they use their notebooks as a source of words. Teaching attributes of written sentences with spelling/vocabulary words helps students be successful. (Their ability to sound out words they have not been taught increases as they learn additional phonograms.) The interactive dialogue and the written sentences make the learning multisensory and help teachers check students' understanding.

After students are familiar with the attributes of simple sentences, teachers begin explicit instruction in identifying (labeling) types of sentences. Primary-grade children begin with declarative and interrogative sentences and then learn exclamatory and imperative sentences. Use simple terms and examples.

Written Compound Sentences—Section H and Above
Primary-grade children were introduced to the term *compound* when they wrote spelling/ vocabulary words *into* and *today* in sections A–G. After students of any age accurately write the four types of simple sentences, teachers introduce compound sentences.

Teaching Compound Sentences: Example Dialogue

Steps 1, 2, and 3

TEACHER:	"Class, you already know what to include in simple sentences. Today, I will teach you a new kind of sentence.
(Review.)	Think back to when you wrote the words *into* and *today* in your notebooks. You learned that these words are called *compound* words. Today, you will learn to compose *compound sentences.*
(Explain/demonstrate.)	"A compound sentence is two sentences related to the same thought and joined with connecting words. Look at these sentences while I demonstrate how to connect two sentences about the same thought:
	" 'Ann plays tag. Ann plays baseball.'
(Model thinking.)	"These sentences are related because they are about games Ann plays. I may combine them by changing the period (full stop) after the first sentence to a comma and then adding the connecting word *and* before writing the second sentence. Read the new sentence with me:
	" 'Ann plays tag, and Ann plays baseball.' "

Step 4

TEACHER:	"Explain a compound sentence. Then tell me which
(Check for understanding.)	connecting word and what punctuation may be used."
STUDENTS:	"A compound sentence has two separate, related sentences connected by a comma before *and*."
TEACHER:	"What does the comma before *and* mean?"
STUDENTS:	"The comma before the word *and* means that two separate, related sentences are combined."
TEACHER:	"That is a good explanation."

Step 5

TEACHER:	"Look at these sentences. First, tell me if they can be
(Provide practice.)	combined, and then tell me your reasoning.
	" 'The dog is small. He is white.' "
STUDENTS:	"These sentences may be combined because they both describe how the dog looks."
TEACHER:	"Good reasoning. You understand that the words *small* and *white* both describe the dog. Tell me what to do to write a compound sentence."

| STUDENTS: | "Put a comma after the first sentence; add the connecting word *and*. Do not write *he* with a capital." |
| TEACHER: | (Provide additional simple sentences that may be combined and some that may not. Have children independently write compound sentences that use a comma before *and*.) |

Step 6

| TEACHER:
(Check application.) | (Make certain children use compound sentences appropriately when they write paragraphs later.) |

After students have practiced using a comma before the connecting word *and*, teachers use the same procedure to introduce compound sentences using the connecting word *but*: "Ann plays tag, but Ann does not play baseball." Then teachers extend students' knowledge by introducing compound sentences using the connecting word *or*: "Each day we play tag, or we play baseball." Although primary-grade children may not have been introduced to the term *conjunction*, they have learned to use the *connecting* words *and*, *but*, and *or*.

Written Complex Sentences—Section H and Above

Beginning with the conjunction *if* in section H, primary-grade children learn the attributes of easy complex sentences using the procedure in the *Teacher Guide* for the appropriate grade level. They can compose simple, easy compound sentences. The following dialogue introduces complex sentences to primary-grade children.

Teaching Complex Sentences: Example Dialogue

Steps 1, 2, and 3

TEACHER: (Review.)	"Class, you have been doing very well writing compound sentences that used the connecting words *and, but, or* with two related sentences.
(Explain/demonstrate.)	"In today's spelling lesson, you wrote the connecting word *if*. I said, 'You may play outside *if* it does not rain.' The connecting word *if* is different from the words *and, but, or*. They join two related sentences that can each stand alone. A *complex* sentence also has two parts, but one part cannot stand alone.
(Model thinking.)	"I will say the sentence again and break it into two parts. 'You may play outside.' This part can stand alone because it

continued

has a pronoun *(you)* and a verb *(play)* and it makes sense. Listen to the second part, 'if it does not rain.' This part has a pronoun *(it)* and a verb phrase *(does rain)*. The two parts are related, but the second part *depend*s on the other part to make sense. We call it the *dependent* part (clause). The connecting word *if* is always used with a dependent part."

Step 4

TEACHER: (Check for understanding.)	"Explain a complex sentence. Then tell me which connecting word you learned today."
STUDENTS:	"A complex sentence has two related parts, one that can stand alone and one that cannot stand alone. We learned the connecting word *if*."
TEACHER:	"That is a good explanation. What do we call the part that cannot stand alone? Why do we call it that?"
STUDENTS:	"We call it the dependent part because it depends on the other part."
TEACHER:	"When may the connecting word *if* be used?"
STUDENTS:	"With a part that cannot stand alone."

Continue steps 5 (provide practice) and 6 (check application) using different complex sentences that use the conjunction *if*. When students have mastered simple complex sentences using *if*, explain and demonstrate complex sentences that begin with dependent clauses followed by a comma. See procedures in the *Teacher Guide* for the appropriate grade level.

Morphology and Parts of Speech—Section L and Above

Another tool for preparing students to write compositions is to teach them to think about and discuss the structure of language. The study of word structure begins in the spelling lesson when teachers explicitly teach the meanings of *syllable, vowel,* and *consonant.* They explain and demonstrate that *open syllables* end with a vowel that says its second sound *(me,* rule 4). They also explain and demonstrate that *closed syllables* end with one or more consonants causing the vowel to say its first sound *(at, in, on).* In the writing lesson, beginners are taught the meanings of base words, suffixes, and prefixes included in the week's spelling words. Primary-grade children are taught to add the suffix *s* to verbs when the subject is third person singular and to compose oral, then written, sentences: e.g., "He *sits* quietly." They are also taught to add the suffixes *ed* and *ing*, respectively, to form the past tense and to show that the action is happening now. ("Bob planted a garden." "Janie is singing.") Word analysis and the meaning and usage of affixes expand as students encounter more difficult spelling words.

Students learn to categorize different kinds of *words* according to the jobs they perform. Being able to name, define, and explain characteristics of a category requires higher-level thinking. It enables students to understand why words behave differently from each other and why position in a sentence affects meaning and sometimes punctuation. Preschool and primary-grade children are familiar with, and enjoy, categorizing different kinds of animals, colors, and objects. They extend that ability in the integrated writing lesson. Interactive dialogue in the whole group improves retention because students learn to explain the purpose of each part of speech and participate in meaningful language practice.

Many kindergartners who have been taught The Spalding Method learn the names for the parts of speech by the end of the year. In the whole group, teachers use words in sections A–G for beginners of any age because students can spell and read these words, and the words include seven of the eight parts of speech. With beginners of any age, initial lessons are done orally in the whole group. Nouns followed by verbs are introduced first because they form the foundation for writing simple sentences. Do not have students write the parts of speech in their notebooks. When the notebooks become cluttered, they are difficult for students to read. The following sample dialogue introduces the term *noun*. Each step in this procedure is identified only in the first sample dialogue.

Teaching Nouns

Teaching Nouns: Example Dialogue

Steps 1 and 2

TEACHER:	"Class, you have composed oral sentences that show you know the meaning of unfamiliar spelling words and how to use them. You have already learned to *group* (categorize) objects by color, size, and shape. Today, I'm going to teach you to group *words*.
(Name and define.)	"You learned that a sentence tells about persons, places, or things. *Nouns* are words that name persons, places, or things.
(Explain/demonstrate.)	"I will write *Nouns* as a big heading on the board. Then I will make three columns under *Nouns* labeled *Persons, Places,* and *Things*. Together we will read words in sections A–G for *reading*. I will stop you when we get to the first word that is a noun. Next, I will list words on the board under those headings (categories)."
	(Have students read words in sections A–G for *reading* in unison. Stop them when they read *man*.)

Step 3

TEACHER:	"I will think out loud as I decide whether *man* names a person, place, or thing. I know *man* names a person because
(Model thinking.)	

continued

I can talk with a man. So I will write *man* under the heading *Persons*. Read on."

(Have students continue reading words in sections A–G. Stop them when they read *bed*.)

"I will think out loud as I decide whether *bed* names a person, place, or thing. I know *bed* is a thing because I can touch a bed, but it can't talk. I will write it under the category *Things*."

(Have students read words in sections A–G for *reading* in unison. Stop them when they read *street*. If anyone identified *today*, say you will explain *today* in the next lesson.)

"I know *street* is a place I can walk to, but it is also a thing I can touch, so I will write street under *Places* and *Things*."

Step 4

TEACHER: (Check for understanding.)	"What is a noun?"
STUDENTS:	"A noun names a person, place, or thing."
TEACHER:	"Good definition. How do you decide whether a word is a person, place, or thing?"
STUDENTS:	"You can talk to a person, touch a thing, and go to a place."
TEACHER:	"Good explaining how to decide."

Step 5

TEACHER: (Provide practice.)	"Now it is your turn to identify words that are nouns. Read on until I tell you to stop. Then tell me whether the word is a person, place, or thing and how you decided." (Have students continue reading words in sections A–G. Stop students when they read *hand*.)
STUDENTS:	"*Hand* is a thing. You can touch it, but it can't talk."
TEACHER:	"Good thinking. You know that a thing can be touched, but it cannot talk." (In the whole group, have students identify nouns in the new spelling words and categorize them as persons, places, or things. Have students use nouns in oral and written sentences in successive lessons.)

Step 6

TEACHER: (Check application.)	(Have children use nouns appropriately in sentences they compose independently. Have them explain how the noun is used: subject, object.)

Daily, questions to check for understanding and oral practice help students rapidly identify nouns. After students are able to categorize and label persons, places, and things, teachers explain that some nouns are *concepts*. A *concept* can be described but cannot be touched. Teachers introduce a new category besides *Person, Place,* and *Thing* on the *Noun Categories* poster and list each *concept* as encountered in the Spalding Spelling/Vocabulary Word List thus far (*chance, charge, time,* and *today* in sections A–G, and *day* in section H). Older students learn that nouns that are concepts, attributes, or qualities are called *abstract* nouns. Students' knowledge of nouns continues to grow as they proceed through the grades. The daily and weekly lesson objectives in the "Planning" section of the *Kindergarten Through Sixth-Grade Teacher Guides* include additional grade-appropriate noun objectives such as forming plurals, using nouns as subjects or objects, forming possessives, and categorizing nouns as concrete and abstract.

Teaching Action Verbs

A sentence is not complete without a verb. The *definitions* of action, linking, and helping verbs are provided in the "Delivery" section of the *Kindergarten Through Sixth-Grade Teacher Guides*. In the following sample dialogues, the focus is on introducing the names for these high-frequency words. Each step in the following dialogue for verbs is the same as for nouns. The dialogue on pages 97 and 98 introduced the *function* of action verbs *do* and *go*. The following dialogue introduces the term *action verb* and defines it.

Teaching Action Verbs: Example Dialogue

TEACHER: "Class, you have had a great deal of practice categorizing (grouping) nouns as persons, places, and things. Today, we are going to name a new category of words. Words that show action are called *action verbs*. Turn to page 1 of your notebook. The second word is *do*. When we talked about this word, I gave you this sentence:
"'*Do* your work.'
"The word *do* shows *action*. I will list *do* under the heading *Action Verbs* because *do* tells what is happening. Tell me about the word *go* and explain your reasoning."

STUDENTS: "*Go* also shows action because you move when you go somewhere. List it under *Action*."

TEACHER: "Yes. The word *go* shows action. Look at this sentence:
"'I see the dog.'
"Which word shows action?"

STUDENTS: "It is hard to tell because you are not moving when you *see*."

TEACHER: "*See* is an action word because your eyes are moving."
(Have children continue to identify action words correctly in succeeding lessons. Make certain children continue to use action verbs appropriately in sentences.)

Teaching Linking Verbs

During initial instruction, teachers use forms of the verb *be* (*am, is, are, was, were*) alone as *linking verbs*. The following sample dialogue introduces linking verbs and then compares action and linking verbs.

Teaching Linking Verbs: Example Dialogue

TEACHER: "You already know how to decide if a word is an action verb. Today, I will teach you to name a new kind of verb. A *linking verb* is used alone to connect two nouns. Look at this sentence:

" 'Bob is a boy.'

"The word *is* links the nouns *Bob* and *boy*. I will list it under the heading *Linking Verbs*. The sentence is about Bob. The noun that follows *is* identifies Bob. Look at this sentence:

" 'I am your teacher.'

"I know the word *am* is also a *linking verb* because it links the speaker, *I*, with the noun *teacher*. The words *am* and *is* are called *linking verbs* because they connect two nouns. They do not show action. Look at this sentence:

" 'Mr. Brown is a teacher.'

"Why do we call the word *is* a linking verb instead of an action verb?"

STUDENTS: "Linking verbs connect two nouns. Action verbs show motion."

TEACHER: "Those are good explanations. The word *is* does not tell what Mr. Brown is doing. It tells us he is a teacher. The word *is* links *Mr. Brown* and *teacher*."
(Have children categorize verbs in sections A–G as action or linking. Then have them write sentences on the board that use linking verbs *am, is,* and *are* with nouns. Discuss and revise as needed. Make certain children continue to use linking verbs appropriately in sentences.)

After students can accurately use *am, is,* and *are* as linking verbs to connect nouns, teachers use the same procedure to identify linking verbs that connect nouns with adjectives. ("Bob is *tall*.")

Teaching Helping Verbs

Teachers introduce the use of helping (auxiliary) verbs when the words *can, will,* and *may* are written in the spelling/vocabulary list. During those lessons, teachers explain that all forms of the verb *be* are also *helping* (auxiliary) *verbs*. The following sample dialogue introduces the term *helping verb* and extends students' learning to categorizing verbs as action, linking, or helping. The same steps apply.

Teaching Helping Verbs: Example Dialogue

TEACHER:	"Class, we have been categorizing action and linking verbs. Today, I have listed a third heading, *Helping* (auxiliary) *Verbs*. Some verbs help other verbs. When I dictated the word *can* in sections A–G, I gave this sentence: " 'I can sing.' "We talked about the meaning of *can*. When used with *sing*, it means *able to sing*. I could have used a different action verb. I could have said, " 'I can walk.' "I know that *sing* and *walk* are action verbs. The word *can* adds more information. It tells that *I* am *able to* sing or walk. "Tell me what a helping verb does."
STUDENTS:	"A helping verb helps an action verb."
TEACHER:	"Good explanation of a helping verb. Now, listen to this: " 'Jose can talk.' "Tell me under which headings I should place *can* and *talk* and then tell me why."
STUDENTS:	"Place *can* under *Helping Verbs* because *can* means you are able to talk. Write *talk* under *Action Verbs* because it shows action."
TEACHER:	"Yes. The word *can* helps the action verb *talk*." (Make certain children use *can* as a helping verb meaning *able to* in succeeding lessons. Have children continue to use helping verbs appropriately in sentences.)

In subsequent lessons, teachers introduce the helping verbs *will, am,* and *may*. They explain that the helping verb *may* means the subject has permission: "I *may* sing." The helping verb *will* means the action will occur in the future: "I *will* sing." The helping verb *am* means the action is happening now: "I *am* singing." Teachers explain and demonstrate that all forms of the verb *be* (*am, is, are, was, were*) can be linking or helping verbs.

Although most verbs show action, linking and helping verbs are important because they are frequently used in writing and reading. These verbs will be practiced again after students are introduced to pronouns. (See dialogue on page 114.)

Teachers use the procedure in the "Delivering" section of the *Kindergarten Through Sixth-Grade Teacher Guides* and the words in sections A–G to teach the names for all parts of speech. They remind students of the use of each part of speech as they now name it. In the whole group, teachers have students categorize these words. For example, in one lesson, teachers have them identify each verb; in another lesson, the students identify pronouns. For convenient reference, words in the order of introduction are available on a Spalding Word Analysis CD. These words can be sorted by alphabet, rules, parts of speech, and syllable patterns.

Teaching Subject Pronouns

The concepts of *person* and *tense* can be explained using simple terms and whole-group activities. These multisensory activities teach students correct usage for speaking and for writing compositions.

Teaching Subject Pronouns with Present Tense Action Verbs: Example Dialogue

TEACHER: (Before class begins, write the sentence pattern below on the board.) "Today, we are going to practice using subject pronouns with action verbs. Listen as I read this pattern. Then I will teach you how to decide which pronoun to use." (Read singular, then plural sentences.)

Singular	*Plural*
I see.	We see.
You see.	You see.
He sees. She sees. It sees.	They see.

"Now read the pattern with me. This time point to yourself when you say, '*I* see,' because *I* refers to the speaker (first person). Point to one other person when you say, '*You* see,' because you are *talking to* one person (second person). Point to a boy when you say, '*He* sees,' because you are *talking about* a male (third person). Point to a girl when you say, '*She* sees,' because you are talking about a female (third person). Point to an imaginary animal when you say, '*It* sees,' because you are talking about an animal (third person). Point to all of us when you say, '*We* see,' because you are talking about all of us seeing (first person plural). Point to the whole class when you say, '*You* see,' because you are *talking to* the whole class. Point to children on the other side of the room when you say, '*They* see,' because you are *talking about* a group of children."
(Have children read the pattern again.)

TEACHER: "Why did you point to yourself when you said, 'I see'?"

STUDENTS: "I pointed to myself to show that I was speaking."

TEACHER: "Good explanation. Why did we point to a boy when we said, 'He sees'?"

STUDENTS: "We pointed to one boy because we were *talking about* one boy."

TEACHER: "Why did we point to all of us when we said, 'We see'?"

STUDENTS: "We pointed to all of us because all of us were doing the seeing."

TEACHER: "Good explanation. Now tell me when to use the pronoun *I*."

STUDENTS: "When I am the speaker, I use the pronoun *I*."

TEACHER: "Yes. Tell me when to use the pronoun *he, she,* or *it*."

STUDENTS: "Use the pronoun *he* when *talking about* one male, *she* when *talking about* one female, and *it* when *talking about* one animal (or thing)."

TEACHER:	"Good explanation. Tell me when to use the pronoun *we*."
STUDENTS:	"Use the pronoun *we* when including others."
TEACHER:	"Yes. Use the pronoun *we* when you are part of a group. Now, tell me which pronoun to use when *talking about* another group of people."
STUDENTS:	"Use the pronoun *they*."
TEACHER:	"Class, you really understand how to use the subject pronouns." (Make certain children use subject pronouns correctly in succeeding lessons. Have children use subject pronouns with present tense action verbs in sentences.)

Choral reading of these patterns with other action verbs provides additional multisensory practice that improves retention. When students have learned these patterns well, teachers model adding direct-object nouns to expand the sentence: "I *see* the dog." "She (He) *sees* the dog." "I *run* the race." "She (He) *runs* the race."

After students have practiced subject pronouns with present tense verbs (*I see, you see,* and so on) and direct objects ("I *see* the boy"), teachers extend the practice to subject pronouns/past tense verb patterns. They begin with regular verbs in sections A–G (*look/looked, like/liked, live/lived, land/landed, play/played*) because students can add the past tense suffix *ed*. Then teachers use the pattern to practice the past tense of irregular verbs in sections A–G (*do/did, see/say, run/ran, make/made*).

Subject pronoun/verb patterns help students visualize abstract concepts of *person* (first, second, third) and *tense* (changes in the form of verbs to indicate the time of the action). Teachers constantly check students' understanding of the meaning of first- and third-person pronouns because they are needed for writing first- and third-person compositions (see page 119). *Terms for first, second, and third person need not be introduced initially, but the concept is taught.*

When students can accurately use subject pronouns with common regular and irregular action verbs in sections A–G, teachers use the pattern to practice subject pronouns with linking and helping verbs.

Teaching Subject Pronouns with Linking and Helping Verbs: Example Dialogue

TEACHER:	(Before class begins, write the sentence pattern below on the board.) "Now let's use subject pronouns to review what we learned about linking and helping verbs. Remember that the verbs *am, is,* and *are* may be both linking and helping verbs. Let's read the sentences listed under *Linking Verbs* together." (Students join teacher in reading the first column.)

continued

	Linking Verbs	*Helping Verbs*
	I am happy.	I am singing.
	You are happy.	You are singing.
	He is happy.	He is singing.
	She is happy.	She is singing.
	It (bird) is happy.	It (bird) is singing.
	We are happy.	We are singing.
	You are happy.	You are singing.

TEACHER: "Why are the verbs *am, are,* and *is* in these sentences called linking verbs?"

STUDENTS: "They are called linking verbs because they tell *how* the person or animal feels."

TEACHER: "Good. Now read the sentences under *Helping Verbs* in unison." (Students read.) "Why are the verbs *am, are,* and *is* in these sentences called helping verbs?"

STUDENTS: "They are called helping verbs because they help the action verb *singing.*"

TEACHER: "What do the helping verbs *am, is,* and *are* tell us about the *time* of the singing?"

STUDENTS: "They tell us the singing is happening *now.*"

(Have students continue comparing linking and helping verbs in successive lessons. Be certain children use linking and helping verbs appropriately in sentences.)

Teaching Composition

To write fine compositions, students need to draw on prior knowledge of vocabulary and many spelling and language rules and concepts. These prerequisites are introduced and practiced in the integrated lessons so students can apply them automatically when composing different types of writing. Becoming an accomplished writer takes years of practice as students grow in their knowledge and command of the English language.

Composition instruction starts with teaching beginners of any age to write sentences that relate to a single topic. After the students can independently compose simple sentences, teachers introduce related sentences. This occurs in week sixteen in the first-grade lesson objectives.

Related Sentences

Beginners of any age first learn the concept of related thoughts during discussion of compound sentences. Students who understand the concept of related thoughts avoid the common tendency to wander from one topic to another. Each step in the procedure is identified in the following dialogue.

Teaching Related Sentences: Example Dialogue

Steps 1 and 2

TEACHER: (Review terms.)	"Class, you can identify the *subject of a sentence* written on the board. Daily you use nouns and pronouns as subjects of good sentences. You have learned that the pronouns *I* and *we* are called *first-person* pronouns because they take the place of the speaker. You have also learned that we use the pronoun *he, she,* or *it* when we are talking about a male, a female, or a thing. Today, I will show you how to use these skills to write related sentences about a single subject.
(Explain/demonstrate.)	"Read the definition on the board with me. " 'A *topic* is the subject of two or more sentences.' "When two or more sentences are about one subject, we say those sentences are related to one topic. Look at these sentences: " 'I have a pet dog. His name is Sandy.'
(Model thinking.)	"I know that these sentences are related because they both talk about one topic, my pet dog. Read these sentences with me: " 'I have a pet dog.' " 'I had eggs today.' "I know these sentences are not related, because one sentence is about my pet, and the second sentence is about what I ate for breakfast.
(Check for understanding.)	"Explain in your own words why these sentences are not related. Use the new word you just learned."
STUDENTS:	"The two sentences are not about one topic. One is about a pet and the other is about eggs."
TEACHER:	"Good. You explained that a topic is the subject of two or more sentences. Related sentences are about one topic.
(Provide practice.)	"Our topic today is pets. I will call on several children to give two sentences about a real or an *imaginary* pet. Use the pronoun *I* to show that you are the speaker. In the first sentence, say, " 'I have a pet _____.' "In the second sentence, say, " 'His (or her) name is _____.' "
STUDENTS:	"I have a pet cat. Her name is Boots." "I have a pet fish. His name is Spot."

continued

| TEACHER: | "Good. You composed sentences about the topic *pets*." (Have students continue to compose related sentences about real or imaginary pets until you are certain they understand the concept.) |
| (Check application.) | (In successive lessons, have children use words to compose related sentences. Hold them accountable for editing for English conventions.) |

The Writing Process in Three Basic Types of Compositions

While students are still practicing related sentences, teachers introduce the writing process.

In the reading lesson, beginners are introduced to three basic types of writing: *narrative*, *informative* (expository), and a combination of the two, which we call *informative-narrative*. In the writing lesson, students draw on their knowledge of vocabulary, spelling, sentence construction, and related thoughts to compose each type of writing. Putting all this together requires higher-level thinking. Just as explicit, sequential instruction is required for learning how the language works, so students need to be taught the *writing process*. Although the process is presented as a series of stages (see the "Delivering" section of the *Kindergarten Through Sixth-Grade Teacher Guides*), writers frequently move from one stage to another. For example, during the revising stage, the writer may see a need to return to the prewriting stage to collect more information. Daily practice of the writing process helps students become logical thinkers and good communicators.

Teachers follow the sequence for teaching types of compositions as introduced in the grade-appropriate lessons in the "Planning" section of the *Kindergarten Through Sixth-Grade Teacher Guides*. Children easily progress from writing two or three statements about familiar topics, such as pets or toys, to writing a short first-person informative-narrative paragraph (four to six sentences) about the topic. The initial paragraph is a simple progression from related sentences.

Teaching Informative-Narrative Paragraphs

The following sample dialogue takes place after children have been taught the basic attributes of paragraphs. For beginners, we recommend that prewriting and composing take at least one lesson. Revising, editing, and publishing may take another lesson or two. This dialogue demonstrates writing a short informative-narrative paragraph in first person and does not include all the elements of a narrative. Each step in the procedure is identified only in the first example dialogue.

Teaching First-Person Informative-Narrative Writing: Example Dialogue

Prewriting

TEACHER:
(Review terms/elements.)

(Before class begins, display an organizer as shown below.)
"Class, in the reading lesson today, I read a short first-person informative-narrative paragraph that had one or two characters, a setting, one event, and factual information. We knew it was first person because the author used first-person pronouns.

(Explain/demonstrate.)

"The first stage in the writing process is called *prewriting* because we plan what we want to write. During prewriting, I consider my audience and purpose for writing, my topic, and whether I will be a part of the paragraph. Today, I will model planning an informative-narrative paragraph. I will use this worksheet to help me organize my thoughts."
(Complete the organizer, as shown below, as you discuss each decision.)

(Model thinking.)

"I will think out loud as I make these decisions. Beside the word *Audience*, I will write, 'My class,' because I am writing for you.
"Beside *Topic*, I will write, 'My pet dog,' because my class enjoys hearing about my dog.
"Beside *Author's Purpose*, I will write, 'To inform in an interesting way.'
"I will write, 'First person,' beside *Point of View*. This means I will participate in the story to make my paragraph more interesting. I may use the pronouns *I, me,* and *my*.
"Beside *Character*, I will write the pronoun *I,* because I am describing my dog.

Informative-Narrative Organizer

Audience_____

Topic_____

Author's Purpose_____

Point of View_____

Character(s)_____

Facts_____

_____

_____

_____

"Because this is not just a narrative about my dog, I will decide which facts I want my students to know about my pet. When I was writing related sentences, I told them his name and color. Under *Facts*, I will write his name, Sandy, and his color, tan and white; and I will add *huge* to describe his size.

(Check for understanding.)
STUDENTS:

"Class, what decisions did I make during the prewriting stage?"
"Audience." "Topic." "Purpose." "Point of view."

continued

TEACHER:	"Great! Which elements did I choose?"
STUDENTS:	"One character." "Facts."
TEACHER:	"Yes. I am the only character because I wanted to emphasize facts about my pet."

Composing

TEACHER: (Explain/demonstrate.)	"Now that I have finished planning what I want to write, I will use my organizer to compose a paragraph. This is the second stage of the writing process, which is called *composing*. During this stage, I compose sentences that include the elements on my organizer.
(Model thinking.)	"I will think out loud as I write. I will begin with the related sentences I already wrote about my pet. " 'I have a pet dog. His name is Sandy.' "Now I will tell his color. I will write, " 'He is tan and white.' "To describe his size, I will add, " 'He is huge.' "Now that I have included everything from my organizer, I will put my paragraph away. Later, I will decide how to improve my paragraph.
(Check for understanding.)	"Explain what I did during the composing stage."
STUDENTS:	"You wrote sentences about your dog." "You included everything on the organizer."
TEACHER:	"You told me two very important points about *composing*. I wrote sentences that were *only* about my topic and checked my organizer to see that I didn't forget anything." (Continue the writing process in the next lesson.)

Revising

| TEACHER:
(Explain/demonstrate.) | "Now it is time to improve my paragraph. We call this the *revising* stage. I will read my paragraph to see if I used precise language to describe my topic. I will also check to see if all sentences are in a logical order to make my purpose clear. Last, I will ask if I have included enough information about my topic."
(Use a different-color chalk for revising.) |

(Model thinking.)	"Now, I will think out loud as I check for these things: "The first sentence says, " 'I have a pet dog.' "I will add *sheep* to tell you what kind of dog. The second sentence tells his name and the third his color. To the sentence about his size, I will add to my description by writing, " 'Sandy is huge and he has a big, bushy tail.' "Now I must write a sentence to signal that my paragraph is finished. I will write, " 'I am glad Sandy is my pet' "I have added information and precise language. I reread my paragraph to see if my sentences are in a logical order. They clearly show that I am informing about my pet, not telling a story. I think I have enough facts about my topic because I have described my pet. "Next, I will add a title. A phrase that signals what my paragraph is about helps the reader. I will write, " 'My pet.'
(Check for understanding.)	"Tell me what I checked in the revising stage."
STUDENTS:	"Precise language." "Information." "Order." "Clear purpose." "Title." "A sentence that signaled that you were finished."
TEACHER:	"Yes. We improve our informative-narrative paragraph by revising for precise language and information, sentence order, clear purpose, and meaning."

Editing

TEACHER:	
(Explain/demonstrate.)	"The next stage in the writing process is called *editing*. We *edit* for capitalization, punctuation, spelling, grammar, indentation, and margins." (Use another color chalk for editing.)
(Model thinking.)	"I will think out loud as I check for capitals. I must capitalize *pet* in the title because every important word in a title must be written with a capital. Next, I check punctuation. I forgot to put a comma between the parts of

continued

	the compound sentence. I forgot a period (full stop) at the end of the last sentence. I spelled all words correctly. I must indent the first word to show that these are related sentences.
(Check for understanding.)	"Class, tell me what I checked in the *editing* stage."
STUDENTS:	"Capitals." "Commas." "Periods (full stops)." "Spelling." "Indents."

Publishing

TEACHER:	"The final stage of the writing process is *publishing*. Now I share my finished paragraph with others. I could share my final copy by posting it on the class bulletin board, in the library, or in the office. Today, I will read my paragraph aloud and then put it on our class bulletin board." (Read to class):

My Pet

I have a pet sheepdog. His name is Sandy. He is tan and white. Sandy is huge, and he has a big, bushy tail. I am glad Sandy is my pet.

(Follow procedures.)	(In the whole group, guide children as they use the writing process to compose one or more informative-narrative paragraphs. Write these on the board. As children compose each new class paragraph, review the decisions made in each stage until the writing process becomes automatic. In successive lessons, have children independently use the writing process to write short informative-narrative paragraphs. Hold them accountable for editing for English conventions.)

For beginners, the informative part of the paragraph is limited to two or three declarative sentences. The narrative part is limited to one or two characters. As students progress through the grades, teachers require them to include more narrative elements and more specific facts. For example, if students are studying early settlers in fourth-grade social studies, teachers might assign a first-person informative-narrative composition on that topic, in which students pretend to be a settler. They would have students use the facts they have learned in social studies in their compositions. This integration reinforces students' comprehension of important social studies facts and enables teachers to assess their knowledge of both social studies and informative-narrative writing.

Teachers follow the same procedure to write third-person informative-narrative paragraphs. They remind students that the writer does not participate in the paragraph when writing in third person. For the initial example, we recommend using the same topic to emphasize the difference between first-person and third-person writing. For example, the third-person informative-narrative paragraph would look like this.

Jane's Pet

Jane has a pet sheepdog. His name is Sandy. He is tan and white. Sandy is very large, and he has a big, bushy tail. Jane is glad Sandy is her pet.

Teachers should model and have students write third-person informative-narrative paragraphs on other topics as well.

Teaching Informative Paragraphs

After beginners have independently composed first- and third-person informative-narrative paragraphs, it is easy to teach them informative writing. The following dialogue introduces a simple informative paragraph on a topic of interest to first-grade children.

Teaching Informative Writing: Example Dialogue

Prewriting

(Before class begins, display an organizer as shown below.)

TEACHER: "Class, in the reading lesson today, I read a short informative paragraph about bears. You know that an informative paragraph explains facts about a topic. It is written in third person. It may have a topic sentence that signals the main idea of the paragraph. I have written the definition of a topic sentence on the board. Read it with me.

" 'A topic sentence is one general sentence that states the most important point about the topic.'

"The writer uses a topic sentence to help the reader find the main idea of the paragraph. Read the definition of a concluding sentence.

" 'A concluding sentence shows that the paragraph is finished. Sometimes this is done by restating the main idea.'

"In the prewriting stage, I use a worksheet to plan my informative paragraph. I have listed *Audience, Author's Purpose,* and the elements of informative writing." (Complete the worksheet as you discuss each decision.)

"Now I will think out loud. I have already decided that you are my audience, so I will write, 'My class' beside *Audience.*

continued

"Beside *Topic,* I will write, 'Bears,' because we have been reading about bears.

"Beside *Author's Purpose,* I will write, 'To inform about bears.'

"Beside *Point of View,* I will write, 'Third,' because I know informative paragraphs are written in third person.

"Under *Facts,* I will list facts we have learned about bears in phrases instead of sentences:

" 'furry; eat in summer, sleep in winter; different colors; eat meat fish berries and other food.'

"Beside *Topic Sentence Ideas,* I will write, 'interesting animals.' "

(Ask children to name the elements of informative writing, describe the decisions required in prewriting, and state the purpose of writing topic and concluding sentences.)

Informative Organizer
Audience_____
Topic_____
Author's Purpose_____
Point of View_____
Facts_____
_____
_____
Topic Sentence Ideas_____
_____

Composing

TEACHER: "The next stage is *composing.* During this stage, I will write a topic sentence that states the most important point I want you to know about bears. Then I will write sentences that state facts about bears. Last, I will write a sentence that shows the paragraph is finished. I will think out loud as I compose. The most important point I want you to know is:

" 'Bears are interesting animals.'

"Now I must state facts about bears. I will begin,

" 'All bears are furry.'

"Next I will tell what they eat and when they sleep.

(Leave out the commas when writing the next sentence.)

" 'They eat meat fish berries and other food. Most bears sleep all winter.'

"Next, I want to show that bears can be different sizes and colors.

(Leave out the commas when writing the second sentence.)

" 'Bears may be large or small. Bears are black brown or white.'

"They live in different places, so I will write,

" 'Some bears live in the forest but others live where there are few trees and much ice and snow.'

"I have composed a topic sentence and stated facts about bears. Later, I will improve my paragraph."

(Ask leading questions to help children identify the elements of informative writing included in the composing stage.)

(In the next lesson or lessons, revise, edit, and publish the informative paragraph.)

Revising

TEACHER: "The next stage is *revising*. In this stage, I reread my paragraph to improve it. I like my topic sentence because it clearly states the most important point about my topic. The next three sentences are OK. I will combine the next two sentences to be more precise.

(Leave out the commas.)

" 'Bears may be large or small and their fur may be black brown or white.'

"I will also combine and revise the next two sentences. I will write, 'Some bears live in the forest but others live where there are few trees and much ice and snow.'

"Now I must finish my paragraph. I will write,

" 'People can see bears in zoos.'

"I need a title that signals my topic. I will write the phrase,

" 'All About Bears.' "

(Ask leading questions to help children identify decisions made in the revising stage.)

Editing

TEACHER: "The next stage is *editing* for capitalization, punctuation, spelling, grammar, and indentations. I started all sentences with a capital, but I forgot to use commas between nouns, adjectives, and compound sentences. I will add commas between *meat, fish, berries, and other food*. I will add a comma between *small* and *and*. I will add commas between *black, brown, or white*. I will also add a comma between *forest* and *but*." (Ask leading questions to help children identify what to check for in the editing stage.)

continued

Publishing

TEACHER: "The last stage is publishing. I will think out loud as I decide how to share my informative paragraph. I think I will read my paragraph to my class and then post my final copy on our bulletin board. I must remember to indent." (Read to class:)

All About Bears

Bears are interesting animals. All bears are furry. They eat meat, fish, berries, and other food. Most bears sleep all winter. Bears may be large or small, and their fur may be black, brown, or white. Some bears live in the forest, but others live where there are few trees and much ice and snow. People can see bears in zoos.

(Ask leading questions to help children identify ways to publish their paragraphs. In the whole group, guide children as they use the writing process to compose one or more informative paragraphs. Write these on the board. As children compose each class paragraph, review the decisions made in each stage until children automatically use the writing process. In successive lessons, have children independently use the writing process to write short, informative paragraphs. Hold them accountable for editing for English conventions.)

Teaching Narrative Paragraphs

After first-grade children have independently composed informative paragraphs, teachers follow the same procedure to teach them to compose narrative paragraphs. In the reading lesson, children learn that narratives may be written in first or third person. This dialogue introduces a simple narrative paragraph written in third person. It does not include dialogue, because the appropriate punctuation has not yet been introduced.

Teaching Narrative Writing: Example Dialogue

Prewriting

(Before class begins, display an organizer as shown below.)

TEACHER: "Class, you know the stages of the writing process very well. You used the writing process to write informative-narrative and informative paragraphs. "Today, I will use the writing process to compose a narrative paragraph. You learned in your reading lesson that narratives relate an event or tell a story. A narrative does not have a topic sentence, but it does have a main idea (theme) that the author wants you to understand. In today's reading lesson, I read a short narrative about a helpful little girl. The main idea the author wanted us to understand in that paragraph is that being helpful takes practice.

"Now I will think out loud as I use a narrative organizer.

"Beside *Audience,* I will write, 'my class.'

"Under *Main Idea,* I will write, 'helpfulness.'

"My *Purpose* for writing is to increase understanding of helpfulness.

"I did not participate in the event, so I will write, 'Third,' under *Point of View.*

"Under *Characters,* I will write, 'Lori, Pat, and Mrs. Lopez.'

"Under *Setting (Place/Time),* I will write, 'Playground at recess.'

"Under *Event,* I will write, 'Lori fell off the slide. Pat and Mrs. Lopez helped Lori.'

> **Narrative Organizer**
>
> Audience_____
>
> Main Idea_____
>
> Purpose_____
>
> Point of View_____
>
> Characters_____
>
> Setting(Place/Time)_____
>
> Event (Plot)_____
>
> _____
>
> _____

Composing

TEACHER: "Now that I have finished prewriting, I will compose. I will begin by introducing two of my characters and the setting. I will write,

" 'Lori and Pat went to the school playground at recess. They planned to take turns going down the slide.'

"Now I must introduce an event. I will write,

" 'Lori went to the top of the slide. She looked down and fell to the ground.'

"Next, I must tell what her friend Pat did to help. I will write,

" 'Pat ran as fast as she could to get Mrs. Lopez, the school nurse. Mrs. Lopez ran to Lori and checked her. Then she carried Lori to her office. After a short rest, Lori felt better.'

"Now I must conclude my narrative. I will write,

" 'She was grateful to Pat and Mrs. Lopez for helping her.'

"Identify each element I included in my narrative."

STUDENTS: "The characters are Lori, Pat, and Mrs. Lopez." "The setting is the playground at recess." "The event is Lori's accident and Pat and Mrs. Lopez helping Lori."

continued

TEACHER: "You have correctly identified the characters, setting, and event. Did I include the main idea that I want you to understand?"

STUDENTS: "Pat and Mrs. Lopez were helpful."

TEACHER: "Yes. They were helpful. I want to explain more about what happened, so I must revise. I will put my narrative aside until later, when I will improve it. (Continue the writing process in another lesson.)

Revising

TEACHER: "I will begin *revising* my paragraph by reading every sentence for precise descriptions."

(Use a different-color chalk for revising.)

"In the first sentence, I will insert *morning* before *recess* to tell when the event happened. In the second sentence, I will insert the word *big* before *slide* to show it was a tall slide. The next sentence is OK. To explain how the event happened, I will add *When Lori leaned over to.* I will delete *she,* the past tense ending on *looked,* and the word *and.* I also will add *she* before *fell.* The next sentence is OK. The sentence after that does not tell why Mrs. Lopez checked Lori, so I will insert *for broken bones.* The next sentence is OK. Now I must make my main idea clear, so I will change the last two sentences and write, *After a short rest, Lori felt better because Pat and Mrs. Lopez helped her. Lori was grateful.*

"What did I look for as I revised my paragraph?"

STUDENTS: "You looked for precise language." "You checked to see that your meaning was clear."

TEACHER: "Yes. It is important to check for precise language and a clear main idea when you *revise* a paragraph."

Editing

TEACHER: "Now I must *edit* my paragraph.

"I have capital letters for the names in the first sentence, and periods in the first two sentences. When I combine two sentences, I need a comma to separate the part that cannot stand alone from the part that can stand alone.

"Explain what we check for when we *edit* a paragraph."

STUDENTS: "We check capitalization, punctuation, spelling, grammar, and indentation."

TEACHER: "Yes. Those are the important points to check whenever you *edit.*"

Publishing

TEACHER: "Now I will publish my paragraph by reading it to you and posting it on our class bulletin board." (Read to class:)

Helpful Friends

Lori and Pat went to the school playground at morning recess. They planned to take turns going down the big slide. Lori went to the top of the slide. When Lori leaned over to look down, she fell to the ground. Pat ran as fast as she could to get Mrs. Lopez, the school nurse. Mrs. Lopez ran to Lori and checked her for broken bones. Then she carried Lori to her office. After a short rest, Lori felt better because Pat and Mrs. Lopez helped her. Lori was grateful.

Although kindergartners may write only class paragraphs, they learn that writing is a process, and this will make them better writers in first grade. First-graders independently compose one-paragraph informative narratives about a pet by week twenty-one and independently compose informative paragraphs and then first- and third-person narrative paragraphs by the end of the year. These form the foundation for a multitude of writing tasks needed by students of all ages. Professor Richard Mitchell explained:

The literate person is in control of those techniques special to writing. . . . He can formulate sentences that make sense. He can choose the right word from an array of similar words. He can devise the structures that show how things and statements about things are related to one another. He can generate strings of sentences that develop logically related thoughts, and arrange them in such a way as to make that logic clear to others. . . . Because he can do these things, he can, in reading, determine whether or not someone else can do these things. (1979, 170–171)

Learning to be a proficient writer continues throughout a student's school career and beyond. However, every journey needs to be well planned. This journey begins with well-chosen words correctly placed in simple, compound, and complex sentences and goes on to related sentences and then to artfully written paragraphs and compositions.

The *Kindergarten Through Sixth-Grade Teacher Guides* provide carefully sequenced daily and weekly lesson objectives with definitions of terms and sample paragraphs that can be used as the teacher's model. *The Writing Road to Reading* is designed to ensure that students have the directions they need for a successful journey.

Delivering Integrated Reading Instruction

Spalding reading instruction is divided into three strands: literary appreciation, text structure, and comprehension. To foster a *desire to read*, teachers use fine literature in literary appreciation lessons beginning on the first day of school at every grade level. Books chosen for reading lessons should include good character development, engrossing plots, and well-crafted descriptive prose. *Spalding Series 1 Leveled Readers, Learning to Read and Loving It*, are used to practice phonograms and text fluency in kindergarten and with older beginning readers. *Series 2 Leveled Readers, Reading and Loving It*, are used for the same purposes in first grade and with older beginning readers. Comprehension booklets that have short, interesting passages and literal and inferential questions are used to teach basic text structures and comprehension strategies. The grade-appropriate procedure for teaching each of these skills is found in the "Delivering" section of the *Kindergarten Through Sixth-Grade Teacher Guides*. Abbreviated lessons for teaching text structure and mental actions are included in *The Grade-Level Comprehension Connection User's Guides*.

Literary Appreciation

In literary appreciation lessons, teachers draw students' attention to the way literature connects with, and sometimes reflects, personal feelings and experiences. Initially, the teacher reads expressively. Teachers take time to discuss a well-turned phrase, to admire or censure an event, to reread a part that is an especially good example of skilled writing. A little time spent talking about descriptive language can add to the enchantment. Teachers should ask thought-provoking questions that call for more than factual recall. They should make allusions throughout the day to characters, phrases, or sentences encountered in books read or being read.

Attributes of Fine Literature

To help students determine literary merit, teachers explain and demonstrate how to identify and label five attributes of fine writing: (1) *precise language*, (2) *emotional appeal*, (3) *content*, (4) *insight into people and life*, and (5) *universality*. Knowing these terms provides students with a common vocabulary to use in class discussions. This process develops students' critical discernment and facilitates their own writing.

As the teacher demonstrates and explains the attributes of exemplary writing, students begin to develop taste. As they discuss an author's skillful use of the elements of narrative writing, they better understand how to use these elements in their own writing. Even before children are able to read, they can learn to recognize the attributes of fine literature. As their reading skills mature, so does their appreciation of well-written prose.

Each step in the procedure for teaching attributes of fine literature is identified. This dialogue introduces the first two attributes: precise language and emotional appeal. For young children, these attributes are introduced on separate days.

Teaching Attributes of Fine Literature: Example Dialogue

Precise Language

TEACHER: (Name and define.)	"You have enjoyed listening to the stories we have read each day. Today, I will teach you how authors use precise language to increase your enjoyment and understanding. *Precise language* means that authors *clearly describe* the people or animals, places, and events.
(Explain/demonstrate.)	"First, I will read a sentence or two from a story. Next, I will talk about the language that helps me enjoy and understand the story. We have read *The Ugly Duckling* by Hans Christian Andersen and talked about how much we enjoyed it. You told me your favorite parts. Today, I will pick out some sentences that use *precise language*.

(Model thinking.)	"Listen as I read and think out loud. " 'After a while one shell cracked, then another, and another, and from each egg came a fluffy little yellow creature that lifted its head and cried, "Peep! peep!" ' "When I read that, I could picture and almost hear the baby ducks. Andersen could just have said, 'The ducks hatched,' but that would not have given us a picture. I enjoy the story more when I can picture the people or animals, places, and events.
(Check for understanding.)	"What do we mean when we say an author uses *precise language?*"
STUDENTS:	"The author *clearly describes.*"
TEACHER:	"Yes. The author uses words that help us picture the people or animals, places, and events. What words did Hans Christian Andersen use to describe the baby ducks?"
STUDENTS:	"Fluffy." "Little." "Yellow."
TEACHER:	"Yes. Those words clearly describe the baby ducks. Listen to this sentence and tell me which words help you picture what is happening and why: " 'Then they climbed the slippery bank of the river and waddled after their mother.' "

continued

STUDENTS:	"*Slippery bank* because I can picture the muddy edge of the water." "*Waddled* because I can picture the baby ducks swinging from side to side."
TEACHER: (Provide practice.)	"Good. You identified examples of *precise language.* Now listen to these sentences, and then tell me words that clearly describe: " 'He was no longer a dark, gray bird, ugly to look at.' "Which words did Andersen use to clearly describe the ugly duckling?"
STUDENTS:	"Dark." "Gray." "Ugly to look at."
TEACHER: (Provide practice.)	"Yes. Andersen describes the ugly duckling as dark and gray in contrast to his description of the fluffy little yellow ducks. Fine writers use *precise language* to clearly describe people or animals, places, and events." (For older beginners or remedial readers studying this or any other story, use sentences that provide more complex descriptions. Continue to have children identify precise language in successive reading lessons.)
(Check application.)	(Have children identify the attributes of literature in library books. Have them explain how the authors' use of the attributes enhances their enjoyment and/or understanding.)

Emotional Appeal

TEACHER:	"We have talked about precise language. Today, I want to teach you that fine authors also describe situations or events that cause us to feel in certain ways. We call how we feel *emotions.* When authors clearly describe how people or animals feel, we often remember feeling the same way. Today, I will read more sentences from *The Ugly Duckling.* I will think out loud as I explain how the sentences make me feel. " 'An old duck who saw the new brood coming stared at them and said, "Do look; here is another brood, as if there were not enough of us already; and what a queer-looking fellow one of them is; we do not want him here," and then she flew at him and bit him in the neck.' "I have been picked on before, so I can imagine how sad the ugly duckling must be when the old duck is mean to him. The emotion the ugly duckling was feeling was sadness. Now listen to these sentences:

	" 'Then they threw bread and cake into the water for the new bird, and they said, "This is the finest of all, he is so young and graceful." The poor swan was so happy he did not know what to do, but he was not at all proud. He had been hated for being ugly, and now he heard them say that he was the most beautiful of all the birds. He rustled his feathers and curved his slender neck, and said, "Now, when people see me they will not be angry, they will be glad. I never dreamed of such happiness when I was an ugly duckling." '
	"How would you feel if you had been the ugly duckling and now you are a beautiful swan?"
STUDENTS:	"Happy."
TEACHER:	"Yes, the emotion you would feel is happiness."
(Follow procedures.)	(Have children identify other examples in successive lessons. Make certain that children can identify examples of emotional appeals in library books they read.)

The Ugly Duckling by Hans Christian Andersen can be used in different lessons to teach insights and universality. For example, children learn that making fun of another is hurtful (insight). Children all over the world can relate to feeling ugly or different (universality). Originally written in Danish, *The Ugly Duckling* has been translated into every language in the world. Learning to recognize the attributes of fine literature increases children's enjoyment and their awareness of the writer's skill. Because *literary appreciation* is usually taught using narratives, the elements of narratives are also an area of focus. These basic literary terms introduced in kindergarten form the foundation for analysis of increasingly difficult narratives as students progress through the grades.

Expanding Understanding of Narrative Elements

In lessons on text structure, students are taught to identify and name the *basic* elements of three types of writing. Teachers expand students' understanding of the elements of narrative writing, deepening their appreciation of fine writing. After reading a story for enjoyment, teachers reread sections and explain how to distinguish between *main* and *supporting* characters, to differentiate between *settings* that are important to the story (integral) and those that are not (backdrop), and to discern the sequence of events called *plot*. Knowing these terms provides students with a common vocabulary to use in comparing one story with another. This process develops students' critical discernment and facilitates their own writing.

Each step in the procedure for expanding understanding of narrative elements is identified in the following dialogue. This sample dialogue for *literary appreciation* introduces main and supporting characters *after* children have learned *basic* narrative elements in lessons on *text structure* (page 136).

Expanding Understanding of Narrative Elements: Example Dialogue

TEACHER: (Review terms.)	"In lessons on text structure you have learned that stories are also called *narratives*. We call the parts of narratives *elements*. Every *narrative* has at least one *character*; a time and place, which we call the *setting*; and one or more *events*, which may involve a *problem* and a *solution*. You learned that a *character* in a narrative may be a person, or an animal who behaves like a person.
(Name and define.)	"Today, we will learn about two kinds of *characters*. The *main* character is clearly described. We get to know the character by what he does, by what he says, and by what is said about him. Usually there are other characters who *support* the main character. They are necessary to the story, but they are not described as fully.
(Explain and demonstrate.)	"In our literary appreciation lesson I read *Peter Rabbit*, and we talked about the author, Beatrix Potter. First, I will read some sentences from *Peter Rabbit*. Next, I will explain how I know who the *main* and *supporting* characters are.
(Model thinking.)	"Listen as I read and then think out loud. "'Once upon a time there were four little Rabbits, and their names were—Flopsy, Mopsy, Cotton-tail, and Peter. They lived with their Mother in a sand-bank, underneath the root of a very big fir-tree.' "Beatrix Potter introduced five characters in the first sentence: Flopsy, Mopsy, Cotton-tail, Peter, and Mrs. Rabbit. Now listen to this sentence: "' "Now, my dears," said old Mrs. Rabbit one morning, "you may go into the fields or down the lane, but don't go into Mr. McGregor's garden: your Father had an accident there; he was put in a pie by Mrs. McGregor." ' "I remember from reading the story earlier that Mr. McGregor chased Peter, so I know Mr. McGregor is also a character. Now I will read carefully to decide who this story is mainly about. "' "Now run along, and don't get into mischief. I am going out . . ." Flopsy, Mopsy, and Cotton-tail, who were good little bunnies, went down the lane to gather blackberries. But Peter, who was very naughty, ran straight away to Mr. McGregor's garden, and squeezed under the gate! First he ate some lettuces and some French beans; and then he ate some radishes.' "I think Peter is the *main* character because I have learned so much about him. I learned that he was naughty, and that he

	immediately did what he was told not to do. I even know what he ate. I think that Flopsy, Mopsy, and Cotton-tail are *supporting* characters because I know very little about them, except that they were good little bunnies who did what they were told. I'll read on to be sure."
	(Continue reading the rest of the story.)
	"Now I know that Peter is the main character because I learned so much about him. Flopsy, Mopsy, and Cotton-tail, Mrs. Rabbit, and Mr. McGregor are *supporting* characters. They are necessary to the action, but they are not described in detail.
(Check for understanding.)	"What do we mean by the term *main character*?"
STUDENTS:	"A *main character* is the person or animal who is described the most."
TEACHER:	"Good explanation. What words did the author use to describe Peter more fully?"
STUDENTS:	"Peter was very naughty." "He ran straight to Mr. McGregor's garden." "He ate lettuces, beans, and radishes."
TEACHER:	"Yes. The author told us Peter was naughty and described where he went, what he ate, and the trouble he got into. Tell me what we call the other characters."
STUDENTS:	"Supporting characters."
TEACHER:	"Yes. Why are they called *supporting* characters?"
STUDENTS:	"They are not described as much."
TEACHER:	"That is true. They are necessary to the action, but the author does not describe them as clearly."
(Provide practice.)	(In successive whole-group lessons, have children identify main and supporting characters in different narratives. Have them refer to sentences in the narratives to defend their choices.)
(Check application.)	(Have children independently identify main and supporting characters in library books. Have them refer to sentences in the narratives to defend their choices.)

Fluent and Expressive Reading

Students must be able to read fluently so they can concentrate on deriving meaning from text. As primary-grade children listen to the teacher reading fluently and expressively, they learn that such reading not only provides pleasure but also enhances comprehension. When children read orally from their beginning readers, the teacher identifies those children who have difficulty decoding and those who need instruction reading expressively. (If spelling words have been taught a year ahead as provided in spelling lessons, there will be few words that interrupt fluency and comprehension.)

During oral reading, students also learn that punctuation marks are signals telling which words go together, when to pause, and when to lower or raise their voices. Reading aloud motivates students to practice their reading; in fact, they don't realize they are practicing fluency. They are just enjoying the stories because they can read and understand them.

Text Structure

During lessons on text structure, students learn to identify three *basic* types of writing: narrative, informative, and the combination we call informative-narrative. These basic types of writing form the foundation for analysis of more advanced types of writing as students progress through the grades. Different types of writing require different levels of concentration. Rapid identification of text structure enhances comprehension by helping students focus on the important elements in each type of text and adjust reading speed as needed.

Teaching Narrative Structure

This sample dialogue is a short narrative written in third person for primary-grade children.

Teaching Narrative Structure: Example Dialogue

TEACHER:
(Name, define, explain.)

(Before the lesson begins, display an organizer, as shown below.) "As I have read stories to you, we talked about why authors write stories. You learned that the author's purpose is to entertain and to help you understand people and the world. Today, I will teach you some new terms.

(Refer to narrative poster; see "Resources.")

"Another word for a story is *narrative*. Narratives have several parts. We call the persons in a story *characters*. They can be real or imaginary. We use the term *setting* to describe where and when the story happened. We use the term *plot* for the events that happen to the characters. Sometimes these events cause a *problem* that has to be *solved*.

(Model thinking.)

"Listen carefully as I read. I will think out loud as I decide if this paragraph is a narrative.

" 'Little Tommy was learning to dress himself. One morning he put on all his clothes, even his shoes. He was very excited and ran to show his mother and father. His mother told him how proud she was of him. His father praised Tommy, too, but pointed at Tommy's feet.'

"I *think* this is a narrative because there are three *characters*, Tommy, his mother, and his father. The *setting* is Tommy's home in the morning. The *event*, or *problem*, is that Tommy learns to dress himself. I'll read on to see what happens next.

"Then his father said, 'Tommy, you put your shoes on the wrong feet.'

"'You are trying to fool me,'" said Tommy. 'You know these are my feet.'

(Model thinking.) "Now I *know* this is a story because it has three characters, a setting, and a problem. I'm sure the author's purpose was to entertain because it made me laugh. I think the author wanted me to understand that Tommy put his right shoe on his left foot and his left shoe on his right foot. What did Tommy think his father meant?"

STUDENTS: "Tommy thought his dad meant he put his shoes on someone else's feet."

TEACHER: "Tell me another name for a story."
(Check for understanding.)

STUDENTS: "Another name is *narrative*."

TEACHER: "Yes. Tell me why authors write stories. What is their purpose or reason?"

STUDENTS: "They want to entertain us." "They help us understand people."

TEACHER: "Yes. What are the parts (elements) of stories we learned about today?"

STUDENTS: "Characters." "Setting." "Event (plot)."

TEACHER: "Yes. To show you the parts of a story, I will complete this
(Initial narrative organizer.) narrative organizer.

"Under *Purpose*, I will write, 'To entertain and develop understanding.'

"Under *Characters*, I will write, 'Tommy, his mother, and his father.'

"Under *Setting (Place/Time),* I will write, 'Tommy's home in the morning.'

"Under *Event (Plot)*, I'll write, 'Tommy tried to dress himself.'"

(Provide practice.) (In the whole group, have students use graphic organizers to

continued

(Check application.)	identify the author's purpose, the characters, the setting, and the event or events in other comprehension passages.) (In *literary appreciation* lessons, have children independently identify the author's purpose and the elements of narratives.)

Completing a narrative organizer makes abstract concepts concrete and provides multi-sensory experiences.

Teaching Informative Structure

After students can consistently identify the author's purpose and the elements of narratives, they are ready to learn the characteristics of informative (expository) paragraphs. The facts of informative paragraphs are not discussed in teaching the elements. The focus of these lessons is identifying only the type of writing.

The following sample dialogue for primary-grade children introduces the author's purpose and two elements of informative writing: topic and information.

Teaching Informative Structure: Example Dialogue

	(Before the lesson begins, display an organizer, as shown below.)
TEACHER:	"You can identify characteristics of narratives very well. Today, I will introduce a different type of writing. In your daily writing lessons, you have composed sentences that provide information. When the author's purpose is to provide information, we call the writing *informative*.
(Name, define, explain.)	Information that is true is called a *fact*. If I write, 'The sun comes up in the morning,' we know this is a fact. The *subject* of that sentence is *sun*. If I write more sentences about the sun, I would say that my *topic* is the *sun*.
(Refer to Informative poster; see "Resources.")	"The *topic* is *what* the paragraph is about. *Facts* provide information about the topic. I will read a short paragraph

	and think out loud as I show you how I identify informative writing. Listen carefully.
(Read sentences.)	" 'The U.S. Air Mail Service began in 1918. The first pilots had no radios or parachutes and few instruments. To find their way, they followed roads and railroad tracks and other things they could see from the air.'
(Model thinking.)	"I *think* this is an informative paragraph because the author told me *facts* about the U.S. Mail Service pilots. There are no characters so far. I *think* the author's purpose is to teach me about the first mail service pilots, but I must read on to be sure.
(Read sentences.)	" 'If there were clouds or fog, they could not see where to go. It was dangerous work. The first U.S. Mail pilots were very brave.'
TEACHER:	"Now I *know* that the *topic* of this paragraph is the first pilots to fly for the U.S. Air Mail Service, and the author's purpose is to teach me *facts* about them.
(Check for understanding.)	"Tell me the name of this type of writing."
STUDENTS:	"Informative."
TEACHER:	"Good. Now tell me what the author's purpose is."
STUDENTS:	"The author wants to teach us something."
TEACHER:	"Yes. Informative writing teaches us something. What is the topic?"
STUDENTS:	"First U.S. Air Mail Service pilots."
TEACHER:	"Yes. Now I will complete an informative initial organizer
(Initial informative organizer.)	so you can see the parts of an informative paragraph. "Beside *Author's Purpose*, I will write 'To inform.' "Beside *Topic*, I will write 'First U.S. Air Mail Service pilots.' "Beside *Facts*, I will write, 'began in 1918; no radios, no parachutes, no instruments; followed roads and railroad tracks.' "
(Provide practice.)	(In the whole group, have students identify author's purpose, the topic, and the facts in other informative passages as you fill out a graphic organizer.)
(Check application.)	(In different paragraphs, have students independently identify the author's purpose and the elements of informative writing. Finally, have them identify the elements in science and social studies books.)

After students have learned to write topic sentences in *composition* lessons, teachers have them identify topic sentences in the comprehension booklets and in science and social studies paragraphs. Do not discuss the facts (content) of the informative paragraphs when teaching the elements of informative writing. The focus of these lessons is only on identifying the type of writing.

Teaching Informative-Narrative Structure

When students can easily distinguish between narrative and informative writing, they are ready to learn that authors sometimes combine elements of both. The following sample dialogue for primary-grade children is used to introduce author's purpose and a few elements of informative-narrative writing: characters, setting, topic, and facts about ants.

Teaching Informative-Narrative Structure: Example Dialogue

(Before the lesson begins, display an organizer, as shown below.)

TEACHER:

(Name, define, explain.)
"You have learned to identify narratives and informatives. Today I will introduce another type of writing. Sometimes an author provides information in an interesting or more personal way. He may include one or two characters and a setting along with important factual information.

(Informative-narrative poster; see "Resources.")
"We call that *informative-narrative* writing because it has elements of both kinds of writing. We say the author's purpose is to inform in an interesting way.

(Model thinking.)
"Listen carefully as I think out loud while reading a short informative-narrative paragraph.

" 'I am working very hard,' said the worker ant. 'I must find food in the park and bring it back to my colony. I have antennae on my head to help me smell the food.'

"I *think* this may be an *informative-narrative* paragraph because it has a character, a worker ant who talks, but it also has some facts about how ants find food. I must read on to see if there are more facts.

" 'When I find food, I will eat some and bring the rest back for others to eat. I will leave a trail for other ants to follow. They will bring more food to feed the colony.'

"Now I *know* this is *informative-narrative* writing, because

	there are more facts about how ants find and gather food. The author's purpose is to inform me about ants in such an interesting way that I will remember the facts more easily.
TEACHER: (Check for understanding.)	"Tell me why we call this type of writing informative-narrative."
STUDENTS:	"There are some narrative elements and some informative elements."
TEACHER:	"That is correct. What elements of a narrative are in this paragraph?"
STUDENTS:	"Characters." "Setting." "Event (plot)."
TEACHER:	"Good identification of narrative elements. What are the parts of informative writing?"
STUDENTS:	"Facts."
TEACHER:	"Yes. There are many facts about how ants find food and feed the colony. Tell me the author's purpose."
STUDENTS:	"The author's purpose is to teach us about ants in an interesting way."
TEACHER: (Informative-narrative initial organizer.)	"Yes. To help you see the parts, I will complete this informative-narrative organizer: "First, beside *Characters*, I will write, 'worker ant.' "Beside *Setting*, I will write, 'park.' "Beside *Event*, I will write 'finding food.' "Beside *Topic*, I will write 'ants.' "I will list some *facts* in phrases: 'ants have antennae; find food with antennae; bring food back to colony; mark trail.' "
(Provide practice.)	(In the whole group, have students identify the author's purpose and the narrative and informative elements in other passages as you complete a graphic organizer.)
(Check application.)	(In different paragraphs, have students independently identify the author's purpose and the elements of informative-narrative writing. Finally, have them identify the elements in other content-area books.)

Comprehension: The Five Mental Actions

When students can easily distinguish between the three types of writing, they are ready to learn to consciously use the five mental actions necessary for comprehension.

Skilled comprehension depends on accurate and automatic decoding, a broad vocabulary, background knowledge, and knowing elements of basic text structures. In addition to teaching those prerequisites, teachers can improve students' ability to comprehend text by teaching them to think about their own thinking (metacognition). Explicit instruction in five mental actions begins in kindergarten after children have learned narrative, informative, and informative-narrative text structures (about week twenty-one).

Teaching the First Three Mental Actions

Teachers model identifying and labeling the first three mental actions: *monitoring comprehension*, *making connections*, and *predicting* the type of writing. They explain and demonstrate that these three mental actions are used together, and that they are needed for the fourth and fifth actions: *reformatting* information in text and *mentally summarizing* the author's main idea. Teachers use the short, interesting passages in the grade-level comprehension booklets so the focus can be on the mental actions. The teacher coaches children as they identify and label the first three and then all five mental actions while listening to text.

This sample dialogue occurs after kindergarten and first-grade children *consistently* identify three *basic* types of writing. It introduces the first three mental actions.

Teaching the First Three Mental Actions: Example Dialogue

Modeling Three Mental Actions

TEACHER:	"You are now so good at identifying narratives, informative, and informative-narrative writing that you are ready to learn how to improve your understanding of what you read. As I read the passage, I will stop and tell you what I am thinking. " 'Benjamin Franklin was one of the men who founded America. He was also a scientist and inventor.'
(Model monitoring.)	"I understand every word.
(Model predicting.)	"I *think* this is informative because it has facts about Ben Franklin. I'll read on. " 'If someone in your family wears bifocals, you can thank Benjamin Franklin.'
(Model monitoring.)	"I understand every word except *bifocals*. I'll read on to see if I can figure out the meaning. " 'His vision was poor, and he needed eyeglasses to read, but he was tired of always having to put them on to read, and then take them off again to see things far away.' "
(Model making connections.)	"I think *bifocals* means some kind of eyeglasses.

MENTAL ACTIONS

MONITORING COMPREHENSION
Checking understanding of words, phrases, and sentences to identify unfamiliar words or concepts

MAKING CONNECTIONS
Linking stated information with information already learned to draw conclusions (infer) and elaborate

PREDICTING
Forecasting, supporting, and/or revising forecasts using stated information and information already learned

(Model supporting prediction.)	"I'm quite sure this is an informative paragraph because it has facts about Ben Franklin and eyeglasses. I'll read on to see if it has a solution.
	" 'Franklin needed eyeglasses that would let him see both near and far. He had two pairs of glasses cut in half and put half of each lens in one frame. Bifocals have been improved since Franklin's time, but the idea was his.' "
(Model monitoring.)	"I understand every word.
(Model confirming prediction.)	"I know this is informative because it has facts about Ben Franklin creating bifocals.
	"I used three mental actions to help me understand the paragraph."
	(As you explain each mental action and name it, refer to the mental action posters; see "Resources.")
(Three mental action poster)	"Now, I will teach you the names for the mental actions I used while thinking out loud. The first mental action I used as I read was *monitoring comprehension*. This means I checked my understanding of each word, phrase, and sentence, and I identified a word I didn't understand.
(Three mental action poster)	"To figure out the unfamiliar word, *bifocals*, I *made connections*. I used the fourth sentence to help me figure out the meaning of *bifocals*, so I made connections between sentences.
(Three mental action poster)	"The third action is *making predictions*. Have you ever heard the daily weather reports that *forecast*, or *predict*, the weather? After the second sentence, I predicted that this is an informative paragraph. That helped me focus on identifying facts as I continued to read the passage.
	"Now, I will read the paragraph again. This time I will *describe* and *label* each of the three mental actions as I use them.
	" 'Ben Franklin was one of the men who founded America. He was a scientist and inventor.'
(Model/label monitoring.)	"I understand every word. *I checked my understanding.*
(Model/label predicting.)	"I *think* this is an informative paragraph because it has facts about Ben Franklin. I *predicted* the type of writing. I'll read on.
	" 'If someone in your family wears bifocals, you can thank Benjamin Franklin.'

continued

(Model/label monitoring.)	"I understand every word, except *bifocals*. I checked my understanding and identified an unfamiliar word.
(Model/label making connections.)	"I'll read on.
	" 'His vision was poor and he needed eyeglasses to read, but he was tired of always having to put them on to read, and then take them off again to see things far away.' "
(Model/name monitoring.)	"I understand every word. I *checked my understanding*." (Continue the dialogue, thinking out loud as you complete the story.)
(Check for understanding.)	"When I read sentences and say that I understand every word, which mental action am I using?"
STUDENTS:	"You are *checking your understanding* (monitoring comprehension)."
TEACHER:	"Yes. When we read, we check our understanding of every word. Which mental action do we use when we don't understand a word?"
STUDENTS:	"We *make connections* with what we already know and what is in the story."
TEACHER:	"Good thinking. What mental action do we use when we forecast the type of writing?"
STUDENTS:	"*Predicting*."
TEACHER:	"You've done a good job of naming and defining three mental actions that help us understand what we read."
(Provide practice.)	(In whole-group lessons, have children define the first three mental actions, and then describe their thinking and label the action used as you read different passages.)
(Check application.)	(In whole-group lessons, have students use the first three mental actions as they listen to or read content-area books.)

When introducing the first three mental actions, teachers do not discuss the content of the paragraphs. The focus of these lessons is only on using and naming the mental actions.

Teaching All Five Mental Actions

When students have learned to use the first three mental actions, they learn to consciously use all five mental actions while listening and later while reading all types of writing. The following dialogue introduces the fourth and fifth mental actions.

Teaching All Five Mental Actions: Example Dialogue

TEACHER:
(Review and introduce the fourth and fifth mental actions.)

"Class, you have become very good at identifying and labeling the first three mental actions while listening and reading. You can *monitor your comprehension, make connections* with prior knowledge and the text, and *predict* the type of writing. Today, I will introduce the fourth and fifth mental actions, which will help you understand what you hear, see, and read. The fourth action is called *reformatting.*

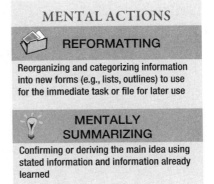

MENTAL ACTIONS

REFORMATTING

Reorganizing and categorizing information into new forms (e.g., lists, outlines) to use for the immediate task or file for later use

MENTALLY SUMMARIZING

Confirming or deriving the main idea using stated information and information already learned

"*Reformatting* means *reorganizing* or *categorizing* information we hear, see, or read. Our brain is like a giant filing system with folders that hold files containing facts we learn. For example, when you learn information about a new country, such as the Netherlands, you create a folder for that country. When you learn facts about the Netherlands, you *reformat,* or place, the information in files and store them in the Netherlands folder. For example, one *file* might be about cities, another about rivers, and so forth. When you learn information in an *organized* way, you can remember and use it quickly.

(Check for understanding.)

"Now, name the mental action we use to file information. Explain what it means and why it helps us learn."

STUDENTS:

"*Reformatting.*" "We categorize information." "Reformatting helps us remember information."

TEACHER:

"Yes. When we *reorganize* information, this helps us remember it quickly.

(Mentally summarizing.)
(Model mentally summarizing.)

"The fifth mental action is called *mentally summarizing.* It means *identifying or figuring out* the *main idea.* We use information stated in the text and information we've already learned and have stored in our brains. You *mentally summarize* when you listen to or read the essential

continued

	information in paragraphs and identify a sentence that states the most important point. We call that sentence the *topic sentence* because it identifies the author's main idea.
(Check for understanding.)	"Name the fifth mental action. Explain its meaning."
STUDENTS:	"*Mentally summarizing*. We use all of the essential information to *identify* or *figure out* the main idea."
TEACHER:	"Yes. *Mentally summarize* means that we consider all essential information, and then identify the paragraph's main idea. Today, I will demonstrate using all five mental actions as I read a paragraph. You will hear me use the first *three* mental actions to help me *reformat* information and *mentally summarize* the main idea. Sometimes, I will use *two* or *three* mental actions together. For example, I may *monitor comprehension*, *make connections*, and *predict* within a single sentence.
	"Listen carefully as I read, think out loud, and name the actions I use.
(Read.)	" 'When you visit the Netherlands you will see windmills in all parts of the country.'
(Model monitoring and making connections.)	*"I understand every word because the author told me the Netherlands is a country.*
	(LABEL) "I used two mental actions. I monitored my comprehension, I identified *Netherlands* as an unfamiliar word, and I made connections between two sentences to understand that Netherlands is a country.
(Model reformatting.)	"I will start a new *folder* and label it *Netherlands* because I didn't know that word before today.
	(LABEL) "I reformatted by filing new information.
(Model predicting type of writing, topic, and topic sentence.)	*"I think this is an informative paragraph about the Netherlands, a country with many windmills. I think the topic is windmills in the Netherlands, and the first sentence is the topic sentence.*
	(LABEL) "I predicted type of writing, topic, and topic sentence.
(Model reformatting.)	*"I will add a file labeled 'windmills' to my Netherlands folder.*
	(LABEL) "I reformatted by filing new information.
	"I'll read on to check if other sentences are about windmills in the Netherlands.

(Read.)	" 'Each windmill is a tower with long wooden arms near the top, like the spokes of a great wheel. The wheel, turned by the wind, moves the pumping machinery inside the tower.'
	"I understand every word.
(Model monitoring.)	**(LABEL)** "I monitored my comprehension.
TEACHER:	*"These two sentences support the first sentence because*
(Model making connections.)	*they tell what windmills are.*
	(LABEL) "I made connections between sentences.
(Model reformatting.)	*"I will add that information to my windmill file.*
	(LABEL) "I reformatted by filing new information.
(Model supporting predictions.)	*"After three sentences, I am almost sure this is an informative paragraph, and the first sentence is the topic sentence about windmills in the Netherlands.*
	(LABEL) "I supported my prediction of type of writing, topic, and topic sentence. I'll read on.
(Read.)	" 'Some of the windmills pump water from the fields into the canals, and the canals carry it out to the ocean. Some windmills grind wheat or do other kinds of work. Nearly every farm in the Netherlands has a windmill.'
(Model monitoring.)	*"I understand every word.*
	(LABEL) "I continued to monitor my comprehension.
(Model making connections.)	*"These sentences support the first sentence because they give more information about windmills. They tell what windmills do.*
	(LABEL) "I made connections between the first sentence and later sentences.
(Model reformatting.)	*"I'll add this new information to my windmill file. Every sentence has only important information about windmills in the Netherlands. This paragraph didn't tell about cities, people, or buildings in the Netherlands, so I do not need to create another file.*
	(LABEL) "I reformatted by filing new information.
(Model confirming predictions.)	*"I am certain this is an informative paragraph about windmills in the Netherlands. The first sentence is the topic sentence (main idea) because all other sentences state facts about windmills in the Netherlands.*
	(LABEL) "I confirmed my predictions that the type of writing is informative; the topic is windmills in the

continued

	Netherlands; and the first sentence is the topic sentence. I mentally summarized by confirming that the first sentence is the main idea.
TEACHER:	"Which mental action did I use when I said, 'I will file this
(Check for understanding.)	information?' "
STUDENTS:	"*Reformatting.*"
TEACHER:	"Yes. *Reformatting* means categorizing and filing information to remember and use it later.
(Check for understanding.)	"Which mental action did I use when I said, 'I know the first sentence is the main idea'?"
STUDENTS:	"*Mentally summarizing.*"
TEACHER:	"Yes. It means confirming a stated main idea. Why is it important to be able to accurately use the first three mental actions?'
STUDENTS:	"*The first three help us use the fourth and fifth.*"
TEACHER:	"Yes. You see how the mental actions work together to help us understand what we hear, see, and read."
(Provide practice.)	(In whole-group lessons, have children define all five mental actions, and then describe their thinking and label the actions used as you read different passages.)
(Check application.)	(In whole-group lessons, have students use all five mental actions as they listen to or read content-area books.

Students who are able to analyze their own thinking while listening and reading increase their comprehension, and thereby significantly improve their performance in language arts and content-area subjects.

Chapter Summary

Chapter 2 presents explicit, interactive, and diagnostic instruction for spelling, writing, and reading lessons. In the spelling lesson, teachers explicitly teach phonemic awareness; phonograms with handwriting; high-frequency vocabulary; and pronunciation, spelling, and language rules of English. In the writing lesson, teachers expand students' knowledge of vocabulary by teaching word meanings and usage, morphology, syntax, and composition using five stages of the writing process. Students learn to compose four types of simple sentences; compound, complex, and related sentences; and narrative, informative, and informative-narrative compositions. In the reading lesson, teachers develop a love of reading by reading fine literature aloud and teaching its attributes. Primary-grade children develop fluent and expressive reading as they read *Spalding Series 1 and 2 Leveled Readers,* and then classics, aloud. Teachers explicitly teach elements of narrative, informative, and informative-narrative text so students can focus on the most important elements when reading a variety of prose. Finally, students learn to consciously use five mental actions to help them identify a stated main idea or derive an implied main idea. *The Writing Road to Reading* is a comprehensive language arts program that has successfully taught students from diverse backgrounds to speak, write, and read well for over five decades. In Chapter 3, we will discuss "Assessing Skills Mastery."

ASSESSING SKILLS MASTERY

CHAPTER OVERVIEW

Environment Conducive to Learning

Spelling Assessments

Writing Assessments

Reading Assessments

IN *THE WRITING ROAD TO READING*, the term *assessment* includes informally observing students' daily behavior and progress, as well as formally measuring their performance on Spalding tests. Chapter 3 considers an environment conducive to learning and assessments for spelling, writing, and reading. Formal assessments include standardized tests that measure students' performance relative to other students in the same categories and criterion-referenced assessments that measure their performance compared with state, district, and/or school standards. Strategies, procedures, and forms for administering, scoring, and recording students' performance on all Spalding pretests and assessments are provided in the "Assessing" section of the *Kindergarten Through Sixth-Grade Teacher Guides*. This chapter describes measuring, scoring, and recording students' performance and identifying students whose behaviors, skills, or procedures are not meeting or exceeding grade-level expectations.

Environment Conducive to Learning

Beginning on academic day one, teachers identify students of any age who are having difficulty adjusting to the established daily routines and procedures. They analyze whether the difficulty is due to hearing, sight, comprehension, or attention problems. Teachers seat these children in the front, where they can be observed. Teachers monitor their progress daily to determine if formal assessment is needed. Early detection and intervention for children with special needs such as dyslexia, ADHD, or autism are the keys to helping these students achieve.

Spelling Assessments

Accurate spelling depends on phonemic awareness, knowledge of phonogram sounds, letter formation, and rules that govern phonogram pronunciation, placement, and spelling. Assessment begins with pretesting to determine students' initial instructional levels.

Pretesting

Kindergartners, and first-graders new to *The Writing Road to Reading*, are *not* pretested. Rather, as teachers introduce the kindergarten or first-grade curricula, routines, and procedures, they carefully observe children's behavior to identify those experiencing difficulty. For first-grade children who had Spalding in kindergarten, and for all older students, teachers analyze prior scores on standardized achievement tests of reading and language (if available).

On the first academic day of school, teachers pretest first-graders who had Spalding in kindergarten and all students in second grade and above on phonemic awareness, phonogram sounds and formation, and spelling using the Spalding Spelling Assessment forms and procedures found in the *First Through Sixth-Grade Teacher Guides*. Refer to "Recommended Language Arts Scope and Sequence" beginning on page 418 in Part Two to identify objectives students should master at each grade level.

Diagnostic Assessments

Phonemic Awareness

For the first academic day, the spelling objective at every grade level is phonemic awareness. After teachers model segmenting sounds in spoken words and blending sounds into spoken words, they carefully observe children who have difficulty hearing vowel or consonant sounds. A vowel is a speech sound made when the air leaving the lungs is vibrated in the voice box (larynx or Adam's apple) and released. The mouth remains *open* as you say each vowel sound, *but* the *shape* of the mouth changes. Vowel sounds are determined by how the mouth is shaped as the air passes through. A consonant is a speech sound that occurs when the airflow is obstructed (blocked) in different ways. For students having difficulty with these sounds, see page 165 in Chapter 4 and the instructional tips accompanying the phonograms listed starting on page 208 in Part Two. Next, teachers observe students' responses and performance when the symbols for speech sounds are introduced.

Systematic Phonics

Informal assessment begins with the introduction of phonograms. Teachers carefully observe students' pronunciations and letter formations of phonograms introduced each day. Immediate identification and correction can prevent problems from developing. Each day, teachers also provide short diagnostic assessments to help them identify skills that need to be retaught and students who need additional teacher-directed small-group instruction (see Chapter 5).

Oral Phonogram Reviews

Daily oral phonogram reviews measure students' ability to see the phonogram and say the sound or sounds—the skill needed for reading words. To identify students who are mispronouncing any speech sound, teachers *listen* carefully as students pronounce phonograms. In addition to making immediate corrections, they record phonograms that many students have mispronounced. Then they reteach and include these in daily reviews until automaticity is achieved. Although the majority of students will master the sounds quickly, teachers continue to listen for students who need additional help as more difficult phonograms are introduced. To monitor the progress of these students, teachers administer the *Individual Assessment for Oral Phonograms* found in the "Assessing" section of the *Kindergarten Teacher's Guide.*

Written Phonogram Reviews

Daily written phonogram reviews measure students' ability to hear a sound or sounds, identify the correct phonogram, and write it legibly. These prerequisites are critical for students' success in spelling and writing words in their notebooks. Writing phonograms is more difficult than hearing and saying them. Therefore, recording performance on daily and weekly written phonogram reviews identifies students who need additional help in small groups. After students begin writing words in their notebooks, teachers assess their performance in a variety of ways.

Spelling Notebooks

After students have written the grade-appropriate number of words in their notebooks, teachers check notebooks for legible handwriting and accurate spelling, markings, and rule notations. To prevent errors, teachers carefully observe students (1) during dictation; (2) as they proofread their notebooks using the model on the board; (3) as they proofread a partner's notebook, identifying errors with tiny pencil checks; and (4) as they correct their own errors before submitting notebooks for the teacher's final assessment. After following this procedure for just a few weeks, teachers are surprised that even primary-grade children have remarkably accurate notebooks. Teachers record phonograms, rules, and handwriting concepts that require reteaching and additional practice. Teachers also carefully observe the last step in spelling dictation each day—reading the newly dictated words two ways: for spelling and for reading.

Reading for Spelling

Daily reading for spelling measures students' ability to decode newly dictated words. Teachers correct mispronunciations immediately and record words mispronounced by the majority of students. They also observe as students read previously written words, to ensure transfer to long-term memory. Students whose pronunciation or segmentation is inaccurate need extra teacher-directed small-group instruction.

Reading for Reading

Daily reading for reading measures word fluency: i.e., automatic word recognition. Teachers correct mispronunciations immediately and record words mispronounced by the majority of students.

They also observe as students read previously written words, to ensure transfer to long-term memory. Students who hesitate while reading or who read slowly require additional teacher-directed small-group instruction.

Daily Quizzes

Daily quizzes measure short-term memory. Teachers provide daily quizzes on words written in the notebook the previous day, to correct errors before these can be retained in memory. They place tiny checks beside students' misspelled words, and then record common errors such as incorrect phonograms, misapplication of rules, and incorrect letter formation, so that the relevant skills can be retaught in small groups and reviewed the next day.

Weekly Quizzes

Weekly quizzes measure short-term memory of the week's spelling words and letter formation. Teachers record errors involving phonograms and application of rules so that the necessary skills can be retaught in small groups and reviewed the next week.

Vocabulary

Teachers informally assess students' understanding of the structure of the language. First, they listen carefully as students analyze daily spelling words for (1) phonograms that use sounds other than the first or use an unfamiliar sound, (2) syllable patterns, and (3) rule application. Then they measure students' performance by assigning a few words to write in syllables and then explain the pronunciation, spelling, marking, and/or syllable patterns. They record errors and identify students who need extra help.

Monthly Progress-Monitoring Assessments for Systematic Phonics and Spelling of High-Frequency Vocabulary

On approximately the same day each month, teachers measure long-term retention of spelling words using one of eight monthly Spalding Spelling Assessments that are aligned to the Spalding Spelling/Vocabulary Word List. Test 1 is both the pretest and the posttest: i.e., the end-of-year outcome assessment. The goal is for students to spell one year above their grade placement so they can decode unfamiliar words encountered in subject-area reading. Each month, teachers record students' progress on the grade-appropriate forms and record errors of phonograms, application of rules, and letter formation. Students' scores on the monthly spelling assessments also measure mastery of spelling and syllable patterns on grade-level vocabulary (see Chapter 5 for evaluation and differentiated instruction).

Writing Assessments

Pretesting

Pretests measure students' knowledge of grade-appropriate vocabulary; attributes of four types of simple, compound, and complex sentences; conventions of paragraph construction; and elements of informative-narrative, informative, and narrative writing.

Diagnostic Assessments

Vocabulary with Sentence Construction

Informal assessments begin on academic day one with careful listening to students' oral language. Teachers pay attention to students' responses to directions, ask questions to check for understanding, observe students' participation in class discussions, and note their sentence construction. After students have mastered the attributes of written declarative sentences, teachers assign one or two declarative sentences and then the other types of simple, compound, and complex sentences. Teachers record spelling errors and grammar errors, identify students who need teacher-directed small-group instruction, and identify skills that need to be retaught.

Oral Sentence Construction

At the beginning of each year, teachers at every grade level introduce or review the attributes of four types of simple sentences, then compound sentences, and last complex sentences. Informal assessment of sentence construction begins when teachers listen carefully to students' simple, compound, and complex oral sentences that demonstrate meaning and usage of unfamiliar spelling words. They record vocabulary that the majority of students found difficult and errors in sentence construction so that the relevant skills can be retaught in whole-group or small-group instruction.

Written Sentence Construction

Formal assessment begins as students compose written sentences that demonstrate meaning and usage of unfamiliar words from the week's spelling lesson. Each day, teachers model sentences, including unfamiliar spelling words in the types of sentences that have been previously introduced. Then, students compose one or two written sentences. As teachers assess students' sentences, they record errors in vocabulary and in sentence construction. Teachers frequently record two scores for these daily writing assignments: a spelling score on any words included in students' notebooks and a writing score based on correct grammar, word order (syntax), and conventions such as capitalization and punctuation. (See Sentence and Paragraph Written Checklists in the "Assessing" section of the *Kindergarten Through Sixth-Grade Teacher Guides*.)

Composition

After teachers introduce related sentences and paragraphs of three types, conventions such as margins and indentation are also assessed. Teachers also assess whether students include grade-appropriate attributes of fine literature introduced in the reading lessons. The grade-appropriate writing assessment in the "Assessing" section of the *Kindergarten Through Sixth-Grade Teacher Guides* makes recording students' progress easy.

Monthly Progress-Monitoring Assessments

Measuring students' ability to compose simple sentences, compound and complex sentences, and three types of paragraphs assesses their monthly progress. Maintaining student portfolios enables parents to see a record of their child's progress throughout the year. After new skills have been taught, teachers may also have students improve sentences or paragraphs in their portfolios. In this way, they can assess students' ability to revise their work as they learn more; revising is an essential skill at each grade.

Reading Assessments

Pretesting

Administering the Fluent and Expressive Reading Checklist during the first week of school each year identifies students who are reading at a grade-appropriate level of accuracy and speed and those who need teacher-directed small-group instruction from the beginning. (See Fluent and Expressive Reading Checklists in the "Assessing" section of the *Kindergarten Through Sixth-Grade Teacher Guides.*)

Diagnostic Assessments

Daily and weekly assessments measure knowledge of attributes of fine literature; fluent and expressive reading; knowledge of text structures; and ability to identify, label, and use five mental actions to comprehend text. These assessments identify students who need additional teacher-directed small-group instruction.

Literary Appreciation and Fluent and Expressive Reading

Beginning on day one, teachers at every grade level introduce or review attributes of fine literature while referring to the Spalding Attributes of Fine Literature poster (see Part Two, "Resources," page 432). Informal assessment begins immediately as teachers listen to students identify examples of the attributes in grade-appropriate narrative passages, then informative passages, and last informative-narrative passages. Formal assessment of attributes is not recommended for the reading lesson, because attributes are tools for enhancing students' enjoyment of fine literature. However, teachers assess students' ability to incorporate attributes in their own narrative, informative, and informative-narrative compositions.

After modeling fluent and expressive reading of fine literature, teachers have primary-grade children chorally, and individually, read *Spalding Series 1* and *2 Leveled Readers* to informally measure this skill. Daily oral reading by every child, even if only a few sentences are read, is essential because oral reading measures what each child is doing in silent reading. Teachers record errors and identify children who need additional help.

Text Structure

At the beginning of each grade, teachers review narrative, then informative, and last informative-narrative text structure using the Spalding Elements of Narrative, Informative, and Informative Narrative posters (see "Resources" in Part Two). After students have mastered the elements of three types of writing in the whole group, teachers informally assess their ability to discriminate among the three types. Teachers read a few sentences from a passage as students use Spalding Text Structure Cards (see "Resources") to identify the type of writing. Teachers then continue reading additional sentences as students use the cards to confirm or revise their identification of the type of writing. Each week, teachers assess students' ability to identify and label the three types of writing using passages in the Spalding comprehension booklets.

Mental Actions

After teachers, at each grade level, introduce or review the first three mental actions using the first Spalding Mental Action Poster (see "Resources"), they informally assess students' ability to think about their own thinking.

Each day, teachers read a short passage aloud and listen carefully as students identify and label the first three mental actions: *monitoring comprehension, making connections,* and *making predictions.* Then, teachers read a short passage as students use the first three Spalding Mental Action Cards (see "Resources") to indicate which mental actions they are using. In this way, they identify students who need teacher-directed small-group instruction.

Next, teachers model identifying and labeling the last two mental actions: *reformatting* and *mentally summarizing,* using the second Mental Action Poster. They assess students' ability to identify and label all five mental actions by having students raise the appropriate Mental Action Cards as the teacher continues to read the passages aloud.

Monthly Progress-Monitoring Assessments

Text Structure

Each month, teachers administer the monthly reading assessment to measure long-term retention of this skill, because the ability to automatically identify elements of each type of writing enhances reading comprehension and improves students' compositions. (See *User's Guides for McCall-Harby* and *McCall-Crabbs Books A-E* in Part Two, "Resources," page 432.)

Five Mental Actions

Formal assessment begins as teachers use the Spalding comprehension booklets to assess long-term retention of content in the passages. Students read short grade-appropriate passages and answer questions that measure both basic and higher-level thinking. Students record answers on the *Spalding Reading Assessment* forms in the "Assessing" section of the *Kindergarten Through Sixth-Grade Teacher Guides.* These assessments provide teachers with valuable documentation of students' progress for sharing with parents.

Chapter Summary

Chapter 3 describes informal and formal spelling, writing, and reading assessments throughout the grades. Spalding spelling assessments measure students' proficiency in eight areas of instruction. Spalding writing assessments measure their competency in grade-appropriate vocabulary, sentence construction, and use of the writing process to compose three text types. Spalding reading assessments measure students' knowledge of the attributes of fine literature, their knowledge of the elements of three types of writing, and their application of five mental actions in reading grade-appropriate passages.

Chapter 4 will focus on using informal and formal assessment data to evaluate instruction to determine why performance was not as expected. Examples of differentiated instruction for students who exceeded grade-level objectives and for those who need reteaching and additional practice are provided.

Chapter 4 EVALUATING SKILLS MASTERY

CHAPTER OVERVIEW

Evaluating Students' Characteristics and Achievement

Differentiating Instruction

Evaluating Assessment Data to Differentiate Instruction

IN THE SPALDING METHOD, teachers continually evaluate assessment data to monitor and adjust spelling, writing, and reading instruction to meet individual students' needs. Romalda Spalding often referred to the ability to identify each student's *growth* point (instructional level) as the *art* of teaching. Although monitoring students' achievement and appropriately adjusting instruction may be the hardest part of teaching, it is also the most rewarding. When teachers develop this ability, they are rewarded with successful, eager learners who are motivated to expand their knowledge and understanding.

To identify individual instructional levels, teachers need to understand that reading and writing are complex processes composed of many subskills, which are acquired in stages (see Chapter 1). They also need to know that to master any skill, students must analyze the task, practice to the point of automaticity, and develop attention control (see Chapter 1). Finally, teachers must know how to move seamlessly from modeling to coaching to scaffolding and then to fading—often within a single lesson (see Chapter 2). As teachers evaluate assessment data, asking themselves the following questions helps them discern why individual students have not mastered lesson objectives.

Evaluation Questions

Did I . . .

1. correctly identify *each* student's level of reading development?

2. teach *all* evidence-based reading and writing components?

3. model, check for understanding, coach, scaffold, and fade appropriately?

4. provide sufficient opportunities for *all* students to analyze the task, to practice to the point of automaticity, and to develop attention control?

"Recommended Language Arts Scope and Sequence" beginning on (page 418) includes the sequenced, cumulative, evidence-based spelling, writing, and reading components stated as outcome (end-of-year) objectives for kindergarten through eighth grade. These objectives list the skills and concepts that need to be introduced and practiced, mastered, and/or reinforced at each grade. Challenge objectives are also provided for students who master grade-level objectives. The *First Through Sixth-Grade Teacher Guides* duplicate the scope and sequence objectives for the grade below and above so teachers can use these to adjust instruction.

Chapter 4 considers evaluating students' characteristics and achievement, differentiating instruction, and evaluating assessment data to differentiate instruction.

To effectively evaluate assessment data, teachers must first understand that individual students may be at different developmental levels for reading and writing. Typically, in general education classrooms, 80 percent of students will have mastered the previous year's grade-level objectives; 15 percent will need some additional support; and the remaining 5 percent will need intensive support. Knowing this, teachers can use the guidelines for differentiating instruction in the present chapter and the grade-specific instructional strategies in the "Evaluating" section of the *Kindergarten Through Sixth-Grade Teacher Guides* to adjust instruction to meet individual needs.

Evaluating Students' Characteristics and Achievement

Declining test scores nationwide and research findings over the last two decades have resulted in an increased interest in general education, greater collaboration between general and special education teachers, revised definitions of learning disabilities, and greater understanding of diverse students.

Students Who Struggle

Students who have average or above-average intelligence, yet struggle to achieve at the level of their age peers, may not have been taught prerequisite subskills; or their primary language may not be English; or they may have one or more learning disabilities that are defined by the federal IDEA Act of 2004 as follows:

Specific learning disability means a disorder in one or more of the basic psychological processes involved in understanding or in using language, spoken or written, that may manifest itself in the imperfect ability to listen, think, speak, read, write, spell, or to do mathematical calculations, including conditions such as perceptual disabilities, brain injury, minimal brain dysfunction, dyslexia, and developmental aphasia. Specific learning disability does not include learning problems that are primarily the result of visual, hearing, or motor disabilities of mental retardation, or emotional disturbance, or of environmental, cultural, or economic disadvantage. (Regulations: Part 300, A, 300.9, c, 1, i)

Dr. Sally Shaywitz, a neuroscientist and professor of pediatrics at Yale and codirector of the Yale Center for the Study of Learning and Attention, describes dyslexia, arguably the most severe disability, in *Overcoming Dyslexia*:

> Dyslexia is a complex problem that has its roots in the very basic brain systems that allow man to understand and express language. . . . The tentacles of the disorder reach out from deep within the brain and affect not only how a person reads but surprisingly, a range of other important functions as well, including the ability to spell words, to retrieve words, to articulate words, and to remember certain facts. (2003, 5)

The question arises: Do children with dyslexia and related disorders learn differently? Drs. Jack Fletcher and Reid Lyon summarized more than thirty years of research, conducted by the National Institute of Child Health and Human Development, on the complex process of reading, how children learn to read, and what causes them to fail. Studies with both beginning and disabled readers demonstrated that problems in word recognition arise from inability to break words and syllables into individual phonemes (sounds). Fletcher and Lyons noted:

> The NICHD research has *not* found the processes underlying reading disability to be *qualitatively* different from those processes associated with early reading proficiency. Reading problems occur as part of a natural, unbroken continuum of ability. What causes good reading also leads to poor reading when the processes are deficient. (1998, 62)

Furthermore, a 400-page report, *Preventing Reading Difficulties in Young Children* (Snow, Burns, and Griffin, 1998), also reviewed research on normal reading development and instruction; on risk factors useful in identifying groups and individuals at risk of reading failure; and on prevention, intervention, and instructional approaches to ensure optimal reading outcomes. This report pointed out that it is now possible to identify children at risk of reading difficulties even before they go to school, and to provide interventions to support language and literacy development.

> There is converging research support for the proposition that getting started in reading depends critically on mapping the letters and the spelling of words onto the sounds and speech units that they represent. Failure to master word recognition impedes text comprehension. (321)

> Our analyses of the research literature in reading acquisition leads us to conclude that, in order to prevent reading difficulties, formal instruction in reading needs to focus on the development of two sorts of mastery: word recognition skills and comprehension skills. (322)

> Although context and pictures can be used as a tool to monitor word recognition, children should not be taught to use them to substitute for information provided by the letters in the word. (323)

In the "Executive Summary," the report concluded:

> There is little evidence that children experiencing difficulties learning to read, even those with identifiable learning disabilities, need radically different sorts of supports than children at low risk, although they may need more intensive support. (2)

Sally Shaywitz sums up the evidence.

> As a result of extraordinary scientific progress, reading and dyslexia are no longer a mystery; we now know what to do to ensure that each child becomes a good reader and how to help readers of all ages and at all levels. . . . At last we know the specific steps a child or adult must take to build and then reinforce the neural pathways deep within the brain for skilled reading. (2003, ix)

> All readers—dyslexic readers included—must take the same steps. The difference is simply in the effort involved and the time it takes to master the alphabetic principle. (51–52)

Students with language disabilities generally have difficulty with one or more of the following tasks:

1. Remembering (naming) colors, objects, letter names, phonogram sounds, songs, etc.
2. Pronouncing phonogram sounds and words
3. Segmenting and blending spoken words
4. Acquiring grade-appropriate vocabulary and oral sentence construction
5. Following directions
6. Understanding concepts and relationships
7. Giving consistent responses (e.g., they may remember or recognize a phonogram or word one day but not the next)
8. Spelling and reading words accurately and automatically
9. Composing sentences and comprehending text
10. Seeing relationships
11. Understanding figurative language
12. Finding patterns
13. Working independently

This chapter will explain how to monitor and adjust instruction to provide the extra time and attention needed for struggling students to learn to read, write, and spell proficiently.

Students Who Learn Easily

In every class, there are also some students who are able to learn at rates and levels of complexity in advance of their age peers. Students who learn easily typically demonstrate these characteristics:

1. Rapid recognition of phonograms and words
2. Rapid recognition of structures, patterns, and relationships
3. Ability to recognize and solve problems rapidly
4. Keen ability to generalize and abstract
5. Ability to infer, reformat, and summarize
6. Intense curiosity
7. High motivation
8. Acute perception
9. Pleasure in working independently

These students need challenge to ensure that they reach their highest potential, do not become disengaged, and do not cause disruptions because they are bored.

When teachers are aware of the strengths and weaknesses of diverse students, they are better able to monitor and adjust instruction appropriately.

Differentiating Instruction

New models of instruction have developed in reaction to the failure of the *discrepancy* model for identifying special education students. Waiting until there is evidence of a discrepancy between a student's intelligence and achievement has delayed intervention by as much as three years. New models stress early identification and intervention beginning with prekindergarten and kindergarten in the general education classroom.

The Florida Center for Reading Research (FCRR) defines *differentiated instruction* as "matching instruction to meet the different needs of learners in a given classroom" (2006, 1). The FCRR recommends that general education classrooms include two hours each day of explicit, structured, multisensory, research-based whole-group and small-group instruction. The *Response to Intervention* (RTI) is a three-tier system mandated by the 2004 reauthorization of IDEA; it is implemented in ninety-minute general education classrooms, with each tier increasing in instructional time and intensity. The goal is to teach effectively, intervene early, and assess progress regularly so that 80 to 90 percent of students attain a high level of achievement.

For more than fifty years, The Spalding Method has incorporated a combination of explicit, interactive, diagnostic instruction in the whole group followed by interventions and enhancements in small groups. Within both the whole group and small groups, Spalding teachers differentiate the levels of instruction, the questions they ask, and the activities they assign to demonstrate students' mastery. The Spalding model described below is also effective in multigrade classrooms, where differentiating instruction is essential.

Whole Group

Teachers explain the purpose of each new task to enhance students' attention and increase their motivation to learn. Then, they provide explicit, interactive, diagnostic instruction using the sequential, cumulative lesson objectives and multisensory activities provided in the "Planning" section of the *Kindergarten Through Sixth-Grade Teacher Guides*.

Teachers ask students who learn easily questions that require higher-level thinking; e.g., making connections, reformatting, or summarizing. In this way, students having difficulty benefit from interaction with their peers. (Frequently, students with dyslexia excel in forming concepts and comprehending text if they are not asked to read or write.) Teachers ask struggling students, or those new to Spalding, questions that require knowledge, understanding, or application of skills and concepts just modeled. As soon as these students master basic skills and concepts, teachers also ask them questions that require higher-level thinking.

If the *majority* of the students still do not master a given objective after one or more clear, concise models in the whole group, teachers provide additional models, review distinguishing characteristics, and provide additional practice.

After whole-group instruction, teachers lead individual or small-group instruction and provide independent activities based on student observations and assessment data. These flexible groups vary in size, students, number of days, and type of structure. Teachers provide ample practice for students having difficulty and challenge for students who learned the skills or concepts after the first model in the whole group. Instruction varies in content, process or activities, products or outcomes, and learning environments. Teacher-directed small-group reinforcements and independent enhancement activities occur during the ninety-minute time block for spelling, writing, and reading.

Teacher-Directed Individual or Small Group

Teacher-directed individual or small-group activities always include explicit reteaching (modeling) of skills or concepts, specific directions, coaching as students attempt the skills, and supervised practice until students achieve mastery. Teachers prepare struggling students for learning as a member of the class by preteaching a difficult skill or concept that will be introduced during the next day's whole-group lesson. Daily practice assignments are differentiated so students can master the lesson objectives; e.g., oral, rather than written, sentences are assessed until sufficient phonogram sounds and letter formation have been mastered.

Extra practice is an essential part of teaching if all students are to learn. Scheduling the *Parent Introduction to Spalding* course enables parents to enhance students' learning at home (see chapter 6, page 194). If parents cannot help, teachers must arrange for extra time in school so that struggling students do not fall behind the class. In addition to in-class small-group reteaching, extra practice may be provided in resource rooms or before or after school as needed and approved by administration and parents. *Before-school* or *after-school* sessions help students new to Spalding or those who continue to struggle obtain the extra practice they need. Mrs. Spalding often admonished, *"The teacher cannot be said to have taught unless and until the student learns."*

Independent Activities and Assignments

Independent assignments and activities should always align with the objective and enhance students' learning. Some activities, such as phonogram bingo, may be fun, but they do not enhance learning. Such activities are distractions from the goal of reading enjoyable books. Other activities, such as crossword puzzles or word searches using spelling words, are a waste of time because they do not relate to a real-life skill. A wide range of independent assignments and activities can be used to expand students' knowledge, skills, procedures, or concepts. Four general strategies that expand students' learning follow:

1. *Expand* the day's lesson objective to the next level of difficulty; e.g., compose the same *number* of sentences that demonstrate meaning and usage of unfamiliar words (in the week's spelling lesson) but include past tense verbs, proper nouns, or prepositional phrases.
2. *Integrate* spelling, writing, reading, science, or social studies content within the lesson objective; e.g., use selected spelling words to create a one-paragraph narrative, or compose an informative-narrative paragraph that includes facts from the week's social studies lesson.
3. *Encourage reflection;* e.g., read a book of the students' or the teacher's choice and share reflections in the whole group.
4. *Encourage exploration* aligned to the lesson objective; e.g., research a topic of personal interest and present an oral report in the whole group.

Evaluating Assessment Data to Differentiate Instruction

Evaluating students' spelling, writing, and reading pretest data enables teachers to (1) establish the class instructional level, (2) identify skills that need to be retaught, and (3) differentiate instruction as early as the first week of school.

Evaluating students' weekly and monthly assessment data enables teachers to maintain the correct level of difficulty and plan small-group interventions and enhancements that follow the sequence in the Spalding curricula.

Differentiated Spelling Instruction: Teacher-Directed Individual or Small-Group Instruction and Independent Activities

Following each day's whole-group spelling instruction, teachers evaluate students' performance on oral or written phonogram reviews and spelling quizzes and provide individual or small-group reteaching for struggling students and independent assignments for students who mastered the objectives. Grade-specific examples of differentiated instruction in spelling, writing, and reading are found in the "Evaluating" section of the *Kindergarten Through Sixth-Grade Teacher Guides.* A few examples are listed here, in the order in which the evidence-based components are presented in the *Teacher Guides.*

Phonemic Awareness: Examples

Most students develop phonemic awareness rather quickly. However, students with language disabilities and those whose primary language is not English may need extra help, in small groups, with segmenting spoken words into individual phonemes (sounds), and blending sounds in spoken words. Students who quickly understand that words consist of individual sounds may do wordplay with rhymes or use phonograms to form words.

Systematic Phonics with High-Frequency Vocabulary: Examples

At the beginning of the year, small-group instruction will focus on accurate and automatic pronunciation of phonogram sounds, legible and neat letter formation, and accurate and automatic segmenting and blending of sounds of high-frequency vocabulary. Teachers who have difficulty pronouncing the sounds should listen to the phonogram CD (see "Resources") until they can correctly pronounce each phonogram, because incorrect pronunciation impedes children's progress in written phonogram reviews, spelling dictation, writing, and reading. Teachers should also evaluate their own handwriting because it is the model for students.

After establishing a daily handwriting focus in the whole group, teachers evaluate students' daily written phonogram reviews to identify students who need extra practice. Initially, more children will have difficulty writing phonograms because they must hear the sounds, correctly pronounce the sounds, and then visualize and legibly write the correct phonograms.

As the year progresses, teachers evaluate students' spelling and marking of words written in their notebooks; their spelling and handwriting on quizzes; and their application of rules, syllable structure, and syllable division.

Independent activities range from using phonograms for word formation to reading books.

Differentiated Writing Instruction: Teacher-Directed Individual or Small-Group Instruction and Independent Activities

A large language gap exists among students from various socioeconomic backgrounds. Students whose primary language is not English or those who have had low verbal experiences at home need extensive help with vocabulary and sentence construction. Individual or small-group instruction will include additional models and practice composing oral sentences using the week's spelling words; reteaching parts of speech; and word structure such as identifying base words, word roots, and affixes. On the other hand, students whose families read to them, travel, and have extensive family discussions come to school with a rich spoken vocabulary. These students may independently compose sentences that use spelling words they have previously entered in their notebooks; categorize spelling words into parts of speech; and compose narrative, informative, and informative-narrative paragraphs or reports.

Differentiated Reading Instruction: Teacher-Directed Individual or Small-Group Instruction and Independent Activities

At the beginning of the year, teachers will provide additional models and extra practice identifying and labeling the attributes of literature and the elements of narrative, informative, and informative-narrative text structures. As the year progresses, small-group instruction will focus on identifying and labeling first three and then five mental actions used in comprehending text. Independent assignments for students who learn basic skills easily will range from reading fine literature independently to identifying and labeling examples of the attributes of literature in books they read or explaining how use of the five mental actions helped them comprehend a particular book or passage.

Chapter Summary

Chapter 4 defines specific learning disabilities and describes characteristics of diverse students. It also identifies and describes basic principles for differentiating spelling, writing, and reading instruction in the whole group, for individual students, or in teacher-directed flexible small groups for students who struggle, and individual activities and assignments for students capable of working independently. Although monitoring each student's instructional level may be time consuming, it also brings great rewards when teachers experience the joy of seeing achievement increase for *all* students.

The Writing Road to Reading is a comprehensive language arts program that has successfully taught children to speak, write, and read well for more than five decades. Chapter 5 will discuss integrating knowledge domains for successful reading and explain why The Spalding Method works.

WHY *THE WRITING ROAD TO READING* WORKS: INTEGRATING KNOWLEDGE DOMAINS

CHAPTER OVERVIEW

The Reading Process

Reading Development

Skill Learning

Effective Instruction

A SUCCESSFUL LANGUAGE ARTS PROGRAM integrates knowledge of four major research domains: the reading process, the learning sequence (how children move from being novices to being skilled readers), skills acquisition, and delivery of effective instruction. *The Writing Road to Reading* has been grounded in sound principles of learning and instruction since the inception of its program. Studying under the eminent New York neurologist Dr. Samuel T. Orton, Dr. William McCall at Columbia Teachers College, and linguists of the day, Romalda Spalding gained extensive knowledge about essential components of reading instruction, what produces success, and what causes some children to fail. Although much has been learned in the last eighty years, Dr. Orton "foresaw many principles of contemporary neuropsychology that awaited new technology for their verification" (Farnham-Diggory, 1992, 297). Dr. Stanislas Dehaene, director of the Cognitive Neuroimaging Unit in Saclay, France, describes Dr. Orton as "the founding father of the psychology of reading and dyslexia" (Dehaene, 2009, 207). Drawing on that knowledge and on more than twenty-five years of experience working with children who had difficulty learning to read, Mrs. Spalding wrote *The Writing Road to Reading*. Farnham-Diggory observed that "the Spalding system capitalizes on a body of psychological principles that are dead right in contemporary theoretical terms" (1992, xviii).

During the last four decades, research has focused on the complex process of reading and how children *learn* to read and write. Technology, such as CAT scans and MRIs, has helped researchers to identify principal subprocesses; to discover where in the brain, and under what conditions, these subprocesses are activated; and to understand how they interact. Dehaene, in *Reading in the Brain* (2009), provides insight into how brain structure determines reading processes:

> It simply is not true that there are hundreds of ways to learn to read. Every child is unique, . . . but when it comes to reading, all have roughly the same brain that imposes the same constraints and the same learning sequence. (218)

. . . In the final analysis, all these findings lean toward a fundamental universality of reading circuits. . . . People the world over . . . solicit the same brain areas as they read. (118–119)

The Reading Process

The century-old debate over the reading process can be compared to the fable of the blind men and the elephant. Just as each blind man thought the part he touched was the entire elephant, some people have viewed reading as "getting meaning from print" and have thought that this was all there is to it. Others have thought that learning the code was all there is. Neuroscience and reading research findings document that learning to read accurately and fluently is a *complex* process requiring coordination of many cognitive subprocesses; e.g., feature and letter recognition; spatial placement; orthographic (sound-letter) relationships; and lexical (vocabulary), syntactic (grammar), and semantic (comprehension) factors. It is important to note here that although the reader may not be aware of them, all these subprocesses are simultaneously active during skilled reading.

Congress directed the National Institute of Child Health and Human Development (NICHD) "to convene a national panel to assess the status of research-based knowledge, including the effectiveness of various approaches to teaching children to read." The *Report of the National Reading Panel* (2000, 1-1) identified five essential *instructional* components that had sufficient experimental evidence to be included in their report: phonemic awareness, systematic phonics, vocabulary, text fluency, and comprehension strategies. This section of Chapter 5 includes descriptions of principal reading subprocesses, research citations for each, how each subprocess is taught in *The Writing Road to Reading*, and how the subprocesses relate to the five research-based components identified in the National Reading Panel's report.

Phonemic Awareness

The understanding that spoken words and syllables consist of sequences of elementary speech sounds is a powerful predictor of success in learning to read (Adams, 1990). Research findings demonstrate that phonemic awareness (PA) is more highly related to learning to read than are general intelligence, reading readiness, and listening comprehension (Stanovich, 1986, 1993). Furthermore, PA is the most important core and causal factor separating normal and disabled readers (Share and Stanovich, 1995); and it is equally important in learning to spell (Ehri and Wilce, 1987; Treiman, 1985, 1993). Instruction in PA is strongest when the sounds are presented with the symbols (Ball and Blachman, 1991; Byrne and Fielding-Barnsley, 1993, 1995; Hatcher, Hulme, and Ellis, 1994).

The National Reading Panel compared (1) the effects of six common PA tasks, (2) the effect of PA alone and PA with phonics instruction, and (3) the length of PA instruction. According to the *Report of the National Reading Panel* (2000):

Blending and segmenting instruction exerted a significantly larger effect size on reading development than did multiple skill instruction. . . . Teaching children to manipulate phonemes using letters produced bigger effects than teaching without letters. (2-4)

. . . PA instruction is more effective when it makes explicit how children are to apply PA skills in reading and writing tasks. PA instruction does not need to consume long periods of time. In these analyses, programs lasting less than 20 hours were more effective than longer programs. (2-6)

The report concluded, "PA instruction helped all types of children improve their reading" (2-5).

Later studies comparing phonological awareness training alone with training that integrated these components confirmed that integrating phonological awareness training with alphabetic instruction was more effective—measured in terms of growth of reading and spelling during first grade—than phonological training alone (Fuchs et al., 2001).

Chapter 1 provides strategies for explicitly teaching children to segment spoken words or syllables into individual phonemes and blend individual phonemes into spoken words. Phonemic awareness training is immediately coordinated with letter formation and both are reinforced in daily oral and written phonogram reviews and spelling dictation.

Feature Recognition

Feature recognition is the ability to distinguish vertical, diagonal, and horizontal lines, and curves. The parts of the brain specialized for distinguishing lines and curves are activated by looking at print, although the reader may not be conscious of the fact (Farnham-Diggory, 1992). Thus shapes of letters are not remembered as holistic patterns. Rather, the visual system analyzes each letter into these elementary features. Therefore, to be fluent at recognizing letters, students need to be familiar with the distinctive features of each letter (Adams, 1990). Spalding children are explicitly taught the six features used to write the twenty-six manuscript letters. These are illustrated, and strategies for teaching them are found, in Chapter 2, page 42.

Letter Recognition

Letter recognition is the ability to group features into patterns, automatically recognizing letters as wholes. Previously, poor readers' errors with letter orientation were often considered a sign of neurological dysfunction or immaturity. Yet this is usually not the case:

Letter reversals seem to be merely a symptom of low print knowledge. . . . Training children to attend to the relevant contrasts between letters has been shown to hasten their ability to recognize and distinguish between them. (Adams, 1990, 65)

Letter recognition and letter formation are also important in learning to write. Dr. Steve Graham, Currey Ingram Professor of Special Education and Literacy at Vanderbilt University, asserts (2009–2010) that early handwriting instruction improves not only legibility, but also the *quantity and quality* of writing:

If children cannot form letters—or cannot form them with reasonable legibility and speed—they cannot translate the language in their minds into written text. . . . Just as young readers must learn to decode fluently so they can focus on comprehension, young writers must develop fluent, legible handwriting (and must master other transcription skills like spelling) so they can focus on generating and organizing ideas. (20)

. . . There is considerable scientific evidence, collected over a span of almost 100 years, demonstrating that directly teaching handwriting enhances legibility and fluency. (21)

Spalding provides explicit handwriting instruction in combining features into manuscript letters followed by practice forming letters in daily written phonogram reviews. To assist recall, students explain which features are used to form each manuscript letter. Strategies are taught in Chapter 2.

Orthographic Unit Recognition (Decoding-Systematic Phonics)

Orthographic unit recognition is the ability to link letters (graphemes) to one or more specific speech sounds (phonemes). Early and systematic emphasis on decoding leads to better achievement than late or more haphazard approaches (Adams, 1990; Beck and Juel, 1995; Chall, 1996a; Stanovich, 1994). Research findings demonstrate that "the critical component of reading that must be taught is the relationship of print to speech" (Fletcher and Lyon, 1998, 57). Recognizing a relatively small set of common letter-sound units enables the reader to construct any number of words.

The *Report of the National Reading Panel* (2000) reviewed studies comparing systematic phonics instruction, nonsystematic phonics instruction, and no phonics instruction and concluded:

Systematic phonics instruction makes a bigger contribution to children's growth in reading than alternative programs providing unsystematic or no phonics instruction. (2-92)

. . . Systematic phonics instruction in kindergarten and 1st grade is highly beneficial. Children at these developmental levels are quite capable of learning phonemic and phonics concepts. (2-93)

Although there are various systematic phonics approaches, this report found that:

The hallmark of systematic phonics programs is that they delineate a planned, sequential set of phonic elements and they teach these elements explicitly and systematically. (2-99)

Dahaene (2009) explains that reading instruction must develop an efficient neuronal hierarchy that enables children to recognize letters and graphemes and easily turn them into speech sounds:

All other essential aspects of the literate mind—the mystery of spelling, the richness of vocabulary, the nuances of meaning, and the pleasures of literature—depend on this crucial step. There is no point in describing the delights of reading to children if they are not provided the means to get there. Without phonological decoding of written words their chances are significantly reduced. Considerable research, both with children and with illiterates, converges on the fact that grapheme-phoneme conversion radically transforms the child's brain and the way in which it processes speech sounds. This process whereby written words are converted into strings of phonemes must be taught explicitly. It does not develop spontaneously and must be acquired. (219)

Learners also benefit from instruction that requires them to move beyond phoneme-grapheme correspondences to analyzing words for spelling and reading (Treiman, 1992). Students trained in spelling outperformed control students on several measures: reading of nonsense words, timed reading of words, timed oral reading of passages, and segmenting and spelling (Uhry and Shepherd, 1993). Students advance from initially sounding out and blending letters to processing by spelling patterns or chunks. Repeated reading of these patterns helps to consolidate the connections, increasing the efficiency of reading. With sufficient repetition of words, learners are able to retrieve entire words from memory. Those words in memory can be used to read or spell unknown words by analogy, i.e., applying word parts or patterns from known words to new words (Ehri, 1997). Teaching spelling provides information about words that facilitates reading. Lessons using this reciprocity build strength in literacy acquisition skills (Cramer, 1998). Learning to read and learning to spell are related because both depend on knowledge of the alphabetic system and both use memory of the specific spellings of words. The correlation between children's spelling and reading comprehension is high because both depend on children's proficiency with language (Ehri, 2000; Snow et al., 2005, 6).

Finally, direct, systematic spelling and handwriting instruction improves academic performance (Gentry and Graham, 2010):

Learning to write letters and spell words reinforces the letter naming, phonemic, and word-deciphering skills required in developing literacy. . . . Research provides clear evidence that spelling should be taught systematically. The right words and patterns must be presented at the right time in the student development. (2)

Learning to write by hand plays a key role in developing literacy, and handwriting skills remain crucial for success throughout school. The mental processes involved in handwriting are connected to other important learning functions, such as storing and retrieving information from memory, manipulating letters, and linking them to sounds when reading, spelling, and writing. Effective handwriting instruction begins with teaching the manuscript alphabet, which helps students master the seemingly abstract forms of 26 uppercase and lowercase letters, punctuation symbols, and numerals—114 symbols in all—that they must decode while learning to read. These printed uppercase and lowercase letters closely resemble the type used in children's books, which reinforces letter recognition. (3)

In the spelling lesson, Spalding's systematic, explicit phonics instruction teaches students to precisely say and write seventy common sound-symbol relationships (phonograms) and to apply pronunciation and spelling rules when saying and writing high-frequency vocabulary from dictation. (See Chapter 2.)

Spatial Placement

The spatial placement subprocess enables readers to recognize or anticipate where particular letters are likely to be located, enhancing their ability to spell and read (Farnham-Diggory, 1992). Dehaene explains:

> Good decoding skills do not arise from associations between letters and speech sounds alone—letters must also be perceived in their proper orientation, at the appropriate spatial location, and in their correct left-right order. In the young reader's brain, collaboration must take place between the visual pathway, which recognizes the identity of letters and words, and the dorsal pathway, which codes for their location in space and programs eye movements and attention. When any of these actors stumbles, reading falls flat on its face. (2009, 298)

Spalding students are explicitly taught to apply rules that govern placement of phonograms within words. For example, they learn that the letter *y* most frequently occurs at the end of a word. They expect certain letters and letter combinations to occur in specific places, and they learn to differentiate the "legal" from "illegal" positions of letters in print. For example, *ai*, *au*, *oi*, and *ui* do not occur at the end of English words.

Lexical Subprocess (Vocabulary)

Understanding the words we must know to communicate effectively is a cornerstone of comprehension. Beginning in infancy, the brain stores the meaning of words, and word parts (prefix, base word or word root, and suffix). The lexical process, which includes understanding the vocabulary and the morphology of language, enables the listener or reader to access those meanings (Farnham-Diggory, 1992). Research from as early as the 1920s identified vocabulary as a significant factor in the development of reading skills.

The *Report of the National Reading Panel* (2000) identified vocabulary instruction as the first part of comprehension instruction. Even though there were insufficient experimental studies for statistical analysis, the report recommended several strategies:

> Vocabulary should be taught both directly and indirectly. Repetition and multiple exposures to vocabulary items are important. Learning in rich context, incidental learning, and use of computer technology all enhance the acquisition of vocabulary. Direct instruction should include task restructuring as necessary and should actively engage the students. Finally, dependence on a single vocabulary instruction method will not result in optimal learning. (14)

The Spalding Spelling/Vocabulary Word List is the foundation for vocabulary instruction. Children learn to pronounce and spell high-frequency words in spelling lessons, and they are explicitly taught the meanings and usage of these words as well as word parts and parts of speech in writing lessons. Vocabulary is extended through use of fine literature in reading lessons and extensive independent reading. (See Chapters 1 and 2.)

In *The Writing Road to Reading*, explicit instruction in phonemic awareness, systematic phonics (including feature and letter formation, handwriting, and spatial placement), and high-frequency vocabulary are all integrated in spelling lessons (see Chapter 1).

Syntactic Subprocess (Grammar and Sentence Construction)

Language acquisition studies show that even very young children acquire knowledge of speech production, word meanings, classes of words (nouns, verbs), conversational formats, rhymes, and grammar. (A detailed summary may be found in Farnham-Diggory, 1992; and in Dahaene, 2009, 197–199.) However, when children arrive at school, they need direct instruction in the written structure of the English language, including parts of speech; word order; and rules of capitalization, punctuation, and grammar. Learning spelling rules, meanings of roots and affixes, word origins, and development of the English language will support vocabulary development, word recognition, and spelling (Moats, 2005/2006, 14).

Moats (2000) explains the importance of teachers' knowledge of language:

The teacher who understands language and how children are using it can give clear, accurate, and organized information about sounds, words, and sentences. The teacher who knows language will understand why students say and write the puzzling things that they do and will be able to judge what a particular student knows and needs to know about the printed word. (1)

Spalding teachers expand students' knowledge of language structure, rules, conventions, sentence construction, and composition in the writing lesson (see Chapters 1 and 2).

Semantic Subprocess (Text Comprehension)

Comprehension is the essence of reading. The *Report of the National Reading Panel* (2000) identified three predominant research themes:

(1) Reading comprehension is a cognitive process that integrates complex skills and cannot be understood without examining the critical role of vocabulary development; (2) active interactive strategic processes are critically necessary to the development of reading comprehension; and (3) the preparation of teachers to best equip them to facilitate these complex processes is critical and intimately tied to the development of reading comprehension. (4-1)

According to this report, text comprehension is enhanced when readers (1) actively connect ideas in print to their prior knowledge and experiences, (2) construct mental representations, (3) use cognitive strategies, and (4) use reason strategically when their comprehension breaks down (14). Teachers should demonstrate such strategies until students are able to carry them out independently. Finally, the report recommended that teachers use a multiple-strategy method, including comprehension monitoring, cooperative learning, use of graphic and semantic organizers, posing questions, use of story structure, and summarization.

The Institute of Education Sciences (IES), a branch of the National Center for Education Evaluation and Regional Assistance in the U.S. Department of Education, publishes guides that combine researchers' expertise with the best available evidence about current educational challenges.

In September 2010, IES published *Improving Reading Comprehension in Kindergarten Through 3rd Grade*. Dr. Timothy Shanahan, a professor at the University of Illinois, chaired this panel. The members defined reading comprehension as "the process of simultaneously extracting and constructing meaning through interaction and involvement with written language" (Shanahan et al., 2010-4038, 5). They also asserted "the teaching of reading comprehension should begin in kindergarten and elementary school" (5). Five recommendations were proposed to improve reading comprehension:

1. Teach students how to use reading comprehension strategies.
2. Teach students to identify and use the text's organizational structure to comprehend, learn, and remember content.
3. Guide students through focused, high-quality discussion on the meaning of text.
4. Select texts purposefully to support comprehension development.
5. Establish an engaging and motivating context in which to teach reading comprehension. (1)

The IES panel defined a comprehension *strategy* as:

Intentional mental actions during reading that improve reading comprehension. Deliberate efforts by a reader to better understand or remember what is being read. (11)

A comprehension strategy is *not* either of the following:

Instructional activities such as completing worksheets. Worksheets rarely include instruction in what students should do actively in their heads to improve comprehension.

Exercises that are aimed at giving students practice with skills such as sequencing or drawing conclusions, but that lack explicit instruction in how to think in these ways during reading. (11)

There is strong evidence for the effectiveness of six strategies: activating prior knowledge/predicting; questioning; visualization; monitoring, clarifying, or fix-up; inference training; and retelling (10–11).

Spalding students are explicitly taught to consciously think about their thinking (metacognition). They monitor their comprehension and identify unfamiliar words, phrases, or sentences; make connections both within the text and with prior knowledge; make predictions; and reformat and summarize information to identify stated main ideas or derive implied main ideas. Students practice these cognitive strategies (mental actions) on all types of print (see Chapter 2).

Text Fluency

The *Report of the National Reading Panel* (2000) identified fluency training as one of the five essential instructional components, stating that "fluent readers can read text with speed, accuracy, and proper expression" (3-1). Although fluency is a prerequisite for reading comprehension, it is often neglected in the classroom. Text fluency depends on rapid word recognition. A decade earlier, Adams reported:

> Research indicates that the most critical factor beneath fluent word reading is the ability to recognize letters, spelling patterns, and whole words, effortlessly, automatically, and visually. Moreover, the goal of all reading instruction—comprehension—depends critically on this ability. (1990, 14)

Slow reading of words clogs working memory with word-level processing and prevents understanding at the content level. Thus both rapid reading of high-frequency words and rapid decoding as a means to enhance text understanding appear critical for typical reading development.

As important as fluent and accurate word reading is, it is insufficient to guarantee text fluency, according to the *Report of the National Reading Panel*. Repeated oral reading with feedback and guidance leads to meaningful improvement in reading expertise for good readers as well as for those who struggle (2000, 3-3). The panel also found that well-described instructional approaches that encourage repeated oral reading result in increased reading proficiency. Conversely, this panel found no evidence supporting the effectiveness of independent silent reading as a means of improving reading achievement. Rather, the report encouraged teachers to informally and formally assess oral reading accuracy, rate, and comprehension regularly (3-4).

Spalding students read high-frequency spelling words daily to develop rapid word recognition, then read text orally to develop fluent and expressive reading. Mrs. Spalding abhorred the old basal readers with their mind-deadening vocabulary. Thus the question arises: Is there evidence supporting decodable books?

Decodable Books

Jenkins and his colleagues (2003) found that alphabetic knowledge is enhanced when students read words that link specific graphemes with their pronunciations; that practice with reading decodable text helps beginners store those connections in memory, thus developing a sight vocabulary; and finally that practice helps them sound out unfamiliar words. Practice with decodable books may also enhance motivation and build confidence, especially for children who are becoming discouraged. Jenkins et al. alert educators:

> Finding storybooks that complement phonics instruction can be daunting. Even storybooks that are labeled decodable may not be readable by individual students, because a

text's decodablity depends on the match between the phonic elements featured in it and the phonic elements students have been taught. (2003, 185)

Responding to that need, SEI commissioned the development of twenty kindergarten and twenty-four first-grade books that provide practice with specific phonograms as they are learned. Series 1, Book 1 can be read after kindergartners have learned the first thirty phonograms. Each successive book provides practice with previously introduced phonograms as well as new ones.

The Reading Process: Summary

Knowing the principal processes that are active during skilled reading and writing and how they interact helps teachers diagnose problems when students have difficulty. It is important to understand that vocabulary development, knowledge of sentence structure, and listening comprehension all begin in early childhood and contribute to the natural development of speech. However, feature and letter recognition, spatial placement, sound-symbol relationships, and spelling are common only to societies that have a written language. Research has confirmed that these are not learned naturally; they must be taught. (Adams, 1990; Adams and Bruck, 1995; Dehaene, 2009; Liberman and Liberman, 1992; Moats, 2000). Furthermore, even those processes that begin in early childhood (vocabulary development, knowledge of sentence structure, and listening comprehension) are enhanced by explicit, systematic instruction in school. The neuroscientist Steven Pinker expressed the consensus among scientists:

Language is a human instinct, but written language is not. Language is found in all societies, present and past. . . . Compare all this with writing. Writing systems have been invented a small number of times in history. . . . Until recently, most children never learned to read or write; even with today's universal education, many children struggle and fail. A group of children is no more likely to invent an alphabet than it is to invent the internal combustion engine. Children are wired for sound, but print is an optional accessory that must be painstakingly bolted on. This basic fact about human nature should be the starting point for any discussion of how to teach our children to read and write. (1999, ix–x)

In The Spalding Method, all children receive explicit, interactive, diagnostic instruction in each instructional component. Grade-level and lesson objectives are sequential and cumulative, and all practice activities are multisensory. Children who have dyslexia or related language disabilities are taught until proficiency is reached. To prevent reading failure, classroom instruction must incorporate what we know about how children learn to read and why children fail to learn to read. To determine the scope and sequence of instruction, teachers need to understand how students progress from learning to read to reading to learn.

Reading Development

The late Dr. Jeanne Chall developed a framework for organizing an instructional sequence for reading while she served as the director of the Reading Laboratory at Harvard University. Chall (1983a) noticed that the facts of beginning reading fit a developmental rather than a single process. This suggests that readers are doing *different* things in relation to printed matter at each successive stage. According to analysis of school results, laboratory experiments, and clinical findings, the first task in learning to read is learning the relation between sounds and letters—decoding.

Teachers who know the developmental stages of reading are able to plan lessons that meet students' instructional needs at each stage. As we identify the first four stages, including the instructional components that should be emphasized from preschool through eighth grade, we will explain how The Spalding Method provides such instruction. (For more detailed descriptions of all six stages, see Chall, 1996b.) Chall noted that the ages or grade levels associated with each stage are *approximations* to identify where the instructional emphasis *typically* takes place. In many schools, Stage 1 begins in kindergarten.

Stage 0: Prereading (Birth–Age 6)

From birth to kindergarten, children develop three types of knowledge. First, they learn a basic vocabulary (e.g., labels for persons, places, things, events, and procedures in their environment). They develop a range of knowledge (facts and concepts) about letters, words, books, and the world around them. During these years, children also develop communication skills. The foundation for all communication is the ability to describe the people and events in their lives and the facts and concepts they have learned. Students who have traveled, have been read to extensively, or have watched educational television are at an advantage. They can draw on an extended vocabulary and quite a wide range of knowledge. Research has shown that the abilities, knowledge, and skills acquired during the prereading stage are substantially related to success with reading at Stage 1.

Stage 1: Decoding (Grades 1–2, Ages 6–7)

The essential aspect of Stage 1 is learning the relationship between spoken sounds in words and the written symbols representing those sounds. Children learn to identify letters that represent speech sounds, to recognize differences between similar words (*bun/bug*), and to know when they have made a mistake. Experimental research has indicated that children go through phases in making oral reading errors (Biemiller, 1970).

In the first phase, children make word substitutions that are semantically and syntactically correct. Next, their errors have a graphic resemblance to the printed word. In the final phase, readers rely mostly on graphic exactness and somewhat on word meaning. Less skilled readers remain in the first phase, relying on word substitutions associated with meaning or a part of speech. Good readers pass through these stages quickly. They do not skip words or rely on context to decode words. Rather, eye movement studies show that they see all the letters and read virtually every word (Foorman et al., 1997; Rieben and Perfetti, 1991; Vellutino and Scanlon, 1991; Vellutino, Scanlon, and Tanzman, 1994).

In The Spalding Method, children are directly taught to read and write seventy common phonograms and to blend these phonograms into high-frequency words. Daily oral and written phonogram reviews develop sound-symbol mastery. Reading the Spelling/Vocabulary Word List two ways (for spelling and for reading) helps children automatically decode unfamiliar words in books and read fluently.

Although the first 700 words in the word list should be in the spoken vocabulary of kindergarten and first-grade children, The Spalding Method provides example dialogues for teaching the usage and meaning of any unfamiliar words (see pages 96–102). Beginning on the first day of school, appropriate oral sentence structure is taught, followed by the conventions of written sentences (see pages 103–105). Reading children's literature aloud and discussing what is read will enable kindergarten and first-grade children to expand their vocabulary, their knowledge of facts and concepts, and their communication skills. (See Chapters 1 and 2.) In this way, children who may not have had these advantages in their preschool environment or who have great difficulty learning language are helped to catch up.

Even though decoding is the *primary* emphasis at this stage, children are also introduced to the attributes and elements of fine writing, the structure of different types of writing, and the use of mental actions for comprehension while listening to stories read aloud. Listening comprehension skills transfer quickly to reading.

Stage 2: Confirmation and Fluency (Grades 2–3, Ages 7–8)

Chall described Stage 2 as a consolidation of what is learned through reading familiar print and what is already known to the reader. By reading familiar stories, children can concentrate on the print because they know the content. This enables them to move beyond accuracy to fluency (automaticity). During Stages 1 and 2, most new information is still learned through listening and observing and through the muscular (kinesthetic) sense because the instructional emphasis is on *learning* to read. *Emphasis* means that extra time is allotted to the skills that need to be mastered at that stage. However, it does not mean that other skills are ignored.

In The Spalding Method, first-grade and older children are pretested at the beginning of each year so teachers know where to begin instruction (see Chapter 3). Daily oral and written phonogram reviews and spelling dictation procedures, including reading words two ways, develop instant word recognition and fluent reading. Although the primary emphasis is still on mastery of decoding, instant word recognition, and fluency, instructional time is also spent on literary appreciation and listening comprehension. It is important to remember that decoding must be automatic before the instructional emphasis can shift to reading comprehension. The reader cannot pay attention to more than one thing at a time. Children cannot focus on meaning while struggling to decode words.

Stage 3: Reading for Information (Grades 4–8, Ages 9–13)

In Stages 1 and 2, children learn to connect print to speech. In Stage 3, they learn to connect print to ideas. Thus, the emphasis shifts from *learning to read* to *reading to learn*. At this stage, children read for information. Chall pointed out that the importance of prior knowledge becomes apparent at this stage. What a child already knows is the most important element in what he or she is able to learn. In addition, children also need to learn a process for finding information in a paragraph, chapter, or book.

At the beginning of this stage, learning by reading is still less efficient than learning by listening and observing. The *primary* instructional emphasis shifts from *listening* comprehension to *reading* comprehension. By eighth grade, the efficiency of reading should equal and begin to surpass the other means of gaining information.

Chapter 2 provides strategies and dialogues for explicitly teaching text structure and listening and reading comprehension. Children are explicitly taught to use five mental actions to comprehend text. They also learn basic research skills: identifying essential information in a paragraph, chapter, or book to determine the main idea or ideas; note-taking; and summarizing.

Reading Development: Summary

Chall's stages of reading development provide a useful framework for teachers to use in lesson planning. The instructional emphasis in kindergarten and first grade is on Stage 1 skills and reinforcing Stage 0 skills. Pretesting first-grade and older students reveals students' stage of reading development and tells teachers where to begin instruction. Research findings have clearly established that Stage 1 and Stage 2 skills must be at the automatic level before children are able to comprehend easily and efficiently. The Spalding Method provides explicit instruction for Stages 0 through 3. It also provides procedures for pretesting students and guidance for lesson planning. (See Chapters 3 and 4 and the *Kindergarten Through Sixth-Grade Teacher Guides*.)

Skill Learning

Over the past 100 years, a wealth of helpful information has been reported in the experimental literature on *skill learning*. The literature includes laboratory studies of every type of skill and studies of skill development in every vocation—from athletes to business entrepreneurs. Farnham-Diggory noted:

> Skill-acquisition in any field appears to include learning phases of three fundamental types: analysis, practice to the point of automaticity, and attention-management. When you learn a skill, you go in and out of these phases repeatedly. . . . You cannot be in more than one of these learning phases at the same time. . . . Each phase of skill learning has its own logical requirements, and they are not interchangeable. (1992, 89)

We will discuss the requirements of each phase, and then explain how they are incorporated in The Spalding Method.

Analytical Phase (Task Analysis)

Dr. Orton taught Mrs. Spalding to divide every task into its parts, sequence the parts, and then directly teach each part. Spalding students are also taught to analyze each task. For example, during spelling lessons, students analyze the features of the alphabet letters, the sounds of spoken words, the appropriate phonogram when there are several possibilities, and the pronunciation of words when more than one pronunciation is possible.

During integrated spelling/writing lessons, students analyze the parts of speech and the rules and concepts of language. In composition lessons, they analyze their purpose for writing, their choice of a particular type of writing, and their use of the conventions of writing. During reading lessons, children analyze the attributes of fine literature; the elements of narrative, informative, and informative-narrative writing; and their use of mental actions for comprehension. With each of these analyses, children are required to explain their reasoning.

Practice to the Point of Automaticity

Basic, or first-order, subskills must be automatic so there will be enough working memory available to focus on second- or third-order subskills. For this to occur, practice must be "well beyond the point where the action feels smooth and efficient" (Farnham-Diggory, 1992, 92). Psychologists call this *overlearning*. It is actually programming a part of the brain, the cerebellum, to carry out an action automatically.

Learning a routine to the point of automaticity involves perceptual information, motor actions, and knowledge. One example is the routine of signing your name. When first learning to write, you try to remember letters and the rules for making them—jobs handled by other parts of the brain. As you practice writing your name, you first notice features of individual letters (feature recognition). With practice, the features are grouped and whole letters are *perceived* (letter recognition). With sufficient practice, a group of letters is perceived as a whole (your first name).

In the beginning, working and kinesthetic memory tell your pencil to move up and around, back and forth. Each *motor action* receives a separate command. With practice, all these *motor actions* for writing your name are activated with a single command.

Working memory also retrieves the particular letters in your first name (knowledge). At first, working memory retrieves one letter at a time (maybe not even in the right order); but with practice, a single command retrieves all the letters of your name as a package.

The process of automating an activity is the process of shifting control from other parts of the brain (the cortex) to the cerebellum. When writing your name is automated, you can sign your name while talking to a friend; you begin and end at a fixed point; you finish once you start; it's difficult to start in the middle or recover if interrupted; and it's extremely difficult to change your signature once learned.

When a routine becomes automated, grouping of perceptual information, motor actions, and knowledge has occurred. In this way, a symbol (your name) has come to control a large amount of information in a small amount of workspace.

At the beginning of learning a new task, practice is short but frequent to achieve accurate performance of the skill. Practice must be *distributed* over time to achieve automaticity (overlearning). A few examples of how The Spalding Method provides practice to automaticity follow.

In the spelling lessons, students review new phonograms daily until they can say and write these automatically. They read spelling words two ways until they can read the words fluently and spell them accurately (see Chapter 2).

In integrated spelling/writing lessons, students compose oral (then written) sentences that demonstrate understanding of *unfamiliar* words. They compose sentences that demonstrate knowledge of the attributes of simple (later compound, complex) sentences. In composition lessons, students write related sentences, then informative-narrative (then informative, and finally narrative) paragraphs that include the elements of each type of writing and the attributes of paragraphs (see Chapter 2).

In reading lessons, students read aloud daily to develop fluency, identify attributes of fine literature, identify elements of narratives (then informatives, and finally informative narratives), and use and label three (then five) mental actions while listening to or reading paragraphs. In Spalding spelling, writing, and reading lessons, students have extensive practice of perceptual, motor, and knowledge routines.

Attention Management

When routines become automated, space becomes available in working memory to choose among them. How you make those choices is an important part of learning any skill. Farnham-Diggory explained:

> In general, attention-management involves the construction of higher-order timesharing programs. . . . The attention-management program says, in effect, "When this-and-this happens, switch your attention here. When that-and-that happens, switch your attention there." Learning to construct these higher-order timesharing programs is essential to skill development. (1992, 94)

Since attention *can* be focused on only one task at a time, students develop attention control by actively participating in each part of the lesson. A few examples of how The Spalding Method requires active participation follow.

In the spelling lessons, students respond in unison during oral and written phonogram reviews and spelling dictation, and all students write phonograms and spelling words. In integrated spelling/writing lessons, students participate in discussions about parts of speech and compose oral (then written) sentences. In composition lessons, students participate in group discussions of related sentences and the writing process. They compose group, then individual, informative-narrative, informative, and narrative paragraphs.

In reading lessons, students participate in group discussions of the attributes and elements of literature, read in unison and independently, answer questions, and use mental actions while listening or reading.

Part of attention management is teaching students to switch attention (focus) from one task to another. For example, in spelling lessons, students focus on reading individual sounds or syllables when reading for spelling, then focus on recognizing whole words when reading for reading.

In integrated spelling/writing lessons, students focus on the meaning of an unfamiliar word, then switch attention to checking their use of English conventions (e.g., capitalization and punctuation). In composition lessons, they switch attention from composing to revising for content and, finally, to editing.

In reading lessons, students switch attention to decoding when they encounter an unfamiliar word, and then reread the entire sentence to focus again on comprehension. Further description of these phases of skill learning is provided in *Cognitive Processes in Education* (Farnham-Diggory, 1992).

Skill Learning: Summary

We know that to be effective and successful, instruction must adhere to the principles of skill learning. Children acquire the requisite language skills most easily when teachers analyze each skill, present its component parts in a logical order, and provide appropriate practice until automaticity is reached and the student's mind is able to focus on more sophisticated tasks. Farnham-Diggory noted:

Spalding's method fully incorporated the three critical skill learning principles. . . . There is extensive training in *analyzing* print, in *analyzing* the nature of the sound stream of the spoken language, and in *analyzing* the writing process. There are enormous amounts of *practice*. Students cycle back, over and over again, through materials they have learned earlier. And *attention management* strategies are explicitly taught. There are specific routines for directing your mind through spelling and reading activities. (1987, 13)

But providing instruction at the appropriate level of difficulty, providing sufficient practice, and providing training in attention management are still not enough. There is another set of principles teachers need to teach effectively.

Effective Instruction

A successful model of instruction takes into consideration the nature of learning, how curricula should be organized, how classrooms should be managed, and what constitutes achievement. A model of cognitive apprenticeship was described by Dr. Allan Collins and his colleagues (1989) at the Center for the Study of Reading at the University of Illinois. This model is an instructional delivery system that is easily applied to any subject; it involves students in every lesson; it makes lessons more meaningful; and it develops students' critical thinking skills. In Chapter 2, under the heading "Explicit, Interactive, Diagnostic Instruction," we defined terms used in the Collins model and explain how this model of instruction is incorporated in The Spalding Method. In this chapter, we will list Collins's six principles of effective instruction and briefly provide a few examples of implementation in The Spalding Method.

Modeling

In *modeling,* an expert carries out a task while apprentices observe and conceptualize the processes required to accomplish it. Modeling is especially helpful in cognitive tasks in which the expert thinks out loud to reveal the reading process. Examples of modeling (demonstrating and explaining) in The Spalding Method follow.

During spelling lessons, teachers model the precise formation of features and letters, and the precise pronunciation of each new phonogram and each word in spelling dictation. During integrated spelling/writing lessons, teachers model composing sentences that demonstrate correct meaning and usage of unfamiliar or difficult spelling words. For composition lessons, teachers model thinking out loud while composing clear, logical informative-narrative (then informative, and finally narrative) paragraphs. For literary appreciation lessons, teachers model thinking out loud while identifying and explaining each attribute of literature. For text structure lessons, they model identifying elements of each type of writing while reading short passages. For listening (then reading) comprehension lessons, they model the use of five mental actions while reading paragraphs and then, later, passages.

Coaching

During *coaching*, the teacher helps students bring their performance closer to that of the teacher. All students need some type of assistance in performing a new task. Help ranges from stating the information needed to complete the task (e.g., telling which phonogram to use when more than one is possible) to signaling to remind students of previous learning (e.g., using fingers during dictation). A few examples of effective coaching during Spalding lessons follow.

During oral phonogram reviews, teachers cover the card and say the sounds correctly as soon as a phonogram is mispronounced. In writing lessons, as students compose oral sentences teachers prompt by giving additional examples and by providing specific, immediate feedback when grammar or word sequence is incorrect. In reading lessons, teachers guide as students identify examples of precise language, determine whether a passage is an informative narrative or a narrative, or name and label the mental action they used.

Scaffolding and Fading

Scaffolding and *fading* are an ongoing process of providing support as long as needed and withdrawing support when students can perform the task independently. Examples of scaffolding and fading in The Spalding Method follow.

In spelling lessons, teachers can usually fade quickly with regard to single-sound consonants and easy multiletter phonograms, but they scaffold with regard to multisound consonants, vowels, and difficult multiletter phonograms until mastery is achieved. They fade for easy words and syllables but scaffold when words or syllables have difficult phonograms or when more than one spelling is possible. In writing lessons, teachers can usually fade quickly for attributes of *simple sentences* but will scaffold for compound and complex sentences. They fade with regard to composing related sentences but scaffold for using the writing process to compose three types of writing. In reading lessons, teachers can fade as soon as first-grade students accurately identify *precise* language in literary appreciation lessons, but teachers scaffold all year on difficult concepts (e.g., insight and universality). In text structure lessons, they fade as soon as students can identify clear examples of narratives and informatives, but scaffold all year on more difficult informative-narrative passages. Teachers may fade quite quickly regarding the first three mental actions but continue to provide support in identifying implied main ideas.

During this process of modeling, coaching, scaffolding, and fading, teachers require students to participate so the students can become independent learners and the teachers can diagnose those who need additional help and those who need challenge.

Articulation

Students' *articulation* requires constant interaction between teacher and students. Students answer questions that check for understanding, they repeat directions, and they explain a process, procedure, or rule. This interaction enables the teacher to identify students who understand the new learning and those who need more practice in small groups. Articulation also benefits the students because they must thoroughly understand concepts or procedures in order to explain them to others. A few examples of student articulation in The Spalding Method follow.

In spelling lessons, students explain the formation of individual letters and how language rules apply to spelling words. In writing lessons, they explain attributes of *simple* (then compound, then complex) sentences. In composition lessons, students identify types of writing and identify the elements to include. In reading lessons, they explain the attributes and elements of literature and the five mental actions.

Reflection

Reflection means that students think about how new learning influences their performance of motor tasks, their problem-solving skills, or their thinking process. A few examples of how The Spalding Method teaches reflection follow.

In spelling lessons, teachers ask students to compare their pronunciation and letter formation today with what they did yesterday. In writing lessons, teachers have students reflect on their improvement in writing sentences and paragraphs. Saving some of students' work in file folders (portfolios) enables them to compare their progress frequently. In reading lessons, teachers might ask students to reflect on how an author's use of emotional appeal affected their opinion of a character.

Exploration

Exploration means moving students into new domains, where they work independently on projects. In The Spalding Method, students independently compose paragraphs and passages, read library books of their choice or the teacher's choice, and report to the class, or select their own topic for a research paper.

Effective Instruction: Summary

Interactive instruction provides teachers with a great deal of information to identify students who need extra help in small groups, those who can complete assignments independently, and those who need extra challenge. When teachers believe students are ready to apply a skill to a new situation, they require independent performance. On the other hand, if students are not ready, teachers may need to return to modeling, coaching, or scaffolding in the whole group or in small groups.

Chapter Summary

In this chapter we explained that *The Writing Road to Reading* is effective because it integrates four knowledge domains: the reading process, reading development, skill learning, and effective instruction. We reviewed research about how children learn to read; what children must know and be able to do to be articulate speakers, fluent readers, accurate spellers, and accomplished writers; and what effective teachers must know and do to ensure that all students will be successful learners. A successful reading program must include explicit instruction in all the essential instructional components in an appropriate sequence for the child's stage of reading development; it must incorporate principles common to all skill learning with principles of effective instruction. Finally, we demonstrated how The Spalding Method includes all these factors.

Spalding Education International (SEI) provides parent and teacher courses that elaborate on the information in this book. In Chapter 6, we will discuss SEI's mission, validation of *The Writing Road to Reading*, and professional development for teachers, including courses and certification opportunities, parent courses, and SEI services.

ADVANCING LITERACY

ROMALDA SPALDING devoted a lifetime to advancing literacy. The need today is as great as or greater than when she began her quest. Dr. Reid Lyon, former chief of the Child Development and Behavior Branch at the National Institute of Child Health and Human Development (NICHD), stated in testimony before a congressional committee, on January 22, 2001:

> The NICHD considers that teaching and learning in today's schools is not only a critical educational and social issue, but a significant public health issue as well. Our research has shown that if children do not learn to use language to communicate ideas and perspectives, read and write, calculate and reason mathematically, and be able to solve problems strategically, their opportunities for a fulfilling and rewarding life are seriously compromised. Specifically, in our NICHD longitudinal studies, we have learned that school failure has devastating consequences with respect to self-esteem, social development, and opportunities for advanced education. (Lyon, 2001, 1)

Mrs. Spalding's *The Writing Road to Reading* program spread through a field network, centered in Maricopa County, Arizona. Administrators from six districts formed a consortium to fund the training of local teachers to become Spalding instructors. A pilot project, comparing Spalding with the program in use in one district, was initiated (see "Evidence-Based Validation," below). When the results of the experimental study demonstrated significant gains in students' achievement, Mrs. Spalding was persuaded to form a nonprofit foundation—Spalding Education Foundation, now Spalding Education International (SEI)—to perpetuate her method and to maintain consistent instruction. SEI instituted rigorous Spalding certification requirements for teachers and instructors.

Mission

Spalding Education International, a nonprofit 501(c)(3) corporation, is committed to developing skilled readers, critical listeners, and accomplished writers and spellers. SEI is governed by a volunteer board of directors dedicated to advancing literacy through courses and other services for teachers, administrators, and parents. In addition, SEI actively pursues outreach to the business sector, community leaders, literacy organizations, and other groups that share a commitment to literacy.

The text *The Writing Road to Reading* provides the knowledge and procedures needed to achieve rapid mastery of the basic elements of English. Adult disabled readers and individuals of any age studying English as a second language enjoy success when taught by this method. Experience also demonstrates that general and special education students make great gains when teachers use *The Writing Road to Reading*.

Because the first years in school are the most important for rapidly acquiring the basic elements of English, this book introduces phonograms with handwriting instruction, and with the accompanying procedures, from a kindergarten and first-grade perspective. Explicit procedures for introducing and practicing the rules of English spelling are also included in this text. Other evidence-based components of language instruction are introduced with procedures and thirty-two weeks of lesson objectives in the companion *Kindergarten Through Sixth-Grade Teacher Guides*. SEI is committed to maintaining excellence in its literacy mission. This book and the method it teaches will lead to better-prepared teachers and increased student literacy.

Evidence-Based Validation

From the beginning, Mrs. Spalding was interested in validating and improving her method. To continually measure students' achievement, she collected, over forty years, a large volume of standardized test scores from public and private school administrators throughout the country. All median reading and spelling scores for the various Spalding student populations showed considerable gains above the U.S. norms in every grade.

Data Collection

Dr. Robert Aukerman, in his text *Approaches to Beginning Reading* (1984), validated Mrs. Spalding's finding. He investigated and described more than 100 different approaches to beginning reading. Aukerman devoted ten pages to The Spalding Method, citing national test scores from many Spalding schools in twelve states. He stated:

> A rather significant and up-to-date body of data has been assembled showing the *indisputable* success that many schools are enjoying with The Spalding Method. . . . They cover scores on standardized achievement tests in reading, and are the results reported by the schools for children of a wide range of backgrounds and intelligence. Moreover, they are from a representative sampling of small and large schools, public, parochial, and private (Arizona, California, Hawaii, Idaho, Illinois, New Hampshire, Texas, and Virginia). It should be noted, also, that the class sizes range all the way from a small class of only eight students to the large classes of 50 or more. In all, 20 schools of varied types and localities are represented with more than 120 *different teachers*. (541)

The Spalding Method was observed in several Honolulu schools in 1967 and again in 1982. In January, for example, in a first-grade class the children were reading at an almost unbelievable level of comprehension, voice inflection, knowledge of word attack. . . . Scores that are consistently far beyond the national norms and testimonials of gains made by illiterate adults, new arrivals from the rim of the Pacific, learning disabled children, and others who had not previously learned to read in regular classrooms using standard means should be proof enough of the effectiveness of *The Writing Road to Reading.* (545–546)

The average grade-level score of the fourteen first grades in his sample was 2.8; that of the sixteen second grades, 3.76; and that of the twelve third grades, 5.24.

Over the years, SEI expanded on this data collection, reporting Arizona Spalding students' achievement scores on the Iowa Test of Basic Skills annually from 1986, when SEI was formed, until statewide testing ended in 1991. When the legislature resumed statewide standardized, norm-referenced testing in 1996 using the Stanford Achievement Test, SEI resumed reporting students' scores. Under state guidelines, schools administered the tests in the spring of each year, and the publisher scored the tests. Using the scores published by the Arizona Department of Education, SEI reported grade-level comparisons of reading and language scores for schools using Spalding with district and state scores. Standardized test scores from schools in other states in which Spalding was taught were also included. Schools were included in the annual Spalding *Special Report on Student Achievement* if the administration formally adopted Spalding as the basic language arts program and Spalding training and follow-up had been provided for the entire faculty. In reading, Spalding students' percentile rank scores ranged from ten to forty-two points higher than district and state norms. The difference would have been even greater if Spalding schools were not included in the district and state averages. The Arizona State Department of Education again discontinued testing all students at every grade level in 2004.

Clinical Studies
Two longitudinal studies were reported in *Clinical Studies of Multisensory Structured Language Education for Students with Dyslexia and Related Disorders* in 1995.

El Paso Independent School District
The effects of Spalding language arts instruction on special education students in a resource-room setting were studied by the El Paso Independent School District. The primary purpose of this longitudinal study was to quantify students' growth when The Spalding Method was used. During the third year, more than 500 boys and girls in grades one through eight who met the Texas Education Agency's eligibility criteria for a handicapping condition were studied. Students made statistically significant gains in reading, writing, and spelling as assessed by the *Brigance Diagnostic Comprehensive Inventory of Basic Skills*, a written composition, and the *Morrison-McCall Spelling Scale* (North, 1995).

Middletown High School, Delaware

The Spalding Method was used in a seven-year longitudinal study with the entire special education population at Middletown High School in Delaware, to determine whether high school is too late to improve the literacy skills of low-performing students. Statistical analyses of preachievement and postachievement test scores for 111 students demonstrated significant improvements in word recognition, passage comprehension, and spelling. Convincing evidence was found that, with appropriate instruction, high school is not too late to improve the literacy skills of most special education students (Hoerl and Koons, 1995).

Quasi-Experimental Studies

Previously published quasi-experimental studies that demonstrate exemplary student achievement in Spalding schools are noted below.

Honolulu, Hawaii

In 1954, the first quasi-experimental study of The Spalding Method was conducted in twenty-four large schools in Hawaii (it was reported in detail in the first edition of *The Writing Road to Reading*, 1957). The experimental group consisted of 369 children; the control classes consisted of 328. Mrs. Spalding trained all teachers in the experimental group; the control group used the existing program. All students were tested on the Metropolitan Achievement Test, a nationally standardized measure. Scores in the experimental group were significantly higher than those in the control group.

Peoria Unified School District, Arizona

In the early 1980s, the Peoria (Arizona) Unified School District's standardized achievement test scores were at or below the 50th percentile rank. A pilot study was designed to compare the effectiveness of The Spalding Method with the district's adopted program. Kindergarten through third-grade classes were matched in five schools: one high-socioeconomic school, two middle-socioeconomic schools, and two low-socioeconomic schools. Mrs. Spalding trained the twenty pilot teachers. By the end of the pilot year 1985–1986, the percentile rank scores in reading comprehension of Peoria's Spalding classes ranged from the upper 80s to the high 90s on the state-adopted Iowa Test of Basic Skills. Scores for the control classes remained at or below the 50th percentile rank. The Governing Board adopted Spalding for kindergarten through third grade in 1986. A decline in learning disability resource room populations was noted after classroom instruction incorporated The Spalding Method.

The pilot project was extended into grades four through eight as a spelling program in 1986. Matched classes compared Spalding with a commercial spelling program. Spelling scores, measured by the Iowa Test of Basic Skills in April of the pilot year 1987–1988, demonstrated that Spalding-trained students had a 5 percentile-rank advantage over other students. Statistical analysis was done by a researcher at Arizona State University. The Peoria Governing Board adopted Spalding for spelling in grades four through eight in 1988. Results of this study and other pilot studies were reported in the *Annals of Dyslexia* (North, 1991), published by the Orton Dyslexia Society (now International Dyslexia Association).

Reading Research Center, University of Delaware

In the Foreword to this edition, Dr. Sylvia Farnham-Diggory explains why The Spalding Method works. In her text *Cognitive Processes in Education* (1992), she described an experimental study conducted at the Reading Research Center:

> We have also conducted evaluation studies of several types. When our program was first introduced, local schools routinely administered a standardized test called the Comprehensive Test of Basic Skills (CTBS) at the end of each year. Since only a few classrooms had begun to adopt our program, it was a simple matter to find a matching classroom that had not. . . . Except for the reading program, children from experimental and control classrooms received the same curriculum. At the end of the school year, we compared a first, second, and third grade to their respective control classrooms on the CTBS total reading scale. The percentile ranks for our Intensive Literacy (Spalding) first-, second-, and third-grade classrooms were 66th, 67th, and 67th, respectively, while the percentile ranks for the control classrooms were 43rd, 54th, and 47th, respectively. These differences were significant statistically and were also meaningful intuitively. The control classes were testing at or below average . . . , whereas the Intensive Literacy classes had moved well above average. (307–308)

Spalding has also been shown to be effective with at-risk students.

Tasmanian Office of Education

A quasi-experimental study conducted by the Tasmanian Office of Education (Australia) in 1999, of at-risk students—including students with attention deficit disorder (ADD) and dyslexia—in grades one and two at the Youngtown Primary School, showed significant progress on three assessments. In eight months of teaching, first-grade students made twelve months', fourteen months', and sixteen months' progress on the *Morrison-McCall Spelling Test*, *Wadding Bray Spelling Test*, and *South Australian Spelling Test*, respectively. Second-grade progress in eight months of teaching was fourteen, ten, and nineteen on the above assessments.

Arizona State University: Final Summary Report—
Evaluation Study of The Writing Road to Reading

The following description and excerpts are from the five-page summary report available under "Research" on the Spalding Web site, at www.spalding.org.

Dr. Gary Bitter, a professor at Arizona State University; and Dr. Mary Aleta White, a senior research specialist at Arizona State University, conducted a four-year quasi-experimental study (2006–2007 through 2009–2010) to evaluate the effectiveness of Spalding's *Writing Road to Reading* program (WRTR). The purpose of the study was to determine whether Spalding students from various backgrounds and types of schools demonstrated statistically significant learning gains and how those gains compared with the progress of children in control schools using other core reading programs. How well teachers implemented the WRTR program was a companion research question.

To study implementation by teachers, the researchers collected data through classroom observations and survey questionnaires. Researchers employed the Dynamic Indicators of Basic Early Literacy Skills (DIBELS) to measure changes in students' reading skills. The DIBELS tests were administered at the beginning, middle, and end of each school year.

This study was conducted in 5 experimental (Spalding) and 6 control schools, matched by gender, ethnicity, socioeconomic status, and language ability, with an average of 47 teachers and an average of 1,000 students each year. Complete descriptions and information are provided in Tables 1–7 in the complete report available on the research page at www.spalding.org. Classes in the experimental group used the Spalding curriculum an average of 90 minutes each day, while control classes used either Houghton Mifflin or Harcourt an average of 80 minutes each day. Another analysis of reading achievement was available in the third-year study because all second-grade students are required to complete the state's norm-referenced achievement test, TerraNova. The chart below represents a sample of the study students (three control and three experimental schools) and their Normal Curve Equivalent (NCE) scores on the TerraNova reading portion. As would be expected from reviewing the DIBELS scores, the Spalding students' NCE scores were significantly higher than the control students on the state test ($p < .01$).

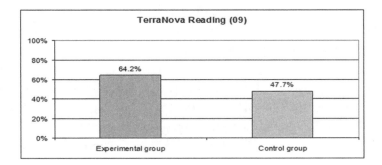

Student NCE reading scores from Spring, 09 AZ TerraNova exam

As shown in the chart below, additional analyses of the extent to which experimental students experienced learning gains by the end of each grade level show that they exceeded the DIBELS decision rules benchmarks for achievement each year (as well as at each testing period). Unfortunately, since the middle of their second-grade year, the average control student is not meeting the DIBELS assessment for low-risk scores. Their achievement level averages a score approximately five points below the low-risk threshold.

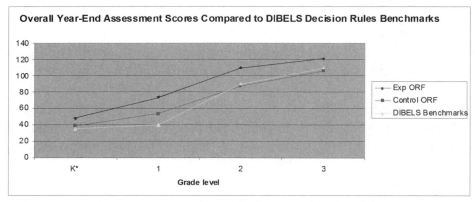

K, Spring 2007 is Phoneme Segmentation Fluency; all others are Oral Reading Fluency

Overall year-end assessment scores compared to DIBELS decision rules benchmarks

In addition to measures of statistical significance, researchers frequently calculate and report measures of practical significance, known as the effect size. This is a way to help educators decide whether a statistically significant difference between programs translates into a meaningful difference—one that would justify a program adoption, for instance. Using the entire treatment group, the effect size for Fall 2009 was .7; for Winter 2010 it was .6; and in Spring 2010 the effect size was .4. This means the intervention has a positive, medium effect (average of 0.54) on student achievement. Converting effect size to percentiles means the average student in the Spalding sample, at the end of the year, scores higher than 69% of the control student sample.

Using longitudinal group scores (students who were in the kindergarten group), the effect size for Fall 2009 was .9; for Winter 2010 was .8; and for Spring 2010 was .6. This means that the intervention has a large effect size (average of 0.78) on student reading achievement. In converting effect size to percentiles, the average student in the longitudinal Spalding group would score higher than 79% of the control student sample.

Summary

According to the four-year results, students who used *The Writing Road to Reading* program demonstrate higher and statistically significant learning as measured by DIBELS. Since both the control groups and the experimental groups used detailed teacher guides evaluated by the Arizona Department of Education for research-based reading components, theoretically, they should have produced similar results. This was not the case. The four-year findings strongly suggest that use of *The Writing Road to Reading* program is an effective method for enhancing performance on critical early literacy skills.

SEI Services

Spalding Professional Development: Courses

In testimony before a congressional committee, Dr. Reid Lyon reported that many teachers feel unprepared to address students' individual learning needs and feel particularly unprepared to provide adequate reading instruction. He cited a survey conducted by the National Center for Educational Statistics: it indicated that only 20 percent of teachers surveyed felt adequately prepared to teach their students. According to Lyon, the problem is insufficient information about reading development and inadequate reading instruction during undergraduate and even graduate studies, "with the average teacher completing only one or two reading courses" (2001, 3).

Recognizing this deficiency, SEI provides professional development for general and special education teachers, speech and language therapists, psychologists, and administrators. To meet the needs of diverse populations, SEI provides courses for teachers, parents, and interested citizens. SEI recognizes that information and methodology presented in a training course are best retained when there is follow-up instructional support. Experienced Spalding instructors go on-site to model correct instructional procedures, coach, and answer teachers' questions. To facilitate correct implementation and consistent exemplary student achievement across all grade levels, seminars for administrators are conducted. Professional development seminars are held regularly for Spalding Certified Teacher Instructors to share research and hone professional skills. The content of all Spalding courses, whether online, in-services, or seminars, reflects the original philosophy and precepts of Romalda Spalding's total language arts approach to literacy.

SEI contracts with various colleges and universities, departments of education, school districts, schools, civic organizations, social agencies, and corporations. To maintain the integrity and effectiveness of The Spalding Method, only SEI-certified personnel may teach SEI-approved Spalding courses (see "Spalding Certification" below). All SEI-approved courses are scheduled by contacting the course administrator at Spalding Education International. All Spalding-approved basic training courses are posted on the Spalding Web site, at www.spalding.org.

Writing Road to Reading 1 (WRTR 1)

Writing Road to Reading 1 is a forty-five-hour course designed for general and special education teachers, administrators, curriculum specialists, psychologists, speech pathologists, and reading specialists. Participants will acquire the content knowledge (phonemic awareness, systematic phonics taught in spelling, vocabulary, fluency, syntax, and text comprehension) and structured, explicit, sequential procedures necessary to provide evidence-based reading instruction. Three credit hours may be obtained from many colleges and universities.

Writing Road to Reading 2 (WRTR 2)

Writing Road to Reading 2 is a forty-five-hour course designed for general and special education teachers, administrators, curriculum specialists, psychologists, speech pathologists, and reading specialists. The focus is on comprehension strategies and the writing process. Teachers will also learn strategies for applying spelling and language rules and for differentiating integrated language arts instruction to meet the needs of all students. Three credit hours may be obtained from many colleges and universities.

Parent Introduction to Spalding

The *Parent Introduction to Spalding* is a ten-hour overview of Spalding's WRTR program for parents with children in Spalding schools. The focus is on reinforcing spelling, the foundation for reading and writing.

Spalding for Home Educators 1 (SHE 1)

Spalding for Home Educators 1 is a fifteen-hour course that provides the information parents need to teach kindergarten through sixth-grade students how to spell accurately, read fluently, and write competently. It focuses on teaching *basic* language skills, developing a love of reading, understanding the structure of the language, and using Spalding materials. This course is available at established sites or online.

Spalding for Home Educators 2 (SHE 2)

Spalding for Home Educators 2 expands on the information in SHE 1 and on all the Spalding teaching procedures needed for teaching grades three and above.

Spalding Coaching 1 (SC 1)

Spalding Coaching 1, a fifteen-hour course, prepares Spalding Certified Teachers (SCTs) and Spalding Certified Teacher Instructors (SCTIs) to coach teachers using The Spalding Method. Participants learn to consciously use effective instructional practices, continuously increase knowledge and understanding of basic skills and processes, refine delivery skills, implement self-analysis to be better prepared to teach these skills, and conduct effective postobservation conferences.

Spalding Certification

Spalding certification ensures that Romalda B. Spalding's concern for students' intellectual and physical well-being will be manifested by those carrying out her quest of "literacy for all." SEI certification at any level signifies professional competence because these individuals not only have completed the required courses but also have been formally observed working with students. To ensure that practitioners of the method will have an appropriate level of training, SEI established the following certification levels: Spalding Authorized Tutor, Spalding Certified Teacher, Instructor, and Executive Trainer. Each level of certification requires additional course work and classroom observations teaching students to ensure appropriate implementation of the WRTR program. A certification brochure and application form are available at www.spalding.org.

School Accreditation

Just as certification ensures that qualified instructors provide instruction, so accreditation signifies that the school administration and staff are committed to raising students' achievement by consistent use of the WRTR program throughout the grades. The designation

Spalding Accredited School is evidence for parents and others that a school has voluntarily met demanding external standards for The Spalding Method.

Quarterly Publications

SEI publishes the *Spalding News*, a quarterly journal that provides current reading research, news from Spalding classrooms, information about in-service workshops, answers to readers' questions, and instructional tips. SEI also publishes *Teacher Talk,* a newsletter, for Spalding certified personnel.

Spalding Materials Distribution

SEI holds the copyright to *The Writing Road to Reading*, published by HarperCollins. In addition, SEI holds sole rights to all SEI-authorized educational materials. A list of authorized materials is found in "Resources," beginning on page 431. An instructional materials catalog is available from the SEI office (see "Resources") or through the SEI Web site: www.spalding.org.

Chapter Summary

Spalding courses are now taught around the world. The efficacy of *The Writing Road to Reading* has made it popular among homeschooling parents and among teachers and administrators searching for a better way to teach reading. Spalding Certified Teachers and Instructors represent a unique cadre of highly trained specialists dedicated to advancing literacy in their schools and communities and to encouraging others to obtain Spalding training. Spalding Accredited Schools demonstrate the exemplary student achievement possible when teachers receive the instruction they need. SEI is dedicated to validating and improving the WRTR program. We invite all who are interested in participating in this effort to contact:

Spalding Education International
23335 North 18th Drive, Suite 102
Phoenix, AZ 85027
Phone: (623) 434-1204
Fax: (623) 434-1208
Web site: www.spalding.org
E-mail <staff@spalding.org>

Part Two

INSTRUCTIONAL MATERIALS

Children's Literature: Recommendations
Phonograms
Phonogram Reviews and Cue Words
Rules of Pronunciation, Spelling, and Language
Morphology
Primary and Intermediate Spelling/Vocabulary Notebooks—
  Sample Pages
Spalding Spelling/Vocabulary Word List: Order of Instruction
Spalding Spelling/Vocabulary Word List: Alphabetized
Recommended Language Arts Scope and Sequence
Resources

CHILDREN'S LITERATURE: RECOMMENDATIONS

BECOMING A NATION OF READERS: The Report of the Commission on Reading recommends, "Parents should read to preschool children and informally teach them about reading and writing" (Anderson et al., 1985, 117). Children whose parents follow this advice enjoy a considerable advantage. Their vocabulary and knowledge of syntax are enlarged, and they are better prepared for more formal classroom instruction.

Knowing how to read is vital. However, of equal consequence is what is read. Spalding Education International (SEI), of course, is dedicated to advancing literacy; but we know that books are not neutral: each carries a message, embodies a value system, or implies a model to emulate. Fine literature explicitly or implicitly sets forth standards of conduct. It teaches about character, nobility, duty, and other virtues as well as the consequences of their absence.

We recommend that each class have its own classroom library, including collections of poetry. We also recommend that book choices be purposeful and deliberate. As parents and educators, our task is to provide guidance regarding what is worthwhile and what is not. Some say it is enough for children's books to just entertain, because that will encourage children to read more. SEI believes that books of little merit confer few benefits. However, even if entertainment is all that justifies a book's selection, it should not degrade the reader, either by style or by content. To ascertain appropriateness for your classroom and circumstances, it is important to read each book before reading it aloud or having students read it.

Books included in the *Kindergarten Through Sixth-Grade Teacher Guides* are listed here as a resource so that listening comprehension, text structure, and literary appreciation may be taught from the first day of class. Teachers at all grade levels read fine literature aloud to demonstrate fluent, expressive reading and to foster a love of reading. An additional list of trade book titles is provided at the Spalding Web site: www.spalding.org. Neither list is exhaustive, but both are intended to provide some guidance, as we believe each represents some of the better children's books available.

Suggested grade-level designations are based upon the phonograms being taught, children's interests, the level of language used, and a determination of merit. In addition, teachers should be guided by children's progress and abilities.

All children benefit greatly from listening to fine literature read aloud by their teachers. However, kindergarten, first-grade, and struggling older readers need practice reading the phonograms before they are able to read books chosen solely for literary merit. This following list is organized by level of difficulty as students progress through the Spalding Spelling/Vocabulary Word List.

Decodable Beginning Readers

Learning to Read and Loving It: Series 1 Leveled Readers

Purpose
The purpose of *Learning to Read and Loving It*, the *Series 1 Leveled Readers*, is to provide practice with the phonograms that are introduced each week. Having beginners read in unison a few pages of a book each day provides practice in rapid word recognition and text fluency.

General Information
Series 1 Level 1 Readers include eight narratives starting after the first thirty phonograms have been introduced and practiced. (See academic week 10 in the "Planning" section of the *Kindergarten Teacher's Guide*.) Level 2 Readers include eight informative books to be read in weeks 18 through 25. Level 3 Readers include four informative-narrative selections to be read in weeks 26 through 29. The following timeline lists the book number and title, the number of the week introduced in the *Teacher's Guide*, and the phonograms practiced.

Book Number and Title	Week Introduced	Phonograms Practiced
1. *Sam and Puff*	10	26 + *sh, ee, th, ow*
2. *A Trip to the Park*	11	30 + *ou, oo, ch, ar*
3. *Ben Visits the Farm*	12	34 + *ay, ai, oy, oi*
4. *Mother Helps Tim*	13	38 + *er, ir, ur, wor, ear*
5. *Her First Nurse Works Early*	14	38 + *er, ir, ur, wor, ear*
6. *The Flying Fish*	15	43 + *ng, ea, aw, au, or*
7. *Grandma's Helper*	16	48 + *ck, wh, ed*
8. *The New Suit*	17	51 + *ew, ui*
9. *Learning About Horses*	18	53 + *oa, gu*
10. *Learning About Dogs*	19	55 + *ph, ough*
11. *Learning About Cows*	20	57 + *oe, ey*
12. *Learning About Sheep*	21	59 + *igh, kn*
13. *Learning About Wild Cats*	22	61 + *gn, wr*
14. *Learning About Birds*	23	63 + *ie, dge*
15. *Learning About Deer*	24	65 + *ei, eigh*
16. *Learning About Bears*	25	67 + *ti, si, ci*
17. *Touring the Public Library*	26	70 (selected)
18. *A Visit to the County Fair*	27	70 (selected)

Book Number and Title	Week Introduced	Phonograms Practiced
19. *A Tour of the Fire Station*	28	70 (selected)
20. *A Trip to the Animal Shelter*	29	70 (selected)

Additional Beginning Decodable Readers from Various Publishers

Additional decodable books are recommended for children to practice reading in unison and individually.

Author	Title	Publisher	Grade
Appleton-Smith, Laura	*The Sunset Pond*	Flyleaf	K–1
Appleton-Smith, Laura	*Jen's Best Gift Ever*	Flyleaf	K–1
Appleton-Smith, Laura	*Frank the Fish Gets His Wish*	Flyleaf	K–1
Appleton-Smith, Laura	*Meg and Jim's Sled Trip*	Flyleaf	K–1
Dr. Seuss	*Green Eggs and Ham*	Random House	K–1
Eastman, P. D.	*Go, Dog, Go*	Random House	K–1
Eastman, P. D.	*Are You My Mother?*	Random House	K–1
Krauss, Ruth	*The Carrot Seed*	Scholastic Books	K–1
Le Seig, Theodore	*Ten Apples Up on Top*	Random House	K–1
Lopshire, Robert	*Put Me in the Zoo*	Random House	K–1

Reading and Loving It: Series 2 Leveled Readers

Purpose

The purpose of *Reading and Loving It*—the *Series 2 Leveled Readers*—is to provide practice with the phonograms introduced and reinforced each week. In Spalding schools, *Series 2* readers are used in first grade, but they are also appropriate for older struggling readers. Having beginners read in unison, and individually, a few pages of a book each day provides practice in rapid word recognition and text fluency.

General Information

If you are using the *Spalding First-Grade Teacher's Guide*, use *Series 1 Leveled Readers* for weeks 2–4 while all of the seventy phonograms are being introduced/reinforced. Then, begin *Series 2 Level 1*, which includes twelve third-person narrative, informative, and informative-narrative selections (weeks 5–16). Level 2 includes four first-person narrative and informative-narrative selections (weeks 17–20). Level 3 includes four third-person informative selections (weeks 21–24). Level 4 includes four narrative, informative, and informative-narrative selections (weeks 25–28). The following timeline lists the book number and title, the number of the week introduced in the *Teacher's Guide*, and the phonograms practiced.

Book Number and Title	Week Introduced	Phonograms Practiced
1. *Teamwork Pays Off*	5	26 + *sh, ee, th, ow, ou, oo, ch, ar, ay, ai, oy, oi, er, ir, ur, wor, ear, ng, ea*
2. *Taking a Detour*	6	same as book 1
3. *Rescuing a Whale*	7	45 + *aw, au, or, ck, wh, ed, ew, ui, oa, gu, ph*
4. *Making New Friends*	8	56 + *ough, oe, ey, igh, kn, gn, wr, ie, dge, ei, eigh, ti, si, ci*
5. *Plants: Redwoods, Cacti, Tulips*	9	70 (selected)
6. *Vertebrates: Dogs, Horses, Whales*	10	70 (selected)
7. *Vertebrates: Lizards, Snakes, Birds*	11	70 (selected)
8. *Invertebrates: Starfish, Butterflies, Spiders*	12	70 (selected)
9. *The Thrifty Pilgrims*	13	70 (selected)
10. *Gardening Takes Patience*	14	70 (selected)
11. *Cleanup Cooperation*	15	70 (selected)
12. *Effort Rewarded*	16	70 (selected)
13. *Finding Courage*	17	70 (selected)
14. *Success Through Perseverance*	18	70 (selected)
15. *A Science Fair*	19	70 (selected)
16. *Building a House*	20	70 (selected)
17. *Matter: Solids, Liquids, Gases*	21	70 (selected)
18. *Energy Sources and Uses*	22	70 (selected)
19. *Earth Materials: Renewable/ Non-renewable*	23	70 (selected)
20. *Sky Objects: Sun, Stars, Moon, Planets*	24	70 (selected)
21. *Sharing Is Fun*	25	70 (selected)
22. *Weather: Climate, Humidity, Wind Chill*	26	70 (selected)
23. *Sending a Letter*	27	70 (selected)
24. *The Amazing Ben Franklin*	28	70 (selected)

Children's Literature

We recommend classroom sets of several titles at each grade level to be used for instruction and for practice in fluency. Additional recommended books are listed at the Spalding Web site, www.spalding.org.

First Grade

Author	Title	Publisher
De Regniers, Beatrice	*May I Bring a Friend?*	Atheneum
Flack, Marjorie	*Angus and the Ducks*	Doubleday
Flack, Marjorie	*The Story About Ping*	Viking
Galdone, Paul	*The Gingerbread Boy*	Houghton Mifflin
Galdone, Paul	*Three Billy Goats Gruff*	Houghton Mifflin
Galdone, Paul	*The Three Little Pigs*	Houghton Mifflin
Hader, B. and E.	*The Big Snow*	Simon and Schuster
Hoban, Lillian	*Arthur's Pen Pal*	Perfection Learning
Keats, Ezra	*Whistle for Willie*	Viking
Leaf, Munro	*The Story of Ferdinand*	Viking
Piper, Watty	*The Little Engine That Could*	Philomel
Rey, H. A. and Margaret	*Curious George* (series)	Houghton Mifflin

Second Grade

Author	Title	Publisher
Coerr, Eleanor B.	*Sadako and the Thousand Paper Cranes*	Penguin
Dalgliesh, Alice	*The Bears on Hemlock Mountain*	Aladdin
Grimm, Jacob	*The Wolf and the Seven Kids*	Silver Burdett
Lindgren, Astrid	*Pippi Longstocking* (series)	Viking
McCloskey, Robert	*Blueberries for Sal*	Viking
McCloskey, Robert	*One Morning in Maine*	Viking
McCloskey, Robert	*Time of Wonder*	Viking
Merriam, Eve	*Blackberry Ink*	William Morrow
Parish, Peggy	*Amelia Bedelia* (series)	Perfection Learning
Perrault, Charles	*Cinderella*	North-South
Peterson, John	*The Littles* (series)	Perfection Learning
Politi, Leo	*Song of Swallows*	Atheneum
Thurber, James	*Many Moons*	Harcourt Children's Books
Williams, Margery	*The Velveteen Rabbit*	Running Press Kids
Yolen, Jane	*Owl Moon*	Putnam

Third Grade

Author	Title	Publisher
Butterworth, Oliver	*The Enormous Egg*	Little, Brown
Cleary, Beverly	*Henry Huggins* (series)	HarperCollins
Cleary, Beverly	*Ramona the Pest* (series)	Perfection Learning

Author	Title	Publisher
Dalgliesh, Alice	*The Fourth of July Story*	Aladdin
D'Aulaire, I. and E.	*Abraham Lincoln*	Beautiful Feet Books
D'Aulaire, I. and E.	*Benjamin Franklin*	Beautiful Feet Books
Lawson, Peter	*Rabbit Hill*	Viking
Lawson, Robert	*Ben and Me*	Perfection Learning
MacLachlan, Patricia	*Sarah Plain and Tall*	HarperCollins
Milne, A. A.	*Winnie-the-Pooh*	Dutton Juvenile
Simon, Seymour	*Jupiter*	HarperCollins
Simon, Seymour	*Saturn*	HarperCollins
White, E. B.	*Charlotte's Web*	HarperCollins
White, E. B.	*Stuart Little*	HarperCollins
Wilder, Laura Ingalls	*Little House* (series)	HarperCollins

Fourth Grade

Author	Title	Publisher
Aesop	*The Fables of Aesop*	Chronicle
Aldrin, Buzz	*Buzz Aldrin, Reaching for the Stars*	HarperCollins
Cleary, Beverly	*Dear Mr. Henshaw*	HarperCollins
Dejong, Meindert	*The House of Sixty Fathers*	Perfection Learning
Furgang, Kathy	*The Declaration of Independence and John Adams*	PowerKids
Forbes, Esther	*America's Paul Revere*	Sandpiper
Grimm, J. and W.	*Household Stories by the Brothers Grimm*	Fili-Quarian Books
Henry, Marguerite	*Benjamin West and His Cat Grimalkin*	Checkerboard
Kipling, Rudyard	*Just So Stories*	Candlewick
Krumgold, Joseph	*. . . and now Miguel*	Perfection Learning
Lewis, C. S.	*Chronicles of Narnia* (series)	HarperCollins
Seldon, George	*The Cricket in Times Square*	Farrar, Straus and Giroux
Spyri, Johanna	*Heidi*	Indy Publish
Travers, P. L.	*Mary Poppins* (series)	Harcourt Children's Books
Wilder, Laura Ingalls	*Farmer Boy*	HarperCollins

Fifth Grade

Author	Title	Publisher
Burnett, Frances	*The Secret Garden*	Oxford University Press
Burnford, Sheila	*The Incredible Journey*	Delacorte
Carroll, Lewis	*Alice's Adventures in Wonderland*	Houghton Mifflin
Christopher, Matt	*Great Moments in Baseball History*	Little, Brown
Daugherty, James	*Landing of the Pilgrims*	Random House
DeJong, Meindert	*The Wheel on the School*	HarperCollins
Forbes, Esther	*Johnny Tremain*	Houghton Mifflin
Freedman, Russell	*Lincoln: A Photobiography*	Perfection Learning
George, Jean	*My Side of the Mountain*	Dutton
Grahame, Kenneth	*The Wind in the Willows*	Candlewick
Latham, Jean	*Carry on, Mr. Bowditch*	Houghton
Lowery, Lois	*Number the Stars*	Houghton Mifflin
O'Dell, Scott	*Island of the Blue Dolphins*	Sandpiper
Park, Linda Sue	*A Single Shard*	Clarion
Sperry, Armstrong	*Call It Courage*	Aladdin

Sixth Grade

Author	Title	Publisher
Alcott, Louisa May	*Little Men*	Signet Classics
Alcott, Louisa May	*Little Women*	Signet Classics
Brink, Carol	*Caddie Woodlawn*	Simon and Schuster
Byars, Betsy	*The Summer of the Swans*	Simon and Schuster
Defoe, Daniel	*Robinson Crusoe*	Modern Library
Fields, Rachel	*Hitty: Her First Hundred Years*	Simon and Schuster
Rawlings, Marjorie	*The Yearling*	Collier Macmillan
Rink, Paul	*Admiral Richard Byrd: Alone in the Antarctic*	Sterling
Rollyson, Carl	*Marie Curie: Honesty in Science*	iUniverse
Sandburg, Carl	*Abe Lincoln Grows Up*	Graphia
Shirer, William	*The Sinking of the Bismarck: The Deadly Hunt*	Sterling
Stevenson, Robert Louis	*Treasure Island*	Signet Classics
Wyss, Johann David	*The Swiss Family Robinson*	Sterling
Yates, Elizabeth	*Amos Fortune, Free Man*	Perfection Learning
Zim, H. S., and R. H. Baker	*Stars: A Guide to the Constellations, Sun, Moon, Planets, and Other Features of the Heavens*	Golden

PHONOGRAMS

THE WRITING ROAD TO READING introduces seventy common phonograms to all novice readers whether they are kindergarten children or adult disabled readers. Seventeen additional phonograms are introduced in the order needed for writing spelling words in the spelling/vocabulary notebook. To aid teachers, the first seventy phonograms, with their sounds, are listed on the following pages.

The seventy phonograms are listed in the order of *instruction*, as the left-hand column of the table indicates. Students of all ages first learn the sounds of the letters that begin at two on the clock; then they learn the sounds of the letters that begin with a line. The remainder of the phonograms are introduced in the order needed for writing spelling words in the spelling/vocabulary notebook. All seventy phonograms are introduced before students write words in section N. The chart just below identifies the phonograms needed to write and read words in sections A through Z in the Spelling/Vocabulary Word List.

Phonogram Numbers	Phonograms	Notebook Sections
1–45	*a* through *ea*	A–G
46 through 53	*aw* through *ui*	H and I
54 through 62	*oa* through *gn*	J and K
63 through 70	*wr* through *ci*	L and M
71 through 87	*tch* through *pn*	L through Z

The middle column of the table lists the symbols that represent phonogram sounds and sample words that illustrate correct pronunciation. The sample words are given as an aid to the teacher's pronunciation; they are not to be memorized by students as *key* words. When a phonogram represents more than one sound, the sounds are listed in the order of frequency of use. The phonogram sounds should be *precise* (short, clipped) so students will recognize phonograms in words they read. Vowel and consonant sounds should not be elongated (e.g., aaaa or ssss); and vowel sounds should not be added to consonant sounds (e.g., *buh* for /b/). If pronunciation is not precise, it affects students' written reviews and their spelling, writing, and reading lessons.

The right-hand column of the table provides instructional tips: (1) directions for pronouncing phonogram sounds precisely and (2) information to help students pronounce and spell words. For example, children learn that phonogram *a* says /ă/ when it is a *closed* syllable, i.e., when it is followed by one or more consonants (*at, bath*); and that it usually says /ā/ at the end of a syllable (*na vy*), but that it *may* say /ah/ at the end of a syllable (*fa ther*), after *w* (*want*), and before *l* (*al so*). During phonogram reviews, children discuss and explain how phonograms work in words. Rules are taught, but students do not memorize the rules by rote. Rather, they explain the reason for using a phonogram when more than one is possible.

Phonograms (In order of instruction)	Sounds/Sample Words	Instructional Tips
a	Sound each separately. ă at ā na̱ vy ah fa̱ **the̱r**	**1** *a usually* says *ā* at the end of a syllable (rule 4). *a may* say *ah* at the end of a syllable, after a *w*, and before an *l*.
c	Sound each separately. k can s cent	**2** *c* before *e, i,* or *y* says *s* but followed by any other letter says *k* (rule 2).
d	d lid	**3** Press tip of tongue against upper ridge behind teeth, then voice sound. Keep jaw still.
f	f if	**4** Gently bite on lower lip and blow (unvoiced).
g	Sound each separately. g bag j gem	**5** *g* before *e, i,* or *y may* say *j* and followed by any other letter says *g* (rule 3).
o	Sound each separately. ŏ odd ō o̱ pen o͞o dŏ	**6** *o usually* says *ō* at the end of a syllable (rule 4). *o may* say *ō (most)* when followed by two consonants (rule 19).
s	Sound each separately. s us z aš	**7**

Phonograms (In order of instruction)	Sounds/Sample Words	Instructional Tips
qu	*kw* qu̲it	**8** Raise back of tongue to soft palate and release breath (unvoiced). *q* is always followed by *u* saying the consonant sound *w* (rule 1).
b	*b* rib	**9** Close lips to form a line, then voice sound.
e	Sound each separately. *ĕ* **end** *ē* **me̲**	**10** *e usually* says *ē* at the end of a syllable (rule 4).
h	*h* **him**	**11** Open mouth and release breath (unvoiced).
i	Sound each separately. *ĭ* **big** *ī* **sḭ lent**	**12** *i usually* says *ĭ* (rule 5). *i may* say *ī* at the end of a syllable (rule 5). *i may* say *ī (find)* when followed by two consonants (rule 19).
j	*j* **jam**	**13** Keep jaw still.
k	*k* **ink**	**14**
l	*l* **lag**	**15** Broaden tip of tongue against ridge behind teeth and voice sound.

Phonograms (In order of instruction)	Sounds/Sample Words		Instructional Tips
m	*m*	ham	16 Close lips and voice sound.
n	*n*	win	17 Press tongue against roof of mouth and voice sound.
p	*p*	map	18 Close lips to form line, then release breath (unvoiced).
r	*r*	rat	19 Move back of tongue upward and back at the same time forming contact with upper molars and back edges of tongue. Keep position and voice sound. (*r* is not pronounced *er.*)
t	*t*	bat	20 Press tongue against roof of mouth and release breath (unvoiced).
u	Sound each separately. ŭ up ū mu̱²sic o͝o pu̱³t		21 *u usually* says *ū* at the end of a syllable (rule 4).
v	*v*	viv id	22 Gently bite on lower lip and voice sound (feel vibration). Teach students to hear and feel the difference between *f* and *v*.
w	*w*	wit	23 Round lips, then release breath while voicing sound. Keep jaw still. (*w* is not pronounced *wh*.)

Phonograms (In order of instruction)	Sounds/Sample Words	Instructional Tips
x	*ks* **box**	**24** *x* has two sounds blended.
y	Sound each separately. *y* **yet** *ĭ* **gym** *ī* **m̲y̲**	**25** The consonant sound *y* is used *only* at the beginning of a syllable, *usually* the first one. *y usually* says *ĭ*, but *may* say *ī (my)* at the end of a syllable (rule 5). *y*, not *i*, is used at the end of English words (rule 6).
z	*z* **zest**	**26** Words beginning with the sound *z* are *always* spelled with a *z*, never an *s* (rule 27).
sh	*sh* **di̲s̲h**	**27** *sh* is used at the beginning or end of a base word, at the end of a syllable, but not at the beginning of a syllable after the first one except for the ending *ship* (rule 13).
ee	*ē* **s̲e̲e**	**28**
th	Sound each separately. *th* **t̲h̲in** *th* **t̲h̲is** (2)	**29** Place extreme tip of tongue barely between teeth and release breath (unvoiced). Place extreme tip of tongue barely between teeth and release breath with voice (feel vibration).
ow	Sound each separately. *ow* **h̲o̲w** *ō* **l̲o̲w** (2)	**30**

Phonograms (In order of instruction)	Sounds/Sample Words Sound each separately.		Instructional Tips	
ou	*ow*	r**ou**nd		31
	$\bar{o}$	s**ou**l [2]		
	$\overline{oo}$	y**ou** [3]		
	$\breve{u}$	c**ou**n try [4]	Pronounce as in *up*.	
oo	Sound each separately.			32
	$\overline{oo}$	b**oo**t		
	$o\breve{o}$	f**oo**t [2]		
ch	Sound each separately.			33
	ch	mu**ch**		
	k	s**ch**ool [2]		
	sh	**ch**ef [3]		
ar	*ar*	f**ar**		34
ay	$\bar{a}$	d**ay**		35
ai	$\bar{a}$	p**ai**nt		36
oy	*oy*	b**oy**	Say quickly with one impulse of voice.	37
oi	*oi*	p**oi**nt	Say quickly with one impulse of voice.	38
er	*er*	h**er**		39
ir	*ir*	f**ir**st		40
ur	*ur*	n**ur**se [5]		41

Phonograms (In order of instruction)	Sounds/Sample Words	Instructional Tips
wor	*wor* w<u>or</u>ks	**42** *wor* has two phonograms or *may* say *er* after *w* (rule 8).
ear	*er* <u>ear</u> ly	**43**
ng	*ng* ra<u>ng</u>	**44** Raise back of tongue as if to say *k*. Keep position, and voice sound through nose (nasal). Do not pronounce *g*.
ea	Sound each separately. *ē* <u>ea</u>t *ĕ* h<u>ĕa</u>d *ā* br<u>ēa</u>k	**45**
aw	*aw* l<u>aw</u>	**46** Drop jaw and resonate from vocal cords.
au	*au* <u>au</u> thor	**47** Drop jaw and resonate from vocal cords.
or	*or* f<u>or</u>	**48**
ck	*k* ne<u>ck</u>	**49**
wh	*wh* <u>wh</u>en	**50** Blow softly on palm of hand. Air should be felt in saying *wh*. (*wh* is not pronounced *w*.)
ed	Sound each separately. *ĕd* grad <u>ed</u> *d* lov<u>ĕd</u> *t* <u>wr</u>e<u>ck</u> <u>ĕd</u>	**51** Keep jaw still. Keep jaw still.

Phonograms (In order of instruction)	Sounds/Sample Words	Instructional Tips	
ew	Sound each separately. $\overline{oo}$ gr<u>ew</u> $\bar{u}$ f<u>ew</u> (2)	Sound the same as *ui*.	52
ui	Sound each separately. $\overline{oo}$ fr<u>ui</u>t $\bar{u}$ s<u>ui</u>t (2)	Sound the same as *ew*.	53
oa	$\bar{o}$ b<u>oa</u>t		54
gu	*g* <u>gu</u>ess		55
ph	*f* <u>ph</u>one	Gently bite on lower lip and blow (unvoiced).	56
ough	Sound each separately. $\bar{o}$ th<u>ough</u> (2) $\overline{oo}$ thr<u>ough</u> (2) $\breve{u}f$ r<u>ough</u> (3) $\breve{o}f$ c<u>ough</u> (4) aw th<u>ough</u>t (5) ow dr<u>ough</u>t (6)		57
oe	$\bar{o}$ t<u>oe</u>		58
ey	Sound each separately. $\bar{a}$ th<u>ey</u> (2) $\bar{e}$ k<u>ey</u> (2) $\breve{i}$ val l<u>ey</u> (3)		59
igh	$\bar{i}$ s<u>igh</u>		60
kn	*n* <u>kn</u>ot	Press tongue against roof of mouth and voice sound.	61

Phonograms (In order of instruction)	Sounds/Sample Words	Instructional Tips	
gn	*n* **si̱g̱n**	Press tongue against roof of mouth and voice sound.	62
wr	*r* **w̱ṟap**	Move back of tongue upward and back at the same time forming contact with upper molars and back edges of tongue. Keep position and voice sound. (*r* is not pronounced *er.*)	63
ie	Sound each separately. *ē* **fie̱ld** *ī* **pie̱** *ĭ* **lil ie̱s**		64
dge	*j* **bri̱ḏg̱e**	Keep jaw still.	65
ei	Sound each separately. *ē* **con ce̱it** *ā* **ve̱il** *ĭ* **for fe̱it**		66
eigh	*ā* **we̱ig̱ẖ**		67
ti	*sh* **na̱ ti̱on**		68
si	Sound each separately. *sh* **ses si̱on** *zh* **vi si̱on**		69
ci	*sh* **fa̱ ci̱al**		70

PHONOGRAM REVIEWS AND CUE WORDS

PROVIDE DAILY ORAL AND WRITTEN PHONOGRAM REVIEWS immediately after introducing phonograms in the grade-appropriate sequence provided in the "Planning" section of the *Kindergarten Through Sixth-Grade Teacher Guides*. One purpose of the daily oral phonogram review (OPR) is to practice *precise* pronunciation of the sound or sounds of each phonogram. Another purpose is to teach students which phonogram to write when more than one phonogram represents the same sound.

Review the sounds of the first twenty-six phonograms using the instructional strategies and procedure for OPR Step 1 in the "Delivering" section of the grade-appropriate *Teacher's Guide*. Begin Step 2 OPR after multiletter phonograms have been introduced.

1. During OPR Step 2, show the phonograms a second time. When two phonograms represent the same sound (*ay/ai*), stop and explain. In the case of *ay* and *ai*, for example, *ay* is often *used at the end of a word*, but *ai* is *not used*, because English words do not end in *i*. Teach students the cue words listed below so they will know which phonogram to write during the written phonogram review (WPR).

2. Do not have students memorize a rule by rote. Rather, ask questions that check their knowledge and understanding; e.g., show *ay* and ask, "Where may I use this phonogram?" In this example, students should respond, "At the end of English words."

3. After students understand a rule, ask questions that require them to apply it to words not previously written in their notebooks; e.g., show *ai* and ask, "May I use this phonogram in the word *play*? Why or why not?" Students should respond in this case, "No. The sound /ai/ occurs at the end."

4. Explain that during WPR you will dictate the sound, they will say it, and then you will give the cue word they have been taught. They will say the sound softly again just before they write the phonogram. Note that a phonogram may have more than one sound.

Number(s)	Phonogram(s)	Cues/Rules	WPR Cues
1–26	*Single letters*	none	none
27–34	*sh, ee, th, ow, ou, oo, ch, ar*	none	none
35	*ay*	"used at the end of a word"	Say sound only.
36	*ai*	"not used at the end of a word, because English words do not end in *i*"	not used
37	*oy*	"used at the end of a word"	Say sound only.
38	*oi*	"not used at the end of a word, because English words do not end in *i*"	not used
39–43	*er, ir, ur, wor, ear*	"word" (*her, first, nurse, early*)	*her, first, nurse, early* ("*wor*" does not need cue.)
44–45	*ng, ea*	none	none
46	*aw*	"used at the end of a word"	Say sound only.
47	*au*	"not used at the end of a word, because English words do not end in *u*"	not used
48	*or*	none	none
49	*ck*	2 letters "used after a single vowel that says its first sound"	2 letters
50–51	*wh, ed*	none	none
52	*ew*	"used at the end of a word"	Say sound only.

Number(s)	Phonogram(s)	Cues/Rules	WPR Cues
53	*ui*	"not used at the end of a word, because English words do not end in *i*"	not used
54	*oa*	"word" (*boat*)	*boat*
55	*gu*	none	none
56	*ph*	2 letters	2 letters
57	*ough*	none	none
58	*oe*	"word" (initially *toe*)	none
59	*ey*	none	none
60	*igh*	3 letters (initially)	none
61	*kn*	2 letters "used only at the beginning of a word"	2 letters—beginning
62	*gn*	2 letters "used at the beginning or end of a word"	2 letters
63	*wr*	2 letters	2 letters
64	*ie*	none	none
65	*dge*	3 letters "used after a single vowel that says its first sound"	3 letters
66	*ei*	none	none
67	*eigh*	4 letters	4 letters
68	*ti*	tall	tall
69	*si*	none	none
70	*ci*	short	short

Number(s)	Phonogram(s)	Cues/Rules	WPR Cues
71	*tch*	3 letters "used after a single vowel that says its first sound in a 1-syllable word"	Say sound only.
72	*eo*	"word" (*people*)	*people*
73	*eau*	3 letters	3 letters
74	*augh*	4 letters	4 letters
75	*ce*	"word" (*ocean*)	*ocean*
76	*gh*	"word" (*ghost*)	*ghost*
77	*gi*	"word" (*region*)	*region*
78	*our*	"word" (*journey*)	*journey*
79	*di*	"word" (*soldier*)	*soldier*
80	*cu*	"word" (*biscuit*)	*biscuit*
81	*aigh*	"word" (*straight*)	*straight*
82	*sc*	"word" (*scene*)	*scene*
83	*ge*	"word" (*pigeon*)	*pigeon*
84	*rh*	"word" (*rhyme*)	*rhyme*
85	*eu*	none	none
86	*sci*	"word" (*conscientious*)	*conscientious*
87	*pn*	"word" (*pneumonia*)	*pneumonia*

RULES OF PRONUNCIATION, SPELLING, AND LANGUAGE

FOR CONVENIENT REFERENCE, all rules introduced in *The Writing Road to Reading* are listed here, by *rule number* and *rule page*. The rule number is followed by the rule, explanations, instructional tips, and example words as needed.

For beginners of any age, rules that apply to phonogram pronunciation and spelling (rules 1–8, 12–20, 23, 25, 27, 29) are introduced, practiced, and reviewed in the spelling lesson. Language rules (rules 9–11, 21–22, 24, 26, 28) are introduced in the writing lesson before they are needed to spell words that illustrate the rules. Students apply all rules when spelling words and when writing sentences and compositions.

For kindergarten through second-grade students, the teacher demonstrates how the rules work in words. Children then write the words that illustrate each rule in their primary notebooks. Students in grade three and above write words that illustrate the first sixteen rules in the first six pages of the intermediate spelling/vocabulary notebook. All students learn to apply the rules by participating in practice activities described in Chapter 2.

Students need daily practice in applying the rules. Just memorizing a rule does not mean students understand or are able to apply it. Spalding Word Builder Cards (see "Resources") are used to provide guided and independent practice of rules 9, 10, 11, 21, 22, and 24.

Rule Page 1 (Rules 1–7)

1. The letter *q* is always followed by *u* and together they say *kw* (*queen*). The *u* is not considered a vowel here.
2. The letter *c* before *e*, *i*, or *y* says *s* (*cent, city, cycle*), but followed by any other letter it says *k* (*cat, cot, cut*).

   The *c* is not numbered, because the letter following *c* identifies the sound.
3. The letter *g* before *e*, *i*, or *y* may say *j* (*page, giant, gym*), but followed by any other letter it says *g* (*gate, go, gust*). The letters *e* and *i* following *g* do not always make the *g* say *j* (*get, girl, give*).

   The *g* is not numbered, because the letter following *g* usually identifies the sound.
4. Vowels *a*, *e*, *o*, and *u* usually say *ā*, *ē*, *ō*, and *ū* at the end of a syllable (*na vy, me, o pen, mu sic*).

   This rule helps students pronounce the vowel correctly in unfamiliar vowel-consonant-vowel (vcv) words (*re port*).
5. The letters *i* and *y* usually say *ĭ* (*big, gym*), but may say *ī* (*si lent, my, type*).
6. The letter *y*, not *i*, is used at the end of an English word (*my*).
7. There are five kinds of silent final *e*'s. (In short words such as *me*, *she*, and *he*, the *e* says *ē*, but in longer words where a single *e* appears at the end, the *e* is silent.
   We retain the first four kinds of silent *e*'s because we need them. (See Chapter 2.) The fifth kind is probably a relic from Old English.

   The abbreviation for rule 7 is not written in student notebooks, but the job of the silent final *e* is marked for each word as encountered. During dictation, including reading of the Spelling/Vocabulary words, for spelling, the silent *e*'s are sounded (*t ī m ē*).

Rule Page 2 (Rule 8)

8. There are five spellings for the sound *er*. The phonogram *or* may say *er* when it follows w (*work*).

   During phonogram reviews and in reading multisyllable Spelling/Vocabulary words, for spelling, students say the blended sound *wer*. When reading or writing one-syllable words (*work*) in the notebook, students say *wer k*. (They learn that the *w* influences the sound of *or*.) It is helpful for primary teachers to use the Primary Rule Page 2 poster for the five spellings of *er*. Add each word that uses one of the five spellings when encountered in the Spelling/Vocabulary Word List.

Rule Page 3 (Rules 9–10)

9. For *one*-syllable words that have *one* vowel and end in *one* consonant (*hop*), write another final consonant (*hop + ped*) before adding suffixes (endings) that begin with a vowel. (Referring to rule 9 as the one-one-one rule helps students remember the criteria for applying the rule. This rule does not apply to words ending in *x* because *x* has two sounds.)
10. Words of *two* syllables (*begin*) in which the second syllable (*gin*) is accented and ends in *one* consonant, with *one* vowel before it, need another final consonant

(*be gin´* + *ning*) before adding a suffix (ending) that begins with a vowel. (Refer to rule 10 as the two-one-one rule. This rule is applied more consistently in American English than in British English.)

Rule Page 4 (Rule 11)

11. Words ending with a silent final *e* (*come*) are written without the *e* when adding a suffix (ending) that begins with a vowel.

Rule Page 5 (Rule 12)

12. After *c* we use *ei* (*receive*). If we say *a,* we use *ei* (*vein*). In the list of exceptions, we use *ei*. In all other words, the phonogram *ie* is used.

Rule Page 6 (Rules 13–16)

13. The phonogram *sh* is used at the beginning or end of a base word (*she, dish*), at the end of a syllable (*fin ish*), but never at the beginning of a syllable after the first one except for the suffix (ending) *ship* (*wor ship, friend ship*).

14. The phonograms *ti, si,* and *ci* are the spellings most frequently used to say *sh* at the beginning of a second or subsequent syllable in a base word (*na tion, ses sion, fa cial*).

15. The phonogram *si* is used to say *sh* when the syllable before it ends in an *s* (*ses sion*) or when the base word has an *s* where the base word changes (*tense, ten sion*).

16. The phonogram *si* may also say *zh,* as in *vi sion*.

Additional Rules (Rules 17–29)

17. We often double *l, f,* and *s* following a single vowel at the end of a one-syllable word (*will, off, miss*). Rule 17 sometimes applies to two-syllable words like *recess.*
    While reading the word (e.g., *will*) for spelling, students say the extra consonant sound (e.g., *w i l l*).

18. We often use *ay* to say *ā* at end of a base word, never *a* alone.
    Students just say the sound *ā*.

19. Vowels *i* and *o* may say *ī* and *ō* if followed by two consonants (*find, old*).

20. The letter *s* almost never follows *x*. The phonogram *x* includes an *s* sound (*ks*).

21. *All,* written alone, has two *l*'s, but when it is written with another syllable, only one *l* is written (*al so, al most*).

22. *Till* and *full,* written alone, have two *l*'s, but when they are written with another syllable, only one *l* is written (*un til, beau ti ful*).
    Students also need practice explaining how the addition of these suffixes (endings) changes word meanings and usage.

23. The phonogram *dge* may be used *only* after a single vowel that says *ă, ĕ, ĭ, ŏ,* or *ŭ* (*badge, edge, bridge, lodge, budge*).

24. When adding a suffix (ending) to a word that ends with a consonant and *y,* use *i* instead of *y* unless the ending is *ing.*
    Students also need practice explaining how the addition of these suffixes (endings)

changes word meanings and usage (plurals of nouns: *baby/babies;* verb tense: *try/tried*).

25. The phonogram *ck* may be used only after a single vowel that says ă, ĕ, ĭ, ŏ, or ŭ (*back, neck, lick, rock, duck*).

26. Words that are the names or titles of people, places, books, days, or months are capitalized (*Mary, Honolulu, Amazon River, Bible, Monday, July*).

    Initially, students need to explain their use of capitals so they do not use them indiscriminately.

27. Words *beginning* with the sound *z* are always spelled with *z*, never *s* (*zoo*).

28. The phonogram *ed* has three sounds and is used to form the past tense of verbs. If the verb ends in the sound *d* or *t*, adding *ed* makes another syllable that says *ed* (*hand ed, land ed, paint ed, plant ed*). If the verb ends in an unvoiced consonant, the suffix (ending) *ed* says *t* (*looked, liked, jumped, washed*). In all other verbs, the suffix (ending) *ed* says *d* (*lived, killed, played, belonged*).

29. Words are usually divided between double consonants within a base word.

    During dictation of words, have students pronounce both consonants to spell the words correctly. When reading words for reading, have students read double-consonant words in normal speech.

MORPHOLOGY

MORPHOLOGY is the study of the structure of words. The Greek word *morpheme* means the smallest unit of meaning in a word. As children progress through the grades, they encounter thousands of words they have not been directly taught. To be independent readers, they must be able to accurately and automatically pronounce (decode) words so they can connect these words with their spoken vocabulary or identify them as unfamiliar. Knowing English word structure facilitates rapid pronunciation of unfamiliar multisyllable words because the arrangement of vowels and consonants influences the vowel sounds.

Definitions

The following definitions provide a common vocabulary during class discussions of word structure.

- A *base word* is a unit of meaning that can stand alone (e.g., *book*) and is the foundation for many related words when affixes are added (e.g., *book, books; please, pleas ant, un pleas ant; cov er, cov er ing, re cov ered*).
- A *word root* is a unit of meaning derived from other languages that cannot stand alone but is the foundation for many English words when affixes are added. About 60 percent of all English words have Latin or Greek origins (e.g., *re port, re port ed, re port ing*).
- A *prefix* is a letter or group of letters added to the beginning of a base word or word root to change the meaning completely (*un happy*) or to clarify by making the word more specific (*re cover*).
- A *suffix* is a letter or a group of letters added to the end of a base word or word root. Suffixes may add information to the meaning of the word (*help ful*), or they may indicate number (*boys*), time (*lat er*), part of speech (*catch/catch er*), and tense (*com ing*).
- A *syllable* is a single word or the part of a word that is pronounced by a single impulse of the voice. There is at least one vowel in every syllable (e.g., *a, at, cat*).

Syllable Types

- An *open syllable* ends with a vowel. The vowel *usually* says its second sound (commonly called long: *me*). Examples follow:

  - 1 vowel   a, I
  - 1 consonant + 1 vowel   me, do, go, so
  - 1 multiletter consonant sound + 1 vowel   s<u>he</u>, <u>the</u>
  - 1 consonant + 1 multiletter vowel sound   s<u>ee</u>, n<u>ow</u>, y<u>ou</u>

- A *closed syllable* has one or more consonants following a single vowel or multiletter vowel sound. A single vowel usually says its first sound (short: *and*). Examples follow:

  - 1 vowel + 1 consonant   at, on, it, is
  - 1 vowel + 2 consonants   and, old, all, will, last, must
  - 1 consonant + 1 vowel + 1 consonant   can, run, man, ten, tan, tin
  - 2-letter vowel sound + 1 consonant   <u>out</u>, <u>oil</u>
  - 1 consonant, 2 letter vowel sound +   g<u>oo</u>d, y<u>our</u>, l<u>oo</u>k, b<u>ir</u>d, f<u>ee</u>d,
    1 consonant
  - 2-letter consonant sound + 1 vowel +   <u>th</u>is, <u>ch</u>ip
    1 consonant
  - 2 or 3 consonants + 1 vowel sound +   str<u>ee</u>t, gr<u>ee</u>n
    1 consonant
  - 2-letter consonant sound + 1 vowel +   <u>ch</u>ild, <u>th</u>ank, <u>th</u>ink
    2 consonants

- A *syllable* with a *silent final e* has one vowel followed by one or more consonants and a silent final *e*. The single vowel usually says its second sound. Examples follow:

  - 1 consonant + 1 vowel + 1 consonant +   time, like, make, late
    1 silent final *e*
  - 1 consonant + 1 vowel + 2 consonants +   paste, fence, waste
    1 silent final *e*

- A *consonant + le syllable* has one consonant followed by *le*. The *e* is silent. Examples follow:

  - open syllable + *ble, cle, dle, fle, gle, kle,*   a•ble, <u>ea</u>•gle, bi•cy•cle
    ple, sle, tle, zle
  - closed syllable + *ble, cle, dle, fle, gle, kle,*   lit•tle, an•kle, ap•ple
    ple, sle, tle, zle

Syllable Division Patterns

Knowing common syllable patterns also facilitates rapid pronunciation of unfamiliar words. Syllable patterns that help students decode unfamiliar words are listed in the order of *introduction*.

1. In a consonant + *le* pattern (c + *le*), the word is divided before the consonant plus *le*.

   lit•tle (A–G)   ap •ple (H)   a•ble (L)   gen•tle (M)   un•cle (O)

2. In a vowel-consonant-vowel (vcv) or consonant-vowel (cv) pattern, the word is divided after the first vowel.

   o•ver (A–G)   be•long (H)   pa•per (I)   ze•ro (I)   be•tween (K)

   Vowels *a, e, o, u* usually say /ă/, /ē/, /ō/, /ū/ at the end of a syllable (rule 4). Vowels *i* and *y* *usually* say /ĭ/ (*big, gym*), but they may say /ī/ (*si•lent, my*: rule 5).

3. In a consonant-vowel-consonant (cvc) or vowel-consonant (vc) pattern, the word is divided after the consonant that follows the vowel.

   riv•er (I)   ver•y (I)   sev•en (J)   cov•er (J)   an•y (K)

4. A compound word (cw) is divided between the base words.

   in•to (A–G)   to•day (A–G)   Sun•day (I)   in•side (J)   af•ter•noon (K)

   If either base word has more than one syllable (afternoon), divide it as a single word.

5. Multiletter phonograms (digraphs/diphthongs/*r*-controlled vowels) are *not* divided regardless of other patterns, such as vcv or vccv.

   moth•er (A–G)   oth•er (H)   au•thor (H)   broth•er (K)   flow•er (L)

   Demonstrate the *sound* of the word if the letters in a multiletter phonogram (phg) were mistakenly divided.

   (mot•her   ot•her   aut•hor   brot•her   flo•wer)

6. In a vowel-consonant-consonant-vowel (vccv) pattern, the word is usually divided between the consonants.

   yel•low (H)   win•ter (I)   let•ter (I)   din•ner (I)   hap•py (J)

   In a vowel-consonant-consonant-consonant-vowel (vcccv) pattern the word is usually divided after the first consonant in the series.

   coun•try (L)   con•tract (M)   dis•trict (O)   ad•dress (O)   en•trance (P)

7. Prefixes (p) *always* include vowels, making them separate syllables.

   re•port (J)   ex•tra (M)   un•a•ble (M)   re•cov•er (M)   re•turn (M)

8. Suffixes (s) usually include vowels, making them separate syllables.

   plant•ed (I)   on•ly (K)   set•ting (K)   com•ing (K)   eas•y (K)

   The suffix *ed* forms a separate syllable in only one case: when the base word ends in the sound /d/ or /t/ (*ground ed, plant ed*). The suffix *y* often combines with the preceding consonant to form a syllable (*guil•ty*).

9. In a vowel-vowel pattern, adjacent vowels that are not muliletter phonograms form separate syllables.

   tri • al (P)   pe •ri •od (Q)

Tip: When more than one pattern explains a division, either is correct. Example: re•port (vcv and/or p). Older students or gifted primary-grade students may recognize that *re* is a prefix (p).

PRIMARY AND INTERMEDIATE SPELLING/VOCABULARY NOTEBOOKS—SAMPLE PAGES

DURING CONSTRUCTION of the primary and intermediate spelling/vocabulary notebooks, children learn to analyze the *written* spelling of high-frequency words, using their minds to apply the rules of the language, not rote memorization. Construction of the notebook, therefore, is the central activity for student achievement in this method because it is the foundation for other language arts instruction.

Primary Notebook

Children in kindergarten through grade two write the Spalding Spelling/Vocabulary words in a *sewn* pink-and-white, stiff-cover composition book containing thirty-four leaves, each having twelve lines with ⅝-inch (1.6-cm) spacing. Writing the words in manuscript begins on page 1 of the primary notebook after children have learned the first forty-five phonograms and developed fine-motor skills—usually about midyear for kindergarten children and after three or four weeks for first-grade children. While kindergartners are developing fine-motor skills, the teacher writes words in sections A–G on chart paper or the board, as illustrated on example pages 229–234. Children read the words for spelling and for reading. Kindergartners write sections A–I in their notebooks. The more words children analyze and read from their notebooks, the faster they become independent readers. Second-grade children are pretested to determine where to begin dictation in the Spelling/Vocabulary Word List.

1

A-G	
me r.4	can
do³	see
and	run
go r.4	the² r.4
at	in
on	so r.4
a r.4	no r.4
it	now
is²	man
she r.4	

2	
ten	an
tan	my r.5, 6
tin	up
ton	last
bed	not
top	us
he r.4	am
you	good
will r.17	
we r.4	

3

t<u>ime</u>	<u>red</u>
h<u>ave</u>=₂ blu<u>e</u>=₂	<u>of</u>=
<u>chance</u>=₃ <u>charge</u>=₃	b<u>e</u> r.4
lit tl<u>e</u>=₄	but
<u>are</u>=₅ (no job e)	[2]<u>th</u>is
	³<u>a</u>ll r.17
lit tl<u>e</u>=₄	³[y<u>our</u>
<u>a</u> g<u>o</u> r.4	³[y<u>ou</u>
<u>old</u> r.19	<u>out</u>
<u>bad</u>	t<u>ime</u>

4

may r.18	by r.5,6
in to³	have₂
him	are₅
to³ day r.18	had
look²	o ver r.4
did	must
like	make
six	street
boy	say r.18
book²	come₅

	5
hand	[big
ring	bag
[live	beg
[live₌₂	bog
kill r.17	[bug
late	moth er
let	three
	land
	cold r.19
	hot

6

<u>h</u>at	<u>f</u>ur
<u>ch</u>ild r.19	<u>gr</u>een
<u>i</u>ce	<u>oi</u>l
<u>pl</u>ay r.18	<u>p</u>aint
⌈ <u>s</u>ea	<u>p</u>ool
⌊ <u>s</u>ee	⌈ <u>t</u>ooth
<u>b</u>ird	⌊ <u>t</u>eeth
<u>c</u>ool	<u>w</u>orm r.8
<u>e</u>arth	
<u>f</u>eed	

Intermediate Notebook

Students in grade three and above write words in a *sewn* blue-and-white, hardcover composition book, containing fifty leaves, each having twenty-three lines with ⅜-inch (1.0-cm) spacing. The intermediate notebook has two parts: rule pages and the Spalding Spelling/Vocabulary Word List. Rule pages, including phonograms and example words for the first sixteen rules, multiletter phonograms, and additional, less common phonograms, are illustrated on pages 237–251. See Chapter 2 for detailed procedures for teaching each rule page.

Older students begin writing spelling/vocabulary words after they have learned to say and write all seventy phonograms in manuscript and cursive writing and have written all numbers. Pretest to determine in which section of the Spalding Spelling/Vocabulary Word List to begin dictation. Students begin writing the spelling/vocabulary words in the middle of the notebook, where the stitching makes it open easily. (See Chapter 3, page 151, for pretest procedures.)

1

Consonants

b c d f g h j k l m n p qu r s t v w x y z
c before e, i or y says $\overset{2}{c}$
g before e, i or y may say $\overset{2}{g}$

Vowels^2

a	at	na vy	fâ ther
e	end	me	
i	{ big	si lent	
y	{ gym	my	
o	odd	o pen	dŏ
u	up	mu šic	pŭt

silent
final e's
{ time
have   blue
chance   charge
lit tle
are (no job e)

Her	first	nurse =5
serve =2	sir	turn
herd	bird	hurt
dinner	third	burn
perfect	girl	church
nerve =2	fir	fur
berth	birth	purpose
western	skirt	surprise =5
merge =3	circle =4	hurdle =4
grocery	firm	Thursday
perch	thirst	Saturday
sterling	squirt	further
verse	squirm	disturb
clerk =5	chirp	curtain
certain	confirm	curve =2

2

works   early.

worm   learn
word   heard
world   search
worth   earn
wor thy   earth
worse   ear nest
  worst   pearl
worry   rehearse
worship

hop	hopping
set	set ting
run	running
red	red dish
hot	hot test
mud	mud dy
flat	flat ten
writ	writ ten
ship	shipped [3] shipper
stop	stopped [3] stopper

	ing	ice	[4] ous
	er	ish	ist
Endings which	3 ed	age	i ble
begin with a	est	{ance	{able [4]
vowel	y	{ant [3]	{a bly [4]
	al	{ence	{ancy
	en	{ent [3]	{ency

3

be̱gin′   be̱gin ning

for̲got′   for̲got ten
con trŏl′   con trol la ble ₌₄
oc cur′   oc cur rence ₌₃
ex cel′   ex celled̂
ad mit′   ad mit tance ₌₃
trans mit′   trans mit ter
ac quit′   ac quit tal
o̱ mit′   o̱ mit ted

en′ter   en ter ing
prof′it   prof it a̱ ble ₌₄
brid′get   brid get ed
ed′it   ed it ing

hope   hoping

come	coming
fierce	fiercest
write	writer
change	changed
serve	service
nerve	nervous
desire	desirable
settle	settling
ease	easy
rehearse	rehearsal

Endings beginning with a vowel

ing	ice	ous
er	ish	ist
ed	age	ible
est	ance	able
y	ant	ably
al	ence	ancy
en	ent	ency
or		

4

ie	cei
believe	receive
belief	perceive
fierce	ceiling
brief	receipt
niece	conceit
priest	
field	
chief	
siege	
achieve	
piece	
pie	
lie	
prairie	
mischief	
friend	

5

ei says "ā"   Exceptions[2]

their   Neither
veil   foreign
heir   sovereign
{ rein   seized (the)
{ reign   counterfeit (and)
vein   forfeited
surveillance   leisure.
skein

                               either
                               weird
                               protein
                               heifer

ti	si
na tion	ses sion
col lec tion	com pres sion
po ten tial	dis cus sion
pa tient	de pres sion
am bi tion	ad mis sion
sub stan tial	or
in fec tion	(tense) ten sion
in flu en tial	(manse) man sion
con fi den tial	
im par tial	
su per sti tious	si
tor ren tial	
pa la tial	vi sion
	di vi sion
	oc ca sion
	ex plo sion

6

ci

(face) facial
(space) spacious
(finance) financial

(music) musician
(electric) electrician
(physic) physician

social
special
especially
ancient
crucial
efficient
suspicious

Multiletter Phonograms

sh

ee

2 th

{ er
{ ir
{ ur
{ wor
{ ear

{ 2 ow
{ 4 ou

2 oo

3 ch

ar

{ ay
{ ai

{ oy
{ oi

ng

3 ea

{ aw
{ au

or

ck

wh

7

3 ed   { kn
                             { gn

{ 2 ew
{ 2 ui   wr

     oa   3 ie
                             3 ei

     qu
                             dge
     ph
                             eigh

6 ough
                             { ti
     oe   { 2 si
                             { ci

3 ey

igh

Additional Phonograms

tch	ca<u>tch</u>
eo	p<u>eo</u>ple₌₄
eau	b<u>eau</u>ty
augh	d<u>augh</u>ter
	<u>laugh</u>ter
ce	o<u>ce</u>an
gh	<u>gh</u>ost
gi	re<u>gi</u>on
our	j<u>our</u>ney³
di	sol<u>di</u>er

8

cu	bis**cui**t
aigh	str**aigh**t
sc	**sc**ene
ge	pi**ge**ons[2]
rh	**rh**yme
eu	**Eu**rope
sci	con**sci**en**tio**us[4]
pn	**pneu**m**o**ni**a**[3]

SPALDING SPELLING/ VOCABULARY WORD LIST: ORDER OF INSTRUCTION

THE SPALDING SPELLING/VOCABULARY (S/V) Word List consists of more than 2,300 high-frequency words. Chapter 2 describes in detail how S/V words are used to teach spelling, reinforce handwriting, and develop fluent word recognition. Chapter 2 also provides explicit, interactive, diagnostic procedures and example lessons for using these words to teach sentence construction and parts of speech. Below, the S/V words are listed in the order of instruction. Starting on page 404, S/V words are listed alphabetically, to facilitate lesson planning.

The basic 1,000 high-frequency words were compiled by Dr. Leonard P. Ayres at Columbia Teachers College. In this edition, additional words (*extensions*) either are included in the core vocabulary identified in the *Collins COBUILD English Dictionary* (1995) or provide practice with phonograms and rules. *Merriam-Webster's Collegiate Dictionary*, Eleventh Edition, is the authority for pronunciation and syllable division.

Dr. Ayres divided words by sections. The first seven sections, A through G, are combined in *The Writing Road to Reading* because there are so few words in these sections. Kindergartners, first-graders, and older severely disabled readers begin with sections A–G. First-graders are pretested to determine which rules and phonograms need to be emphasized. Second-grade students and older students are pretested to determine in which section to begin. (See Chapter 3, "Assessing Skills Mastery"; and the "Assessing" section in the *Kindergarten Through Sixth-Grade Teacher Guides*).

As noted above, the following table lists the S/V words in the order of instruction. In the left-hand column, the original words are printed in boldface type; additional words are printed in italics. Some words are bracketed together to demonstrate relationships that need to be taught in integrated spelling/writing lessons.

The middle column lists rules that apply to S/V words. In this edition, all rules are listed throughout sections A–Z for convenient reference and for use in lesson planning. This enables upper-grade teachers to quickly find words (in earlier sections of the S/V list) to use for additional rule practice.

The right-hand column lists instructional tips that provide facts specific to particular words or information needed for students' success (e.g., the correct phonogram to use when several are possible). Most words in the Spelling/Vocabulary Word List have a single pronunciation.

Alternative pronunciations and spellings are designated as British English (B.E.) and marked accordingly, as specified in the *Collins* COBUILD *English Dictionary*.

Instructional tips are based on the explicit, interactive, diagnostic model of instruction described in Chapter 2. Initially, teachers *model*: they provide complete information to prevent students from making errors. Then, they *coach*: they guide as students attempt to independently say, write, mark, and read each word. Finally, support is provided only when needed, so that students can do the thinking and responding. (For a detailed explanation of this progression from modeling by the teacher to independence on the part of the students, see Chapters 2 and 5.) *When students no longer need a tip, it should no longer be used.*

To facilitate students' independence, instructional tips are gradually phased out. If first-grade students complete writing section N, they are introduced to all 29 rules; *specific* tips are provided for the majority of words. However, beginning in section O, *specific* tips are provided only to avoid common errors of spelling or pronunciation, such as writing the wrong vowel in unaccented syllables and choosing the wrong phonogram among possible alternatives. To avoid repetition, *general tips* are provided only the *first* time they apply. There are four kinds of *general tips*:

1. General tip for rule 29 words: "Continue to require correct pronunciation for spelling and reading throughout the section."
2. General tip for words that have a final phonogram *y* saying /ĭ/: "Continue to require precise pronunciation of the vowel in the unaccented syllables throughout the section." (By section Z, this statement includes all vowels in the unaccented syllable.)
3. General tip for words that end in *ct*, *pt*, *bt*: "Continue to require precise pronunciation throughout the section."
4. General tip for base and derived words: "Continue to dictate the base word first throughout the section." (See Morphology, page 224, for the definition of a base word.)

SPALDING SPELLING/VOCABULARY WORD LIST

Sections A–G
113 Words for Spelling, Writing, and Reading

Spelling Word	Rule(s)	Instructional Tips
m<u>e</u>	r. 4	In *me,* the *e* says $\bar{e}$ at the end of a syllable. Remind children that a syllable is a word or part of a word that is said in one impulse (beat) of the voice.
dŏ³		After children say the sounds for *do,* say, "Use the phonogram that says $\breve{o}$, $\bar{o}$, $\overline{oo}$. Write a three above the <u>o</u> to show the third sound, $\overline{oo}$."
and		
g<u>o</u>	r. 4	In *go,* the *o* says $\bar{o}$ at the end of a syllable.
at		
on		
<u>a</u>	r. 4	In the word *a,* the *a* says $\bar{a}$ at the end of a syllable. Say $\bar{a}$ for spelling. In reading, the accent is almost never on the word *a* (*a man, a house*).
it		
iš²		After children say the sounds for *is,* say, "Use the phonogram that says *s, z.* Write a two above the *s* to show the second sound, *z.*"
<u>sh</u>e	r. 4	Underline the two-letter phonogram that says *sh* at the beginning of a word (r. 13). In *she,* the *e* says $\bar{e}$ at the end of a syllable.
can		In the word *can,* say, "Use the phonogram that says *k, s.*"

Spelling Word	Rule(s)	Instructional Tips
s**ee**		After children say the sounds for *see*, say, "Use the phonogram that says *ē*."
run		
²the	r. 4	After children say the sounds for *the*, say "Use the phonogram that says *th*, *t͡h*. Write two above and between the letters *t* and *h* to show the second sound, *t͡h*." For spelling, say *ē* distinctly. For reading, the *e* is not accented.
in		
s**o**	r. 4	In *so*, the *o* says *ō* at the end of a syllable.
n**o**	r. 4	In *no*, the *o* says *ō* at the end of a syllable.
n**ow**		After children say the sounds for *now*, say, "Use the phonogram that says *ow*, *ō*."
man		
ten *tan* *tin* *ton*		In *ten*, use the phonogram that says *ĕ*, *ē*. In *tan*, use *ă*, *ā*, *ah*. In *tin*, use *ĭ*, *ī*. In *ton*, use *ŏ*, *ō*, *o͞o*. Have children say *ŏ* precisely. British English (B.E.): *Ton* is colloquial.
bed		
top		
h**e**	r. 4	In *he*, the *e* says *ē* at the end of a syllable.

Spelling Word	Rule(s)	Instructional Tips
y$\overset{3}{\underline{ou}}$		After children say the sounds for *you*, say, "Use the phonogram that says *ow*, $\bar{o}$, $\overline{oo}$, $\breve{u}$. Write three above and between the *o* and *u* to show the third sound, $\overline{oo}$." (*You* is one of the few words that end with *ou*.)
will	r. 17	After children say the sounds for *will*, say, "Write another *l* because the *l* is often doubled following a single vowel at the end of a one-syllable word." For spelling, say both *l*'s.
w$\underline{e}$	r. 4	In *we*, the *e* says $\bar{e}$ at the end of a syllable.
an		
m$\underline{y}$	r. 5, 6	In *my*, the *y* may say $\bar{\imath}$. The letter *y*, not *i*, is used at the end of an English word.
up		
last		B.E.: l$\overset{3}{\breve{a}}$st.
not		
us		
am		
g$\overset{2}{\underline{oo}}$d		After children say the sounds for *good*, say, "Use the phonogram that says $\overline{oo}$, $\breve{oo}$. Write two above and between the *o*'s to show the second sound, $\breve{oo}$."

Spelling Word	Rule(s)	Instructional Tips
time ha<u>v</u>e₂ blu<u>e</u>₂ <u>ch</u>an<u>ce</u>₃ char<u>ge</u>₌₃ lit tl<u>e</u>₄ <u>are</u>₅ (no job e)		Rule 7 explains silent final *e*'s. The *e* lets the *i* say *ī* (job 1). English words do not end in *v* or *u* (job 2). The *e* lets *c* say *s* and *g* say *j* (job 3). Every syllable must have a vowel (job 4). Remnant of Old English (job 5).
lit tl<u>e</u>₄		Use two hands to demonstrate two syllables (two impulses of the voice). Children say *lit* and write *lit*, then say *tle* and write *tle* (job 4). For spelling, be sure they say both *t*'s (rule 29).
<u>a</u> g<u>o</u>	r. 4	Children say *ā* and write it, then *go* and write it. Say *ā* for spelling, but accent *go* when reading.
old	r. 19	In *old*, the *o* says *ō* because it is followed by two consonants. It is not necessary to write the two above *o*, because rule 19 explains which sound is used.
bad		
red		
o<u>f</u>		Say *ŏf* for spelling but *ŏv* for reading. Both must be learned. Underline the *f* twice to indicate an uncommon sound for *f*.
b<u>e</u>	r. 4	In *be*, the *e* says *ē* at the end of a syllable.
but		
t̲his		Write two above and between the letters *t* and *h* to show the second sound, *th*.

Spelling Word	Rule(s)	Instructional Tips
ằll	r. 17	After children say the sounds for *all*, say, "Use the phonogram that says *ă, ā, ah*." For spelling say both *l*'s. B.E.: The sound of *a* may be altered when followed by an *l*.
[yọ̃ur [yọ̃u		Skip a space after the word *all*. Dictate the base word, *you*, first, then the derived word, *your*, on the line above.
<u>ou</u>t		After children say the sounds for *out*, say, "Use the phonogram that says *ow, ō, ōō, ŭ*."
t<u>i_e</u>		In *time*, the *e* lets the *i* say *ī* (job 1 on primary notebook page 3 and intermediate notebook rule page 1).
m<u>ay</u>	r. 18	After children say the sounds for *may*, say, "Use the phonogram that says *ā* at the end of a base word."
in tõ̊		After children say the syllable *to*, say, "Use the phonogram that says *ŏ, ō, ōō*."
him		
tõ̊ d<u>ay</u>	r. 18	After children say the syllable *day*, say, "Use the phonogram that says *ā* at the end of a base word."
lo̊̃ok		After children say the sounds for *look*, say, "Use the phonogram that says *ōō, ŏŏ*."
did		

Spelling Word	Rule(s)	Instructional Tips
li**ke**		After children say the sounds for *like,* say, "Use *k.*" The silent *e* lets the *i* say *ī* (job 1 on primary notebook page 3 and intermediate notebook rule page 1).
six		
b**oy**		After children say the sounds for *boy,* say, "Use the phonogram that says *oy* at the end of a word."
b**oo**²k		After children say the sounds for *book,* say, "Use the phonogram that says *ōō,* *ŏŏ.*"
b**y**	r. 5, 6	In *by,* the *y* says *ī.* The letter *y,* not *i,* is used at the end of an English word.
ha**ve**₂		English words do not end with a *v* (job 2). Refer to the five kinds of silent *e* on primary notebook page 3 or intermediate notebook rule page 1.
are₅		In *are,* the silent *e* has no job (job 5). Refer to primary notebook page 3 or intermediate notebook rule page 1.
had		
o v**er**	r. 4	Before spelling dictation, write, "H**er** f**ir**st n**ur**se₅ w**or**ks **ear** ly," on Rule Page 2 poster. After children say the syllable *ver,* say, "The *er* in *her* is the one we use most often."
must		
m**ake**		After children say the sounds for *make,* say, "Use the phonogram that says *k.*" The *e* lets the *a* say *ā* (job 1).

Spelling Word	Rule(s)	Instructional Tips
str**ee**t		After children say the sounds for *street*, say, "Use the phonogram that says *ē*." Say each phonogram separately.
s**ay**	r. 18	After children say the sounds for *say*, say, "Use the phonogram that says *ā* at the end of a base word."
com**e**₅		For spelling, say *ŏ*. In *come*, the silent *e* has no job (job 5). Refer to primary notebook page 3 or intermediate notebook rule page 1.
hand		
ri**ng**		For spelling, say *ĭ* and *ng* precisely.
l**i**v**e** l**i**v**e**₂		In *live*, the *e* lets the *i* say *ī* (job 1) and keeps the word from ending in a *v* (job 2). Mark only the first job. The *i* says *ĭ*, but the silent *e* is needed because English words do not end with *v* (job 2).
hill	r. 17	For spelling, say both *l*'s.
l**ate**		In *late*, the *e* lets the *a* say *ā* (job 1).
let		
big *bag* beg *bog* *bug*		Emphasize precise pronunciation of the vowel sounds. .

Spelling Word	Rule(s)	Instructional Tips
mo<u>th</u> <u>er</u> (with ² above th)		For spelling, say ŏ. After children say the syllable *moth,* say, "Use the phonogram that says ŏ, ō, o͞o." After the syllable *er,* say, "Use the *er* of *her.*"
<u>three</u>		After children say the sounds for *three,* say, "Use the phonogram that says ē."
land		
cold	r. 19	In *cold,* the o says ō because it is followed by two consonants.
hot		
hat		
<u>ch</u>ild	r. 19	In *child,* the i says ī because it is followed by two consonants.
<u>i</u><u>ce</u>		In *ice,* the e lets the i say ī (job 1) and lets the c say s (job 3). Mark only the first job.
pl<u>ay</u>	r. 18	After children say the sounds for *play,* say, "Use the phonogram that says ā at the end of a base word."
[s<u>ea</u> s<u>ee</u>		After children say the sounds for *sea,* say, "Use the phonogram that says ē, ĕ, ā." The phonograms *ee* and *ea* (each saying ē) show that the words have different meanings. After children say the sounds for *see,* say, "Use the phonogram that says ē."

The three usual ways for a vowel to say ā, ē, ī, ō, or ū have now been introduced:
1. By ending the syllable *(mē).*
2. By being followed by a consonant and a silent *e (time).*
3. By having two consonants follow an *i* or an *o (old, child).*
When reading, teach children to try the first sound unless one of these conditions exists.

Spelling Word	Rule(s)	Instructional Tips
b<u>ir</u>d		After children say the sounds for *bird*, say, "Use the *er* of *first*."
c<u>oo</u>l		After children say the sounds for *cool*, say, "Use the phonogram that says $\overline{oo}$, $\breve{oo}$."
<u>ear</u>th		After children say the sounds for *earth*, say, "Use the *er* of *early*."
f<u>ee</u>d		After children say the sounds for *feed*, say, "Use the phonogram that says $\bar{e}$."
f<u>ur</u>		After children say the sounds for *fur*, say, "Use the *er* of *nurse*."
gr<u>ee</u>n		After children say the sounds for *green*, say, "Use the phonogram that says $\bar{e}$."
<u>oi</u>l		After children say the sounds for *oil*, say, "Use the phonogram *oi* that is not used at the end of a word."
p<u>ai</u>nt		After children say the sounds for *paint*, say, "Use $\bar{a}$ that is not used at the end of a word."
p<u>oo</u>l		After children say the sounds for *pool*, say, "Use the phonogram that says $\overline{oo}$, $\breve{oo}$."
t<u>oo</u>th **t<u>ee</u>th**		After children say the sounds for *tooth*, say, "Use the phonogram that says $\overline{oo}$, $\breve{oo}$." After children say the sounds for *teeth*, say, "Use the phonogram that says $\bar{e}$."
w<u>or</u>m	r. 8	For spelling, say *wer m*.

Section H
73 Words for Spelling, Writing, and Reading

Spelling Word	Rule(s)	Instructional Tips
d**ay**	r. 18	After children say the sounds for *day*, say, "Use the phonogram that says $\bar{a}$ at the end of a base word."
eat		After children say the sounds for *eat*, say, "Use $\bar{e}$, $\breve{e}$, $\bar{a}$."
sits sit		Skip a space. Dictate the base word, *sit*, first.
lot		Use the sentence, "Weeds are growing in the vacant *lot*."
box		
sc**h**<u>oo</u>l		After children say the sounds for *school*, say, "Use *ch*, *k*, *sh*. Use $\overline{oo}$, $\breve{oo}$."
be lo**ng**	r. 4	
d<u><u>oo</u></u>r fl<u><u>oo</u></u>r		After children say the sounds for *door*, say, "Use $\overline{oo}$, $\breve{oo}$." For spelling, say $\overline{oo}$. Underline the *oo* twice to indicate an uncommon sound. For reading, say *dor*.
yes		
lo̅w		After children say the sounds for *low*, say, "Use *ow*, $\bar{o}$."
soft		
stands stand		Skip a space. Dictate the base word, *stand*, first. After children say the sounds for *stands*, say, "Use *s*, *z*."
y**ar**d		

Spelling Word	Rule(s)	Instructional Tips
bri<u>ng</u>		For spelling, say *ĭ* and *ng* precisely.
te**ll**	r. 17	For spelling, say both *l*'s.
f<u>i</u>v<u>e</u>		In *five,* the *e* lets the *i* say *ī* (job 1) and keeps the word from ending in a *v* (job 2). Mark only the first job.
bȧ̆ll	r. 17	After children say the sounds for *ball,* say, "Use *ă, ā, ah.*" For spelling, say both *l*'s. B.E.: The sound of *a* may be altered when followed by an *l*.
l<u>aw</u>		After children say the sounds for *law,* say, "Use *aw* that is used at the end of English words."
ask		After children say the sounds for *ask,* say, "Use *k.*" B.E.: ȧ̆sk.
just		
wa<u>y</u>	r. 18	After children say the sounds for *way,* say, "Use *ā* that is used at the end of a base word."
get		
h<u>o</u>m<u>e</u>		The *e* lets the *o* say *ō* (job 1).
mu<u>ch</u>		
cȧ̆ll	r. 17	After children say the sounds for *call,* say, "Use *ă, ā, ah.*" For spelling, say both *l*'s. B.E.: The sound of *a* may be altered when followed by an *l*.

Spelling Word	Rule(s)	Instructional Tips
lo**ng**		
lo**ve**₂		For spelling, say ŏ. The *e* is needed, since English words do not end in *v* (job 2).
then		
h**ouse**₅		After children say the sounds for *house,* say, "Use *ow, ō, ōō, ŭ.*" The *e* has no job (job 5).
y**ea**r		After children say the sounds for *year,* say, "Use *ē, ĕ, ā.*"
tŏ		After children say the sounds for *to,* say, "Use *ŏ, ō, ōō.*"
I	r. 5	The pronoun *I* is always capitalized. Explain that early printers thought the lowercase *i* looked insignificant as a word.
aš		After children say the sounds for *as,* say, "Use *s, z.*"
send		
a lone *lone* one	r. 4	Skip two spaces after the word *send.* On the third line, dictate the base word, *one.* For spelling, say letter names *o, n, e,* because *one* is not phonetic. For reading, say *won.* On the second line, write *lone* (job 1). On the first line, write *alone* (job 1). B.E.: For reading, say *wun.*
haš		After children say the sounds for *has,* say, "Use *s, z.*"

Spelling Word	Rule(s)	Instructional Tips
some͟e₅		For spelling, say ŏ. The *e* has no job (job 5).
if		
h**ow**		After children say the sounds for *how*, say, "Use *ow, ō*."
h**er**		After children say the sounds for *her*, say, "Use *er* of *her*."
²t͟hem		
²ot͟h **er**		After children say the syllables, say, "In the first syllable, use ŏ, ō, o͞o. In the second syllable, use *er* of *her*."
b**ā** by	r. 4, 6	For spelling, say *bā bĭ*. The accent is on the first syllable.
well	r. 17	For spelling, say both *l*'s.
a b**ou**t	r. 4	For spelling, say *ā bout*. For reading, the *ā* is not accented.
⎡men ⎣man		Skip a space. Dictate the base word, *man*, first.
f**or**		
⎡ran ⎣run		Skip a space. Dictate the base word, *run*, first.
w³²ȃs		After children say the sounds for *was*, say, "Use ă, ā, *ah*, and *s, z*." B.E.: The sound of *a* may be altered after *w*.
²t͟hat		

Spelling Word	Rule(s)	Instructional Tips
hi$\overset{2}{s}$		After children say the sounds for *his,* say, "Use *s, z.*"
led		
l<u>ay</u>	r. 18	
ap pl<u>e</u>₄	r. 29	For spelling, say both *p*'s (rule 29). Every syllable must have a vowel (job 4).
<u>ate</u>		In *ate,* the *e* lets the *a* say *ā* (job 1).
<u>au</u> <u>thor</u>		After children say the syllables, say, "Use the *au* that is not used at the end of English words." For spelling, say *or,* not *er.*
br<u>e</u>$\overset{2}{a}$d		After children say the sounds for *bread,* say, "Use *ē, ĕ, ā.*"
br<u>ow</u>n		After children say the sounds for *brown,* say, "Use *ow, ō.*"
dog		
<u>ea</u>ts		After children say the sounds for *eats,* say, "Use *ē, ĕ, ā.*"
fast		B.E.: f$\overset{3}{a}$st.
f<u>oo</u>d		After children say the sounds for *food,* say, "Use $\overline{oo}, \overline{oo}$."
jump		
sl<u>ee</u>p		After children say the sounds for *sleep,* say, "Use the phonogram that says *ē.*"

Spelling Word	Rule(s)	Instructional Tips
wȧsh		After children say the sounds for *wash*, say, "Use ă, ā, ah." B.E.: The sound of *a* may be altered after *w*.
yel lōw	r. 29	For spelling, say both *l*'s (rule 29). After children say the syllables, say, "Use *ow, ō*."

Section I
90 Words for Spelling, Writing, and Reading

Spelling Word	Rule(s)	Instructional Tips
nine		In *nine,* the *e* lets the *i* say ī (job 1).
face		After children say the sounds for *face,* say, "Use *k, s.*" In *face,* the *e* lets the *a* say ā (job 1) and the *c* say *s* (job 3). Mark only the first job.
miss	r. 17	For spelling, say both *s*'s.
[rides ride		Skip a space. Dictate the base word, *ride,* first. In *ride,* the *e* lets the *i* say ī (job 1).
tree		After children say the sounds for *tree,* say, "Use the phonogram that says ē."
sick	r. 25	After children say the sounds for *sick,* say, "Use two-letter *k.*"
got		
north		

Spelling Word	Rule(s)	Instructional Tips
wh<u>i</u>t<u>e</u>		The phonogram *wh* has no sound but air can be felt on the hand held before the lips. Have children blow air out and feel it on their hands as they say *white* (not *wite*). In *white,* the *e* lets the *i* say *ī* (job 1).
spent		
f<u>o͞o</u>t **f<u>ee</u>t**		After children say the sounds for *foot,* say, "Use o͞o, o͝o." After children say the sounds for *feet,* say, "Use the phonogram that says *ē*."
bl<u>ow</u>s **bl<u>ow</u>**		Skip a space. Dictate the base word, *blow,* first. After children say the sounds for *blow,* say, "Use *ow, ō*." After children say the sounds for *blows,* say, "Use *s, z*."
blo<u>ck</u>	r. 25	After children say the sounds for *block,* say, "Use two-letter *k*."
spri<u>ng</u>		For spelling, say *ĭ* and *ng* precisely.
riv <u>er</u>		After children say the syllables, say, "In the last syllable, use *er* of *her.* This *er* is used most often at the end of words."
plant <u>ed</u> **plant**	r. 28	Skip a space. Dictate the base word, *plant,* first. After children say the syllables for *planted,* say, "Use *ĕd, d, t*."
cut		

Spelling Word	Rule(s)	Instructional Tips
so<u>ng</u> *si<u>ng</u>* *sa<u>ng</u>* *su<u>ng</u>*		Emphasize precise pronunciation of the vowel sounds.
win t<u>er</u>		
st<u>one</u>		In *stone*, the *e* lets the *o* say *ō* (job 1).
fr<u>ee</u>		After children say the sounds for *free*, say, "Use the phonogram that says *ē*."
l<u>ake</u> *l<u>ace</u>*		In *lake*, the *e* lets the *a* say *ā* (job 1). After children say the sounds for *lace*, say, "Use *k, s*." The *e* lets the *a* say *ā* (job 1) and the *c* say *s* (job 3). Mark only the first job.
p<u>age</u>		After children say the sounds for *page*, say, "Use *g, j*." The *e* lets the *a* say *ā* (job 1) and the *g* say *j* (job 3). Mark only the first job.
ni<u>ce</u>		After children say the sounds for *nice*, say, "Use *k, s*." The *e* lets the *i* say *ī* (job 1) and the *c* say *s* (job 3). Mark only the first job.
end		
få̃ll	r. 17	After children say the sounds for *fall*, say, "Use *ă, ā, ah*." For spelling, say both *l*'s. B.E.: The sound of *a* may be altered when followed by an *l*.
went		

Spelling Word	Rule(s)	Instructional Tips
ba<u>ck</u>	r. 25	After children say the sounds for *back*, say, "Use two-letter *k*."
<u>a</u> w<u>ay</u>	r. 4, 18	For spelling, say *ā way*. In reading, the *a* is not accented.
p<u>a</u> p<u>er</u>	r. 4	
p³ut		After children say the sounds for *put*, say, "Use *ŭ, ū, ŏo*."
<u>each</u>		After children say the sounds for *each*, say, "Use *ē, ĕ, ā*."
s<u>oo</u>n		After children say the sounds for *soon*, say, "Use *ōo, ŏo*."
c<u>a</u>m<u>e</u>		In *came*, the *e* lets the *a* say *ā* (job 1).
Sun d<u>ay</u>	r. 26, 18	After children say *Sun day* in syllables, say, "Use a capital letter because *Sunday* is the name of one day. Like a person's name, it must be written with a capital letter."
sh<u>o</u>²w		After children say the sounds for *show*, say, "Use *ow, ō*."
[Mon d<u>ay</u> *m<u>oo</u>n*	r. 26, 18	After children say *Mon day* in syllables, say, "Use a capital letter because *Monday* is the name of one day and must be written with a capital letter."
yet		
find	r. 19	In *find*, the *i* says *ī* because it is followed by two consonants.

Spelling Word	Rule(s)	Instructional Tips
gi$\underline{ve}_2$		In *give*, the *e* is needed, since English words do not end in *v* (job 2).
n$\overset{2}{\underline{e}}$w		After children say the sounds for *new*, say, "Use $\overline{oo}$, $\bar{u}$ that is used at the end of a word."
let t$\underline{er}$	**r. 29**	For spelling say both *t*'s.
t$\underline{ake}$		In *take*, the *e* lets the *a* say $\bar{a}$ (job 1).
Mr. = $\underline{Mis}$ t$\underline{er}$	**r. 26**	Say, "I will write the word *Mister* in syllables. Now I will demonstrate how to write an abbreviation for *Mister*. I will use a capital *M* because this abbreviation is always written with a person's name. I will use the first and last letters and a period to show that it is an abbreviation." Have students follow your model on the board. B.E.: Full stop (period) is not used. *Mr* is the international alternative.
af t$\underline{er}$		B.E.: $\overset{3}{a}$f t$\underline{er}$
thi$\underline{ng}$		For spelling, say $\breve{i}$ and *ng* precisely.
wh$\overset{3}{\text{a}}$t		Have children blow air as they say *what*, not *watt*. Use $\breve{a}$, $\bar{a}$, *ah*. B.E.: The sound of *a* may be altered after *wh*.
$\overset{2}{\underline{th}}$an		
its, hi$\overset{2}{\text{s}}$, h$\underline{er}$ *it's = it (i)$\overset{2}{\text{s}}$*		Demonstrate writing bracketed words *(its, his, and her)* on the first line to show they are possessive pronouns. (An apostrophe is not used with *its*, because *its* is not a contraction.) Demonstrate writing *it's = it (i)$\overset{2}{\text{s}}$*. The apostrophe replaces the *i* of *is*.

Spelling Word	Rule(s)	Instructional Tips
vėr y	r. 6	Have children say *vĕr ĭ*. Put a one above the *ĕ* to show it is not *er*.
<u>or</u>		B.E.: Pronounce *or* for spelling.
<u>th</u>ank		For spelling, say *th ă n k*.
d<u>ea</u>r		After children say the sounds for *dear*, say, "Use *ē, ĕ, ā*."
west		
sold	r. 19	In *sold*, the *o* says *ō* because it is followed by two consonants.
told	r. 19	In *told*, the *o* says *ō* because it is followed by two consonants.
best		
f<u>or</u>m		B.E.: Pronounce *or* for spelling.
f<u>ar</u>		B.E.: Pronounce *ar* for spelling.
g<u>a</u><u>ve</u>		In *gave*, the *e* lets the *a* say *ā* (job 1) and keeps the word from ending in a *v* (job 2). Mark only the first job.
<u>a</u> l<u>i</u><u>ke</u>	r. 4	For spelling, say *ā like*. For reading, the *a* is not accented. The *e* lets the *i* say *ī* (job 1).
add		For spelling, say both *d*'s.
br<u>a</u><u>ve</u>		In *brave*, the *e* lets the *a* say *ā* (job 1) and keeps the word from ending in a *v* (job 2). Mark only the first job.
c<u>or</u>n		

Spelling Word	Rule(s)	Instructional Tips
dan*ce*₃		In *dance*, the *e* lets the *c* say *s* (job 3).
din n*er*	r. 29	For spelling, say both *n*'s.
do*ll*	r. 17	For spelling, say both *l*'s.
e*gg*		For spelling, say both *g*'s.
fr*ui*t		After children say the sounds for *fruit*, say, "Use o͞o, *ū*, that is not used at the end of English words."
l*o͝o*ks		After children say the sounds for *looks*, say, "Use o͞o, o͝o."
pi*ck*	r. 25	After children say the sounds for *pick*, say, "Use two-letter *k*."
ri*ch*		
z*oo*	r. 27	Words beginning with the sound *z* are always spelled with a *z*, never an *s*.
zip	r. 27	
z*e* r*o*	r. 27, 4	

Section J
105 Words for Writing, Reading, and Spelling

Spelling Word	Rule(s)	Instructional Tips
sev en		Say *ĕn*, not *ĭn*.
f*or* get		
hap py	r. 29, 6	For spelling, say both *p*'s and *ĭ*. For reading, say the word in normal speech.
n*oo*n		After children say the sounds for *noon*, say, "Use o͞o, o͝o."

Spelling Word	Rule(s)	Instructional Tips
<u>th</u>ink		Say ĭ precisely.
sis t<u>er</u>		
cast		B.E: cằst.
c<u>ar</u>d		
s<u>ou</u>th		After children say the sounds for *south*, say, "Use *ow, ō, ōō, ŭ*."
d<u>ee</u>p		After children say the sounds for *deep*, say, "Use the phonogram that says *ē*."
in s<u>ide</u>		Job 1.
bl<u>ue</u>₂		Job 2.
post	r. 19	
t<u>ow</u>n		After children say the sounds for *town*, say, "Use *ow, ō*."
st<u>ay</u>	r. 18	
grand		
<u>ou</u>t s<u>ide</u>		Job 1.
d<u>ar</u>k		
band		
<u>g</u>a<u>me</u>		Job 1.
b<u>oa</u>t		After children say the sounds for *boat*, say, "Use the *ō* of *boat*."
rest		

Spelling Word	Rule(s)	Instructional Tips
<u>ea</u>st		After children say the sounds for *east*, say, "Use ē, ĕ, ā."
[son *sun*		For spelling, say ŏ.
<u>h</u>elp		
h<u>ar</u>d		
r<u>ace</u>		In *race*, the *e* lets the *a* say *ā* (job 1) and the *c* say *s* (job 3). Mark only the first job.
cov <u>er</u>		

[f<u>ire</u>
 	
  w<u>ire</u>
 	
  t<u>ire</u>
		Say *fire* as one syllable. Children say *fire*, not *fi er* (job 1).
		Say *wire* as one syllable (job 1).
		
		Say *tire* as one syllable (job 1).
		B.E.: *Noun* spelling is t<u>yr</u> e.

<u>a</u><u>ge</u>		In *age*, the *e* lets the *a* say *ā* (job 1) and the *g* say *j* (job 3). Mark only the first job.
gold	r. 19	

[read   (a book)
  [rĕăd   (a book)
  red
		After the children say the sounds for *read*, say, "Use ē, ĕ, ā." Write (*a book*) after *read*. Write (*a book*) after *rĕăd*.

f<u>ine</u>		Job 1.
can not		For spelling and reading, say both *n*'s. This is not r. 29, because it is a compound word.

Spelling Word	Rule(s)	Instructional Tips
M<u>ay</u> m<u>ay</u>	r. 26, 18 r. 18	
l<u>i</u><u>ne</u>		Job 1.
left		
<u>sh</u>ip	r. 13	After children say the sounds for *ship*, say, "Use the phonogram that says *sh* at the beginning of a word" (r. 13).
tr<u>ai</u>n		After children say the sounds for *train*, say, "Use *ā* that is not used at the end of a word."
s<u>aw</u>		
p<u>ay</u>	r. 18	
<u>large</u>₌₃		Job 3.
n<u>ea</u>r		After children say the sounds for *near*, say, "Use *ē, ĕ, ā*."
d<u>ow</u>n		After children say the sounds for *down*, say, "Use *ow, ō*."
<u>why</u>	r. 5, 6	Have children blow as they say *wh ī* (not *w ī*).
bill	r. 17	
wȧnt		B.E.: The sound of *a* may be altered after *w*.
*girl*s² girl		Skip a space. Dictate the base word, *girl*, first. After children say the sounds for *girl*, say, "Use *er* of *first*."

Spelling Word	Rule(s)	Instructional Tips
p<u>ar</u>t		
still	r. 17	
pl<u>ace</u>		In *place,* the *e* lets the *a* say *ā* (job 1) and the *c* say *s* (job 3). Mark only the first job.
r<u>e</u> p<u>or</u>t	r. 4	
nev <u>er</u>		
f<u>ou</u>nd		After children say the sounds for *found,* say, "Use *ow, ō, ōō, ŭ.*"
s<u>ide</u>		Job 1.
kind	r. 19	
l<u>ife</u>		Job 1.
h<u>ere</u>		Job 1.
c<u>ar</u>		
w<u>or</u>d	r. 8	For spelling, say *wer d.*
ev <u>er</u> y	r. 6	For spelling, the *y* says *ĭ.*
un d<u>er</u>		
most	r. 19	
m<u>a</u><u>de</u>		Job 1.
[s<u>ai</u>d say<u>s</u>² s<u>ay</u>	r. 18	After *made,* skip two spaces. Write the base word, *say.* On the second line, write *says.* For spelling, say *says².* For reading, say *ses².* On the first line, write *said.* For spelling, say *said.* For reading, say *sĕd.*

Spelling Word	Rule(s)	Instructional Tips
w**or**k	r. 8	For spelling, say *wer k.*
our		After children say the sounds for *our,* say, "Use *ow, ō, o͞o, ŭ.*"
m**ore**		Job 1. Use of job 1 reinforces correct spelling.
when		Have children blow as they say *wh* (not *w*).
from f**or**m		*From* has four phonograms. *Form* has three phonograms.
wind w*ind*² (a toy)	r. 19	(An *i* does not have to say *ī* when followed by two consonants.) Write the two over *i* to distinguish *wind*² from *wind.* Write (*a toy*) after *wind*², then r. 19.
print		
air		After children say the sounds for *air,* say, "Use *ā* that is not used at the end of a word."
fill	r. 17	
a lo**ng**	r. 4	For spelling, say *ā long.* For reading, the *a* is not accented.
lost		
nam**e**		Job 1.
r**oo**m		After children say the sounds for *room,* say, "Use *o͞o, o͝o.*"
h**o**p**e**		Job 1.

Spelling Word	Rule(s)	Instructional Tips
s<u>a</u>m<u>e</u>		Job 1.
glad		
wi<u>th</u>²		
m<u>i</u>n<u>e</u>		Job 1.
<u>ch</u>a<u>i</u>r		After children say the sounds for *chair*, say, "Use *ā* that is not used at the end of a word."
<u>for</u> got		
<u>g</u>u<u>ess</u>	r. 17	
ha<u>ng</u>		Make sure children say *ă* and *ng* correctly.
m<u>ea</u>t		After children say the sounds for *meat*, say, "Use *ē, ĕ, ā*."
m<u>ouse</u>₅		After children say the sounds for *mouse*, say, "Use *ow, ō, ōo, ŭ*" (job 5).
<u>ph</u>o<u>n</u>e		After children say the sounds for *phone*, say, "Use two-letter *f*" (job 1).
st<u>ore</u>		Job 1. Use of job 1 reinforces correct spelling.
sup p<u>er</u>	r. 29	For spelling, say both *p*'s. For reading, say the word in normal speech.
<u>thr</u>o<u>u</u>²<u>gh</u>		After children say the sounds for *through*, say, "Use *ō, ōo, ŭf, ŏf, aw, ow*."
<u>t</u>o<u>e</u>		After children say the sounds for *toe*, say, "Use *ō* of *toe*."

Section K
120 Words for Spelling, Writing, and Reading

Spelling Word	Rule(s)	Instructional Tips
b<u>e</u> c<u>a</u>m<u>e</u>	r. 4	Job 1.
bro<u>th</u>² <u>er</u>		For spelling, say ŏ.
r<u>ai</u>n		After children say the sounds for *rain*, say, "Use *ā* that is not used at the end of a word."
k<u>ee</u>p		After children say the sounds for *keep*, say, "Use the phonogram that says *ē*."
st<u>ar</u>t		
m<u>ai</u>l *m<u>a</u>l<u>e</u>* *f<u>e</u> m<u>a</u>l<u>e</u>*	 r. 4	After children say the sounds for *mail*, say, "Use *ā* that is not used at the end of a word." Job 1. Job 1.
eye I	 r. 5	*Eye* is not phonetic. Say the names of the letters *e y e*. The pronoun "I" is always capitalized.
gl<u>a</u>ss	r. 17	B.E.: *glȁss*.
p<u>ar</u> ty	r. 6	For spelling, the *y* says *ĭ*.
up on		
tw<u>o</u>³ twin tw<u>ice</u> twel<u>ve</u>₂ twen ty b<u>e</u> tw<u>ee</u>n	 r. 6 r. 4	For spelling, say *t w oo*. (We probably once said *two* sounding the *w* as we still do in *twin*, *twice* (job 1), *twelve* (job 2), *twenty*, and *between*, each of which relates to *two*.) For spelling, say *tĭ*. After children say the syllable *tween*, say, "Use the phonogram that says *ē*."

Spelling Word	Rule(s)	Instructional Tips
<u>²</u> **the̲y**		
w<u>ou</u>l̲d		For spelling, say *w ow l d*. Underline *ou* twice because *ŏŏ* is an uncommon sound for *ou*. Underline *l* twice because it is silent. (The *l* came from *will*, the present tense of *would*.) For reading, say *wŏŏd*.
c<u>ou</u>l̲d		For spelling, say *c ow l d*. (The *l* was added to conform to *would* and *should*.) For reading, say *cŏŏd*.
<u>sh</u><u>ou</u>l̲d	r. 13	For spelling, say *sh ow l d*. The phonogram *sh* is used at the beginning of a base word to say *sh*. (The *l* comes from *shall*.) For reading, say *shŏŏd*.
<u>a</u>n y	r. 6	For spelling, say, *ăn ĭ*. Underline *a* twice because *ĕ* is an uncommon sound for *a*. For reading, say *ĕn ĭ*.
m<u>a̲</u>n y	r. 6	For spelling, say *măn ĭ*. For reading, say *mĕn ĭ*.
cit y	r. 2, 6	For spelling, *y* says *ĭ*.
on ly	r. 19, 6	The base word is *one*. Normally the *e* would be retained, since the ending *ly* does not begin with a vowel (exception to rule 11). The *o* may say *ō* when followed by two consonants.
<u>wh</u>èr̲e̲₅ ¹		For spelling and reading, say *wh*, not *w*. Write a one above the *e* to show it is not *er*. Job 5.
w<u>ee</u>k		After children say the sounds for *week*, say, "Use the phonogram that says *ē*."
w<u>ea̲</u>k		After children say the sounds for *weak*, say, "Use *ē*, *ĕ*, *ā*."

Spelling Word	Rule(s)	Instructional Tips
f<u>i</u>rst		After children say the sounds for *first*, say, "Use *er* of *first*."
[sent cent	r. 2	After children say the sounds for *sent*, say, "Use *s, z*." After children say the sounds for *cent*, say, "Use *k, s*."
mi<u>le</u>		Job 1.
s<u>ee</u>m		After children say the sounds for *seem*, say, "Use the phonogram that says *ē*."
<u>e</u> ven	r. 4	For spelling, say *věn*, not *vĭn*.
wi<u>t̲h̲</u> <u>out</u>		For spelling, say *t̲h̲*.
af t<u>er</u> n<u>oo</u>n		B.E.: *åf t<u>er</u> n<u>oo</u>n*.
Fri d<u>ay</u>	r. 26, 5, 18	
[<u>h̲</u>our <u>ou</u>r		For spelling, say *h*. Underline *h* twice because it is silent.
wi<u>f</u><u>e</u>		Job 1.
st<u>a</u><u>te</u>		Job 1.
J<u>u</u> l<u>y</u>	r. 26, 4, 5, 6	
he<u>a̲</u>d		After children say the sounds for *head*, say, "Use *ē, ě, ā*."
st<u>o</u> ry	r. 4, 6	For spelling, say *rĭ*.
<u>o</u> pen	r. 4	After children say the syllables, say, "Use *ě, ē*."

Spelling Word	Rule(s)	Instructional Tips
s͟h͟o͟rt	**r. 13**	The phonogram *sh* is used at the beginning of a base word to say *sh*.
la͟ dy	**r. 4, 6**	For spelling, say *dĭ*.
re͟a͟ch		After children say the sounds for *reach*, say, "Use *ē, ĕ, ā*."
bet te͟r	**r. 29**	For spelling, say both *t*'s. For reading, say the word in normal speech.
wå ter		B.E.: The sound of *a* may be altered after *w*.
ro͟u͟nd		
cost		
pri͟c͟e		Job 1.
be͟ come͟₅	**r. 4**	Job 5.
class	**r. 17**	B.E.: *clåss*.
ho͟rse͟₅		Job 5.
ca͟re͟		Job 1.
try͟	**r. 5, 6**	
mȯ͟v͟e͟₂		After children say the sounds for *move*, say, "Use *ŏ, ō, ō͞o*." Job 2.
de͟ la͟y	**r. 4, 18**	
po͟u͟nd		
be͟ hind	**r. 4, 19**	

Spelling Word	Rule(s)	Instructional Tips
<u>a</u> r<u>ou</u>nd	r. 4	For spelling, say *ā round*. For reading, say the word in normal speech.
b<u>ur</u>n		After children say the sounds for *burn*, say, "Use *er* of *nurse*."
cam<u>p</u>		
b<u>ea</u>r³ / **b<u>are</u>**		After children say the sounds for *bear*, say, "Use *ē, ĕ, ā*." Job 1. B.E.: *bĕar*².
cl<u>ea</u>r		After children say the sounds for *clear*, say, "Use *ē, ĕ, ā*."
cl<u>ea</u>n		After children say the sounds for *clean*, say, "Use *ē, ĕ, ā*."
spell	r. 17	
p<u>oo</u>r		After children say the sounds for *poor*, say, "Use *o̅o̅, ŏŏ*."
fin i<u>sh</u>	r. 13	After children say the syllables, say, "Use the phonogram that says *sh* at the end of a syllable."
h<u>ur</u>t		After children say the sounds for *hurt*, say, "Use *er* of *nurse*."
m<u>ay</u> b<u>e</u>	r. 18, 4	
<u>a</u> cross	r. 4, 17	For spelling, say *ā cross*. For reading, say the word in normal speech.
tŏ³ n<u>igh</u>t		After children say the sounds for *night*, say, "Use the three-letter *ī*."
ten<u>th</u>		

Spelling Word	Rule(s)	Instructional Tips
s<u>ir</u>		After children say the sounds for *sir*, say, "Use *er* of *first*."
[th<u>e</u>s<u>e</u> th<u>o</u>s<u>e</u>		After children say the sounds for *these*, say, "Use *s, z*." Job 1. Job 1.
club		
[s<u>ee</u>n s<u>ee</u>		Skip a space. Dictate the base word, *see*, first. After children say the sounds for *see*, say, "Use the phonogram that says *ē*."
felt		
f<u>u</u>ll	r. 17	After children say the sounds for *full*, say, "Use *ŭ, ū, o͝o*."
f<u>ai</u>l		After children say the sounds for *fail*, say, "Use *ā* that is not used at the end of a word."
[*set <u>ting</u>* *set*	r. 9	Skip a space. Dictate the base word, *set*, first. After children say the syllables, say, "Write *set* and add another consonant *t* before adding the suffix *ing* that begins with a vowel." One-one-one rule.
st<u>a</u>mp		
li<u>ght</u>		After children say the sounds for *light*, say, "Use three-letter *ī*."
[com <u>ing</u> com<u>e</u>₅	r. 11	Skip a space. Dictate the base word, *come*, first. Job 5. After children say the syllable *come*, say, "Write *come* without the *e* before adding the suffix *ing*, which begins with a vowel."

Spelling Word	Rule(s)	Instructional Tips
ni<u>gh</u>t		After children say the sounds for *night,* say, "Use three-letter *ī.*"
pass	**r. 17**	B.E.: *pȃss.*
<u>sh</u>ut	**r. 13**	The phonogram *sh* is used at the beginning of a base word.
[**ea̋s y** **ea̋s̲e₅**	**r. 11, 6**	Skip a space. Dictate the base word, *ease,* first. After children say the syllable, say, "Write *ease* without the *e* before adding the suffix *ĭ.* Use *y, ĭ, ī.*" After children say the sounds for *ease,* say, "Use *ē, ĕ, ā* and *s, z.*" Job 5.
<u>bo</u>ne		Job 1.
cl<u>ou</u>d		
dr<u>aw</u>		
drink		For spelling, say *ĭ* correctly.
g<u>ar</u> den		After children say the syllables, say, "Use *ĕ, ē.*"
g<u>oo</u>s̲e₅		After children say the sounds for *goose,* say, "Use *ōō, ŏŏ.*" Job 5.
[*hop <u>p̲ing</u>* *hop*	**r. 9**	Skip a space. Dictate the base word, *hop,* first. (One-one-one rule.)
<u>kn</u>ife		After children say the sounds for *knife,* say, "Use two-letter *n* that is used at the beginning of a base word." Job 1.
m<u>ou</u>th		

Spelling Word	Rule(s)	Instructional Tips
o͟ak		After children say the sounds for *oak*, say, "Use ō of *boat*."
pe͟a͟ch		After children say the sounds for *peach*, say, "Use ē, ĕ, ā."
po͟le		Job 1.
qu͟een	r. 1	After children say the sounds for *queen*, say, "Use the phonogram that says ē."
r͟ope		Job 1.
se͟a͟ s̆on		After children say the syllables, say, "In the first syllable, use ē, ĕ, ā." For spelling, say s̆ŏn, not s̆ŭn.
si͟gn	r. 19	After children say the sounds for *sign*, say, "Use two-letter *n* that is used at the end of a word."
spa͟c͟e		Job 1.
wag on		For spelling, say, ŏn, not ŭn.
wh͟ea͟t		After children say the sounds for *wheat*, say, "For spelling, use *wh* and ē, ĕ, ā."
win do͟w͟		After children say the syllables for *window*, say, "Use ow, ō."

Section L
133 Words for Spelling, Writing, and Reading

Spelling Word	Rule(s)	Instructional Tips
catch catch er kitch en bŭtch er		After children say the sounds for *catch*, say, "Use the additional phonogram *tch* that always follows a single vowel that does not say *ā, ē, ī, ō, ū* (*cătch, ĕtch, pĭtch, nŏtch, bŭtcher*). The phonogram *tch* says *ch*.
black	r. 25	After children say the sounds for *black*, say, "Use two-letter *k*."
warm		For spelling, say *ar*. For reading, say *or*.
un less	r. 17	
cloth ing clothes clothe	r. 11	Skip two spaces. On the third line, dictate the base word, *clothe*. On the second line, dictate *clothes*. On the first line, dictate the word *clothing*. Write *clothe* without the *e* before adding the suffix *ing*, which begins with a vowel.
be gan be gin be gin ning	r. 4 r. 4 r. 4, 10	Skip one space and dictate the base word, *begin*. On the first line, write *began*. After children say the syllables, say, "The accent is on *gin*, which has one vowel, *ĭ*, followed by one consonant, *n*. Write another *n* before adding the suffix *ing*, which begins with a vowel." Rule 10.
a ble₄	r. 4	
gone₅ go	 r. 4	Skip a space. Dictate the base word, *go*, first.

Spelling Word	Rule(s)	Instructional Tips
done₅ do		Skip a space. Dictate the base word, *do*, first. For spelling *done*, say ŏ.
su̲it		Say sounds separately.
tra̲ck	r. 25	
wa̲tch		After children say the sounds for *watch*, say, "Use the additional phonogram *tch* to say *ch*." B.E.: The sound of *a* can be altered after *w*.
da̲sh	r. 13	After children say the sounds for *dash*, say, "Use the phonogram that says *sh* at the end of a base word."
fe̲ll	r. 17	
fi̲ght		After children say the sounds for *fight*, say, "Use three-letter ī."
buy by	r. 5, 6 r. 5, 6	For spelling, say each sound *b ŭ ī*. For reading, say *bī*. The *u* is silent.
stop ping stop	r. 9	Skip a space. Dictate the base word, *stop*, first. One-one-one rule.
wa̲lk ta̲lk cha̲lk		For spelling, say *l*. For reading, say *wăk*, *tăk*, *chăk*. B.E.: The sound of *a* may be altered after *w*. B.E.: The sound of *a* may be altered when followed by an *l*.
gra̲nt		

Spelling Word	Rule(s)	Instructional Tips
s<u>oa</u>p		After children say the sounds in *soap*, say, "Use the ō of *boat*."
n<u>ew</u>s̶² n<u>ew</u>²		Skip a space. Dictate the base word, *new*, first.
sm<u>ȧ</u>ll *sm<u>ȧ</u>ll <u>er</u>* *sm<u>ȧ</u>ll est*	r. 17	B.E.: The sound of *a* may be altered when followed by an *l*.
w<u>ar</u>		For spelling, say *ar*. For reading, say *or*.
sum m<u>er</u>	r. 29	For spelling, say both *m*'s. For reading, say the word in normal speech.
<u>a</u> bo<u>ve</u>₂	r. 4	For spelling, say *ā bove*. For reading, the *a* is not accented.
ex press	r. 20, 17	The letter *s* almost never follows *x*.
t<u>ur</u>n		After children say the sounds for *turn*, say, "Use *er* of *nurse*."
les son	r. 29	For spelling, say both *s*'s. For reading, say the word in normal speech.
ha<u>l</u>f		For spelling, say *l*. For reading, say *haf*. B.E.: *hȧl̶f*.
fa³ <u>ther</u>²		
<u>a</u> y <u>thing</u>		For spelling, say *ăn ĭ*. For reading, say *ĕn ĭ*.
t<u>a</u> b<u>le</u>₄	r. 4	
h<u>igh</u>		After children say the sounds for *high*, say, "Use three-letter ī."

Spelling Word	Rule(s)	Instructional Tips
J**une**	**r. 26**	
right **write** **wrote**		After children say the sounds for *right*, say, "Use three-letter *ī*." After children say the sounds for *write*, say, "Use two-letter *r*."
d**ate**		
r**oa**d *r**ode*** r**ide**		After children say the sounds for *road*, say, "Use the *ō* of *boat*."
M**arch** *m**ar**ch*	**r. 26**	
next		
in d**ee**d		After children say the syllable *deed*, say, "Use the phonogram that says *ē*."
f**ou**r		After children say the sounds for *four*, say, "Use *ow, ō, ōo, ŭ*." B.E.: For reading, say *faw*.
h**er** self		
p**ow** **er**		After children say the syllables, say, "In the first syllable, use *ow, ō*."
wi**sh**	**r. 13**	After children say the sounds for *wish*, say, "Use *sh* that is used at the end of a word."
b**e** c**au**s**e**₅ c**au**s**e**₅	**r. 4**	Skip a space. Dictate the base word, *cause*, first. After children say the sounds for *cause*, say, "Use *au* that is not used at the end of a word."

Spelling Word	Rule(s)	Instructional Tips
w<u>or</u>ld	r. 8	For spelling, say *wer l d*.
c<u>o</u>⁴un try	r. 6	After children say the syllables, say, "Use *ow, ō, ōo, ŭ*." For spelling, say *trĭ*.
[m<u>ee</u>t m<u>ea</u>t		After children say the sounds for *meet*, say, "Use the phonogram that says *ē*." After children say the sounds for *meat*, say, "Use *ē, ĕ, ā*."
an o<u>th</u>² <u>er</u>		For spelling, say the syllables *ăn ŏth er*.
[*tripp<u>ĕ</u>d*³ trip	r. 9, 28	Skip a space. Dictate the base word, *trip*, first. (One-one-one rule.)
list		
p<u>eo</u> pl<u>e</u>₄		After children say the syllables, say, "In the first syllable, use additional phonogram *eo* to say *ē*."
ev <u>er</u>		
held		
<u>ch</u>ur<u>ch</u>		After children say the sounds for *church*, say, "Use *er* of *nurse*."
[on<u>ce</u>₃ one		Skip a space. Dictate the base word, *one*, by letter names, first. For spelling, say *o n s e*. Say, "Use *k, s*." For reading, say *wonce*. B.E.: For reading, say *wunce*.
o<u>w</u>²n		After children say the sounds for *own*, say, "Use *ow, ō*."
b<u>e</u> f<u>or</u>e	r. 4	Use of job 1 reinforces correct spelling.

Spelling Word	Rule(s)	Instructional Tips
knŏw² nō	r. 4	After children say the sounds for *know*, say, "Use two-letter *n* that is used at the beginning of a base word and *ow, ō*."
wĕre₅ whĕre¹₅ thĕre²¹₅ here		Although these four words have the same last three letters, they are not all alike. Each is phonetic. Put a one above the *ĕ* to show it is not *er*.
dĕ²ad		After children say the sounds for *dead*, say, "Use *ē, ĕ, ā*."
leāve₂		After children say the sounds for *leave*, say, "Use *ē, ĕ, ā*."
ear ly	r. 6	For spelling, say *lĭ*.
clŏ²se *close*		
flow er *flour*		After children say the syllables for *flower*, say, "In the first syllable, use *ow, ō*." After children say the sounds for *flour*, say, "Use *ow, ō, ōō, ŭ*." For spelling, say *r*, not *er*. The word is only one syllable.
noth ing		For spelling, say *nŏth*.
ground		After children say the sounds for *ground*, say, "Use *ow, ō, ōō, ŭ*."
lead (the way) led (the way) lĕ²ad (pencil)		Write *(the way)* after *lead*. Write *(the way)* after *led*. After children say the sounds for *lead*, say, "Use *ē, ĕ, ā*." Write *(pencil)* after *lead*.
such		

Spelling Word	Rule(s)	Instructional Tips
m<u>or</u>n <u>ing</u>		
h<u>ow</u> ev <u>er</u>		
mind	r. 19	
<u>sh</u>all	r. 13, 17	
<u>a</u> l<u>one</u>	r. 4	For spelling, say *ā*. For reading, the *a* is not accented.
<u>or</u> d<u>er</u>		
<u>th</u><u>ir</u>d		After children say the sounds for *third*, say, "Use *er* of *first*."
pu<u>sh</u>³	r. 13	After children say the sounds for *push*, say, "Use the phonogram that says *sh* at the end of a base word."
p<u>oi</u>nt		
wi<u>th</u>² in		
bod y	r. 6	For spelling, *y* says *ĭ*.
f<u>ie</u>ld	r. 12	After children say the sounds for *field*, say, "Use *ē, ī, ĭ*."
be l<u>o</u>ng<u>s</u>²	r. 4	
<u>ch</u>ee<u>s</u>²<u>e</u>₅		After children say the sounds for *cheese*, say, "Use the phonogram that says *ē*."
<u>ear</u>n		After children say the sounds for *earn*, say, "Use *er* of *early*."
e<u>dge</u>	r. 23	After children say the sounds for *edge*, say, "Use three-letter *j*."

Spelling Word	Rule(s)	Instructional Tips
fẽ**ath** **er**		After children say the syllables, say, "In the first syllable, use ē, ĕ, ā. The phonogram *ea* saying *ĕa* never ends a syllable."
fen**ce**₃		
fun **ny**	r. 9, 6	For spelling, say *nĭ*. One-one-one rule.
g**o** **ing**	r. 4	
hon e̊**y**		After children say the *syllables*, say, "In the last syllable, use ā, ē, ĭ."
let te**r**s̊	r. 29	For spelling, say both *t*'s. For reading, say the word in normal speech.
o̊r an**ge**₌₃		For spelling, say ŏ, not *or*.
po**ck** et	r. 25	For spelling, say ĕt, not ĭt.
[sh**o̊e**s̊	r. 13	Skip a space. Dictate the base word *shoe* first. Say, "Write *shoe* and add the suffix s̊." For reading, say *sho̊s̊*.
sh**o̊e**₌₅	r. 13	
st**ai**r̊s		After children say the sounds in *stairs*, say, "Use ā that is not used at the end of a word."
str**ea**m		After children say the sounds for *stream*, say, "Use ē, ĕ, ā."
tå**l**ks		For spelling, say *t å l k s*. For reading, say *tåks*. B.E.: The sound of *a* may be altered when followed by an *l*.
t**i** ny	r. 5, 6	For spelling, say *tī nĭ*.
w**or**d̊s	r. 8	For spelling, say *wer d z*.

Section M
123 Words for Spelling, Writing, and Reading

Spelling Word	Rule(s)	Instructional Tips
trust		
ex trä³	r. 20	The letter *s* almost never follows *x*. After children say the syllables, say, "In the last syllable, use ă, ā, ah."
dress	r. 17	
be̲ si̲de̲	r. 4	
te̲a̲c̲h		After children say the sounds for *teach,* say, "Use ē, ĕ, ā."
hap pen	r. 29	For spelling, say both *p*'s. For reading, say the word in normal speech.
be̲ gun	r. 4	
col lect	r. 29	For spelling, say each sound in the second syllable.
fi̲le̲		
pro̲ vi̲de̲	r. 4	
si̲ght		
sto͞od²		
[*fixĕd³* fix	r. 28	Skip a space. Dictate the base word, *fix,* first. Rule 9 does not apply to words ending in *x* (exception to r. 9), because *x* has two sounds, *ks* (*ox, oxen*).
bo̲rn		

Spelling Word	Rule(s)	Instructional Tips
goe$\overset{2}{s}$ g<u>o</u>	r. 4	Skip a space. Dictate the base word, *go*, first. Say, "Write *go* and add *e$\overset{2}{s}$*." For spelling and reading, say *g* <u>*oe*</u> $\overset{2}{s}$.
hold	r. 19	
drill	r. 17	
<u>ar</u> my	r. 6	For spelling, say *ĭ*.
pr<u>e</u>t ty	r. 29, 6	For spelling, say *prĕt tĭ*. For reading, say *prĭt ĭ*.
st<u>o</u>l<u>e</u>		
in com<u>e</u>₅		
bo<u>ugh</u>t		After children say the sounds for *bought*, say, "Use *ō*, *ōō*, *ŭf*, *ŏf*, *aw*, *ow*."
p<u>ai</u>d p<u>ay</u>	r. 18	Skip a space. Dictate the base word, *pay*, first.
en t<u>er</u>		
r<u>ai</u>l r<u>oa</u>d		
un <u>a</u> bl<u>e</u>₄	r. 4	
ti<u>ck</u> et	r. 25	For spelling, say *ĕt*, not *ĭt*.
ac c<u>ou</u>nt	r. 29	For spelling, say both *k*'s. For reading, say the word in normal speech.
driv en	r. 11	After children say the syllables, say, "Write the base word, *drive*, without the *e* before adding the suffix *en* which begins with a vowel."
r<u>e</u> al	r. 4	This is a two-syllable word.

Spelling Word	Rule(s)	Instructional Tips
re̱ cov er̲	r. 4	After children say the syllables for *recover*, say, "In the second syllable, use ŏ, ō, o͞o."
m**ou**n t**ai**n		For spelling, say *t**ai**n*. For reading, say *t'n*.
sp**ea**k		After children say the sounds for *speak*, say, "Use ē, ĕ, ā."
past		B.E.: *p$\overset{3}{a}$st*.
mi**gh**t		
con tract		For spelling, say each sound in the second syllable.
d**ea**l		After children say the sounds for *deal*, say, "Use ē, ĕ, ā." This is a one-syllable word.
[$\overset{3}{a}$l most	r. 21, 19	Skip a space. Dictate the base word, *all*, first. After children say the syllable *al*, say, "Write one *l* when *all* is used as a prefix." B.E.: The sound of *a* may be altered when followed by an *l*.
[$\overset{3}{a}$ll	r. 17	
[brou$\overset{5}{gh}$t		Skip a space. Dictate the base word, *bring*, first.
[bri**ng**		
less	r. 17	
e̱ vent	r. 4	
[off	r. 17	
[o**f**		
[tru**e**₂		For spelling, say ū.
[*tru**th***		The silent final *e* is no longer needed, because ū is not at the end of the word.

Spelling Word	Rule(s)	Instructional Tips
t<u>oo</u>k²		
<u>a</u> g<u>ai</u>n	r. 4	For spelling, say *gain*. For reading, say *gĕn*. B.E.: The pronunciation *<u>a</u> g<u>ai</u>n* is accepted.
in f<u>or</u>m		
bo<u>th</u>	r. 19	
h<u>ea</u>rt		For spelling, sound each phonogram *h ĕ ar t*. For reading, say *h<u>ar</u>t*. The *e* is silent.
mon<u>th</u>		
[<u>ch</u>il dren [<u>ch</u>ild	r. 19	Skip a space. Dictate the base word, *child*, first. After children say the syllables, say, "In the second syllable, use ĕ, ē." (We often keep the base word in one syllable, but here we do not.)
[b<u>ui</u>ld [b<u>ui</u>lt		For spelling, say each phonogram *b ŭ ĭ l d*. For reading, say *bild*. For spelling, say each phonogram *b ŭ ĭ l t*. For reading, say *bilt*.
un d<u>er</u> stand		
fol l<u>ow</u>²	r. 29	For spelling, say both *l*'s. For reading, say the word in normal speech.
<u>ch</u>ar<u>ge</u>=3		
mem b<u>er</u>		
<u>c</u>a<u>se</u>		

Spelling Word	Rule(s)	Instructional Tips
whi̲l̲e		For spelling and reading, say *wh*, not *w*.
ặl so̲	**r. 21, 4**	After children say the syllables, say, "Write one *l* when *all* is used as a prefix." B.E.: The sound of *a* may be altered when followed by an *l*.
re̲ tu̲r̲n	**r. 4**	After children say the syllables for *return*, say, "Use *er* of *nurse*."
of fic̲e̲₃	**r. 29**	For spelling, say both *f*'s. For reading, say the word in normal speech.
gre̯ặt		After children say the sounds for *great*, say, "Use *ē, ĕ, ā*."
⎡ Miss **⎣ miss**	**r. 26, 17** **r. 17**	
wh̲ǒ̲		For spelling, say *wh ǒ*. For reading, say *hǒ*.
⎡ di̯e̲d **⎣ di̲e̲**	**r. 11, 28** **r. 12**	Skip a space. Dictate the base word, *die*, first. After children say the sounds for *die*, say, "Use *ē, ī, ĭ*." After children say the sounds for *died*, say, "Write *die* without the *e* and add the suffix *ed, d, t*. The letters *ie* together say *ī*, and *ed* says *ĕd*."
⎡ *chang ing* **⎣ change**	**r. 11**	Skip a space. Dictate the base word *change*, first. After children say the syllables, say, "Write *change* without the *e* and add the suffix *ing*, which begins with a vowel."
fĕ̲w		
⎡ plĕ̯ăṣ ant **⎣ plĕ̯ặs̲e̲₅**	**r. 11**	Skip a space. Dictate the base word, *please*, first. After children say the sounds for *please*, say, "Use *ē, ĕ, ā*, and *s, z*." Say, "Write *please* without the *e* and add the suffix *ant*, which begins with a vowel."

Spelling Word	Rule(s)	Instructional Tips
pic tu<u>re</u> *pit<u>ch</u> <u>er</u>* *pi<u>tch</u>*		For spelling, say *ture*, not *cher*. Skip a space. Dictate the base word, *pitch*, first. After the children say the sounds for *pitch*, say, "Use the additional phonogram *tch* to say *ch*."
mon e<u>y</u>		After children say the syllables, say, "Use *ā, ē, ĭ*."
r<u>e</u>ad y	r. 6	After children say the syllables for *ready*, say, "Use *ē, ĕ, ā*." For spelling, *y* says *ĭ*.
<u>o</u> mit	r. 4	
<u>an</u> y w<u>ay</u>	r. 18	For spelling, say *ăn ĭ*. For reading, say *ĕn ĭ*.
e<u>igh</u>t		After children say the sounds for *eight*, say, "Use four-letter *ā*."
br<u>ea</u>k fast		B.E.: *br<u>ea</u>k fàst*. After children say the syllables, say, "Use *ē, ĕ, ā* in the first syllable."
<u>ch</u>an<u>ce</u>₃		
clim<u>b</u>	r. 19	For spelling, say *k l ī m b*.
cof f<u>ee</u>	r. 29	For spelling, say both *f*'s. For reading, say the word in normal speech.
col <u>or</u>		For spelling, say *or*, not *er*. B.E.: Spelling is *col <u>ou</u>r*.
con t<u>ai</u>ns		
d<u>ai</u> ly *d<u>ay</u>*	r. 6 r. 18	Skip a space. Dictate the base word, *day*, first. After children say the syllables in *daily*, say, "Use *ā* that is not used at the end of a word."

Spelling Word	Rule(s)	Instructional Tips
_ea_ gl_e_4		After children say the syllables, say, "Use ē, ĕ, ā."
fan cy	r. 6	For spelling, say cĭ.
fl_y_	r. 5, 6	
f*ŏr* est		After children say the syllables, say, "The first syllable has three separate sounds."
free_ze_5		After children say the sounds for _freeze_, say, "Use the phonogram that says ē."
gen tl_e_4	r. 3	
gr*ŏw*		After children say the sounds for _grow_, say, "Use _ow_, ō."
h_ole_s		
h_o_ tel	r. 4	
_i_ r_on_	r. 5	For spelling, say ī ron. For reading, say ī _ern_. B.E.: i r_on_.
liv ing li_ve_2	r. 11	Skip a space. Dictate the base word, _live_, first. After children say the syllable _liv_, say, "Write _live_ without the _e_ before adding the suffix _ing_, which begins with a vowel."
mon k*ĕy*		After children say the syllables, say, "Use ā, ē, ĭ."
m_y_ self	r. 5, 6	
n_oi_s_e_5		
pen cil	r. 2	

Spelling Word	Rule(s)	Instructional Tips
p<u>ie</u> [2]	r. 12	After children say the sounds for *pie,* say, "Use ē, ī, ĭ."
p<u>u</u>ll [3]	r. 17	
<u>s</u><u>ew</u> (needle) s<u>ow</u> (seeds) [2] s<u>o</u>	r. 4	After children say the sounds for *sew,* say, "Use o͞o, ū." Write (*needle*) after *sew.* After children say the sounds for *sow,* say, "Use ow, ō." Write (*seeds*) after *sow.*
st<u>ea</u>m		After children say the sounds for *steam,* say, "Use ē, ĕ, ā."
<u>t</u>hr<u>ea</u>d [2]		After children say the sounds for *thread,* say, "Use ē, ĕ, ā."
<u>t</u>hun d<u>er</u>		
tr<u>ie</u>d [2 2] tr<u>y</u>	r. 24, 28 r. 5, 6	Skip a space. Dictate the base word, *try,* first. After children say the sounds for *tried,* say, "Use ĭ, ī, and add the suffix *ed, d, t.* The letters *ie* together say ī and the suffix says e̋d.
v<u>ei</u>n [2]	r. 12	After children say the sounds for *vein,* say, "Use ē, ā, ĭ."

Section N
110 Words for Spelling, Writing, and Reading

Spelling Word	Rule(s)	Instructional Tips
ex cept	r. 20, 2	After children say the syllables, say each sound in the first and second syllables. "Remember the letter *s* almost never follows the letter *x.* Use *ks.*"

Spelling Word	Rule(s)	Instructional Tips
<u>au</u>nt ant		For spelling, say *au n t*.
cap t<u>ure</u>		For spelling, say *ture*, not *cher*.
els<u>e</u>₅		
bri<u>dge</u>	r. 23	After children say the sounds for *bridge*, say, "Use three-letter *j*."
of f<u>er</u>	r. 29	For spelling, say both *f*'s. For reading, say the word in normal speech.
suf f<u>er</u>	r. 29	For spelling, say both *f*'s. For reading, say the word in normal speech.
cen t<u>er</u>	r. 2	B.E.: Spelling is *cen tr<u>e</u>₄*.
front		For spelling, say *ŏ*.
run <u>ning</u> run	r. 9	Skip a space. Dictate the base word, *run*, first. (One-one-one rule.)
r<u>ule</u>		For spelling, say *ū*.
cắr ry	r. 29, 6	After children say the syllables, say, "The first syllable has three separate sounds." For spelling, say *rĭ*.
<u>ch</u>ain		
de²<u>a</u>th		After children say the sounds for *death*, say, "Use *ē, ĕ, ā*."
l<u>ear</u>n		After children say the sounds for *learn*, say, "Use the *er* of *early*."
won d<u>er</u>		B.E.: The sound of *o* may be altered after *w*.

Spelling Word	Rule(s)	Instructional Tips
p<u>ai</u>r (two) pe<u>a</u>r[3] (eat) p<u>are</u> (cut)		Write (*two*) after *pair*. "Use $\bar{a}$, not used." Write (*eat*) after *pear*. "Use $\bar{e}, \breve{e}, \bar{a}$." B.E.: p<u>e</u>ar[2]. Write (*cut*) after *pare*.
<u>ch</u>e<u>ck</u>	r. 25	
pró<u>ve</u>[3]₂		
h<u>ear</u>d h<u>ear</u>		Skip a space. Dictate the base word, *hear*, first. After children say the sounds for *hear*, say, "Use $\bar{e}, \breve{e}, \bar{a}$."
in spect		For spelling, say each sound in the second syllable.
it self		For spelling, say each sound in the second syllable.
ằl way<u>s</u>[2]	r. 21	After children say the syllables, say, "Write one *l* when *all* is a prefix." B.E.: The sound of *a* may be altered when followed by an *l*.
some <u>thing</u>₌₅		
ex pect	r. 20	After children say the syllables, say, "Remember *s* almost never follows an *x*." For spelling, say each sound in the first and second syllables.
n<u>ee</u>d		After children say the sounds for *need*, say, "Use the phonogram that says $\bar{e}$."
<u>th</u>us[2]		

Spelling Word	Rule(s)	Instructional Tips
[wom an wom en		For spelling, say *wom en*. For reading, say *wim en*.
young		After children say the sounds for *young*, say, "Use o*w*, ō, ōō, ŭ."
[fair fare		
dol lar	r. 29	For spelling, say both *l*'s. For reading, say the word in normal speech. For spelling, say *lar*.
eve ning		
plan		
broke		
feel		After children say the sounds for *feel*, say, "Use the phonogram that says ē."
[sure sug ar		For spelling, say *s*. For reading, say *sh*. For spelling, say *s*. For reading, say *sh*.
least		After children say the sounds for *least*, say, "Use ē, ĕ, ā."
sor ry	r. 29, 6	After children say the syllables, say, "The first syllable has three sounds." For spelling, say *rĭ*.
press	r. 17	

Spelling Word	Rule(s)	Instructional Tips
God *god*	**r. 26**	
teach er		After children say the syllables, say, "In the first syllable, use ē, ĕ, ā."
No vem b**er**	**r. 26, 4**	
sub ject		For spelling, say each sound in the second syllable.
A pril	**r. 26, 4**	
his t**o** ry	**r. 4, 6**	For spelling, say *rĭ*.
stud y	**r. 6**	For spelling, *y* says *ĭ*.
him self		For spelling, say each sound in the second syllable.
mat t**er**	**r. 29**	For spelling, say both *t*'s.
u$\overset{2}{s}$e		
$\overset{5}{thought}$		After children say the sounds for *thought*, say, "Use ō, o͞o, ŭf, ŏf, aw, ow."
per son		For spelling, say *sŏn*, not *sŭn*.
no**r** **or**		
Jan $\overset{1}{u}$ ăr y	**r. 26, 4, 6**	After children say the syllables, say, "The third syllable has two sounds." For spelling, *y* says *ĭ*.
m**ea**n		After children say the sounds for *mean*, say, "Use ē, ĕ, ā."

Spelling Word	Rule(s)	Instructional Tips
v<u>ote</u>		
c<u>ou</u>rt (2 over ou)		After children say the sounds for *court*, say, "Use *ow, ō, ōō, ŭ*."
cop y	r. 6	For spelling, *y* says *ĭ*.
act		
[b<u>ee</u>n be (with underline)	r. 4	Skip a space. Dictate the base word, *be*, first. For spelling, say *b<u>ee</u>n*. For reading, say *bĭn*. B.E.: *b<u>ee</u>n*.
yes t<u>er</u> d<u>ay</u>	r. 18	
<u>a</u> mo<u>ng</u>	r. 4	
[<u>ques</u> tion (with = under) *quest* (with underline)	r. 14	Skip a space. Dictate the base word, *quest*, first. For spelling, say *tion*. For reading, say *ch̲on*.
doc t<u>or</u>		For spelling, say *or*, not *er*.
s<u>ize</u>		The letter *z* is usually used at the beginning of a base word. (*Size, dozen, organize, realize*, and *citizen* are exceptions.)
D<u>e</u> cem b<u>er</u>	r. 26, 4, 2	
doz en		After children say the syllables, say, "In the first syllable, use *ŏ, ō, ōō*. In the second syllable, use *ĕ, ē*."
th<u>ere</u>₅ (2 1 over there)		
tax		
num b<u>er</u>		

Spelling Word	Rule(s)	Instructional Tips
Oc to ber	**r. 26, 4**	
rea son		After children say the syllables, say, "Use $\bar{e}, \breve{e}, \bar{a}$."
fifth		For spelling, say *f i f th* precisely.
bak ing *bake*	**r. 11**	Skip a space. Dictate the base word, *bake*, first. After children say the syllables, say, "Write *bake* without the *e* before adding the suffix *ing*, which begins with a vowel."
bowl		After children say the sounds for *bowl*, say, "Use *ow*, $\bar{o}$."
cheap		After children say the sounds for *cheap*, say, "Use $\bar{e}, \breve{e}, \bar{a}$."
cheer ful	**r. 22**	After children say the syllables, say, "Write *ful* with one *l* when used as a suffix."
chick en	**r. 25**	
driv ing *drive*	**r. 11**	Skip a space. Dictate the base word, *drive*, first. After children say the syllables, say, "Write *drive* without the *e* before adding the suffix *ing*, which begins with a vowel."
ech oes *ech o*	**r. 4**	Skip a space. Dictate the base word, *echo*, first. After children say the syllables, say, "Use *ch, k, sh*." After children say the syllables in *echoes*, say, "Write $\bar{o}$ and add *es* to form the plural. For spelling and reading, say *oes*."
fair y	**r. 6**	For spelling, *y* says $\breve{i}$.
knock	**r. 25**	After children say the sounds for *knock*, say, "Use two-letter *n* that is used at the beginning of a base word."

Spelling Word	Rule(s)	Instructional Tips
lĕ**ath** **er**		The phonogram *ea* saying *ĕa* never ends a syllable.
lin en		
mix t**ure**	r. 20	For spelling, say *ture*, not *cher*.
nā **tion**	r. 4, 14	After children say the syllables, say, "In the last syllable, use tall *sh*."
pau**s̆e**₅		
p**eac̲e**₃		After children say the sounds for *peace*, say, "Use *ē, ĕ, ā*."
pĕr mis **sion**	r. 14, 15	After children say the syllables, say, "In the last syllable, use *sh, zh*."
rou̅g̈h		After children say the sounds for *rough*, say, "Use *ō, ōō, ŭf, ŏf, aw, ow*."
s̲o **cial**	r. 4, 14	After children say the syllables, say, "In the last syllable, use short *sh*."
st**eal**		After children say the sounds for *steal*, say, "Use *ē, ĕ, ā*."
st**range**		
trŏ **phy**	r. 4, 6	After children say the syllables, say, "Use two-letter *f*." For spelling, say *phĭ*.
[v**oic̆** e**s̆** v**oic̲e**₃	r. 11	Skip a space. Dictate the base word, *voice*, first. After children say the syllables, say, "Write *voice* and add *s* to form the plural."

Section O
132 Words for Spelling, Writing, and Reading

Spelling Word	Rule(s)	Instructional Tips
eight a̲t̲e̲		
a̲ fra̲i̲d	r. 4	
un cl̲e̲₄		
ra̲t̲h er		B.E.: *ra̲t̲h er*.
com f̲or̲t		For spelling, say *or*, not *er*.
e̲ lec t̲i̲on e̲ lect	r. 4, 14 r. 4	Skip a space. Dictate the base word *elect* first. For spelling, say each sound in the second syllable. After children say the syllables for *election*, say, "In the last syllable, use tall *sh*."
a̲ b̲oa̲rd	r. 4	After children say the syllables, say, "In the last syllable, use *oa* of *boat*."
j̲a̲i̲l		B.E.: Spelling alternative is *ga̲ ol*.
s̲h̲ed	r. 13	
r̲e̲ fu̲s̲e̲	r. 4	
dis trict		For spelling, say each sound in the second syllable.
r̲e̲ stra̲i̲n	r. 4	
roy̲ al		For spelling, say *ăl*, not *ŭl*.

Spelling Word	Rule(s)	Instructional Tips
ob jec <u>tion</u> ob ject	r. 14	Skip a space. Dictate the base word, *object*, first. (*Continue to dictate the base word first throughout the section.*) For spelling, say each sound in the second syllable.
pleas̄ ̆ <u>ure</u> meas̄ ̆ <u>ure</u> treas̄ ̆ <u>ure</u>		After children say the syllables, say, "In the first syllable, use ē, ĕ, ā, and s, z. The phonogram *ea* saying *e²a* never ends a syllable. The second syllable is ū r ē." For spelling, say *ūre*, not *er*.
n<u>a</u> vy	r. 4, 6	For spelling, say *vĭ*.
f<u>or</u> ty fou²r teen fou²<u>r</u>th fou²<u>r</u>	r. 6	Skip three spaces. On the fourth line, dictate the base word, *four*. On the third line, write *fourth*. On the second line, write *fourteen*. On the first line, write *forty*. For spelling *forty*, say *tĭ*.
pop <u>u</u> l<u>a</u> <u>tion</u>	r. 4, 14	After children say the syllables, say, "Use tall *sh* in the last syllable."
prop <u>er</u>		
ju<u>dge</u>	r. 23	
we²a²<u>th</u> er whe²<u>th</u> er		After children say the syllables, say, "In the first syllable, use ē, ĕ, ā." The phonogram *ea* saying *e²a* never ends a syllable. For spelling, say *wh*, not *w*.
w<u>or</u>th	r. 8	For spelling, say *wer th*.
con t<u>ai</u>n		
fig <u>ure</u>		B.E.: For spelling, say *fig <u>ure</u>*.

Spelling Word	Rule(s)	Instructional Tips
sud den	r. 29	For spelling, say both *d*'s. For reading, say the word in normal speech. (*Continue to require precise pronunciation for spelling and reading throughout the section.*)
in stēad		After children say the syllables, say, "In the second syllable, use *ē, ĕ, ā*."
thrōw / *thrēw*		After children say the sounds for *throw*, say, "Use *ow, ō*."
pēr son al		For spelling, say *ăl*, not *ŭl*.
ev ēr y thing		For spelling, *y* says *ĭ*.
rāte		
chīef	r. 12	After children say the sounds for *chief*, say, "Use *ē, ī, ĭ*."
pēr fect		For spelling, say each sound in the second syllable.
sec ond		
slīde		
fār thēr		
dū ty	r. 4, 6	For spelling, say *tĭ*.
in tend		
com pan y	r. 6	For spelling, *y* says *ĭ*.
quite / *quit* / *qui et*	r. 5	

Spelling Word	Rule(s)	Instructional Tips
none͞e₅		
knéw² knów²		After children say the sounds, say, "Use two-letter *n* that is used at the beginning of a base word."
re main	r. 4	
di rec tion di rect	r. 14	For spelling, say *dĭ*. Base word. For spelling, say each sound in the second syllable.
ap pear	r. 29	After children say the syllables, say, "Use *ē, ĕ, ā*." For spelling, say both *p*'s. For reading, say the word in normal speech.
lib er ty	r. 6	For spelling, say *tĭ*.
e nough³	r. 4	After children say the syllables, say, "In the last syllable, use *ō, ōō, ŭf, ŏf, aw, ow*."
fact		For spelling say *f a k t*.
board		After children say the sounds for *board*, say, "Use *oa* of *boat*."
Sep tem ber	r. 26	
sta tion	r. 4, 14	
at tend	r. 29	
pub lic mu šic² pic nic	r. 4	

Spelling Word	Rule(s)	Instructional Tips
frien̄ds² / frie̱nd	r. 12 / r. 12	Base word. After children say the sounds for *friend*, say, "Use *ē, ī, ĭ*." The *ĕ* is an uncommon sound for *ie*." For spelling, say *f r ē n d*. For reading, say *frĕnd*.
dŭr ing		After children say the syllables, say, "In the first syllable, put a 2 over the *u* because it says the second sound."
po̱ li̱ce₃	r. 4	For spelling, say *pō l ĭ ĉ² ē*. The French *i* says *ē*.
un til	r. 22	After children say the syllables, say, "In the last syllable, write *till* with only one *l* when written with another syllable."
tru̱ ly / true̱₂	r. 6	The silent final *e* is no longer needed. For spelling, say *lĭ*. Base word.
who̱le / ho̱le		For spelling, say *wh*. For reading, say *h*.
ad dress	r. 29, 17	
re̱ que̱st	r. 4	
rai̱s̱e²₅		After children say the sounds for *raise*, say, "Use *s, z*."
Au gust	r. 26	After children say the syllables, say, "The last syllable has four sounds."
struc̱ḵ	r. 25	

Spelling Word	Rule(s)	Instructional Tips
get ting get	r. 9	One-one-one rule. Base word.
don't = dŏ³ not	r. 19	
Thurs² day Sat ur day	r. 26, 18 r. 26, 18	
ad mis sion	r. 14, 15	After children say the syllables, say, "In the last syllable, use *sh, zh*." Base word is *admit*.
că¹ nŏe³₅		
cap tain		For spelling, say *tain*.
cau tiŏu⁴s cau tion	r. 14 r. 14	After children say the syllables, say, "In the last syllable, use tall *sh* and *ow, ō, o͞o, ŭ*." Base word.
cel lar	r. 2, 29	For spelling, say *ar*, not *er*.
cov erĕd²	r. 28	
crea ture		After children say the syllables, say, "In the first syllable, use *ē, ĕ, ā*." The second syllable says *ture*.
cur tain		For spelling, say *tain*.
de clarĕd² de clare	r. 4, 11, 28 r. 4	Base word.
dis tance₃ dis tant		

Spelling Word	Rule(s)	Instructional Tips
ex pl<u>ai</u>n	r. 20	
fl<u>oa</u>t <u>ed</u>	r. 28	After children say the syllables, say, "Use ō of *boat* in the first syllable."
<u>g</u>host	r. 19	After children say the sounds for *ghost*, say, "Use the additional phonogram *gh*."
⎡ hol i d<u>ay</u> ⎣ h<u>o</u> ly	r. 24, 18 r. 4, 6	After children say the syllables, say, "In the second syllable, use ĭ, ī, instead of *y*." Base word. For spelling, say *lĭ*.
<u>kn</u><u>ee</u>		After children say the sounds for *knee*, say, "Use two-letter *n* that is used at the beginning of a base word and the phonogram that says ē."
lem on		
⎡ l<u>y</u> ing ⎣ l<u>ie</u>²	r. 5 r. 12	After children say the syllables, say, "In the first syllable, use *y*, ĭ, ī." Base word. After children say sounds, say, "Use ē, ī, ĭ."
n<u>ai</u>l<u>s</u>²		
n<u>ee</u> dl<u>e</u>₄		After children say the syllables, say, "In the first syllable, use the phonogram that says ē."
n<u>o</u> bod y	r. 4, 6	For spelling, *y* says ĭ.
<u>oa</u>r		After children say the sounds for *oar*, say, "Use *oa* of *boat*."
pal a<u>ce</u>₃		For spelling, say ă c ē.
pen ny	r. 29, 6	For spelling, say nĭ.

Spelling Word	Rule(s)	Instructional Tips
reg <u>u</u> <u>lar</u>	r. 4	For spelling, say *ar*, not *er*.
r<u>e</u> p<u>ea</u>ts	r. 4	After children say the syllables, say, "Use *ē, ĕ, ā* in the second syllable."
s<u>ai</u>l <u>or</u>		For spelling, say *or*, not *er*.
sen ten<u>ce</u>₃		
<u>shin</u> <u>ing</u> *shine*	r. 11	Base word.
<u>sur</u> f<u>ace</u>		After children say the syllables, say, "Use the *er* of *nurse* in the first syllable." For spelling, say *face*.
sw<u>ee</u>p <u>ing</u> sw<u>ee</u>ps		After children say the sounds for *sweeps*, say, "Use the phonogram that says *ē*."
thief	r. 12	After children say the sounds for *thief*, say, "Use *ē, ī, ĭ*."
w<u>ai</u>st w<u>aste</u>		
w<u>ai</u>t <u>ing</u>		
w<u>ea</u> ry	r. 6	After children say the syllables, say, "Use *ē, ĕ, ā* in the first syllable." For spelling, say *rĭ*.
<u>writ</u> <u>ing</u> <u>writ</u> <u>er</u> <u>write</u>	r. 11 r. 11	Skip two spaces. On the third line, dictate the base word, *write*. On the second line, dictate *writer*. On the first line, dictate *writing*.

Section P
113 Words for Spelling, Writing, and Reading

Spelling Words	Rule(s)	Instructional Tips
spend		
en joy		For spelling, say *ĕn*, not *ĭn*.
[**aw fŭl³** [**awe₅**	r. 22	Skip a space. Dictate the base word *awe*, first. (*Continue dictating the base word first throughout the section.*) In *awful*, the silent final *e* is not needed. After children say the syllables, say, "When *full* is used as a suffix, we write one *l*."
u̇ s̲u̲² al	r. 4, 11	For spelling, say *al*. Base word is *use*.
com plaint		
au to̲	r. 4	
va̲ ca̲ t̲ion	r. 4, 11, 14	Base word is *vacate*.
[**beau ti fŭl³** [*beau ty*	r. 24, 22 r. 6	After children say the syllables, say, "In the last syllable, write one *l* when *full* is used as a suffix." Base word. After children say the syllables, say, "In the first syllable, the additional phonogram *eau* (French) says *ū*."
flight		
trav el		For spelling, say *el*, not *ul*.
rap id		
re̲ pair	r. 4	

Spelling Word	Rule(s)	Instructional Tips
trŏu̲ bling trŏu̲ ble̲₄	r. 11	After children say the syllables, say, "Use *ow*, *ō*, *o̅o̅*, *ŭ*." Base word. For spelling, say only two syllables.
en tran<u>ce</u>₃		
im p<u>or</u> tan<u>ce</u>₃ im p<u>or</u> tant		
căr rĭ<u>e</u>d căr ry	r. 29, 24, 28 r. 29, 6	After children say the syllables, say, "In the last syllable, use *ĭ*, *ī*, instead of *y* and add the suffix. The letters *ie* together say *ĭ* and the suffix says *ĕd*." Base word. For spelling, say both *r*'s and *rĭ*. (*Continue to require precise pronunciation for spelling and reading throughout the section.*)
loss	r. 17	
f<u>or</u> t<u>une</u>		For spelling, say *tune*, not *chune*.
em p<u>ire</u>		
m<u>ay</u> <u>or</u>		After children say the syllables, say, "Use *ā* that is used at the end of a word." For spelling, say *or*. B.E: For reading, say *ĕr*.
w<u>ai</u>t		
d<u>e</u> gr<u>ee</u>	r. 4	After children say the syllables, say, "Use the phonogram that says *ē*."
prĭṡ on		For spelling, say *ŏn*, not *ŭn*. After children say the syllables, say, "Use *s*, *z*."

Spelling Word	Rule(s)	Instructional Tips
en gine̲₅	r. 3	
vĭs̆ it		After children say the syllables, say, "Use *s, z*."
guest guess	r. 17	
de̲ p̲a̲rt ment	r. 4	
ob ta̲i̲n		
fam i ly	r. 6	
fa̲ v o̲r	r. 4	For spelling, say *or*. B.E.: Spelling is *fa̲ vo̲ur*.
Mrs.	r. 26	Have children write the abbreviation saying the letter name. For reading, say *Mis ŭs̆*. B.E.: Full stop (period) is not used. *Mrs* is the international alternative.
Mr. = M̲is te̲r	r. 26	B.E.: Full stop (period) is not used. *Mr* is the international alternative.
Miss	r. 26, 17	
hŭs̆ band		
a̲ m o̲u̲nt	r. 4	
hu̲ man	r. 4	
vĭĕ̲w		For spelling, say each sound, *v ĭ ĕ̯w*. For reading, say *vū*.
cle̲rk		B.E.: *cle̲rk*. For reading, say *clark*.
thŏugh		

Spelling Word	Rule(s)	Instructional Tips
o'clock = o(f the) clock	r. 4, 25	
sup port	r. 29	
does do		Write *do* and add *es*. For spelling, say each sound, *d oe s*. For reading, say *dus*. Base word.
re gard	r. 4	
es cape		
since		
which		For spelling, say *wh*, not *w*.
length long *strength* *strong*		For spelling, say *ng* precisely. Base word. For spelling, say *ng* precisely. Base word.
de stroy	r. 4	
news pa per	r. 4	
daugh ter *naugh ty* *caught* *taught*	 r. 6	After children say the syllables, say, "In the first syllable, the additional phonogram *augh* says *au*." For spelling *naughty*, say *ti*."
an swer		For spelling, say *s w er*. For reading, say *ser*.
re ply	r. 4, 5, 6	

Spelling Word	Rule(s)	Instructional Tips
s<u>ai</u>l *s<u>a</u>l<u>e</u>*		
cit <u>ie</u>s cit y	r. 2, 24 r. 2, 6	After children say the syllables, say, "In the last syllable, use ĭ, ī instead of *y* and add es̆. The letters *ie* together say ĭ, and *s* says s̆." Base word.
kno̊wn kno̊w		After children say the sounds for each word, say, "Use two-letter *n* that is used at the beginning of a base word and *ow*, ō." Base word.
sev <u>er</u> al		For spelling, say *al*, not *ul*.
de s̊<u>i</u>r<u>e</u>	r. 4	After children say the syllables, say, "Use *s*, *z* in the second syllable."
n<u>ea</u>r ly	r. 6	After children say the syllables, say, "Use ē, ĕ, ā." For spelling, say lĭ.
t<u>oo</u> tw<u>o</u>̊ to̊		After children say the sounds for *too*, say "Use o͞o, ŏo." For spelling, say *t w* o̊. For reading, say to̊.
an i mal		For spelling, say *măl*, not *mŭl*.
b<u>a</u> sin	r. 4	
br<u>ee</u>z<u>e</u>₅		After children say the sounds for *breeze*, say, "Use the phonogram that says ē."
but ton	r. 29	For spelling, say *tŏn*.
cab b<u>a</u>g<u>e</u>=₃	r. 29	For spelling, say ă g ē.

Spelling Word	Rule(s)	Instructional Tips
c<u>are</u> fŭl	r. 22	After children say the syllables, say, "In the last syllable, write one *l* when *full* is a suffix."
cou͞gh		
c<u>ou</u>s̆ in		After children say the syllables, say, "In the first syllable, use *ow*, *ō*, *o͞o*, *ŭ* and *s*, *z*."
dol l<u>ar</u>s̆	r. 29	For spelling, say *ar*, not *er*.
⎡ *ex c<u>use</u>* ⎣ *ex cu<u>s̆</u>e*	r. 20 r. 20	After children say the syllables, say, "Remember *s* almost never follows *x*. Use *ks*."
i<u>s</u> land	r. 5, 19	For spelling, say *ĭs land*.
gr<u>ie</u>f	r. 12	After children say the sounds for *grief*, say, "Use *ē*, *ī*, *ĭ*."
<u>gu</u>ard		
<u>gu</u>il ty	r. 6	
hun gry	r. 6	
lan <u>gu</u>age		After children say the syllables, say, "The phonogram *gu* also says *gw*. The *u* says *w* as it does in *qu* (*kw*)."
⎡ *l<u>augh</u> ter* ⎣ *l<u>augh</u>*		Base word. After children say the sounds for *laugh*, say, "The additional phonogram *augh* also says *ăf*." For reading, say *lăf*. B.E.: *lăf*.
⎡ *l<u>i</u>n ing* ⎣ *l<u>ine</u>*	r. 11	 Base word.

Spelling Word	Rule(s)	Instructional Tips
o cean	r. 4	After children say the syllables, say, "In the last syllable, the additional phonogram *ce* says *sh*."
neph ew		After children say the syllables, say, "Use two-letter *f* and *ōō*, *ū*."
nine teen		
no ticed	r. 4, 11, 28	
no tice	r. 4	Base word.
pas sen gers	r. 29, 3	
re mained	r. 4, 28	
re treat ing	r. 4	After children say the syllables, say, "Use *ē*, *ĕ*, *ā* in the second syllable."
style		After children say the sounds for *style*, say, "Use *y*, *ĭ*, *ī*."
sub tract		For spelling, say each sound in the second syllable.
tai lor		For spelling, say *or*, not *er*.
thumb		For spelling, say *th ŭ m b*.
tri al	r. 5	For spelling, say *ăl*, not *ŭl*.
voy age		
whis per		
wrong		After children say the sounds for *wrong*, say, "Use two-letter *r*."

Section Q
127 Words for Spelling, Writing, and Reading

Spelling Words	Rule(s)	Instructional Tips
some͟e₅time͟s̲²		
en ga͟ge͟		
fi̱ nal	r. 5, 11	Base word is *fine*.
tė̱r ri ble͟₄	r. 29	After children say the syllables, say, "The first syllable has three separate sounds." For spelling, say both *r*'s. For reading, say the word in normal speech. (*Continue to require precise pronunciation for spelling and reading throughout the section.*)
su͟r pri̱se²		After children say the syllables, say, "In the first syllable, use *er* of *nurse*. In the second syllable, use *s, z.*"
pe͟ ri od	r. 4	
ad di t͟ion	r. 29, 14	
em plo͟y		
prop e͟r ty	r. 6	For spelling, say *tĭ*. (*Continue to require precise pronunciation of vowels in unaccented syllables throughout the section.*)
se͟ lect	r. 4	For spelling, say each sound in the second syllable. (*Continue to require precise pronunciation throughout the section.*)
con nec t͟ion con nect	r. 29, 14 r. 29	Skip a space. Dictate the base word, *connect*, first. For spelling, say each sound in the second syllable. (*Continue to dictate the base word first throughout the section.*)

Spelling Word	Rule(s)	Instructional Tips
f**ir**m		After children say the sounds for *firm*, say, "Use the *er* of *first*."
r**e** gion *r**e** li gion*	r. 4 r. 4	After children say the syllables, say, "In the last syllable, the additional phonogram *gi* says *j*."
con vict		For spelling, say each sound in the second syllable.
pr**i** v**a**t**e**₅	r. 5	
com mand	r. 29	
d**e** b**ate**	r. 4	
cr**ow**d		After children say the sounds for *crowd*, say, "Use *ow*, *ō*."
fac t**o** ry	r. 4, 6	
pub li**sh**	r. 13	
rep r**e** ṡent	r. 4	After children say the syllables, say, "In the last syllable, use *s*, *z*."
t**er**m		
sec **ti**on	r. 14	
rel **a** ti**ve**₂ r**e** l**ate**	r. 4, 11 r. 4	Base word.
prog ress *pr**o** gress*	r. 17 r. 4, 17	
en t**ire**		

Spelling Word	Rule(s)	Instructional Tips
pre$\overset{2}{s}$ i dent pre $\overset{2}{s}$<u>i</u>de	r. 11 r. 4	After children say the syllables, say, "Use *s, z*." Base word.
f<u>a</u> m<u>o</u>$\overset{4}{u}$s f<u>ame</u>	r. 4, 11	After children say the syllables, say, "In the last syllable, use *ow, ō, ōō, ŭ*." Base word.
s<u>er</u> <u>ve</u>₂		
es t<u>ate</u>		
r<u>e</u> mem b<u>er</u>	r. 4	
<u>ei</u> $\overset{2}{ther}$	r. 12	After children say the syllables, say, "In the first syllable, use *ē, ā, ĭ*."
ef f<u>or</u>t	r. 29	For spelling, say *or*, not *er*.
d<u>ue</u>₂ d$\overset{2}{\underline{ew}}$		For spelling, say *ū* distinctly.
in cl<u>ude</u>		
al l<u>ow</u>	r. 29	
p<u>o</u> $\overset{2}{si}$ t<u>ion</u>	r. 4, 14	After children say the syllables, say, "In the second syllable, use *s, z*. In the third syllable, use tall *sh*."
le<u>dg</u>e	r. 23	After children say the sounds for *ledge*, say, "Use three-letter *j*."
cl<u>ai</u>m		
pr<u>i</u> m<u>a</u> ry	r. 5, 4, 6	
r<u>e</u> $\overset{2}{s}$ult	r. 4	After children say the syllables, say, "In the last syllable, use *s, z*."

Spelling Word	Rule(s)	Instructional Tips
ap p<u>oi</u>nt	r. 29	
in f<u>or</u> ma <u>ti</u>on	r. 4, 14	
wh[3]<u>o</u>m **wh[3]<u>o</u>**		For spelling, say *wh ō m*. For spelling, say *wh ō*.
[1]<u>a</u>r rest	r. 29	
<u>th</u>[2]em selv<u>es</u>[2] *self* *ca<u>lve</u>s[2]* *ca<u>l</u>f* *ha<u>lve</u>s[2]* *ha<u>l</u>f*		After children say the syllables, say, "In the second syllable, use *v* instead of *f* and add *es*[2]." For spelling, say each sound in the second syllable. Base word. After children say the sounds for *calves*, say, "Use *v* instead of *f* and add *es*[2]." B.E.: *ca[3]<u>lve</u>s[2]*. Base word. B.E.: *ca[3]<u>l</u>f*. After children say the sounds for *halves*, say, "Use *v* instead of *f* and add *es*[2]." B.E.: *ha[3]<u>lve</u>s[2]*. Base word. B.E.: *ha[3]<u>l</u>f*.
spe[1] <u>ci</u>al	r. 14	After children say the syllables, say, "In the last syllable, use short *sh*."
pre<u>s</u>[2] ent **pre[2] <u>s</u>ent**	 r. 4	After children say the syllables, say, "In the first syllable, use *s, z*."
ac <u>ti</u>on **act**	r. 14	After children say the syllables, say, "The base word tells you which phonogram to use." Base word.

Spelling Word	Rule(s)	Instructional Tips
jus tic̲e₃ just		Base word.
gen tl̲e₄ man *gen tl̲e₄*	r. 3 r. 3	Dictate *gentle* first.
en clo̅s̲e		After children say the syllables, say, "In the last syllable, use *s, z*."
a̲ wa̲it	r. 4	
sup po̅s̲e	r. 29	After children say the syllables, say, "In the last syllable, use *s, z*."
won de̲r fu̅l	r. 22	After children say the syllables, say, "When *full* is a suffix, write one *l*."
fo̲r wa̲rd *ba̲ck wa̲rd* to̲ wa̲rd	 r. 25 r. 4	For spelling, say *ar*, not *or*. For spelling, say *to̲ wa̲rd*. For reading, say *toa̲rd*. B.E.: For spelling, say *to̅ wa̲rd*. For reading, say *to̅ wa̲wd*.
al tho̲ugh	r. 21	After children say the syllables, say, "When *all* is a prefix, write one *l*."
prompt		For spelling, say each sound precisely.
at tempt	r. 29	For spelling, say each sound in the second syllable.
who̅s̲e₅ who̅		For spelling, say *wh o̅ s̲ e*. For reading, say *ho̅s̲*. Dictate *who* first.

Spelling Word	Rule(s)	Instructional Tips
[state ment [state		Base word.
per haps		
[their [they	r. 12	After children say the sounds for *their,* say, "Use ē, ā, ĭ." Dictate *they* first.
im pris on		After children say the syllables, say, "In the second syllable, use s, z."
[writ ten [writ	r. 9	One-one-one rule. Base word.
ar range	r. 29	After children say the syllables, say, "The last syllable has two separate consonants between the *a* and the silent *e*."
an kle₄		For spelling, say ăn; say each sound in the second syllable *k, l, ē.*
ap pears	r. 29	After children say the syllables, say, "Use ē, ĕ, ā."
[brace let [brace		Base word.
[breathe₅ [breath		After children say the sounds for each word, say, "Use ē, ĕ, ā." Base word.
calm		For spelling, say c ä l m.

Spelling Word	Rule(s)	Instructional Tips
ci̲r cus	r. 2	After children say the syllables, say, "In the first syllable, use the *er* of *first*."
con sent e̲d	r. 28	
con tin ue̊²d con tin u̲e̲₂	r. 11, 28	After children say the syllables, say, "Write *continue* without the *e* before adding the suffix *e̊²d*, which begins with a vowel." Base word.
då²n ge̲r o̊u̲s⁴	r. 3	After children say the syllables, say, "In the first syllable, put a 2 over the *a* because it is saying its second sound in the middle of a syllable."
deb̲t		For spelling, say *d ĕ b t*.
dri̲e̲²²d dr̲y	r. 24, 28 r. 5, 6	After children say the sounds for *dried*, say, "Use *i* instead of *y* and add the past tense suffix. The phonogram *ie* says *ī* and the suffix says *e̊²d*." Base word.
ex h̲aust	r. 20	For spelling, say *h au s t*.
ex e̲r ci̲s̲²e	r. 20, 2	After children say the syllables, say, "In the last syllable, use *s, z*."
ex plo̲ s̲i̲²on	r. 20, 4, 16	After children say the syllables, say, "In the last syllable, use *sh, zh*."
gram ma̲r	r. 29	For spelling, say *ar*, not *er*.
In di an	r. 26	
jou̲r ne̊³y jou̲r nal cou̲r ag̲e		After children say the syllables, say, "In the first syllable, the additional phonogram *our* says *er*." B.E.: For reading, say *cŭr ag̲e*.

Spelling Word	Rule(s)	Instructional Tips
laid *lay*	r. 18	Base word.
pack age *pack*	r. 25 r. 25	Base word.
phys i cal		After children say the syllables, say, "In the first syllable, use *y*, *ĭ*, *ī* and *s*, *z*. Say *ăl*, not *ŭl*."
praises		After children say the sounds for *praise*, say, "Use *s*, *z*."
prop er ly	r. 6	
searched	r. 28	After children say the sounds for *searched*, say, "Use the *er* of *early*."
smooth		
thir teen		After children say the syllables, say, "In the first syllable, use the *er* of *first*."
throat		After children say the sounds for *throat*, say, "Use *oa* of *boat*."
touch		After children say the sounds for *touch*, say, "Use *ow*, *ō*, *ōō*, *ŭ*."
tow el		After children say the syllables, say, "Use *ow*, *ō*."
um brel la	r. 29	After children say the syllables, say, "In the third syllable, use *ă*, *ā*, *ah*."
weap on		The phonogram *ea* saying *ĕa* never ends a syllable.

Section R
125 Words for Spelling, Writing, and Reading

Spelling Words	Rule(s)	Instructional Tips
$\Big[$ lo̅s̆e̠₅ l$\underline{oo}$se̠₅		After children say the sounds for *lose*, say, "Use ŏ, ō, o͞o and *s, z*."
$\Big[$ com bi na̲ <u>tion</u> com b<u>ine</u>	r. 11, 4, 14	Skip a space. Dictate the base word, *combine*, first. (*Continue to dictate the base word first throughout the section.*) After children say the syllables, say, "Write *combine* without the *e* before adding the suffix *a tion* that begins with a vowel, and use tall *sh*."
av e̊ n<u>ue̠</u>₂		For spelling, say *ū*.
n<u>eigh</u> bor		After children say the syllables, say, "Use four-letter *ā*." For spelling, say *or, not er*. B.E.: Spelling is *n<u>eigh</u> bŏ̈ur*.
$\Big[$ *w<u>eigh</u>t* w<u>eigh</u>		Base word. After children say the sound for *weigh*, say, "Use four-letter *ā*."
w$\overset{3}{e̊}$ar		After children say the sounds for *wear*, say, "Use ē, ĕ, ā." B.E.: *w$\overset{2}{e̊}$ar*.
en t<u>er</u> t<u>ai</u>n		
sal <u>a</u> ry	r. 4, 6	For spelling, say *rĭ*. (*Continue to require precise pronunciation of vowels in unaccented syllables throughout the section.*)

Spelling Word	Rule(s)	Instructional Tips
vis̆ i t<u>or</u> vis̆ it		After children say the syllables, say, "Use *s, z*." For spelling, say *or*, not *er*. Base word.
pub li c<u>a</u> <u>ti</u>on	r. 4, 14	After children say the syllables, say, "Use tall *sh* in the last syllable."
ma <u>ch</u>ĭn<u>e</u>₅		For spelling, say *ch̆ ĭ n ē*. The French *i* says *ē*.
t<u>o</u> <u>w</u>ard	r. 4	For spelling, say *t<u>o</u> <u>w</u>ard*. For reading, say *t<u>oa</u>rd*. B.E.: For spelling, say *tŏ̆ w<u>ar</u>d*. For reading, say *tŏ̆ w<u>aw</u>d*.
suc cess	r. 2, 17	
dr<u>ow</u>n		
<u>a</u> dopt	r. 4	For spelling, say each sound in the second syllable. (*Continue to require precise pronunciation throughout the section.*)
s<u>e</u> c<u>ure</u>	r. 4	
<u>h</u>on <u>or</u>		For spelling, say *hŏn or*. Say *or*, not *er*. B.E.: Spelling is *<u>h</u>on ŏur*.
prom is<u>e</u>₅		
<u>wreck</u>	r. 25	
pr<u>e</u> p<u>are</u>	r. 4	
ves sel	r. 29	For spelling, say both *s*'s. For reading, say the word in normal speech. (*Continue to require precise pronunciation for spelling and reading throughout the section.*)

Spelling Word	Rule(s)	Instructional Tips
bu̲ s̆y²	r. 6	For spelling, say *bŭ s̆ ĭ*. For reading, say *bĭ s̆ĭ*.
pref e̲r en̲c̲e₃ pre̲ f̲er	 r. 4	In *preference*, another *r* is not added, because the accent shifts to the first syllable, *pref*. Base word.
il lus tr̲a tion il lus tr̲ate	r. 29, 4, 11, 14 r. 29	After children say the syllables, say, "Write *illustrate* without the *e* before adding the suffix *a tion* that begins with a vowel." Base word.
dif f̲er ent dif f̲er	r. 29 r. 29	 Base word.
pro̲ vi s̲io̲n² pro̲ v̲id̲e	r. 4, 16 r. 4	 Base word.
ac c̲ord in̲g	r. 29	
ål re̊ad y³ ²	r. 21, 6	After children say the syllables, say, "Write one *l* when *all* is a prefix. In the second syllable, use *ē, ĕ, ā*." The phonogram *ea* saying *e̊a²* never ends a syllable.
at ten tion	r. 29, 14	
ed u̲ c̲a tion	r. 4, 11, 14	After children say the syllables, say, "In the last syllable, use tall *sh*."
di rec to̲r di rect		For spelling, say *or*, not *er*. Base word. For spelling, say each sound in the second syllable.

Spelling Word	Rule(s)	Instructional Tips
p**ur** pos**e**₅		After children say the syllables, say, "In the first syllable, use the *er* of *nurse*."
com mon	r. 29	
di̲ a̲ mond	r. 5, 4	
to̍³ ge**th** **er**²		
con ven **ti**on	r. 14	
in cr**eas**e₅		After children say the syllables, say, "In the last syllable, use ē, ĕ, ā."
man n**er**	r. 29	
f**ea** t**ure**		After children say the syllables, say, "In the first syllable, use ē, ĕ, ā."
ar ti cl**e**₄		
s**er**v ic**e**₃ / s**erv**e₂	r. 11	Base word.
*in j**u** ry* / in j**ure**	r. 4, 11, 6	Base word.
ef fect	r. 29	For spelling, say each sound in the second syllable.
dis trib **ute**		
gen **er** al	r. 3	
to̍³ mor̍¹ r**ow**²	r. 29	For spelling, say each syllable precisely.
con sid **er**		

Spelling Word	Rule(s)	Instructional Tips
a gainst	r. 4	B.E.: May be _a gainst_.
a gain	r. 4	Base word. For spelling, say _gain_. B.E.: May be _a gain_.
com plete		
search		After children say the sounds for _search_, say, "Use the _er_ of _early_."
treas ure		After children say the syllables, say, "In the first syllable, use ē, ĕ, ā and _s_, _z_."
pop u lar	r. 4	For spelling, say _ar_, not _er_.
Christ mas	r. 26	For spelling, say _Chrĭst mas_.
Christ	r. 26, 19	Base word.
in ter est		
ad vice		After children say the syllables, say, "Use _s_, _z_ in the second syllable."
ad vise		
A mer i can	r. 26, 4	
A mer i că	r. 26, 4	Base word.
bar gain		
be neath	r. 4	After children say the syllables, say, "In the last syllable, use ē, ĕ, ā."
be yond	r. 4	

Spelling Word	Rule(s)	Instructional Tips
br<u>o</u> ken br<u>oke</u> br<u>ēă</u>k	r. 4, 11	Base word. After children say the sounds for *break*, say, "Use *ē, ĕ, ā*."
c<u>o</u> c<u>oa</u>	r. 4	After children say the syllables, say, "In the last syllable, use *oa* of *boat*."
col l<u>ar</u>	r. 29	For spelling, say *ar*, not *er*.
com p<u>ă</u>r i son com p<u>are</u>	r. 11	 Base word.
con troll<u>ĕ</u>d con tr<u>ŏ</u>l	r. 10, 19, 28	After children say the syllables, say, "Write *control* with another *l* before adding the suffix that begins with a vowel." Base word.
de<u>b</u>ts		For spelling, say *d ĕ b t s*.
di<u>š</u> as t<u>er</u>		After children say the syllables, say, "In the first syllable, use *s, z*." B.E.: *di<u>š</u> ă<u>s</u> t<u>er</u>*.
<u>ea</u> g<u>er</u>		After children say the syllables, say, "In the first syllable, use *ē, ĕ, ā*."
en <u>e</u> my	r. 4, 6	
ex am pl<u>e</u>₄	r. 20	
ex c<u>īte</u> ment ex cit <u>ing</u> ex c<u>īte</u>	r. 20, 2 r. 20, 2, 11 r. 20, 2	 Base word.

Spelling Word	Rule(s)	Instructional Tips
f<u>ier</u>c<u>e</u>₃	r. 12	After children say the sounds for *fierce*, say, "Use ē, ī, ĭ."
fl<u>ew</u> fl<u>ie</u>s^{2 2} fl<u>y</u>	r. 24 r. 5, 6	After children say the sounds for *flies*, say, "Use *i*, instead of *y* and add *eš*. The *ie* together says ī." Base word.
f<u>or</u> got <u>te</u>n f<u>or</u> got	r. 10	Dictate *forgot* first. After children say the syllables, say, "Write *forgot* with another *t* before adding the suffix that begins with a vowel."
g<u>i</u> gan tic g<u>i</u> ant	r. 3, 5 r. 3, 5	Base word.
g<u>ui</u>de		
h<u>ur</u> ry <u>ing</u> h<u>ur</u> r<u>ie</u>d^{3 2} h<u>ur</u> ry	r. 29 r. 29, 24, 28 r. 29, 6	After children say the syllables, say, "Write *hurry* and add the suffix *ing*. Do not change the *y* to *i* because two *i*'s are not written together." After children say the syllables, say, "In the last syllable, use *i* instead of *y* and add the past tense suffix. The *ie* together says ĭ." Base word.
knowl edge kn<u>o</u>w²	r. 23	For spelling, say *kn <u>ow</u> l.* Base word.
l<u>aw</u> yer		
pär¹ <u>a</u> gra<u>ph</u>	r. 4	After children say the syllables, say, "Use two-letter *f* in the third syllable."
p<u>a</u> <u>t</u>ient p<u>a</u> <u>t</u>ienc<u>e</u>₃	r. 4, 14 r. 4, 14	After children say the syllables, say, "In the second syllable, use tall *sh*."

Spelling Word	Rule(s)	Instructional Tips
p<u>i</u> an ist p<u>i</u> an ō̇s p<u>i</u> an <u>o</u>	 r. 4	After children say the syllables, say, "Italian words ending in *o* add *s* to form plurals." Base word. For spelling, say *pĭ*. The Italian *i* says *ē*.
pi<u>ck</u> les̆² pi<u>ck</u> l<u>e</u>₄	r. 25 r. 25	For spelling, say *l ĕ s̆*. Base word. For spelling, say *l ē*, not *ĕl*.
pris̆² on <u>er</u>		After children say the syllables, say, "In the first syllable, use *s, z*."
r<u>e</u> l<u>ea</u>s<u>e</u>₅	r. 4	After children say the syllables, say, "In the last syllable, use *ē, ĕ, ā*."
r<u>e</u> s̆²<u>ign</u>	r. 4, 19	After children say the syllables, say, "In the last syllable, use *s, z* and two-letter *n*."
r<u>e</u> v<u>ea</u>l	r. 4	After children say the syllables, say, "In the last syllable, use *ē, ĕ, ā*."
sl<u>ee</u>v<u>e</u>₂		After children say the sounds for *sleeve*, say, "Use the phonogram that says *e*."
sol <u>dier</u>	r. 19	After children say the syllables, say, "In the last syllable, the additional phonogram *di* says *j*."
sum <u>ma</u> ry sum	r. 9, 4, 6	One-one-one rule. Base word.
s<u>w</u>ord		For spelling, say *s w or d*.
t<u>o</u> m<u>a</u> to<u>e</u>s² t<u>o</u> m<u>a</u> t<u>o</u>	r. 4 r. 4	After children say the syllables, say, "In the last syllable, write *tō* and add *es̆*. The *oe* together says *ō*." Base word. B.E.: *t<u>o</u> m<u>ȧ</u>³ t<u>o</u>*.

Section S
125 Words for Spelling, Writing, and Reading

Spelling Words	Rule(s)	Instructional Tips
of <u>t</u>en		For spelling, say *ŏf tĕn*. For reading, say *ŏf ĕn*.
mo̲ <u>t</u>ion	r. 4, 14	After the children say the syllables, say, "In the last syllable, use tall *sh*."
<u>the</u> a̲ te̲r	r. 4	Accent is on the first syllable. B.E.: Spelling is <u>the</u> a̲ tre̲₄.
[im pro̲ve̲₂ment **[*im pro̲ve̲₂***		Skip a space. Dictate *improve,* first.
[cen tu̲ ry **[cent**	r. 2, 4, 6 r. 2	Skip a space. Dictate *cent* first. (*Continue to dictate the base word first throughout the section.*) For spelling, say *rĭ*. (*Continue to require precise pronunciation of vowels in unaccented syllables throughout the section.*)
to̲ tal	r. 4	
men <u>t</u>ion	r. 14	After children say the syllables, say, "Use tall *sh*."
a̍r ri̲ve̲	r. 29	For spelling, say both *r*'s. For reading, say the word in normal speech. (*Continue to require precise pronunciation for spelling and reading throughout the section.*)
sup pl<u>y</u>	r. 29, 5, 6	
as sist	r. 29	
dif fe̲r ence̲₃	r. 29	

Spelling Word	Rule(s)	Instructional Tips
ex am i na tion ex am ine₅	r. 20, 11, 4, 14 r. 20	Dictate *examine* first. For spelling, say *ex am ĭnē*. For reading, say *eg zam in*.
par tic u lar	r. 4	
af fair	r. 29	
course₅ coarse₅		After children say the sounds for *course*, say, "Use *ow, ō, ōō, ŭ*." After children say the sounds for *coarse*, say, "Use *oa* of *boat*."
nei ther	r. 12	After children say the syllables, say, "In the first syllable, use *ē, ā, ĭ*."
lo cal	r. 4	
mar riage mar ry	r. 29, 24 r. 29, 6	After children say the syllables, say, "In the last syllable, use *i*, instead of *y* and add the suffix *age*." Base word.
car riage car ry	r. 29, 24 r. 29, 6	After children say the syllables, say, "In the last syllable, use *i*, instead of *y* and add the suffix *age*." Base word.
fur ther		After children say the syllables, say, "In the first syllable, use the *er* of *nurse*."
se ri ous	r. 4	After children say the syllables, say, "In the last syllable, use *ow, ō, ōō, ŭ*."
doubt		For spelling, say *d ou b t*.
con di tion	r. 14	After children say the syllables, say, "Use tall *sh*."

Spelling Word	Rule(s)	Instructional Tips
gov <u>ern</u> ment *gov <u>ern</u>*		For spelling, say *ern*, not *er*. Base word.
<u>o</u> pin <u>i</u>on on <u>i</u>on ŭn <u>i</u>on com pan <u>i</u>on mil l<u>i</u>on b<u>e</u> hav <u>ior</u>	r. 4 r. 29 r. 4, 11	For spelling, say *ĭon*. For reading, say *yon*. The letter *i* says the consonant *y* sound. (Use this tip for the next four words.) For spelling, say *ĭor*. For reading, say *yor*. B.E.: Spelling is *b<u>e</u> hav <u>io</u>ur*.
b<u>e</u> l<u>iev</u>e₂	r. 4, 12	After children say the syllables, say, "In the last syllable, use *ē, ī, ĭ*."
sys tem		After children say the syllables, say, "In the first syllable, use *y, ĭ, ī*."
pos si bly pos si bl<u>e</u>₄	r. 29, 11, 6 r. 29	 Base word.
p<u>iec</u>e₃ p<u>eac</u>e₃	r. 12	After children say the sounds for *piece*, say, "Use *ē, ī, ĭ*." After children say the sounds for *peace*, say, "Use *ē, ĕ, ā*."
c<u>er</u> t<u>ai</u>n ly c<u>er</u> t<u>ai</u>n	r. 2, 6 r. 2	 Base word.
wit ness	r. 17	
in ves ti g<u>a</u>t<u>e</u>		
<u>there</u>₅ f<u>ore</u> b<u>e</u> f<u>ore</u>	 r. 4	

Spelling Word	Rule(s)	Instructional Tips
ple**ās** ant (2,2)	r. 11	After children say the syllables, say, "In the first syllable, use ē, ĕ, ā. The phonogram *ea* saying *ĕa* never ends a syllable." Base word is *please*.
a bil i ty	r. 4, 6	
ap p**ear** an**ce**₃	r. 29	After children say the syllables, say, "In the second syllable, use ē, ĕ, ā. Then add the suffix *ance*."
at m**o** spher ic	r. 4, 11	
at m**o** s**phere**	r. 4	Base word.
au tum**n**		For spelling, say *t ŭ m n*.
can vas		
c**ei**l i**ng**	r. 2, 12	After children say the syllables, say, "In the first syllable, use ē, ā, ĭ."
cel **er** y	r. 2, 6	
sal **a** ry	r. 4, 6	
col l**ege**₌₃	r. 29	
com m**u** ni t**ies** (3,2)	r. 29, 4, 24	After children say the syllables, say, "In the last syllable, use *i*, instead of *y* and add *ĕs*. The *ie* together says *ĭ*."
com m**u** ni ty	r. 29, 4, 6	Dictate *community* first.
cr**e** **a** **t**ion	r. 4, 11, 14	
cr**e** **a** ti**ve**₂	r. 4, 11	
cr**e** **a** t**ed**	r. 4, 11, 28	
cr**e** **ate**	r. 4	Base word.

Spelling Word	Rule(s)	Instructional Tips
con c<u>er</u>t	r. 2	
de cid <u>ed</u>	r. 4, 2, 11, 28	
d<u>e</u> c<u>ide</u>	r. 4, 2	Base word.
d<u>e</u> s̆ign	r. 4, 19	After children say the syllables, say, "In the last syllable, use *s, z.*"
dic <u>tio</u>n ȧr y	r. 14, 6	
el <u>e</u> <u>ph</u>ant	r. 4	After children say the syllables, say, "In the last syllable, use two-letter *f.*"
ev <u>er</u> y bod y	r. 6	
fri<u>gh</u>t en<u>ĕd</u>	r. 28	
fri<u>gh</u>t en		Dictate *frighten* first.
g<u>ro</u> c<u>er</u> y	r. 4, 6	
gr<u>o͞u</u>p		After children say the sounds for *group,* say, "Use *ow, ō, o͞o, ŭ.*"
h<u>ĕa</u>l<u>th</u>		After children say the sounds for *health,* say, "Use *ē, ĕ, ā.*"
lis <u>t</u>en<u>ĕd</u>	r. 28	
lis <u>t</u>en		Base word.
ni<u>ck</u> el	r. 25	
ni<u>ece</u>₃	r. 12	After children say the sounds for *niece,* say, "Use *ē, ī, ĭ.*"

Spelling Word	Rule(s)	Instructional Tips
no̲rth ern so̲uth ern e̲ast ern west e̲rn		After children say the syllables, say, "In the first syllable, use *ow, ō, o͞o, ŭ*."
po̲ et	r. 4	Base word.
po̲ et ic	r. 4	
po̲ e̍ try	r. 4, 6	
po̲ em	r. 4	
po̲ ta t̲o̲e̲s²	r. 4	After children say the syllables, say, "In the last syllable, write *tō* and add *es̍*. The *oe* together says *ō*."
po̲ ta t̲o̲	r. 4	Base word.
pres s̲u̲r̲e		For spelling, say *s ū r ē*. For reading, say the word in normal speech.
pro̲ du̲c̲e	r. 4	
prod uct		
pu̲r cha̲s̲e̲d³	r. 11, 28	After children say the syllables, say, "In the first syllable, use the *er* of *nurse*."
pu̲r cha̲s̲e		Base word.
qu̲ar rel	r. 29	
ra̲ d̲i̲ o̲	r. 4	For spelling, say *dĭ*. The French *i* says *ē*.
re̲ cess̲	r. 4, 2, 17	
sa̲u̲ ce̲r	r. 2	
se̲ cret	r. 4	
si mi la̲r		

Spelling Word	Rule(s)	Instructional Tips
s<u>lei</u>gh		After children say the sounds for *sleigh,* say, "Use four-letter *ā*."
s<u>o</u> c<u>i</u> e ty	r. 4, 2, 5, 6	
s<u>o</u> <u>ci</u>al	r. 4, 14	After children say the syllables, say, "In the last syllable, use short *sh*."
s<u>o</u> lu <u>ti</u>on	r. 4, 14	After children say the syllables, say, "Use tall *sh*."
s<u>ou</u>rc<u>e</u>		After children say the sounds for *source,* say, "Use *ow, ō, ōo, ŭ*."
sp<u>ee</u>ch		After children say the sounds for *speech,* say, "Use the phonogram that says *ē*."
st<u>ea</u>k		After children say the sounds for *steak,* say, "Use *ē, ĕ, ā*."
suc cess f<u>u</u>l	r. 2, 22	
t<u>ai</u>l<u>s</u>		
t<u>a</u>l<u>e</u><u>s</u>		
t<u>ea</u>r		After children say the sounds for *tear,* say, "Use *ē,ĕ,ā*."
t<u>ea</u>r		B.E.: *t<u>ea</u>r*.
t<u>e</u> le phone	r. 4	
<u>through</u> out		After children say the syllables, say, "In the first syllable, use *ō, ōo, ŭf, ŏf, aw, ow*."
traf fic	r. 29	
<u>U</u> nit <u>ed</u> Sta<u>te</u>s	r. 26, 4, 11, 28	
<u>u</u> n<u>ite</u>	r. 4	
<u>u</u> nit	r. 4	Base word.

Spelling Words	Rule(s)	Instructional Tips
val <u>u</u> <u>a</u> bl<u>e</u>₄ val <u>ue</u>₂	r. 4, 11	Base word.
w<u>ore</u> w<u>or</u>n		

Section T
125 Words for Spelling, Writing, and Reading

Spelling Words	Rule(s)	Instructional Tips
c<u>ir</u> c<u>u</u> l<u>ar</u> c<u>ir</u> cl<u>e</u>₄	r. 2, 4 r. 2	Skip a space. Dictate the base word, *circle*, first. (*Continue to dictate the base word first throughout the section.*) For spelling, say *ar*, not *er*. (*Continue to require precise pronunciation of vowels in unaccented syllables throughout the section.*)
<u>ar</u> g<u>u</u> ment <u>ar</u> g<u>ue</u>₂	r. 4	In *argument*, the silent final *e* is not needed. Base word.
vol <u>ume</u>		
<u>or</u> gȧ n<u>ize</u>		After children say the syllables, say, "In the last syllable, use *z*. The letter *z* is usually used at the beginning of a base word." (*Size, dozen, organize, realize,* and *citizen* are exceptions.) B.E.: Spelling is <u>or</u> ga n<u>ise</u>.
sum mon	r. 29	For spelling, say both *m*'s. For reading, say the word in normal speech. (*Continue to require precise pronunciation for spelling and reading throughout the section.*)

Spelling Word	Rule(s)	Instructional Tips
of fi <u>c</u>ial _of fi c<u>er</u>_ of fi<u>ce</u>₃	r. 29, 11, 14 r. 29, 2, 11 r. 29	 Base word.
vic tim		
es ti m<u>ate</u>		
ac ci dent	r. 2	After children say the syllables, say, "In the second syllable, $\overset{2}{\breve{c}}\breve{\imath}$ has two separate phonogram sounds, _s, ĭ_."
in vi t<u>a</u> <u>tion</u> _in v<u>ite</u>_	r. 11, 4, 14 	 Base word.
ac cept	r. 2	For spelling, say each sound in the second syllable. (_Continue to require precise pronunciation throughout the section._)
im pos si bl<u>e</u>₄	r. 29	
con c<u>er</u>n	r. 2	
<u>au</u> t<u>o</u> m<u>o</u> bil<u>e</u>₅	r. 4	
as s<u>o</u> ci <u>a</u> <u>tion</u> as s<u>o</u> <u>ci</u> <u>ate</u>	r. 29, 4, 2, 11, 14 r. 29, 4, 14	After children say the syllables, say, "In the third syllable, $\overset{2}{\breve{c}}\breve{\imath}$ has two separate phonogram sounds, _s, ĭ_." Base word. After children say the syllables, say, "In the third syllable, use short _sh_. The _i_ has two functions: it forms the phonogram _sh_, and it provides the vowel sound for the syllable _shĭ_."

Spelling Word	Rule(s)	Instructional Tips
vắr i o͞us	r. 24	
vắr y	r. 6	Base word.
vẽr y	r. 6	After children say the syllables, say, "In the second syllable, use *i* instead of *y* and add the suffix o͞us."
de̲ ci si̲on	r. 4, 2, 16	After children say the syllables, say, "In the second syllable, *či* has two separate phonogram sounds, *s, ĭ*."
de̲ ci̲de̲	r. 4, 2	Base word.
en ti̲ tle̲₄	r. 5	
po̲ lit i cal	r. 4	
nā ti̲on al	r. 14	
na̲ ti̲on	r. 4, 14	Base word.
re̲ cent	r. 4, 2	
bu̲ si ness	r. 24, 17	After children say the syllables, say, "In the second syllable, use *i* instead of *y* and add the suffix *ness*."
bu̲ sy	r. 6	Base word. For spelling, say *bŭ*. For reading, say *bĭ*.
re̲ fe̲r	r. 4	
min ute̲₅		For spelling, say *ŭ t ē*.
mi̲ nu̲te	r. 5	For spelling, say *n ū t ē*.
ou͞ght		After children say the sounds for *ought*, say, "Use *ō, o͞o, ŭf, ŏf, aw, ow*."
ab senc̲e̲₃		
ab sent		Base word.

Spelling Word	Rule(s)	Instructional Tips
con fer ence₃ con fer		In *conference*, we do not add another *r*, because the accent moves to the first syllable, *con*. Base word.
Wed neš day	r. 26, 18	For spelling, say *Wed neš day*. For reading, say *Wenš day*.
re al ly re al	r. 4, 6 r. 4	 Base word. This is a two-syllable word.
cel e bra tion	r. 2, 4, 11, 14	Base word is *celebrate*.
folks folk	r. 19 r. 19	 Base word.
aches ache		After children say the sounds for *ache*, say, "Use *ch, k, sh*." Base word.
a muše ment	r. 4	
an gri ly an gry an ger	r. 24, 6 r. 6	After children say the syllables, say, "In the second syllable, use *i* instead of *y* and add the suffix *ly*." Base word. For spelling, say *an*.
ap prov al ap prove₂	r. 29, 11 r. 29	 Dictate *approve* first.
a vail a ble₄	r. 4	
a void	r. 4	
ba na na		B.E.: *ba nan a*.

Spelling Word	Rule(s)	Instructional Tips
bis c̲u̲its		After children say the syllables, say, "In the last syllable, the additional phonogram *cu* says *k*."
bot tl̲e̲₄	r. 29	
bot tom	r. 29	
bru̲i̲s̲ĕ̲d *bru̲i̲s̲e̲₅*	r. 11, 28	 Base word.
c̲h̲a̲n̲g̲e̲ a bl̲e̲₄ *c̲h̲a̲n̲g̲e̲*	r. 4	After children say the syllables, say, "Write *change* with the *e* and add the suffix *a ble*. We need the *e* to let the *g* say *j*." Base word.
c̲h̲ap t̲e̲r̲		
c̲h̲im n̲e̲y̲		After children say the syllables, say, "In the last syllable, use *ā, ē, ĭ*."
c̲h̲o̲i̲r̲		For spelling, say *ch oi r*. For reading, say *quire*.
com p̲e̲t̲e̲		
d̲e̲ c̲e̲i̲v̲e̲₂	r. 4, 2,12	After children say the syllables, say, "In the last syllable, use *k, s*, and *ē, ā, ĭ*."
d̲e̲ t̲e̲r̲ mi n̲a̲ t̲i̲o̲n̲ *d̲e̲ t̲e̲r̲ minĕd* *d̲e̲ t̲e̲r̲ min̲e̲₅*	r. 4, 11, 14 r. 4, 11, 28 r. 4	 Base word.
dis cov e̲r̲ i̲e̲s̲ *dis cov e̲r̲ y* *dis cov e̲r̲*	r. 24 r. 6	After children say the syllables, say, "In the last syllable, use *ĭ, ī*, instead of *y* and add *es̲*. The *ie* together says *ĭ*." Dictate *discover* first.

Spelling Word	Rule(s)	Instructional Tips
e̲ lec tric i ty	r. 4, 2, 6	
e̲ lec tri c̲ian	r. 4, 14	
e̲ lec tri cal	r. 4	
e̲ lec tric	r. 4	Base word.
en ter e̊d	r. 28	
e̊r r̲o̲r	r. 29	For spelling, say e̊r ror.
er̲r̲		Base word. For spelling, say er r. For reading, say er.
ex act	r. 20	
ex cep t̲ion̊s̲	r. 20, 2, 14	
fa̲ v̲o̲r a̲ bl̲e̲₄	r. 4	B.E.: Spelling is fa̲ vo̊ur a̲ bl̲e̲₄.
fa̲ v̲o̲r it̲e̲₅	r. 4	B.E.: Spelling is fa̲ vo̊ur it̲e̲₅.
fa̲ v̲o̲r	r. 4	Base word. B.E.: Spelling is fa̲ vo̊ur.
foůght		After children say the sounds for *fought*, say, "Use ō, o͞o, ŭf, ŏf, aw, ow."
fu̲ el	r. 4	
gen u̲ in̲e̲₅	r. 3, 4	
gro̊wth		After children say the sounds for *growth*, say, "Use ow, ō."
hand fůl	r. 22	
ha̲r̲d ly	r. 6	
hymn̲		For spelling, say h ĭ m n.
in ves ti ga̲ t̲ion	r. 4, 11, 14	

Spelling Word	Rule(s)	Instructional Tips
in volvĕd in volv̲e̲₂	r. 11, 28	Base word.
lil i̲e̲s̆ lil y	r. 24 r. 6	After children say the syllables, say, "In the last syllable, use *i* instead of *y* and add *es̆*. The *ie* together says *ĭ*." Base word.
mas siv̲e̲₂ mass	r. 29 r. 17	Base word.
med al met al		
med i cin̲e̲₅	r. 2	
ni̲n̲e̲ ty	r. 6	
r̲e̲ al i̲z̲e	r. 4	The letter *z* is usually used at the beginning of a base word. (*Size, dozen, organize, realize*, and *citizen* are exceptions.) B.E.: *r̲e̲ al i̲s̲̆e*.
rĕḯgn	r. 12	After children say the sounds for *reign*, say, "Use *ē, ā, ĭ*."
s̲e̲ v̲e̲r̲e	r. 4	
slipp̲ĕ̲d slip	r. 9, 28	Base word.
sn̲e̲e̲z̲e̲₅		After children say the sounds for *sneeze*, say, "Use the phonogram that says *ē*."

Spelling Word	Rule(s)	Instructional Tips
sta tion ar y	r. 4, 14, 6	
sta tio ner y	r. 4, 14, 6	
stom ach		After children say the syllables, say, "In the last syllable, use *ch, k, sh.*"
straight		After children say the sounds for *straight,* say, "The additional phonogram *aigh* says *ā.*"
suc ceed	r. 2	After children say the syllables, say, "In the second syllable, use the phonogram that says *ē.*"
te le vi sion	r. 4, 16	
tough		After children say the sounds for *tough,* say, "Use *ō, ōō, ŭf, ŏf, aw, ow.*"
whis tling	r. 11	For spelling, say only two syllables (two vowel sounds) and pronounce the *t.* Base word. For spelling, say *t l ē.*
whis tle		
whole some		
wreath		After children say the sounds for *wreath,* say, "Use *ē, ĕ, ā.*"
wres tling	r. 11	For spelling, say only two syllables (two vowel sounds) and pronounce the *t.* Base word. For spelling, say *t l ē.*
wres tle		

Section U
125 Words for Spelling, Writing, and Reading

Spelling Words	Rule(s)	Instructional Tips
[mē̆ant mean		Skip a space. Dictate the base word, *mean*, first. (*Continue to dictate the base word first throughout the section.*) After children say the sounds in *mean*, say, "Use $\bar{e}, \breve{e}, \bar{a}$."
[ear li est	r. 24	After children say the syllables, say, "In the second syllable, use *i* instead of *y* and add the suffix *est*."
ear ly	r. 6	Base word. For spelling, say *lĭ*. (*Continue to require precise pronunciation of vowels in unaccented syllables throughout the section.*)
dis tin guish	r. 13	After children say the syllables, say, "In the last syllable, the phonogram *gu* says *gw*."
con sid er a tion	r. 4, 14	
[cŏ lo ni al	r. 4, 24	After children say the syllables, say, "In the third syllable, use *i* instead of *y* and add the suffix *ăl*."
col o nies	r. 4, 24	After children say the syllables, say, "In the last syllable, use *i* instead of *y* and add *ĕs*. The *ie* together says *ĭ*."
col o ny	r. 4, 6	Base word.
[as sure		For spelling, say both *s*'s. For reading, say the word in normal speech. (*Continue to require precise pronunciation for spelling and reading throughout the section.*)
sure		Base word. For spelling, say *s ū r ē*.
re lief	r. 4, 12	After children say the syllables, say, "In the second syllable, use $\bar{e}, \bar{i}, \breve{i}$."

Spelling Word	Rule(s)	Instructional Tips
oc cu̲ py̲	r. 29, 4, 5, 6	For spelling, say both *c*'s. For reading, say the word in normal speech.
prob a̲ bly	r. 4, 11, 6	After children say the syllables, say, "Write the word *probable* without the *ē* and add the suffix, which begins with a vowel."
prob a̲ ble̲₄	r. 4	Base word.
for e̅i̅g̅n̅ [1] [3]	r. 12	After children say the syllables, say, "In the second syllable, use *ē*, *ā*, *ĭ* and two-letter *n* that is used at the end of a word."
ex pense̲₅	r. 20	
re̲ spon si ble̲₄	r. 4, 11	
re̲ sponse̲₅	r. 4	Base word.
ap pli ca̲ tio̲n	r. 29, 24, 4, 14	After children say the syllables, say, "In the second syllable, use *i* instead of *y*."
ap ply̲	r. 29, 5, 6	Base word.
dif fi cul ty	r. 29, 6	
dif fi cult	r. 29	Base word.
s̲c̲e̲ne	r. 2	After children say the sounds for *scene*, say, "The additional phonogram *sc* says *s*."
s̲c̲en e̲r y	r. 2, 6	
s̲c̲i̲s̲² s̲o̲r̲s̲²	r. 2, 29	
s̲c̲i̲ ence̲₃	r. 2, 5	
de̲ s̲c̲end	r. 4, 2	
de̲ s̲c̲ent	r. 4, 2	
as cend	r. 29, 2	Rule 29 holds here because *s* and *c* have the same sound.
as cent	r. 29, 2	

Spelling Word	Rule(s)	Instructional Tips
fi̱ nal ly	r. 5, 6	
fi̱ nal	r. 5	Dictate *final* first.
de̱ vel op	r. 4	
en vel op		
en ve̊ lo̲pe		
ci̱r cum sta̲nce̲₃	r. 2	
ci̱r cum fe̱r e̲nce̲₃	r. 2	
ci̱r cl̲e̲₄	r. 2	
is s̲ue̲₂		For spelling, say both *s*'s. For reading, say the words in normal speech.
tis s̲ue̲₂		
må te̲ ri al	r. 4	
sug gest	r. 3	
me̲re		
sen a̲ to̲ ri al	r. 4, 11	
sen a̲ to̲r	r. 4, 11	
sen at̲e̲₅		Base word.
re̲ ce̲iv̲e̲₂	r. 4, 2, 12	After children say the syllables, say, "In the last syllable, use ē, ā, ĭ."
re̲ spect fůl ly	r. 4, 22, 6	
re̲ spect fůl	r. 4, 22	After children say the syllables, say, "In the last syllable, write *full* with one *l*."
re̲ spect	r. 4	Base word. For spelling, say each sound in the second syllable. (*Continue to require precise pronunciation throughout the section.*)

Spelling Word	Rule(s)	Instructional Tips
a grēe ment *a grēe*	r. 4 r. 4	After children say the syllables, say, "Use the phonogram that says *ē*." Base word.
un fọr tụ natẹ₅	r. 4, 11	
mȧ̇ jȯr i ty *ma jor*	r. 6 r. 4	Base word.
e lab o ratẹ₅ *e lab o rạte*	r. 4 r. 4	
cit i zen cit y	r. 2, 24 r. 2, 6	After children say the syllables, say, "In the second syllable, use *i* instead of *y*; and in the last syllable, use *z*. The letter *z* is usually used at the beginning of a base word. (*Size, dozen, organize, realize,* and *citizen* are exceptions.) Base word.
nė̇ ces si ty *nec es sȧ̇r y*	r. 2, 29, 6 r. 2, 29, 6	Base word.
di vịde		
a chievẹš *a chievẹ₂*	r. 4, 12 r. 4, 12	Base word. After children say the syllables, say, "In the second syllable, use *ē, ī, ĭ*."
ac quire		
ȧn cient	r. 14	After children say the syllables, say, "In the last syllable, use short *sh*."

Spelling Word	Rule(s)	Instructional Tips
_an_ y one		
_a_ pie_ce_₃	r. 4, 12	After children say the syllables, say, "In the second syllable, use ē, ī, ĭ."
ap pr_oach_ eš	r. 29	After children say the syllables, say, "In the second syllable, use o of *boat*."
at ta_ck_	r. 29, 25	
at _tor_ nėy	r. 29	After children say the syllables, say, "In the last syllable, use ā, ē, ĭ." For spelling, say *tor*. For reading, say *ter*.
bal an_ce_₃		
cal c_u_ l_a_ _tion_	r. 4, 11, 14	
cal c_u_ l_ate_	r. 4	Base word.
cen tral	r. 2	
cér _e_ m_o_ ny	r. 2, 4, 6	
con c_eal_ĕd	r. 2, 28	After children say the syllables, say, "In the last syllable, use ē, ĕ, ā."
d_e_ li _ciŏus_	r. 4, 14	After children say the syllables, say, "In the last syllable, use short *sh*."
d_e_ scr_ib_ĕd	r. 4, 11, 28	
d_e_ scr_ibe_	r. 4	Dictate *describe* first.
dis ap p_ear_	r. 29	After children say the syllables, say, "In the last syllable, use ē, ĕ, ā."
drop_p_ĕd	r. 9, 28	
drop		Base word.

Spelling Word	Rule(s)	Instructional Tips
el <u>e</u> gant	r. 4	
em p<u>er</u> <u>or</u>		
[es tab li<u>sh</u> ment	r. 13	
es tab li<u>sh</u>ĕd	r. 13, 28	
es tab li<u>sh</u>	r. 13	Base word.
[ex ce<u>l</u> lent	r. 20, 2, 10	In *excellent*, write another *l* even though the accent moves to the first syllable.
ex cel	r. 20, 2	Base word.
ga<u>th</u>² <u>er</u>		
gen <u>er</u> al ly	r. 3, 6	
gr<u>ate</u> fŭl³	r. 22	
[<u>h</u>eĭr²	r. 12	For spelling, say *h eĭ r*.
in hĕr¹ it		After children say the sounds for *heir*, say, "Use *ē, ā, ĭ*."
h<u>oars</u>e₅		B.E.: After children say the sounds for *hoarse*, say, "Use *oa* of *boat*."
<u>i</u> ci cl<u>e</u>₄	r. 5, 2	After children say the syllables, say, "In the second syllable, use *k, s*."
[<u>i</u> den ti f<u>ie</u>d²²	r. 5, 24, 28	After children say the syllables, say, "In the last syllable, use *i* instead of *y* and add the past tense suffix. The *ie* together says *ī*."
<u>i</u> den ti f<u>y</u>	r. 5, 6	Base word.
[ig n<u>o</u> ran<u>ce</u>₃	r. 4, 11	
ig n<u>o</u> rant	r. 4, 11	
ig n<u>ore</u>		Base word.

Spelling Word	Rule(s)	Instructional Tips
in di ca tion in di cate	r. 4, 11, 14	 Base word.
in ter fer ence₃ in ter fere	r. 11	 Base word.
lead er ship lead er	r. 13	 Dictate *leader* first.
mes sen ger mes sage	r. 29, 3 r. 29	 Base word.
mu̅ ši cian mu̅ šic	r. 4, 14 r. 4	 Base word.
pi geon		After children say the syllables, say, "In the last syllable, the additional phonogram *ge* says *j*."
plane plain		
prob lems̆		
re hears al re hearse₅	r. 4, 11 r. 4	 Dictate *rehearse* first.
re mŏv al re mŏved re mŏve₂	r. 4, 11 r. 4, 11, 28 r. 4	 Dictate *remove* first.

Spelling Word	Rule(s)	Instructional Tips
_siege_₃	r. 12	After children say the sounds for _siege_, say, "Use $\bar{e}, \bar{\imath}, \breve{\imath}.$"
val léy	r. 29	After children say the syllables, say, "In the last syllable, use $\bar{a}, \bar{e}, \breve{\imath}.$"
_veg e ta ble_₄	r. 2, 4	

Section V
125 Words for Spelling, Writing, and Reading

Spelling Words	Rule(s)	Instructional Tips
prin ci pal **prin ci ple**₄	r. 2 r. 2	After children say the syllables, say, "In the second syllable, use _k, s._" For spelling, say _ăl_, not _ŭl_. (_Continue to require precise pronunciation of vowels in unaccented syllables throughout the section._)
tes ti mo ny	r. 4, 6	
dis cus sion _dis cuss_	r. 14, 15 r. 17	Skip a space. Dictate _discuss_ first.
ar range ment **ar range**	r. 29 r. 29	Base word. (_Continue to dictate the base word first throughout this section._) For spelling, say both _r_'s. For reading, say word in normal speech. (_Continue to require precise pronunciation for spelling and reading throughout the section._)
ref er ence₃ **re fer**	 r. 4	In _reference_, we do not write another _r_, because the accent shifts to the first syllable, _ref._ Base word.

Spelling Word	Rule(s)	Instructional Tips
ev i den**ce**[3]		
ex p**e** ri en**ce**[3]	r. 20, 4	
ses _si_on	r. 14, 15	
sec r**e** tăr[1] y	r. 4, 6	
as s**o** ci **a** _ti_on	r. 29, 4, 2, 11, 14	After children say the syllables, say, "The third syllable has two separate sounds, *s, ĭ*."
că[3] r**ee**r		After children say the syllables, say, "In the last syllable, use the phonogram that says *ē*."
height high		For spelling, say *h e igh t*. Base word.
ap păr[1] ent	r. 29	
as cend _ing_	r. 29, 2	Rule 29 holds here because *s* and *c* have the same sound.
b**a** si cal ly b**a** sic	r. 4, 6 r. 4	 Dictate *basic* first.
bou[6]gh b_ow_ b_ŏ_[2]_w_		After children say the sounds for *bough*, say "Use *ō, ōō, ŭf, ŏf, aw, ow*." After children say the sounds for *bow*, say, "Use *ow, ō*."
cam pa_ig_n		After children say the syllables, say, "In the last syllable, use two-letter *n* that is used at the end of a word."
cap i tal cap i tol		After children say the syllables for *capital*, say, "In the last syllable, use *ă, ā, ah*; and for *capitol*, use *ŏ, ō, ōō*."

Spelling Word	Rule(s)	Instructional Tips
ce̲ re̲ al	r. 2, 4	
cho͡ice₃		
cho̱²sen cho̱²se cho͡o̱²se₅	r. 4, 11	The base word is often kept in one syllable, but here it is not. Base word.
co͡arse₅		After children say the sounds for *coarse*, say "Use *oa* of *boat*."
col umn̲²s̲		For spelling, say each sound in the second syllable.
co̊¹r rect	r. 29	For spelling, say each sound in the second syllable. (*Continue to require precise pronunciation throughout the section.*)
cu̲r rent	r. 29	After children say the syllables, say, "Use *er* of *nurse* in the first syllable." B.E.: ců¹r rent
de̲²s̲ir a̲ ble̲₄ de̲²s̲ire	r. 4, 11 r. 4	 Base word.
di vi s̲io²n di vi̲de	r. 16	 Base word.
Dr. = D̲oc tor̲	r. 26	B.E.: *Dr* is the international alternative.
dra̲wn dre̲w dra̲w		 Base word.

Spelling Word	Rule(s)	Instructional Tips
e quip ment	r. 4	
e quippĕd	r. 4, 10, 28	
e quip	r. 4	Base word.
ex treme ly	r. 20, 6	
ex treme	r. 20	Base word.
fear fŭl	r. 22	After children say the sounds for *fear*, say, "Use ē, ĕ, ā."
fear		Base word.
func tion al	r. 14	
func tion	r. 14	Base word.
fur ni ture		After children say the syllables, say, "In the first syllable, use *er* of *nurse*."
fu ture	r. 4	
gath er ing		
heav i ly	r. 24	After children say the syllables, say, "In the second syllable, use *i* instead of *y* and add the suffix *ly* or *er*."
heav i er	r. 24	
heav y	r. 6	Base word. The phonogram *ea* saying ĕ never ends a syllable.
hun dred		
im ag ine	r. 11	
im age		Base word.
inch es		

Spelling Word	Rule(s)	Instructional Tips
in de pen dent	r. 4	
in di vid u al	r. 4	
in flu ence₃	r. 4	
in no cent	r. 29, 4, 2	
in stance₃		
⎡ in stru men tal	r. 4	
⎣ in stru ment	r. 4	Base word. For spelling, say *strū*.
lei šure	r. 12	After children say the syllables, say, "Use *ē, ā, ĭ*." B.E.: *lei šure*.
li cense₅	r. 5, 2	B.E.: Spelling for the noun is *li cence₃*; verb is *li cense₅*.
li quid		
⎡ lo ca tion	r. 4, 11, 14	
⎢ lo cat ed	r. 4, 11, 28	
⎣ lo cate	r. 4	Base word.
mag nif i cent	r. 2	
main		
min er als		
meth od		
mod ern		

Spelling Word	Rule(s)	Instructional Tips
[mys te ri o͞us⁴	r. 4, 24	After children say the syllables, say, "In the third syllable, use *i* instead of *y* and add the suffix *o͞us*⁴."
mys te͟r y	r. 6	Base word. After children say the syllables, say, "In the first syllable, use *y*, *ĭ*, *ī*."
oc ca͟² sion	r. 29, 4, 16	
[or͟ di na̋r¹ i ly	r. 24, 6	After children say the syllables, say, "In the fourth syllable, use *i* instead of *y* and add the suffix *ly*."
or͟ di na̋r¹ y	r. 6	Base word.
pe͟r son al i ty	r. 6	
phy͟s² i cal ly	r. 6	After children say the syllables, say, "In the first syllable, use *y*, *ĭ*, *ī*."
plan et		
[plen ti fül³	r. 24, 22	After children say the syllables, say, "In the second syllable, use *i* instead of *y* and add the suffix *ful*."
plen ty	r. 6	Base word.
po͟w er fül³	r. 22	After children say the syllables, say, "In the first syllable, use *ow*, *ō*."
pra͟i ri͟e³	r. 12	After children say the syllables, say, "Use *ā* not used at the end of a word and *ē*, *ī*, *ĭ*."
pre͟ pa͟re͟d²	r. 4, 11, 28	
pre͟ vent	r. 4	

Spelling Word	Rule(s)	Instructional Tips
pr<u>o</u> tec <u>ti</u>on pr<u>o</u> tec ti<u>ve</u>₂ pr<u>o</u> tect	r. 4, 14 r. 4 r. 4	Base word. For spelling, say each sound in the last syllable.
<u>quar</u> <u>ter</u> <u>quart</u>		Base word.
rec og ni <u>ti</u>on rec og n<u>ize</u>	r. 14	Base word. The letter z is usually used at the beginning of a base word. (*Size, dozen, organize,* and *citizen* are exceptions.) B.E.: Spelling is *rec og ni<u>s̲e</u>*.
rec <u>ord</u>s̋ r<u>e</u> c<u>ord</u>s̋	 r. 4	
r<u>e</u> l<u>ieve</u>₂	r. 4, 12	After children say the syllables, say, "In the last syllable, use ē, ī, ĭ."
r<u>e</u> p<u>ea</u>t <u>ed</u> rep <u>e</u> ti <u>ti</u>on	r. 4, 28 r. 4, 14	After children say the syllables, say, "In the second syllable, use ē, ă, ā."
r<u>e</u> qu<u>ir</u>e̋d	r. 4, 11, 28	
sac ri f<u>ice</u>		
sen si b<u>le</u>₄ sen<u>se</u>₅	r. 11	 Base word.
shő<u>u</u>l d<u>er</u>	r. 13	After children say the syllables, say, "In the first syllable, use ow, ō, o͞o, ŭ."

Spelling Word	Rule(s)	Instructional Tips
sit <u>u</u> <u>a</u> <u>tion</u>	r. 4, 11, 14	
sli<u>ght</u> ly	r. 6	
sol em<u>n</u>		For spelling, say ĕ m n.
spĭr it <u>u</u> al spĭr it	r. 4	 Base word.
stĕ̠ad i ly stĕ̠ad y	r. 24, 6 r. 6	After children say the syllables, say, "In the second syllable, use ĭ, ī, instead of y and add the suffix ly." Base word.
tem p<u>er</u> <u>a</u> t<u>ure</u>	r. 4	
<u>thou</u> s̆and		
t<u>y</u> <u>ing</u> tĭ̠e	r. 5 r. 12	After children say the syllables, say, "In the first syllable, use y, ĭ, ī." Base word. After children say the sounds for tie, say, "Use ē, ī, ĭ."
wĭ̠s dom wĭ̠se		 Base word.

Section W
125 Words for Spelling, Writing, and Reading

Spelling Words	Rule(s)	Instructional Tips
<u>or</u> gă ni z<u>a</u> <u>tion</u> <u>or</u> gă n<u>ize</u>	r. 11, 4, 14	Skip a space. Dictate the base word, *organize*, first. (*Continue to dictate the base word first throughout the section.*) B. E.: Spelling is <u>or</u> gan ĭ̠ s̆<u>a</u> <u>tion</u>. Base word. B. E.: Spelling is <u>or</u> gan ĭ̠s̆e.

Spelling Word	Rule(s)	Instructional Tips
e̲ me̲r gen cy	r. 4, 3, 11, 2, 6	For spelling, *y* says ĭ. (*Continue to require precise pronunciation of vowels in unaccented syllables throughout the section.*) Base word is *merge*.
ap pre̲ ci̲ȧ³ tive̲₂	r. 29, 4, 14, 11	
ap pre̲ ci̲ a̲te̲	r. 29, 4, 14	Base word. For spelling, say both *p*'s. For reading, say word in normal speech. (*Continue to require precise pronunciation for spelling and reading throughout the section.*) After children say the syllables, say, "In the third syllable, use short *sh*."
sin ce̲re̲ ly	r. 2, 6	
sin ce̲re̲	r. 2	Base word.
a̲th let ic	r. 11	
a̲th le̲te̲		Base word.
ex tre̲me̲	r. 20	
prac ti cal		
pro̲ ce̲e̲d	r. 4, 2	After children say the syllables, say, "In the last syllable, use the phonogram that says ē."
co̲r di̲al ly	r. 6	B.E.: *co̲r di al ly.*
co̲r di̲al		Base word. After children say the syllables, say, "In the second syllable, the additional phonogram *di* says *j*." B.E.: *co̲r di al.*
c̲har² ac te̲r¹		

Spelling Word	Rule(s)	Instructional Tips
sep a rate	r. 4	
Feb ru ar y	r. 26, 4, 6	
ac tiv i ties ac tiv i ty ac tive	r. 11, 24 r. 11, 6	After children say the syllables, say, "In the last syllable, use *i* instead of *y* and add *es*. The *ie* together says *ĭ*." Dictate *active* first.
ac tu al ac tu al ly	r. 4 r. 4, 6	
an gu lar an gle	r. 4	Base word.
an ti que		For spelling, say *t ĭ qu ē*. The French *i* says *ē* and *qu* says *k*.
an xi e ty anx ious	r. 5, 6	After children say the syllables, say, "In the second syllable, use the phonogram *x* saying *z*, an uncommon sound." For spelling, say *ang sh ous*.
av er age		
bi cy cle	r. 5, 2	After children say the syllables, say, "In the second syllable, use *y, ĭ, ī*."
bou quet		After children say the syllables, say, "In the first syllable, use *ow, ō, oo, ŭ*. In the second syllable, use *qu* to say *k* and *et* to say *ā* in this French word." For spelling, say *boo quet*. For reading, say *boo kā*. B.E.: *bou quet*.
cal en dar		

Spelling Word	Rule(s)	Instructional Tips
cen tu r**ies**	r. 2, 4, 24	After children say the syllables, say, "In the last syllable, use *i* instead of *y* and add *es*. The *ie* together says ĭ."
cen tu ry	r. 2, 4, 6	Dictate *century* first.
cl**i** m**ate**	r. 5	
com po**sed**	r. 11, 28	
com po **si** **tion**	r. 4, 11, 14	
con **se** quence	r. 4	
c**or** n**er**		
cot ton	r. 29	
c**ou**nt less	r. 17	
c**ou**nt		Base word.
d**e** pen dent	r. 4	
d**e** pend**s**	r. 4	
d**e** pend	r. 4	Base word.
d**i** **a** gram	r. 5, 4	
di**s** **ea**s**e**		After children say the syllables, say, "Use *s, z* in both syllables and *ē, ĕ, ā* in the second syllable."
el **e** men t**a** ry	r. 4, 6	
el **e** ment	r. 4	Base word.
emp ty	r. 6	
en v**i** ron ment	r. 5	

Spelling Word	Rule(s)	Instructional Tips
e quiv a lent	r. 4	
e qual i ty	r. 4, 6	
e qual	r. 4	Base word.
ev er y one		
ev er y where		
ex claimed	r. 20, 28	
ex cla ma tion	r. 20, 4, 14	
ex per i men tal	r. 20	
ex per i ment	r. 20	Base word.
ex pres sion	r. 20, 14, 15	
fac tors		
fa tigue		For spelling, say *t ĭ gu ē*. The French *i* says *ē*.
for eign ers	r. 12	
for eign	r. 12	Base word. After children say the syllables, say, "In the last syllable, use *e*, *ō*, and two-letter *n* that is used at the end of a word."
fre quen cy	r. 4, 2, 6	
fre quent	r. 4	Base word.
grad u al ly	r. 4, 6	
grad u al	r. 4	Dictate *gradual* first.
isth mus		For spelling, say *i s th*.

Spelling Word	Rule(s)	Instructional Tips
lev el		
li̇̄ brȧr y	r. 5, 6	
mod el		
mo̱ ment	r. 4	
mos qu̲i̲ to̲	r. 4	For spelling, say *qu ĭ.* The phonogram *qu* says *k* and the Spanish *i* says *ē.*
mus cu̲ lar̲	r. 4	
mus c̆le̲₄	r. 29	Base word. After children say the syllables, say, "In the second syllable, use *k, s.*" (Rule 29 holds here because *s* and *c* have the same sound.)
nȧr ro̲w̲	r. 29	After children say the syllables, say, "In the second syllable, "Use *ow, ō.*"
nat u̲ ral ist	r. 4, 11	
nat u̲ ral ly	r. 4, 11, 6	
nat u̲ ral	r. 4, 11	For spelling, say *nat u ral.* For reading, say *natch u ral.*
na̲ tu̲re̲	r. 4	Base word.
non sense̲₅		
ob s̆er̲ va̲ tion	r. 4, 11, 14	After children say the syllables, say, "In the second syllable, use *s, z.*"
ob s̆erv a̲ to̲ ry	r. 4, 11, 6	
ob s̆er̲ve̲₂		Base word.

Spelling Word	Rule(s)	Instructional Tips
oc cŭr rence₃ oc cŭrréd oc cŭr	r. 29, 10 r. 29, 10, 28 r. 29	B.E.: *oc cŭr rence₃*. Base word. After children say the syllables, say, "In the second syllable, use *er* of *nurse*."
op po̱ ší tion op po̱ šite₅	r. 29, 4, 11, 14 r. 29, 4, 11	Dictate *opposite* first.
phraše		
prac tice₃		B.E.: Spelling for the noun is *prac tice₃*; verb is *prac tise₅*.
pró cess	r. 2, 17	B.E.: *pro̱ cess*.
pro̱ duc tion pro̱ duc tive₂ prod uct	r. 4, 14 r. 4	Base word. For spelling, say each sound in the second syllable. (*Continue to require precise pronunciation throughout the section.*)
pro̱ gram	r. 4	
re̱ sóurce₃fúl re̱ sóurc eš re̱ sóurce₃	r. 4, 22 r. 4 r. 4	Dictate *resource* first. After children say the syllables, say, "In the second syllable, use *ow, ō, o͞o, ŭ*."
rhyme rhythm rhyth mic		After children say the sounds for *rhyme*, say, "Use the additional phonogram *rh* to say *r*, and use *y* instead of *i*." This is a one-syllable word.

Spelling Word	Rule(s)	Instructional Tips
r<u>ou</u>tes		After children say the sounds for *routes*, say, "Use *ow*, *ō*, *ōō*, *ŭ*." B.E.: *rŏutes*.
s<u>afe</u> ty	r. 6	
sc<u>a</u>l<u>e</u>		
sc <u>i</u> en tif ic sc <u>i</u> en tists	r. 2, 5 r. 2, 5	After children say the syllables, say, "In the first syllable, use the additional phonogram *sc* to say *s*."
s<u>e</u> crè cy s<u>e</u> cret	r. 4, 6 r. 4	Base word.
sec <u>tion</u>s	r. 14	
s<u>qua</u>r<u>e</u>		
stan d<u>ar</u>d		
struc tur al struc t<u>ure</u>	r. 11	Base word.
sub stan <u>tial</u> sub stan<u>ce</u>	r. 14	Base word.
ton<u>gue</u>		For spelling, say *t ŏ ng ū ē*.
tr<u>i</u> an gl<u>e</u>	r. 5	
và r<u>i</u> ė ty	r. 24, 5, 6	
v<u>e</u> hi cl<u>e</u>	r. 4	
v<u>i</u> cin i ty	r. 2, 6	

Spelling Word	Rule(s)	Instructional Tips
vol un t<u>ee</u>r		After children say the syllables, say, "In the last syllable, use the phonogram that says *ē*."
wel f<u>are</u>		
y<u>ǎ̊ch</u>t		For spelling, say *y ǎ̊ ch t*.

Section X
125 Words for Spelling, Writing, and Reading

Spelling Words	Rule(s)	Instructional Tips
im m<u>e</u> di <u>ate</u>	**r. 29, 4**	For spelling, say both *m*'s. For reading, say the word in normal speech. (*Continue to require precise pronunciation for spelling and reading throughout the section.*)
con v<u>e</u> n<u>i</u>ent *con v<u>ene</u>*	**r. 4, 11**	Skip a space. Dictate the base word, *convene*, first. (*Continue to dictate the base word first throughout the section.*) For spelling, say *n ĭ ĕ n t*. For reading, say *n yent*. B. E.: *con v<u>e</u> ni ent*.
re c<u>ei</u>p̱t	**r. 4, 2, 12**	After children say the syllables, say, "In the second syllable, use *ē, ā, ĭ*." For spelling, say each sound in the second syllable. For reading, say *re cēt*. (*Continue to require precise pronunciation throughout the section.*)
pr<u>e</u> lim i nǎ̇r y	**r. 4, 6**	For spelling, *y* says *ĭ*. (*Continue to require precise pronunciation of vowels in unaccented syllables throughout the section.*)
dis ap p<u>oi</u>nt	**r. 29**	

Spelling Word	Rule(s)	Instructional Tips
es pḛ́ cial ly	r. 14, 6	After children say the syllables, say, "Use short *sh*."
spḛ́ cial	r. 14	Base word.
an nṵ al	r. 29, 4	
com mit t<u>ee</u>	r. 29, 10	After children say the syllables, say, "In the third syllable, use the phonogram that says *ē*."
com mit	r. 29	Base word.
a<u>d</u> jec ti<u>ve</u>₂		For spelling, say *ad jek tive*.
ad van t<u>age</u>		
af fect	r. 29	
Af ri cå̇	r. 26	
al ti t<u>ude</u>		
an ces t<u>ors</u>²	r. 2	
Ant <u>arc</u> ti cå̇	r. 26	
ap plīḛd	r. 29, 24, 28	After children say the syllables, say, "In the last syllable, use *i* instead of *y* and add *ed*."
ap plỵ ing	r. 29, 5	
ap plỵ	r. 29, 5, 6	Base word.
<u>ar</u> <u>chi</u>² tec t<u>ure</u>		After children say the syllables, say, "In the second syllable, use *ch*, *k*, *sh*."
<u>Arc</u> tic <u>O</u> <u>ce</u>an	r. 26, 4	After children say the syllables, say, "Use the additional phonogram *ce* to say *sh*."
<u>ar</u> ti fi <u>cial</u>	r. 14	After children say the syllables, say, "In the fourth syllable, use short *sh*."

Spelling Word	Rule(s)	Instructional Tips
<u>A</u> sia (2 3)	r. 26, 4, 16	After children say the syllables, say, "In the second syllable, use *sh, zh*."
At lan tic <u>O</u> cean	r. 26, 4	After children say the syllables, say, "Use the additional phonogram *ce* to say *sh*."
<u>Au</u>s tra li ă (3)	r. 26	After children say the syllables, say, "In the first syllable, say *au s*. In the last syllable, say *lĭ ă*." For reading, say *lya*. The letter *i* says the consonant *y* sound.
ben <u>e</u> fi <u>c</u>ial	r. 4, 14	After children say the syllables, say, "In the last syllable, use the short *sh*."
ben <u>e</u> fit	r. 4	Base word.
<u>b</u>ound <u>a</u> rĭĕš (3 2)	r. 4, 24	After children say the syllables, say, "In the last syllable, use *i* instead of *y* and add *eš* (2). The *ie* together says *ĭ*."
<u>b</u>ound <u>a</u> ry	r. 4, 6	Dictate *boundary* first.
bril l<u>i</u>ant	r. 29	For spelling, say *l ĭ ă n t*. For reading, say *yant*. The letter *i* says the consonant *y* sound.
<u>c</u>har ac t<u>er</u> is tics (2 1)		After children say the syllables, say, "In the first syllable, use *ch, k, sh*."
<u>C</u>hi ca g<u>o</u> (3 3)	r. 26, 4	After children say the syllables, say, "In the first syllable, use *ch, k, sh*, and in the second syllable, use *ă, ā, ah*."
<u>c</u>hoc <u>o</u> lat<u>e</u>₅		
civ i l<u>i</u> z<u>a</u> <u>t</u>ion	r. 2, 5, 11, 4, 14	B.E.: Spelling is *civ i lĭ s<u>a</u> <u>t</u>ion*.
civ i l<u>i</u>z<u>e</u>́d (2)	r. 2, 11, 28	B.E.: Spelling is *civ i l<u>i</u>s<u>e</u>d*.
civ i l<u>i</u>z<u>e</u>	r. 2	B.E.: Spelling is *civ i l<u>i</u>s<u>e</u>*.
civ il	r. 2	Base word.

Spelling Word	Rule(s)	Instructional Tips
col <u>o</u> nel	r. 4	For spelling, say *col ō nel*. For reading, say *kernel*.
con gress	r. 17	
con ta gi<u>o</u>u<u>s</u>	r. 4	After children say the syllables, say, "Use the additional phonogram *gi* to say *j* in the last syllable."
[con ti nen tal con ti nent		Base word.
dep<u>th</u>		
[d<u>e</u> scrip <u>ti</u>on d<u>e</u> scrip ti<u>ve</u>₂	r. 4, 14 r. 4	
[d<u>e</u> vel op ment d<u>e</u> vel op	r. 4 r. 4	Base word.
d<u>i</u> ag <u>o</u> nal	r. 5, 4	
d<u>i</u> am e̊ t<u>er</u>	r. 5	
[ef fec ti<u>ve</u>₂ ef fect	r. 29 r. 29	Base word.
[em pl<u>oy</u> <u>ee</u> em pl<u>oy</u>		After children say the syllables, say, "In the third syllable, use the phonogram that says *ē*." Base word.
[<u>Eng</u> land <u>Eng</u> lish	r. 26 r. 26, 13	

Spelling Word	Rule(s)	Instructional Tips
e̱ n<u>or</u> mo<u>u</u>s[4]	r. 4	After children say the syllables, say, "In the last syllable, use *ow ō, ōō, ŭ*."
es sen t<u>ia</u>l	r. 29, 14	
<u>Eu</u> r<u>o</u>pe	r. 26	After children say the syllables, say, "Use the additional phonogram *eu* to say *u*."
e̱ ven t<u>u</u> al ly	r. 4, 6	
ex <u>change</u>	r. 20	
ex is ten<u>ce</u>[=3]	r. 20	
ex ist	r. 20	Base word.
ex pl<u>o</u> r<u>a</u> t<u>io</u>n	r. 20, 4, 11, 14	
ex plor <u>er</u>s̆[2]	r. 20, 11	
ex pl<u>ore</u>	r. 20	Base word.
ex <u>qui</u> s̆ite[2][=5]	r. 20	After children say the syllables, say, "In the last syllable, use *s, z*."
fȧ[1] mil i̱<u>a</u>r i ty	r. 24, 6	After children say the syllables, say, "In the last syllable, use *i* instead of *y* and add the suffix *ar*." For spelling, say *ĭar*. The letter *i* says the consonant *y* sound.
fȧ[1] mil i̱<u>a</u>r	r. 24	
fam i ly	r. 6	Base word.
<u>forth</u>		
fo<u>u</u>[2]<u>rth</u>		After children say the sounds in *fourth*, say, "Use *ow, ō, ōō, ŭ*."
frac t<u>io</u>n al	r. 14	
frac t<u>io</u>n	r. 14	Base word.
grav i ty	r. 6	

Spelling Word	Rule(s)	Instructional Tips
<u>g</u>uard		
hȯr i zon tal		
Il li n<u>oi</u>s	r. 26, 29	For spelling, say *n oi s*. The French *s* is silent.
im ag i n<u>a</u> <u>ti</u>on	r. 3, 11, 4, 14	Base word is *image*.
in d<u>e</u> pen den<u>ce</u>₃	r. 4	
In di an <u>O</u> <u>ce</u>an	r. 26, 4	After children say the syllables, say, "Use the additional phonogram *ce* to say *sh*."
in dus tri al	r. 24	
in dus try	r. 6	Base word.
in tel li gent	r. 29, 3	
in t<u>e</u> ri <u>or</u>	r. 4	
in vent <u>ed</u>	r. 28	
in ven <u>ti</u>on	r. 14	
lat i t<u>ude</u>		
lat t<u>er</u>	r. 29	
Lin co<u>l</u>n	r. 26	For spelling, say *c ŏ l n*.
lon gi t<u>u</u> di nal	r. 3, 4, 11	
lon gi t<u>ude</u>	r. 3	Dictate *longitude* first.

Spelling Word	Rule(s)	Instructional Tips
⌈ ma ch*i*n er y ⌊ ma ch*i*n*e*₅	r. 11, 6	After children say the syllables, say, "In the second syllable, use *ch*, *k*, *sh*." Base word. The French *i* says *ē*.
mag *a* z*i*n*e*₅	r. 4	After children say the syllables, say, "In the third syllable, *zine*, use the French *i* saying *ē*."
m*i*r r*or*	r. 29	
mis tak en	r. 11	Base word is *take*.
⌈ m*oi*s t*u*re ⌊ m*oi*st		 Base word.
N*orth* *A* m*e*r i c*a*	r. 26, 4	
oc c*a* *si*on al ly	r. 29, 4, 16, 6	
⌈ op p*or* t*u* ni ty ⌊ op p*or* t*u*n*e*	r. 29, 4, 11, 6 r. 29	 Base word.
P*a* cif ic *O* c*ean*	r. 2, 26, 4	After children say the syllables for *ocean*, say, "In the second syllable, use the additional phonogram *ce* to say *sh*."
p*a*r ents		
p*e* cu l*i*ar	r. 4	For spelling, say *lĭar*. For reading, say *lyar*.
p*er* pen dic *u* l*ar*	r. 4	
p*er* s*e* v*e*r*e*	r. 4	
r*e* pr*oa*ch*e*d	r. 4, 28	After children say the syllables, say, "In the second syllable, use *ō* of *boat*."

Spelling Word	Rule(s)	Instructional Tips
rev <u>er</u> en<u>ce</u>₃ rev <u>er</u> ent r<u>e</u> v<u>ere</u>	r. 11 r. 11 r. 4	 Base word.
rins<u>ĕd</u>³ rins<u>e</u>₅	r. 11, 28 	 Base word.
s<u>e</u> <u>quence</u>₋₌₃	r. 4	
s<u>e</u> rie̊s²	r. 4, 12	After children say the syllables, say, "In the last syllable, use ē, ī, ĭ."
sim i lȧr¹ i tie̊s³² sim i lȧr¹ i ty sim i l<u>ar</u>	r. 24 r. 6	After children say the syllables, say, "In the last syllable, use i instead of y and add the suffix e̊s. The ie together says ĭ." Base word.
<u>South</u> <u>A</u> mer̊¹ i c̊ả³	r. 26, 4	
trĕach² <u>er</u> y	r. 6	The phonogram ea saying e̊a² never ends a syllable.
ty pi cal t<u>ype</u>	r. 11 	 Base word. After children say the sounds for type, say, "Use y, ĭ, ī."
v<u>er</u> ti cal		

Section Y
124 Words for Spelling, Writing, and Reading

Spelling Words	Rule(s)	Instructional Tips
d<u>e</u> ci s̲ion² d<u>e</u> c<u>ide</u>	r. 2, 4, 16 r. 2, 4	Skip a space. Dictate the base word, *decide*, first. (*Continue to dictate the base word first throughout the section.*)

Spelling Word	Rule(s)	Instructional Tips
prin ci ple̲₄	**r. 2**	
ac com mo̲ da̲te̲	**r. 29, 4**	For spelling, say both *c*'s and *m*'s. For reading, say the word in normal speech. (*Continue to require precise pronunciation for spelling and reading throughout the section.*)
ac cu̲ ra̲ cy	**r. 29, 4, 2, 6**	For spelling, *y* says ĭ. (*Continue to require precise pronunciation of vowels in unaccented syllables throughout the section.*)
ac cu̲ ra̲te̲	**r. 29, 4**	Base word.
ap prox i ma̲te̲	**r. 29, 20**	
ap prox i ma̲te̲₅	**r. 29, 20**	
com men̲ce̲₃	**r. 29**	
com me̲r cial̲	**r. 29, 11, 14**	After children say the syllables, say, "In the last syllable, use short *sh*."
com me̲r̲ce̲₃	**r. 29**	Base word.
com mu̲ ni ca̲ tion̲	**r. 29, 4, 11, 14**	
com mu̲ ni ca̲te̲	**r. 29, 4**	Dictate *communicate* first.
com plex	**r. 20**	
con clu̲ s̲i̲on²	**r. 4, 16**	After children say the syllables, say, "In the last syllable, use *sh*, *zh*."
con struc tion̲	**r. 14**	
con struct		Base word. For spelling, say each sound in the last syllable.
con ve̲r sa̲ tion̲	**r. 11, 4, 14**	
con ve̲rse̲₅		Base word.

Spelling Word	Rule(s)	Instructional Tips
c**ou**n ter f**ei**t³	r. 12	After children say the syllables, say, "In the last syllable, use ē, ā, ĭ."
cul t**u** ral cul t**ure**	r. 4, 11	Dictate *culture* first.
c**u** ri os i ty c**u** ri **ou**s⁴	r. 4, 6 r. 4	Dictate *curious* first. After children say the syllables, say, "In the last syllable, use ow, ō, o͞o, ŭ."
de**s**² **ert** de**s**² **s**²**ert**	 r. 29	
di gest i bl**e**₄ d**i** gest	r. 3 r. 5, 3	Base word.
E gyp **ti**an **E** gypt	r. 26, 4, 14 r. 26, 4	Base word. After children say the syllables, say, "In the second syllable, the phonogram *y* says ĭ."
e lec tron**s**²	r. 4	
e qu**a** to ri al e qu**a** tor e qu**a** **ti**on e qu**a**te	r. 4, 11 r. 4, 11 r. 4, 11, 14 r. 4	The phonogram *ti* says the additional sound *zh*. Base word.
ex pen si**ve**₂	r. 20, 11	
ex pl**a** n**a** **ti**on	r. 20, 4, 14	

Spelling Word	Rule(s)	Instructional Tips
ex ten <u>si</u>on	r. 20, 14	After children say the syllables, say, "In the last syllable, use *sh*, *zh*."
ex ten siv<u>e</u>₂	r. 20	
ex tent	r. 20	
ex tend	r. 20	Base word.
im mens<u>e</u>₅	r. 29	
in tr<u>o</u> du<u>c</u>ĕ́d	r. 4, 11, 28	
in tr<u>o</u> duc <u>ti</u>on	r. 4, 14	
in viš̃ i bl<u>e</u>₄		After children say the syllables, say, "In the second syllable, use *s*, *z*."
l<u>eo</u> p<u>ar</u>d		After children say the syllables, say, "In the first syllable, use the additional phonogram *eo* to say *ē*."
lit <u>er</u> al ly	r. 6	
lit <u>er</u> ằr y	r. 6	
lit <u>er</u> <u>a</u> t<u>ur</u>e	r. 4, 11	
lit <u>er</u> at<u>e</u>₅		Base word.
man <u>u</u> fac tur ing	r. 4, 11	
man <u>u</u> fac t<u>ur</u>e	r. 4	Base word.
Med i t<u>er</u> r<u>a</u> n<u>e</u> an	r. 26, 29, 4	
mem <u>o</u> r<u>a</u> bl<u>e</u>₄	r. 4	
mem <u>o</u> ri al	r. 4, 24	
mem <u>o</u> r<u>iz</u>e	r. 4, 24	B.E.: Spelling is *mem <u>o</u> ri̊š̃e*.
mem <u>o</u> ry	r. 4, 6	Base word.

Spelling Word	Rule(s)	Instructional Tips
men tal ly	r. 6	
mil l̲i̲on a̲i̲r̲e̲₅	r. 29	After children say the syllables, say, "In the second syllable, the phonogram *i* says the consonant sound *y*."
[*mi̲ no̅r i ty*	r. 5, 6	
[*mi̲ no̲r̲*	r. 5	Base word.
[*neg a̲ tiv̲e̲₂*	r. 4, 11	
[*ne̅ ga̅te*	r. 4	Dictate *negate* first.
[*nu̲ me̅r i cal*	r. 4	
[*nu̲ me̲r̲ o̅us*	r. 4	
[*nu̲ me̲r̲ al*	r. 4	Base word.
[*op e̲r̲ a̲ t̲ion*	r. 4, 11, 14	
[*op e̲r̲ a̲ tor*	r. 4, 11	
[*op e̲r̲ a̲te*		Base word.
o̲r̲ c̲h̲es tra̅		After children say the syllables, say, "In the second syllable, use *ch*, *k*, *sh*; and in the last syllable, use *ă*, *ā*, *oh*."
[*o̲ rig i nal*	r. 4, 3	
[*o̲ rig i nat e̲d̲*	r. 4, 3, 11, 28	
[*o̲r̲ i gin*	r. 3	Base word.
pa̲r̲ li̲a̲ ment		For spelling, say *l ĭ ă*.
[*pe̲r̲ ce̲i̲ve̲d̲*	r. 2, 12, 11, 28	After children say the syllables, say, "In the last syllable, use *ē*, *ā*, *ĭ*."
[*pe̲r̲ ce̲i̲ve̲₂*	r. 2, 12	Base word.

Spelling Word	Rule(s)	Instructional Tips
⎡ p<u>er</u> f<u>or</u> man<u>ce</u>₃ ⎣ p<u>er</u> f<u>or</u>m		Base word.
p<u>er</u> mȧ¹ nent		
poš² i tiv<u>e</u>₂		After children say the syllables, say, "In the first syllable, use *s, z*."
⎡ pr<u>e</u> cip i t<u>ou</u>s⁴ ⎣ prec i pi<u>ce</u>₃	r. 4, 2 r. 2	After children say the syllables, say, "In the last syllable, use *ow, ō, o͞o, ŭ*."
pr<u>e</u> vi <u>ou</u>s⁴	r. 4	After children say the syllables, say, "In the last syllable, use *ow, ō, o͞o, ŭ*."
⎡ preš² en<u>ce</u>₃ ⎣ preš² ents		
⎡ prim i tiv<u>e</u>₂ ⎢ pr<u>i</u> mȧr¹ i ly ⎢ pr<u>i</u> m<u>a</u> ry ⎣ pr<u>ime</u>	r. 11 r. 5, 24, 6 r. 5, 11, 4, 6	After children say the syllables, say, "Use *i* instead of *y* and add the suffix *ly*." Base word.
⎡ pr<u>o</u> fes <u>si</u>on al ⎣ pr<u>o</u> fes <u>si</u>on	r. 4, 15 r. 4, 15	Dictate *profession* first.
⎡ pr<u>o</u> jec <u>ti</u>on ⎢ pr<u>o</u> jec t<u>or</u> ⎣ pr<u>o</u> ject	r. 4, 14 r. 4 r. 4	Base word.
⎡ qu<u>a</u>ȧl³ i ti<u>e</u>š³² ² ⎣ qu<u>a</u>ȧl³ i ty	r. 24 r. 6	After children say the syllables, say, "Use *i* instead of *y* and add *eš*². The letters *ie* together say *ĭ* and the ending says *z*." Base word.

Spelling Word	Rule(s)	Instructional Tips
quăn ti tiĕs	r. 24	After children say the syllables, say, "Use *i* instead of *y* and add *ĕs*. The letters *ie* together say *ĭ* and the ending says *z*."
quăn ti ty	r. 6	Base word.
re search	r. 4	After children say the syllables, say, "In the last syllable, use *er* of *early*."
re sĕm blance	r. 4, 11	After children say the syllables, say, "In the second syllable, use *s, z*."
re sĕm ble	r. 4	Base word.
rec om mend	r. 29	
re lā tion ship	r. 4, 11, 14, 13	
re lā tion	r. 4, 11, 14	
re late	r. 4	Base word.
res tau rănt		After children say the syllables, say, "In the last syllable, use *ă, ā, ah*."
scarce ly	r. 6	
schēme		After children say the sounds for *scheme*, say, "Use *ch, k, sh*."
seizĕd	r. 12, 11, 28	After children say the sounds for *seize*, say, "Use *ē, ā, ĭ*."
seize	r. 12	Base word.
se lec tion	r. 4, 14	

Spelling Word	Rule(s)	Instructional Tips
sim pli ci ty	r. 11, 2, 6	
sim pli fi͟e͟d (2 2)	r. 24, 28	After children say the syllables, say, "Use *i* instead of *y* and add *ed*. The letters *ie* together say *ī* and *ed* together say *d*."
sim pli fy͟	r. 11, 5, 6	
sim ple͟₄		Base word.
sub ma͟³ r͟i͟ne͟₅		
ma͟³ r͟i͟ne͟₅		Dictate *marine* first. For spelling, say *r ĭ n ē*. The Latin *i* says *ē*.
su͟ pe͟r in ten dent	r. 4	
sur͟ ge͟on		After children say the syllables, say, "Use *er* of *nurse* and the additional phonogram *ge* to say *j*."
te�…¹ le͙¹ sco͟pe		
te͙¹r ri to͟ ri al	r. 29, 4, 24	After children say the syllables, say, "In the fourth syllable, use *i* instead of *y* and add the suffix *al*."
te͙¹r ri to͟ ry	r. 29, 4, 6	Base word.
thor͟ ou͟gh ly	r. 6	After children say the syllables, say, "In the first syllable, use the phonogram *or* to say *er*, an uncommon sound."
tre͟ men do͞u͟s⁴	r. 4	After children say the syllables, say, "In the last syllable, use *ow*, *ō*, *o͞o*, *ŭ*."

Section Z
125 Words for Spelling, Writing, and Reading

Spelling Words	Rule(s)	Instructional Tips
judg ment judge	r. 23	Skip a space. Dictate the base word, *judge*, first. (*Continue to dictate the base word first throughout the section.*) B.E.: Spelling is *judge ment*.
rec om mend *rec om men ded*	r. 29 r. 29, 28	Base word. For spelling, say both *m*'s. For reading, say the word in normal speech. (*Continue to require precise pronunciation for spelling and reading throughout the section.*)
al le giance₌₃ al lege₌₃	r. 29, 4, 11 r. 29	After children say the syllables, say, "In the third syllable, use the additional phonogram *gi* and add the suffix *ance*. The *gi* says *j*." Base word.
a byss	r. 4, 17	After children say the syllables, say, "In the second syllable, use *y* to say *ĭ*."
ac quain tance₌₃		
a pol o gize	r. 4, 3, 24	B.E.: Spelling is *a pol o gise*.
ap pro pri ate ap pro pri ate₅	r. 29, 4 r. 29, 4	
can tá loupe₅		After children say the syllables, say, "In the last syllable, use *ow, ō, ōō, ŭ*."
cau li flow er		After children say the syllables, say, "In the third syllable, use *ow, ō*."

Spelling Word	Rule(s)	Instructional Tips
cem e̲ te̊r y [1]	r. 2, 4, 6	For spelling, *y* says ĭ. (*Continue to require precise pronunciation of vowels in unaccented syllables throughout the section.*)
[chan de̲ lie̲r [3]	r. 4, 12	After children say the syllables, say, "In the first syllable, use *ch, k, sh* and in the last syllable, use *ē, ī, ĭ.*"
fi nan cie̲r	r. 11	Exception to rule 12. After children say the syllables, say, "In the last syllable, use *ē, ī, ĭ.*"
chau̲f fe̲ur [3]	r. 29	For spelling, say *ch au f f ĕ ur* [3]. For reading, say *chō fur* [3].
com bus ti ble̲₄		
con sci̲ en tio̲u̲s [4]	r. 14	After children say the syllables, say, "In the second syllable, use the additional phonogram *sci*. The *i* has two functions: it forms the phonogram that says *sh* and it provides the vowel sound for the syllable *shĭ.*"
[dis ce̲rn i ble̲₄	r. 29, 2	
dis ce̲rn	r. 29, 2	Base word.
dis ci pline̲₅	r. 29, 2	
dis pense̲₅		
[dis sen sio̲n	r. 29, 14	After children say the syllables, say, "In the last syllable, use *sh, zh.*"
dis sent	r. 29	Base word.

Spelling Word	Rule(s)	Instructional Tips
drǻ mat i cal ly drǻ mat ic drǻ mǻ	r. 6	Base word. After children say the syllables, say, "In the first and last syllables, use ă, ā, ah."
ė cọ nom i cal ė cọ nom ic e con ọ my	r. 4, 24 r. 4, 24 r. 4, 6	Base word.
e lim i nate	r. 4	
ef fi cien cy ef fi cient	r. 29, 2, 14, 6 r. 29, 14	After children say the syllables, say, "In the third syllable, use short sh." Dictate *efficient* first.
em bȧr rass ment em bȧr rass	r. 29 r. 29, 17	Base word.
en děav or		After children say the syllables, say, "In the second syllable, use ē, ĕ, ā." B.E.: Spelling is en děav ọur.
en thu ŝi aŝm	r. 4	After children say the syllables, say, "In the third and last syllables, use s, z."
ex traor di nȧr y	r. 20, 6	After children say the syllables, say, "In the second syllable, say t r ă or."
fȧ tigu ing fȧ tigue	r. 11	Base word. For spelling, say t ĭ gu ē. The French i says ē.

Spelling Word	Rule(s)	Instructional Tips
[_for mal ly_	r. 6	
[_for mal_		Dictate _formal_ first.
fron tier	r. 12	After children say the syllables, say, "In the last syllable, use $\bar{e}, \bar{\imath}, \breve{\imath}$."
guár an tee		After children say the syllables, say, "In the last syllable, use the phonogram that says $\bar{e}$."
gui tar		After children say the syllables, say, "In the first syllable, use two-letter _g_."
[_hu mor óus_	r. 4	After children say the syllables, say, "In the last syllable, use _ow_, $\bar{o}$, $\overline{oo}$, $\breve{u}$."
[_hu mor_	r. 4	Base word. B.E.: Spelling is _hu mŏur_.
[_im pres sive₂_	r. 29	
im pres sion	r. 14, 15	
[_im press_	r. 17	Dictate _impress_ first.
in ces sant	r. 2, 29	
[_Iš rae li_	r. 26	After children say the syllables, say, "In the first syllable, use _s, z_." For spelling, say _r $\bar{a}$ $\bar{e}$_.
[_Iš ra el_	r. 26, 4	Base word.
league₂		After children say the sounds for _league_, say, "Use $\bar{e}$, $\breve{e}$, $\bar{a}$ and two-letter _g_."
[_math e mat i cal_	r. 4	
[_math e mat ics_	r. 4	Dictate _mathematics_ first.

Spelling Word	Rule(s)	Instructional Tips
mil i tăr y mi li tiă	r. 6 r. 14	After children say the syllables, say, "In the last syllable, use tall *sh*."
mis cel la ne ous	r. 29, 2, 4	After children say the syllables, say, "In the last syllable, use *ow*, *ō*, *ōō*, *ŭ*."
mis chie vous mis chief	r. 12 r. 12	B.E.: *mis chie vous* Base word. After children say the syllables, say, "In the last syllable, use *ē*, *ī*, *ĭ*."
mort gage		
mu nic i pal	r. 4, 2	
neu tral Eu rope pneu mo niă lieu ten ant	 r. 26 r. 4	After children say the syllables, say, "In the first syllable, use the additional phonogram *eu* to say *ū*." After children say the syllables, say, "In the first syllable, use the additional phonograms *pn* to say *n* and *eu* to say *ū*. The *ī* says the consonant *y* sound." For spelling, say *l ĭ eu*. B.E.: Pronunciation varies.
oc cur rence₃	r. 29, 10	B.E.: *oc cŭr rence₃*.
pàr al lel	r. 29	
per cent age per cent	r. 2 r. 2	Dictate *percent* first.
per sis tence₃ per sist		Base word.

Spelling Word	Rule(s)	Instructional Tips
phy ší cian	r. 14	After children say the syllables, say, "In the first syllable, use *y* to say *ĭ*, and use short *sh* in the last syllable."
por ce lain	r. 2, 4	
priv i lege		
pro fi cien cy	r. 4, 14, 2, 6	
pro fi cient	r. 4, 14	Base word. After children say the syllables, say, "In the last syllable, use short *sh*."
rec i pe	r. 2, 4	
re flect ed	r. 4, 28	For spelling, say each sound in the second syllable.
ren dez voùs		For spelling, say *rĕn dĕz voùs*. For reading, say *răn dĕ voù*. The French *s* is silent.
re šis tance	r. 4	After children say the syllables, say, "In the second syllable, use *s, z*."
re šist	r. 4	Base word.
rhap so dy	r. 4, 6	After children say the syllables, say, "In the first syllable, use the additional phonogram *rh* to say *r*."
rhi noc er os	r. 5, 2	
rhu barb	r. 4	
salm on		For spelling, say *s ă l m*.
sat el lites	r. 29	

Spelling Word	Rule(s)	Instructional Tips
sat is fac <u>ti</u>on	r. 14	
sat is fac t<u>o</u> ry	r. 4, 6	
sat is f^{2 2}<u>ie</u>d	r. 24, 28	After children say the syllables, say, "Use *i* instead of *y* and add the suffix *ed*. The letters *ie* together say *ī* and *ed* together say *d*."
sat is f<u>y</u>	r. 5, 6	Base word.
<u>sh</u>elv<u>e</u>²s		After children say the sounds for *shelves*, say, "Use *v* instead of *f* and add *e*²*s*."
<u>sh</u>elf	r. 13	Base word.
s<u>o</u> l<u>ar</u>	r. 4	
s³<u>ou</u> v<u>e</u> n¹ir	r. 4	After children say the syllables, say, "In the first syllable, use *ow*, *ō*, *ōō*, *ŭ*."
sov <u>er</u> <u>ei</u>³gn	r. 12	After children say the syllables, say, "In the last syllable, use *ē*, *ā*, *ĭ*."
sp<u>e</u> <u>cie</u>²s	r. 4, 14	After children say the syllables, say, "Use short *sh*. The *i* also combines with the *e* to say *ē*."
sp<u>e</u>¹ cif i cal ly	r. 2, 6	
sp<u>e</u>¹ cif ic	r. 2	
spec i f^{2 2}<u>ie</u>d	r. 2, 24, 28	After children say the syllables, say, "Use *i* instead of *y* and add *ed*. The letter *ie* together say *ī* and *ed* together say *d*."
spec i f<u>y</u>	r. 2, 5, 6	Base word.
suf fi <u>ci</u>ent ly	r. 29, 14, 6	After children say the syllables, say, "In the third syllable, use short *sh*."
syl l<u>a</u> ble²s	r. 29, 4	
syl l<u>a</u> bl<u>e</u>₄	r. 29, 4	Base word.

Spelling Word	Rule(s)	Instructional Tips
te*ch* nol *o* gy te*ch* niques te*ch* ni cal	r. 4, 6	For spelling, say *n ĭ qu ě s*. The French *i* says *ē*. The *qu* says *k*, an uncommon sound. After children say the syllables, say, "In the first syllable, use *ch, k, sh*."
the *o* ry	r. 4, 6	
tor *toise*		For spelling, say *tor toise*. For reading, say *tor tise*.
tran *quil* li ty tran *quil*	r. 10, 6	Base word.
u nique	r. 4	For spelling, say *n ĭ qu ě*. The French *i* says *ē*. The *qu* says *k*, an uncommon sound for *qu*.
u ni v*er* si ty *u* ni v*er* sal *u* ni v*erse*	r. 4, 11, 6 r. 4, 11 r. 4	Base word.
vac *u* um	r. 4	
v*ague* ly v*ague*	r. 6	Base word.
vic t*o* ri *ous* vic t*o* ry	r. 4, 24 r. 4, 6	After children say the syllables, say, "In the last syllable, use *ow, ō, ōō, ŭ*." Dictate *victory* first.
v*i* *o* *lence* v*i* *o* lent	r. 5, 4 r. 5, 4	Dictate *violent* first.
xy lo *phone*	r. 5, 4	After children say the syllables, say, "In the first syllable, use the phonogram *x* to say *z*, an uncommon sound for *x*."

SPALDING SPELLING/VOCABULARY WORD LIST: ALPHABETIZED

THE ALPHABETIZED Spalding Spelling/Vocabulary Word List is a handy reference for parents and teachers. Words can be located quickly when students ask questions about particular markings, spellings, or pronunciations. The list is also useful when words are needed to provide additional practice with specific rules or phonograms. Being able to find words quickly and easily conserves valuable instructional time.

Word	Section	Page	Word	Section	Page	Word	Section	Page
a	A–G	254	allege	Z	395	approaches	U	362
ability	S	346	allegiance	Z	395	appropriate	Z	395
able	L	289	allow	Q	329	approval	T	353
aboard	O	312	almost	M	299	approve	T	353
about	H	266	alone	H, L	265, 295	approximate	Y	388
above	L	291				April	N	308
absence	T	352	along	J	279	architecture	X	381
absent	T	352	already	R	337	Arctic Ocean	X	381
abyss	Z	395	also	M	301	are	A–G	259
accept	T	351	although	Q	331	argue	T	350
accident	T	351	altitude	X	381	argument	T	350
accommodate	Y	388	always	N	306	army	M	298
according	R	337	am	A–G	256	around	K	285
account	M	298	America	R	339	arrange	Q, V	332, 365
accuracy	Y	388	American	R	339			
accurate	Y	388	among	N	309	arrangement	V	365
ache	T	353	amount	P	322	arrest	Q	330
aches	T	353	amusement	T	353	arrive	S	343
achieve	U	361	an	A–G	256	article	R	338
achieves	U	361	ancestors	X	381	artificial	X	381
acquaintance	Z	395	ancient	U	361	as	H	265
acquire	U	361	and	A–G	254	ascend	U	359
across	K	285	anger	T	353	ascending	V	366
act	N, Q	309, 330	angle	W	374	ascent	U	359
			angrily	T	353	Asia	X	382
action	Q	330	angry	T	353	ask	H	264
active	W	374	angular	W	374	assist	S	343
activities	W	374	animal	P	324	associate	T	351
activity	W	374	ankle	Q	332	association	T, V	351, 366
actual	W	374	annual	X	381			
actually	W	374	another	L	293	assure	U	358
add	I	273	answer	P	323	at	A–G	254
addition	Q	327	ant	N	305	ate	H, O	267, 312
address	O	316	Antarctica	X	381			
adjective	X	381	antique	W	374	athlete	W	373
admission	O	317	anxiety	W	374	athletic	W	373
adopt	R	336	anxious	W	374	Atlantic Ocean	X	382
advantage	X	381	any	K	282	atmosphere	S	346
advice	R	339	anyone	U	362	atmospheric	S	346
advise	R	339	anything	L	291	attack	U	362
affair	S	344	anyway	M	302	attempt	Q	331
affect	X	381	apiece	U	362	attend	O	315
afraid	O	312	apologize	Z	395	attention	R	337
Africa	X	381	apparent	V	366	attorney	U	362
after	I	272	appear	O	315	August	O	316
afternoon	K	283	appearance	S	346	aunt	N	305
again	M, R	300, 339	appears	Q	332	Australia	X	382
			apple	H	267	author	H	267
against	R	339	application	U	359	auto	P	320
age	J	276	applied	X	381	automobile	T	351
ago	A–G	257	apply	U, X	359, 381	autumn	S	346
agree	U	361				available	T	353
agreement	U	361	applying	X	381	avenue	R	335
air	J	279	appoint	Q	330	average	W	374
alike	I	273	appreciate	W	373	avoid	T	353
all	A–G	258	appreciative	W	373	await	Q	331

Word	Section	Page
away	I	271
awe	P	320
awful	P	320
baby	H	266
back	I	271
backward	Q	331
bad	A–G	257
bag	A–G	260
bake	N	310
baking	N	310
balance	U	362
ball	H	264
banana	T	353
band	J	275
bare	K	285
bargain	R	339
basic	V	366
basically	V	366
basin	P	324
be	A–G, N	257, 309
bear	K	285
beautiful	P	320
beauty	P	320
became	K	281
because	L	292
become	K	284
bed	A–G	255
been	N	309
before	L, S	293, 345
beg	A–G	260
began	L	289
begin	L	289
beginning	L	289
begun	M	297
behavior	S	345
behind	K	284
believe	S	345
belong	H	263
belongs	L	295
beneath	R	339
beneficial	X	382
benefit	X	382
beside	M	297
best	I	273
better	K	284
between	K	281
beyond	R	339
bicycle	W	374
big	A–G	260
bill	J	277
bird	A–G	262
biscuits	T	354
black	L	289
block	I	269

Word	Section	Page
blow	I	269
blows	I	269
blue	A–G, J	257, 275
board	O	315
boat	J	275
body	L	295
bog	A–G	260
bone	K	287
book	A–G	259
born	M	297
both	M	299
bottle	T	354
bottom	T	354
bough	V	366
bought	M	298
boundaries	X	382
boundary	X	382
bouquet	W	374
bow	V	366
bowl	N	310
box	H	263
boy	A–G	259
brace	Q	332
bracelet	Q	332
brave	I	273
bread	H	267
break	R	340
breakfast	M	302
breath	Q	332
breathe	Q	332
breeze	P	324
bridge	N	305
brilliant	X	382
bring	H, M	264, 299
broke	N, R	307, 340
broken	R	340
brother	K	281
brought	M	299
brown	H	267
bruise	T	354
bruised	T	354
bug	A–G	260
build	M	300
built	M	300
burn	K	285
business	T	352
busy	R, T	337, 352
but	A–G	257
butcher	L	289
button	P	324
buy	L	290
by	A–G, L	259, 290

Word	Section	Page
cabbage	P	324
calculate	U	362
calculation	U	362
calendar	W	374
calf	Q	330
call	H	264
calm	Q	332
calves	Q	330
came	I	271
camp	K	285
campaign	V	366
can	A–G	254
cannot	J	276
canoe	O	317
cantaloupe	Z	395
canvas	S	346
capital	V	366
capitol	V	366
captain	O	317
capture	N	305
car	J	278
card	J	275
care	K	284
career	V	366
careful	P	325
carriage	S	344
carried	P	321
carry	N, P, S	305, 321, 344
case	M	300
cast	J	275
catch	L	289
catcher	L	289
caught	P	323
cauliflower	Z	395
cause	L	292
caution	O	317
cautious	O	317
ceiling	S	346
celebration	T	353
celery	S	346
cellar	O	317
cemetery	Z	396
cent	K, S	283, 343
center	N	305
central	U	362
centuries	W	375
century	S, W	343, 375
cereal	V	367
ceremony	U	362
certain	S	345
certainly	S	345
chain	N	305

Word	Section	Page	Word	Section	Page	Word	Section	Page
chair	J	280	climb	M	302	congress	X	383
chalk	L	290	close	L	294	connect	Q	327
chance	A–G, M	257, 302	clothe	L	289	connection	Q	327
chandelier	Z	396	clothes	L	289	conscientious	Z	396
change	M, T	301, 354	clothing	L	289	consented	Q	333
changeable	T	354	cloud	K	287	consequence	W	375
changing	M	301	club	K	286	consider	R	338
chapter	T	354	coarse	S, V	344, 367	consideration	U	358
character	W	373				construct	Y	388
characteristics	X	382	cocoa	R	340	construction	Y	388
charge	A–G, M	257, 300	coffee	M	302	contagious	X	383
			cold	A–G	261	contain	O	313
chauffeur	Z	396	collar	R	340	contains	M	302
cheap	N	310	collect	M	297	continent	X	383
check	N	306	college	S	346	continental	X	383
cheerful	N	310	colonel	X	382	continue	Q	333
cheese	L	295	colonial	U	358	continued	Q	333
Chicago	X	382	colonies	U	358	contract	M	299
chicken	N	310	colony	U	358	control	R	340
chief	O	314	color	M	302	controlled	R	340
child	A–G, M	261, 300	columns	V	367	convene	X	380
			combination	R	335	convenient	X	380
children	M	300	combine	R	335	convention	R	338
chimney	T	354	combustible	Z	396	conversation	Y	388
chocolate	X	382	come	A–G, K	260, 286	converse	Y	388
choice	V	367				convict	Q	328
choir	T	354	comfort	O	312	cool	A–G	262
choose	V	367	coming	K	286	copy	N	309
chose	V	367	command	Q	328	cordial	W	373
chosen	V	367	commence	Y	388	cordially	W	373
Christ	R	339	commerce	Y	388	corn	I	273
Christmas	R	339	commercial	Y	388	corner	W	375
church	L	293	commit	X	381	correct	V	367
circle	T, U	350, 360	committee	X	381	cost	K	284
			common	R	338	cotton	W	375
circular	T	350	communicate	Y	388	cough	P	325
circumference	U	360	communication	Y	388	could	K	282
circumstance	U	360	communities	S	346	count	W	375
circus	Q	333	community	S	346	counterfeit	Y	389
cities	P	324	companion	S	345	countless	W	375
citizen	U	361	company	O	314	country	L	293
city	K, P, U	282, 324, 362	compare	R	340	courage	Q	333
			comparison	R	340	course	S	344
			compete	T	354	court	N	309
civil	X	382	complaint	P	320	cousin	P	325
civilization	X	382	complete	R	339	cover	J	276
civilize	X	382	complex	Y	388	covered	O	317
civilized	X	382	composed	W	375	create	S	346
claim	Q	329	composition	W	375	created	S	346
class	K	284	concealed	U	362	creation	S	346
clean	K	285	concern	T	351	creative	S	346
clear	K	285	concert	S	347	creature	O	317
clerk	P	322	conclusion	Y	388	crowd	Q	328
climate	W	375	condition	S	344	cultural	Y	389
			confer	T	353	culture	Y	389
			conference	T	353	curiosity	Y	389

Word	Section	Page	Word	Section	Page	Word	Section	Page
curious	Y	389	develop	U, X	360, 383	don't	O	317
current	V	367	development	X	383	done	L	290
curtain	O	317	dew	Q	329	door	H	263
cut	I	269	diagonal	X	383	doubt	S	344
daily	M	302	diagram	W	375	down	J	277
dance	I	274	diameter	X	383	dozen	N	309
dangerous	Q	333	diamond	R	338	Dr.	V	367
dark	J	275	dictionary	S	347	drama	Z	397
dash	L	290	did	A–G	258	dramatic	Z	397
date	L	292	die	M	301	dramatically	Z	397
daughter	P	323	died	M	301	draw	K, V	287, 367
day	H, M	263, 302	differ	R	337	drawn	V	367
dead	L	294	difference	S	343	dress	M	297
deal	M	299	different	R	337	drew	V	367
dear	I	273	difficult	U	359	dried	Q	333
death	N	305	difficulty	U	359	drill	M	298
debate	Q	328	digest	Y	389	drink	K	287
debt	Q	333	digestible	Y	389	drive	N	310
debts	R	340	dinner	I	274	driven	M	298
deceive	T	354	direct	O, R	315, 337	driving	N	310
December	N	309	direction	O	315	drop	U	362
decide	S, T, Y	347, 352, 387	director	R	337	dropped	U	362
decided	S	347	disappear	U	362	drown	R	336
decision	T, Y	352, 387	disappoint	X	380	dry	Q	333
declare	O	317	disaster	R	340	due	Q	329
declared	O	317	discern	Z	396	during	O	316
deep	J	275	discernible	Z	396	duty	O	314
degree	P	321	discipline	Z	396	each	I	271
delay	K	285	discover	T	354	eager	R	340
delicious	U	362	discoveries	T	354	eagle	M	303
department	P	322	discovery	T	354	earliest	U	358
depend	W	375	discuss	V	365	early	L, U	294, 358
dependent	W	375	discussion	V	365	earn	L	295
depends	W	375	disease	W	375	earth	A–G	262
depth	X	383	dispense	Z	396	ease	K	287
descend	U	359	dissension	Z	396	east	J	276
descent	U	359	dissent	Z	396	eastern	S	348
describe	U	362	distance	O	317	easy	K	287
described	U	362	distant	O	317	eat	H	263
description	X	383	distinguish	U	358	eats	H	267
descriptive	X	383	distribute	R	338	echo	N	310
desert	Y	389	district	O	312	echoes	N	310
design	S	347	divide	U, V	361, 367	economic	Z	397
desirable	V	367	division	V	367	economical	Z	397
desire	P, V	324, 367	do	A–G, L, P	254, 290, 323	economy	Z	397
dessert	Y	389	doctor	N	309	edge	L	295
destroy	P	323	does	P	323	education	R	337
determination	T	354	dog	H	267	effect	R, X	338, 383
determine	T	354	doll	I	274	effective	X	383
determined	T	354	dollar	N	307	efficiency	Z	397
			dollars	P	325	efficient	Z	397
						effort	Q	329
						egg	I	274

Word	Section	Page	Word	Section	Page	Word	Section	Page
Egypt	Y	389	equipment	V	368	explosion	Q	333
Egyptian	Y	389	equipped	V	368	express	L	291
eight	M, O	302, 312	equivalent	W	376	expression	W	376
either	Q	329	err	T	355	exquisite	X	384
elaborate	U	361	error	T	355	extend	Y	390
elect	O	312	escape	P	323	extension	Y	390
election	O	312	especially	X	381	extensive	Y	390
electric	T	355	essential	X	384	extent	Y	390
electrical	T	355	establish	U	363	extra	M	297
electrician	T	355	established	U	363	extraordinary	Z	397
electricity	T	355	establishment	U	363	extreme	V, W	368, 373
electrons	Y	389	estate	Q	329			
elegant	U	363	estimate	T	351	extremely	V	368
element	W	375	Europe	X, Z	384, 399	eye	K	281
elementary	W	375				face	I	268
elephant	S	347	even	K	283	fact	O	315
eliminate	Z	397	evening	N	307	factors	W	376
else	N	305	event	M	299	factory	Q	328
embarrass	Z	397	eventually	X	384	fail	K	286
embarrassment	Z	397	ever	L	293	fair	N	307
emergency	W	373	every	J	278	fairy	N	310
emperor	U	363	everybody	S	347	fall	I	270
empire	P	321	everyone	W	376	fame	Q	329
employ	Q, X	327, 383	everything	O	314	familiar	X	384
			everywhere	W	376	familiarity	X	384
employee	X	383	evidence	V	366	family	P, X	322, 384
empty	W	375	exact	T	355			
enclose	Q	331	examination	S	344	famous	Q	329
end	I	270	examine	S	344	fancy	M	303
endeavor	Z	397	example	R	340	far	I	273
enemy	R	340	excel	U	363	fare	N	307
engage	Q	327	excellent	U	363	farther	O	314
engine	P	322	except	N	304	fast	H	267
England	X	383	exceptions	T	355	father	L	291
English	X	383	exchange	X	384	fatigue	W, Z	376, 397
enjoy	P	320	excite	R	340			
enormous	X	384	excitement	R	340	fatiguing	Z	397
enough	O	315	exciting	R	340	favor	P, T	322, 355
enter	M	298	exclaimed	W	376			
entered	T	355	exclamation	W	376	favorable	T	355
entertain	R	335	excuse	P	325	favorite	T	355
enthusiasm	Z	397	exercise	Q	333	fear	V	368
entire	Q	328	exhaust	Q	333	fearful	V	368
entitle	T	352	exist	X	384	feather	L	296
entrance	P	321	existence	X	384	feature	R	338
envelop	U	360	expect	N	306	February	W	374
envelope	U	360	expense	U	359	feed	A–G	262
environment	W	375	expensive	Y	389	feel	N	307
equal	W	376	experience	V	366	feet	I	269
equality	W	376	experiment	W	376	fell	L	290
equate	Y	389	experimental	W	376	felt	K	286
equation	Y	389	explain	O	318	female	K	281
equator	Y	389	explanation	Y	389	fence	L	296
equatorial	Y	389	exploration	X	384	few	M	301
equip	V	368	explore	X	384	field	L	295
			explorers	X	384	fierce	R	341

Word	Section	Page
fifth	N	310
fight	L	290
figure	O	313
file	M	297
fill	J	279
final	Q, U	327, 360
finally	U	360
financier	Z	396
find	I	271
fine	J	276
finish	K	285
fire	J	276
firm	Q	328
first	K	283
five	H	264
fix	M	297
fixed	M	297
flew	R	341
flies	R	341
flight	P	320
floated	O	318
floor	H	263
flour	L	294
flower	L	294
fly	M, R	303, 341
folk	T	353
folks	T	353
follow	M	300
food	H	267
foot	I	269
for	H	266
foreign	U, W	359, 376
foreigners	W	376
forest	M	303
forget	J	274
forgot	J, R	280, 341
forgotten	R	341
form	I, J	273, 279
formal	Z	398
formally	Z	398
forth	X	384
fortune	P	321
forty	O	313
forward	Q	331
fought	T	355
found	J	278
four	L, O	292, 313
fourteen	O	313
fourth	O, X	313, 384

Word	Section	Page
fraction	X	384
fractional	X	384
free	I	270
freeze	M	303
frequency	W	376
frequent	W	376
Friday	K	283
friend	O	316
friends	O	316
frighten	S	347
frightened	S	347
from	J	279
front	N	305
frontier	Z	398
fruit	I	274
fuel	T	355
full	K	286
function	V	368
functional	V	368
funny	L	296
fur	A–G	262
furniture	V	368
further	S	344
future	V	368
game	J	275
garden	K	287
gather	U	363
gathering	V	368
gave	I	273
general	R	338
generally	U	363
gentle	M, Q	303, 331
gentleman	Q	331
genuine	T	355
get	H, O	264, 317
getting	O	317
ghost	O	318
giant	R	341
gigantic	R	341
girl	J	277
girls	J	277
give	I	272
glad	J	280
glass	K	281
go	A–G, L, M	254, 289, 298
god	N	308
God	N	308
goes	M	298
going	L	296
gold	J	276
gone	L	289
good	A–G	256

Word	Section	Page
goose	K	287
got	I	268
govern	S	345
government	S	345
gradual	W	376
gradually	W	376
grammar	Q	333
grand	J	275
grant	L	290
grateful	U	363
gravity	X	384
great	M	301
green	A–G	262
grief	P	325
grocery	S	347
ground	L	294
group	S	347
grow	M	303
growth	T	355
guarantee	Z	398
guard	P, X	325, 385
guess	J, P	280, 322
guest	P	322
guide	R	341
guilty	P	325
guitar	Z	398
had	A–G	259
half	L, Q	291, 330
halves	Q	330
hand	A–G	260
handful	T	355
hang	J	280
happen	M	297
happy	J	274
hard	J	276
hardly	T	355
has	H	265
hat	A–G	261
have	A–G	259
he	A–G	255
head	K	283
health	S	347
hear	N	306
heard	N	306
heart	M	300
heavier	V	368
heavily	V	368
heavy	V	368
height	V	366
heir	U	363
held	L	293
help	J	276

Word	Section	Page	Word	Section	Page	Word	Section	Page
her	H, I	266, 272	illustration	R	337	investigation	T	355
here	J, L	278, 294	image	V	368	invisible	Y	390
herself	L	292	imagination	X	385	invitation	T	351
high	L, V	291, 366	imagine	V	368	invite	T	351
hill	A–G	260	immediate	X	380	involve	T	356
him	A–G	258	immense	Y	390	involved	T	356
himself	N	308	importance	P	321	iron	M	303
his	H, I	267, 272	important	P	321	is	A–G	254
history	N	308	impossible	T	351	island	P	325
hoarse	U	363	impress	Z	398	Israel	Z	398
hold	M	298	impression	Z	398	Israeli	Z	398
hole	O	316	impressive	Z	398	issue	U	360
holes	M	303	imprison	Q	332	isthmus	W	376
holiday	O	318	improve	S	343	it	A–G	254
holy	O	318	improvement	S	343	it's	I	272
home	H	264	in	A–G	255	its	I	272
honey	L	296	incessant	Z	398	itself	N	306
honor	R	336	inches	V	368	jail	O	312
hop	K	287	include	Q	329	January	N	308
hope	J	279	income	M	298	journal	Q	333
hopping	K	287	increase	R	338	journey	Q	333
horizontal	X	385	indeed	L	292	judge	O, Z	313, 395
horse	K	284	independence	X	385	judgment	Z	395
hot	A–G	261	independent	V	369	July	K	283
hotel	M	303	Indian	Q	333	jump	H	267
hour	K	283	Indian Ocean	X	385	June	L	292
house	H	265	indicate	U	364	just	H, Q	264, 331
how	H	266	indication	U	364	justice	Q	331
however	L	295	individual	V	369	keep	K	281
human	P	322	industrial	X	385	kind	J	278
humor	Z	398	industry	X	385	kitchen	L	289
humorous	Z	398	influence	V	369	knee	O	318
hundred	V	368	inform	M	300	knew	O	315
hungry	P	325	information	Q	330	knife	K	287
hurried	R	341	inherit	U	363	knock	N	310
hurry	R	341	injure	R	338	know	L, O, P, R	294, 315, 324, 341
hurrying	R	341	injury	R	338			
hurt	K	285	innocent	V	369			
husband	P	322	inside	J	275			
hymn	T	355	inspect	N	306	knowledge	R	341
I	H, K	265, 281	instance	V	369	known	P	324
			instead	O	314	lace	I	270
			instrument	V	369	lady	K	284
ice	A–G	261	instrumental	V	369	laid	Q	334
icicle	U	363	intelligent	X	385	lake	I	270
identified	U	363	intend	O	314	land	A–G	261
identify	U	363	interest	R	339	language	P	325
if	H	266	interfere	U	364	large	J	277
ignorance	U	363	interference	U	364	last	A–G	256
ignorant	U	363	interior	X	385	late	A–G	260
ignore	U	363	into	A–G	258	latitude	X	385
Illinois	X	385	introduced	Y	390	latter	X	385
illustrate	R	337	introduction	Y	390	laugh	P	325
			invented	X	385	laughter	P	325
			invention	X	385			
			investigate	S	345			

Word	Section	Page
law	H	264
lawyer	R	341
lay	H, Q	267, 334
lead	L	294
leader	U	364
leadership	U	364
league	Z	398
learn	N	305
least	N	307
leather	N	311
leave	L	294
led	H, L	267, 294
ledge	Q	329
left	J	277
leisure	V	369
lemon	O	318
length	P	323
leopard	Y	390
less	M	299
lesson	L	291
let	A–G	260
letter	I	272
letters	L	296
level	W	377
liberty	O	315
library	W	377
license	V	369
lie	O	318
lieutenant	Z	399
life	J	278
light	K	286
like	A–G	259
lilies	T	356
lily	T	356
Lincoln	X	385
line	J, P	277, 325
linen	N	311
lining	P	325
liquid	V	369
list	L	293
listen	S	347
listened	S	347
literally	Y	390
literary	Y	390
literate	Y	390
literature	Y	390
little	A–G	257
live	A–G, M	260, 303
living	M	303
local	S	344
locate	V	369
located	V	369

Word	Section	Page
location	V	369
lone	H	265
long	H, P	265, 323
longitude	X	385
longitudinal	X	385
look	A–G	258
looks	I	274
loose	R	335
lose	R	335
loss	P	321
lost	J	279
lot	H	263
love	H	265
low	A–G	263
lying	O	318
machine	R, X	336, 386
machinery	X	386
made	J	278
magazine	X	386
magnificent	V	369
mail	K	281
main	V	369
major	U	361
majority	U	361
make	A–G	259
male	K	281
man	A–G, H	255, 266
manner	R	338
manufacture	Y	390
manufacturing	Y	390
many	K	282
March	L	292
march	L	292
marine	Y	394
marriage	S	344
marry	S	344
mass	T	356
massive	T	356
material	U	360
mathematical	Z	398
mathematics	Z	398
matter	N	308
may	A–G, J	258, 277
May	J	277
maybe	K	285
mayor	P	321
me	A–G	254
mean	N, U	308, 358
meant	U	358
measure	O	313

Word	Section	Page
meat	J, L	280, 293
medal	T	356
medicine	T	356
Mediterranean	Y	390
meet	L	293
member	M	300
memorable	Y	390
memorial	Y	390
memorize	Y	390
memory	Y	390
men	H	266
mentally	Y	391
mention	S	343
mere	U	360
message	U	364
messenger	U	364
metal	T	356
method	V	369
might	M	299
mile	K	283
military	Z	399
militia	Z	399
million	S	345
millionaire	Y	391
mind	L	295
mine	J	280
minerals	V	369
minor	Y	391
minority	Y	391
minute	T	352
mirror	X	386
miscellaneous	Z	399
mischief	Z	399
mischievous	Z	399
Miss	M, P	301, 322
miss	I, M	268, 301
mistaken	X	386
Mister	I, P	272, 322
mixture	N	311
model	W	377
modern	V	369
moist	X	386
moisture	X	386
moment	W	377
Monday	I	271
money	M	302
monkey	M	303
month	M	300
moon	I	271
more	J	279
morning	L	295
mortgage	Z	399

Word	Section	Page	Word	Section	Page	Word	Section	Page
mosquito	W	377	night	K	287	once	L	293
most	J	278	nine	I	268	one	H, L	265, 293
mother	A–G	261	nineteen	P	326			
motion	S	343	ninety	T	356	onion	S	345
mountain	M	299	no	A–G, L	255, 294	only	K	282
mouse	J	280				open	K	283
mouth	K	287	nobody	O	318	operate	Y	391
move	K	284	noise	M	303	operation	Y	391
Mr.	I, P	272, 322	none	O	315	operator	Y	391
			nonsense	W	377	opinion	S	345
Mrs.	P	322	noon	J	274	opportune	X	386
much	H	264	nor	N	308	opportunity	X	386
municipal	Z	399	north	I	268	opposite	W	378
muscle	W	377	North America	X	386	opposition	W	378
muscular	W	377	northern	S	348	or	I, N	273, 308
music	O, U	315, 364	not	A–G	256			
			nothing	L	294	orange	L	296
musician	U	364	notice	P	326	orchestra	Y	391
must	A–G	259	noticed	P	326	order	L	295
my	A–G	256	November	N	308	ordinarily	V	370
myself	M	303	now	A–G	255	ordinary	V	370
mysterious	V	370	number	N	309	organization	W	372
mystery	V	370	numeral	Y	391	organize	T, W	350, 372
nails	O	318	numerical	Y	391			
name	J	279	numerous	Y	391	origin	Y	391
narrow	W	377	oak	K	288	original	Y	391
nation	N, T	311, 352	oar	O	318	originated	Y	391
			object	O	313	other	H	266
national	T	352	objection	O	313	ought	T	352
natural	W	377	observation	W	377	our	J, K	279, 283
naturalist	W	377	observatory	W	377			
naturally	W	377	observe	W	377	out	A–G	258
nature	W	377	obtain	P	322	outside	J	275
naughty	P	323	occasion	V	370	over	A–G	259
navy	O	313	occasionally	X	386	own	L	293
near	J	277	occupy	U	359	Pacific Ocean	X	386
nearly	P	324	occur	W	378	pack	Q	334
necessary	U	361	occurred	W	378	package	Q	334
necessity	U	361	occurrence	W, Z	378, 399	page	I	270
need	N	306				paid	M	298
needle	O	318	ocean	P	326	paint	A–G	262
negate	Y	391	o'clock	P	323	pair	N	306
negative	Y	391	October	N	310	palace	O	318
neighbor	R	335	of	A–G, M	257, 299	paper	I	271
neither	S	344				paragraph	R	341
nephew	P	326	off	M	299	parallel	Z	399
neutral	Z	399	offer	N	305	pare	N	306
never	J	278	office	M, T	301, 511	parents	X	386
new	I, L	272, 291				parliament	Y	391
			officer	T	351	part	J	278
news	L	291	official	T	351	particular	S	344
newspaper	P	323	often	S	343	party	K	281
next	L	292	oil	A–G	262	pass	K	287
nice	I	270	old	A–G	257	passengers	P	326
nickel	S	347	omit	M	302	past	M	299
niece	S	347	on	A–G	254	patience	R	341

Word	Section	Page	Word	Section	Page	Word	Section	Page
patient	R	341	pleasant	M, S	301, 346	prime	Y	392
pause	N	311	please	M	301	primitive	Y	392
pay	J, M	277, 298	pleasure	O	313	principal	V	365
peace	N, S	311, 345	plentiful	V	370	principle	V, Y	365, 388
peach	K	288	plenty	V	370	print	J	279
pear	N	306	pneumonia	Z	399	prison	P	321
peculiar	X	386	pocket	L	296	prisoner	R	342
pencil	M	303	poem	S	348	private	Q	328
penny	O	318	poet	S	348	privilege	Z	400
people	L	293	poetic	S	348	probable	U	359
perceive	Y	391	poetry	S	348	probably	U	359
perceived	Y	391	point	L	295	problems	U	364
percent	Z	399	pole	K	288	proceed	W	373
percentage	Z	399	police	O	316	process	W	378
perfect	O	314	political	T	352	produce	S	348
perform	Y	392	pool	A–G	262	product	S, W	348, 378
performance	Y	392	poor	K	285			
perhaps	Q	332	popular	R	339	production	W	378
period	Q	327	population	O	313	productive	W	378
permanent	Y	392	porcelain	Z	400	profession	Y	392
permission	N	311	position	Q	329	professional	Y	392
perpendicular	X	386	positive	Y	392	proficiency	Z	400
persevere	X	386	possible	S	345	proficient	Z	400
persist	Z	399	possibly	S	345	program	W	378
persistence	Z	399	post	J	275	progress	Q	328
person	N	308	potato	S	348	project	Y	392
personal	O	314	potatoes	S	348	projection	Y	392
personality	V	370	pound	K	284	projector	Y	392
phone	J	280	power	L	292	promise	R	336
phrase	W	378	powerful	V	370	prompt	Q	331
physical	Q	334	practical	W	373	proper	O	313
physically	V	370	practice	W	378	properly	Q	334
physician	Z	400	prairie	V	370	property	Q	327
pianist	R	342	praise	Q	334	protect	V	371
piano	R	342	precipice	Y	392	protection	V	371
pianos	R	342	precipitous	Y	392	protective	V	371
pick	I	274	prefer	R	337	prove	N	306
pickle	R	342	preference	R	337	provide	M, R	297, 337
pickles	R	342	preliminary	X	380			
picnic	O	315	prepare	R	336	provision	R	337
picture	M	302	prepared	V	370	public	O	315
pie	M	304	presence	Y	392	publication	R	336
piece	S	345	present	Q	330	publish	Q	328
pigeon	U	364	presents	Y	392	pull	M	304
pitch	M	302	preside	Q	329	purchase	S	348
pitcher	M	302	president	Q	329	purchased	S	348
place	J	278	press	N	307	purpose	R	338
plain	U	364	pressure	S	348	push	L	295
plan	N	307	pretty	M	298	put	I	271
plane	U	364	prevent	V	370	qualities	Y	392
planet	V	370	previous	Y	392	quality	Y	392
plant	I	269	price	K	284	quantities	Y	393
planted	I	269	primarily	Y	392	quantity	Y	393
play	A–G	261	primary	Q, Y	329, 392	quarrel	S	348
						quart	V	371

Word	Section	Page	Word	Section	Page	Word	Section	Page
section	Q	328	similar	S, X	348, 387	sow	M	304
sections	W	379	similarities	X	387	space	K	288
secure	R	336	similarity	X	387	speak	M	299
see	A–G, K	255, 261, 286	simple	Y	394	special	Q, X	330, 381
seem	K	283	simplicity	Y	394	species	Z	401
seen	K	286	simplified	Y	394	specific	Z	401
seize	Y	393	simplify	Y	394	specifically	Z	401
seized	Y	393	since	P	323	specified	Z	401
select	Q	327	sincere	W	373	specify	Z	401
selection	Y	393	sincerely	W	373	speech	S	349
self	Q	330	sing	I	270	spell	K	285
senate	U	360	sir	K	286	spend	P	320
senator	U	360	sister	J	275	spent	I	269
senatorial	U	360	sit	H	263	spirit	V	372
send	H	265	sits	H	263	spiritual	V	372
sense	V	371	situation	V	372	spring	I	269
sensible	V	371	six	A–G	259	square	W	379
sent	K	283	size	N	309	stairs	L	296
sentence	O	319	sleep	H	267	stamp	K	286
separate	W	374	sleeve	R	342	stand	H	263
September	O	315	sleigh	S	348	standard	W	379
sequence	X	387	slide	O	314	stands	H	263
series	X	387	slightly	V	372	start	K	281
serious	S	344	slip	T	356	state	K, Q	283, 332
serve	Q, R	329, 338	slipped	T	356	statement	Q	332
service	R	338	small	L	291	station	O	315
session	V	366	smaller	L	291	stationary	T	357
set	K	286	smallest	L	291	stationery	T	357
setting	K	286	smooth	Q	334	stay	J	275
seven	J	274	sneeze	T	356	steadily	V	372
several	P	324	so	A–G, M	255, 304	steady	V	372
severe	T	356	soap	L	291	steak	S	349
sew	M	304	social	N, S	311, 349	steal	N	311
shall	L	295	society	S	349	steam	M	304
she	A–G	254	soft	H	263	still	J	278
shed	O	312	solar	Z	401	stole	M	298
shelf	Z	401	sold	I	273	stomach	T	357
shelves	Z	401	soldier	R	342	stone	I	270
shine	O	319	solemn	V	372	stood	M	297
shining	O	319	solution	S	349	stop	L	290
ship	J	277	some	H	266	stopping	L	290
shoe	L	296	something	N	306	store	J	280
shoes	L	296	sometimes	Q	327	story	K	283
short	K	284	son	J	276	straight	T	357
should	K	282	song	I	270	strange	N	311
shoulder	V	371	soon	I	271	stream	L	296
show	I	271	sorry	N	307	street	A–G	260
shut	K	287	source	S	349	strength	P	323
sick	I	268	south	J	275	strong	P	323
side	J	278	South America	X	387	struck	O	316
siege	U	365	southern	S	348	structural	W	379
sight	M	297	souvenir	Z	401	structure	W	379
sign	K	288	sovereign	Z	401	study	N	308
						style	P	326

Word	Section	Page	Word	Section	Page	Word	Section	Page
subject	N	308	telescope	Y	394	tissue	U	360
submarine	Y	394	television	T	357	to	H, P	265,
substance	W	379	tell	H	264			324
substantial	W	379	temperature	V	372	today	A–G	258
subtract	P	326	ten	A–G	255	toe	J	280
succeed	T	357	tenth	K	285	together	R	338
success	R	336	term	Q	328	told	I	273
successful	S	349	terrible	Q	327	tomato	R	342
such	L	294	territorial	Y	394	tomatoes	R	342
sudden	O	314	territory	Y	394	tomorrow	R	338
suffer	N	305	testimony	V	365	ton	A–G	255
sufficiently	Z	401	than	I	272	tongue	W	379
sugar	N	307	thank	I	273	tonight	K	285
suggest	U	360	that	H	266	too	P	324
suit	L	290	the	A–G	255	took	M	300
sum	R	342	theater	S	343	tooth	A–G	262
summary	R	342	their	Q	332	top	A–G	255
summer	L	291	them	H	266	tortoise	Z	402
summon	T	350	themselves	Q	330	total	S	343
sun	J	276	then	H	265	touch	Q	334
Sunday	I	271	theory	Z	402	tough	T	357
sung	I	270	there	L, N	294,	toward	Q, R	331,
superintendent	Y	394			309			336
supper	J	281	therefore	S	345	towel	Q	334
supply	S	343	these	K	286	town	J	275
support	P	323	they	K, Q	282,	track	L	290
suppose	Q	331			332	traffic	S	349
sure	N, U	307,	thief	O	319	train	J	277
		358	thing	I	272	tranquil	Z	402
surface	O	319	think	J	275	tranquillity	Z	402
surgeon	Y	394	third	L	295	travel	P	320
surprise	Q	327	thirteen	Q	334	treachery	X	387
sweeping	O	319	this	A–G	257	treasure	O, R	313,
sweeps	O	319	thoroughly	Y	394			339
sword	R	342	those	K	286	tree	I	268
syllable	Z	401	though	P	322	tremendous	Y	394
syllables	Z	401	thought	N	308	trial	P	326
system	S	345	thousand	V	372	triangle	W	379
table	L	291	thread	M	304	tried	M	304
tailor	P	326	three	A–G	261	trip	L	293
tails	S	349	threw	O	314	tripped	L	293
take	I	272	throat	Q	334	trophy	N	311
tales	S	349	through	J	280	trouble	P	321
talk	L	290	throughout	S	349	troubling	P	321
talks	L	296	throw	O	314	true	M, O	299,
tan	A–G	255	thumb	P	326			316
taught	P	323	thunder	M	304	truly	O	316
tax	N	309	Thursday	O	317	trust	M	297
teach	M	297	thus	N	306	truth	M	299
teacher	N	308	ticket	M	298	try	K, M	284,
tear	S	349	tie	V	372			304
technical	Z	402	time	A–G	257,	turn	L	291
techniques	Z	402			258	twelve	K	281
technology	Z	402	tin	A–G	255	twenty	K	281
teeth	A–G	262	tiny	L	296	twice	K	281
telephone	S	349	tire	J	276	twin	K	281

Word	Section	Page	Word	Section	Page	Word	Section	Page
two	K, P	281, 324	voices	N	311	why	J	277
tying	V	372	volume	T	350	wife	K	283
type	X	387	volunteer	W	379	will	A–G	256
typical	X	387	vote	N	309	wind	J	279
umbrella	Q	334	voyage	P	326	window	K	288
unable	M	298	wagon	K	288	winter	I	270
uncle	O	312	waist	O	319	wire	J	276
under	J	278	wait	P	321	wisdom	V	372
understand	M	300	waiting	O	319	wise	V	372
unfortunate	U	361	walk	L	290	wish	L	292
union	S	345	want	J	277	with	J	280
unique	Z	402	war	L	291	within	L	295
unit	S	349	warm	L	289	without	K	283
unite	S	349	was	H	266	witness	S	345
United States	S	349	wash	H	268	woman	N	307
universal	Z	402	waste	O	319	women	N	307
universe	Z	402	watch	L	290	wonder	N	305
university	Z	402	water	K	284	wonderful	Q	331
unless	L	289	way	H	264	word	J	278
until	O	316	we	A–G	256	words	L	296
up	A–G	256	weak	K	282	wore	S	350
upon	K	281	weapon	Q	334	work	J	279
us	A–G	256	wear	R	335	world	L	293
use	N	308	weary	O	319	worm	A–G	262
usual	P	320	weather	O	313	worn	S	350
vacation	P	320	Wednesday	T	353	worth	O	313
vacuum	Z	402	week	K	282	would	K	282
vague	Z	402	weigh	R	335	wreath	T	357
vaguely	Z	402	weight	R	335	wreck	R	336
valley	U	365	welfare	W	379	wrestle	T	357
valuable	S	350	well	H	266	wrestling	T	357
value	S	350	went	I	270	writ	Q	332
variety	W	379	were	L	294	write	L, O	292, 319
various	T	352	west	I	273			
vary	T	352	western	S	348	writer	O	319
vegetable	U	365	what	I	272	writing	O	319
vehicle	W	379	wheat	K	288	written	Q	332
vein	M	304	when	J	279	wrong	P	326
vertical	X	387	where	K, L	282, 294	wrote	L	292
very	I, T	273, 352				xylophone	Z	402
			whether	O	313	yacht	W	379
vessel	R	336	which	P	323	yard	H	263
vicinity	W	379	while	M	301	year	H	265
victim	T	351	whisper	P	326	yellow	H	268
victorious	Z	402	whistle	T	357	yes	H	263
victory	Z	402	whistling	T	357	yesterday	N	309
view	P	322	white	I	269	yet	I	271
violence	Z	402	who	M, Q	301, 330, 331	you	A–G	256, 258
violent	Z	402						
visit	P, R	322, 336	whole	O	316	young	N	307
			wholesome	T	357	your	A–G	258
visitor	R	336	whom	Q	330	zero	I	274
voice	N	311	whose	Q	331	zip	I	274
						zoo	I	274

RECOMMENDED LANGUAGE ARTS SCOPE AND SEQUENCE

THE LANGUAGE ARTS scope and sequence provides recommended grade-level objectives to be mastered in spelling, writing, and reading lessons from kindergarten through eighth grade. Each day's lessons include objectives from spelling, writing, and reading because the content and skills are interrelated and interdependent. *Each objective that addresses a skill will be applied to grade-appropriate content* (e.g., language rules applied to grade-level spelling words). At each successive grade, teachers pretest to differentiate instruction. Previously introduced skills are reviewed and applied to new, grade-appropriate content. The teacher's judgment determines the amount of review necessary to maintain mastery throughout the grades. (Labels for concepts taught need not be used initially.)

Code

I/P: *Introduce* and *practice*, but automaticity (mastery) by a majority of students is not expected.

P: *Practice* to achieve automaticity (mastery).

M: *Mastery* means accurate and automatic recall of grade-appropriate content and application of grade-appropriate skills by 80 percent of students 80 percent of the time.

R: *Review* to *reinforce* (1) previously introduced content and (2) application of skills to new, grade-appropriate content.

C: *Challenge* for students who have achieved mastery of grade-level content and skills.

SPELLING SCOPE AND SEQUENCE
Grade-Level Objectives

CODE
I/P: Introduce/Practice
P: Practice
M: Mastery
R: Review/Reinforce
C: Challenge

Phonemic Awareness The student will . . .	K	1	2	3	4	5	6	7	8
segment spoken words into sounds/syllables.	M	R	R	R	R	R	R	R	R
count sounds in spoken words.	M	R	R	R	R	R	R	R	R
blend spoken sounds into words.	M	R	R	R	R	R	R	R	R

Systematic Phonics: Sound-Symbols The student will . . .	K	1	2	3	4	5	6	7	8
explain the purpose of learning phonograms.	M	R	R	R	R	R	R	R	R
explain the purpose of precise handwriting.	I/P	M	R	R	R	R	R	R	R
precisely read 70 common phonograms.	I/P	M	R	R	R	R	R	R	R
precisely say and write 70 common phonograms.	I/P	M	R	R	R	R	R	R	R
precisely read 17 additional phonograms.	—	C	I/P	I/P	P	M	R	R	R

Systematic Phonics: Language Rules The student will . . .	K	1	2	3	4	5	6	7	8
1. write *qu* (a two-letter consonant sound) to say /kw/.	I/P	M	R	R	R	R	R	R	R
2. read *c* before *e, i,* and *y* as /s/.	I/P	M	R	R	R	R	R	R	R
3. read *g* before *e, i, y* as /j/.	I/P	M	R	R	R	R	R	R	R
4. read/mark /ā/, /ē/, /ō/, and /ū/ at the end of an *open* syllable.	I/P	M	R	R	R	R	R	R	R
5. read/mark *i* and *y* at end of an *open* syllable.	I/P	M	R	R	R	R	R	R	R
6. write *y*, not *i*, at the end of a word.	I/P	M	R	R	R	R	R	R	R
7. read/mark/explain jobs of silent *e*'s.	I/P	M	R	R	R	R	R	R	R
8. read /or/ as /er/ after a *w*.	I/P	M	R	R	R	R	R	R	R
9. explain/apply the 1-1-1 rule to one-syllable words (*hop*).	C	I/P	P	M	R	R	R	R	R
10. explain/apply the 2-1-1 rule to multisyllable words (*begin*).	C	I/P	P	P	M	R	R	R	R
11. explain/apply r. 11 to words with final silent *e* (*hope/hoping*).	C	I/P	P	M	R	R	R	R	R
12. write *ie* except after *c*, if we say /ā/ or in exceptions.	—	I/P	P	M	R	R	R	R	R
13. write *sh* to say /sh/ at the beginning/end of words and at the end of syllables.	I/P	M	R	R	R	R	R	R	R
14. write *ti, si, ci* to say /sh/ in syllables after the first one.	—	I/P	P	M	R	R	R	R	R
15. write *si* to say /sh/ if preceding syllable/base word ends in *s*.	—	I/P	P	M	R	R	R	R	R
16. read/mark and explain that *si* may also say /zh/.	—	I/P	P	M	R	R	R	R	R
17. write two *l*'s, *f*'s, or *s*'s after one vowel in one syllable.	I/P	M	R	R	R	R	R	R	R
18. write *ay* to say /ā/ at the end of a word.	I/P	M	R	R	R	R	R	R	R
19. read /ī/ and /ō/ before two consonants when appropriate.	I/P	M	R	R	R	R	R	R	R
20. explain/apply r. 20 (*s* never follows the letter *x*).	C	I/P	P	M	R	R	R	R	R
21. write *all* with one *l* when used as a prefix.	C	I/P	P	M	R	R	R	R	R
22. write *till* and *full* with one *l* when used as a suffix.	C	I/P	P	M	R	R	R	R	R
23. write *dge* to say /j/ after one vowel saying its first sound.	C	I/P	P	M	R	R	R	R	R

SPELLING SCOPE AND SEQUENCE
Grade-Level Objectives

CODE
I/P: Introduce/Practice
P: Practice
M: Mastery
R: Review/Reinforce
C: Challenge

Systematic Phonics: Language Rules The student will . . .	K	1	2	3	4	5	6	7	8
24. write *i,* instead of *y,* when adding vowel suffixes.	C	I/P	P	**M**	R	R	R	R	R
25. write *ck* to say /k/ after one vowel saying its first sound.	I/P	P	**M**	R	R	R	R	R	R
26. capitalize names and titles.	I/P	**M**	R	R	R	R	R	R	R
27. write *z* to say /z/ at beginning of words (*zoo*).	I/P	**M**	R	R	R	R	R	R	R
28. read ending *ed* as /ed/ if the base word ends in *d* or *t* (*grad ed*); read suffix *ed* as /d/ after a voiced consonant (*lived*); read suffix *ed* as /t/ after an unvoiced consonant (*stopped*).	C	I/P	**M**	R	R	R	R	R	R
29. read double consonants in both syllables for spelling (*lit tle*); read double consonant words in normal speech for reading.	I/P	P	**M**	R	R	R	R	R	R

Systematic Phonics: Spelling High-Frequency Words The student will . . .	K	1	2	3	4	5	6	7	8
explain the purpose of spelling dictation.	I/P	**M**	R	R	R	R	R	R	R
precisely say, write, read words in sections A–G.	I/P	**M**	R	R	R	R	R	R	R
precisely say, write, read words in section H.	I/P	**M**	R	R	R	R	R	R	R
precisely say, write, read words in section I.	I/P	**M**	R	R	R	R	R	R	R
precisely say, write, read words in section J.	C	**M**	R	R	R	R	R	R	R
precisely say, write, read words in section K.	—	I/P	**M**	R	R	R	R	R	R
precisely say, write, read words in section L.	—	I/P	**M**	R	R	R	R	R	R
precisely say, write, read words in section M.	—	I/P	**M**	R	R	R	R	R	R
precisely say, write, read words in section N.	—	I/P	**M**	R	R	R	R	R	R
precisely say, write, read words in section O.	—	C	I/P	**M**	R	R	R	R	R
precisely say, write, read words in section P.	—	—	I/P	**M**	R	R	R	R	R
precisely say, write, read words in section Q.	—	—	I/P	**M**	R	R	R	R	R
precisely say, write, read words in section R.	—	—	C	I/P	**M**	R	R	R	R
precisely say, write, read words in section S.	—	—	—	I/P	**M**	R	R	R	R
precisely say, write, read words in section T.	—	—	—	I/P	**M**	R	R	R	R
precisely say, write, read words in section U.	—	—	—	C	I/P	**M**	R	R	R
precisely say, write, read words in section V.	—	—	—	—	I/P	**M**	R	R	R
precisely say, write, read words in section W.	—	—	—	—	I/P	**M**	R	R	R
precisely say, write, read words in section X.	—	—	—	—	C	I/P	**M**	R	R
precisely say, write, read words in section Y.	—	—	—	—	—	I/P	**M**	R	R
precisely say, write, read words in section Z.	—	—	—	—	—	I/P	**M**	R	R

WRITING SCOPE AND SEQUENCE

Grade-Level Objectives

CODE
I/P: Introduce/Practice
P: Practice
M: Mastery
R: Review/Reinforce
C: Challenge

Conventions: Capitalization The student will capitalize . . .	K	1	2	3	4	5	6	7	8
first words of sentences.	I/P	M	R	R	R	R	R	R	R
single-word proper nouns and titles (Mr., etc.).	I/P	M	R	R	R	R	R	R	R
abbreviations.	—	I/P	M	R	R	R	R	R	R
multiword proper nouns.	C	I/P	P	M	R	R	R	R	R
titles of books, poems, short stories.	C	I/P	P	M	R	R	R	R	R
informal letter components.	—	I/P	P	M	R	R	R	R	R
first words of direct quotations.	—	C	I/P	M	R	R	R	R	R
familial titles, races, nationalities.	—	—	C	I/P	M	R	R	R	R
course titles, religious terms, periods of time.	—	—	—	—	C	I/P	M	R	R
formal letter components.	—	—	—	—	C	I/P	M	R	R

Conventions: Punctuation The student will use . . .	K	1	2	3	4	5	6	7	8
periods (full stops) . . .									
at the end of declarative sentences.	I/P	M	R	R	R	R	R	R	R
with abbreviations.	C	I/P	M	R	R	R	R	R	R
question marks.	I/P	P	M	R	R	R	R	R	R
exclamation points.	I/P	P	M	R	R	R	R	R	R
apostrophes in contractions and possessives.	—	I/P	P	M	R	R	R	R	R
commas . . .									
in series, dates, addresses, friendly letters.	—	I/P	P	M	R	R	R	R	R
in compound sentences.	I/P	P	M	M	R	R	R	R	R
in complex sentences.	C	I/P	P	M	R	R	R	R	R
with introductory phrases and clauses.	—	I/P	P	P	M	R	R	R	R
with appositives, direct address, interrupters, quotations.	—	I/P	P	P	P	M	R	R	R
after closing a business letter.	—	—	C	I/P	P	M	R	R	R
to avoid confusion.	—	—	—	C	I/P	P	M	R	R
underlining for titles of books within texts.	—	I/P	P	M	R	R	R	R	R
quotation marks . . .									
with direct quotations.	—	C	I/P	P	M	R	R	R	R
with titles of short works within text.	—	C	I/P	P	M	R	R	R	R
colons . . .									
in time.	I/P	P	M	R	R	R	R	R	R
in lists, after salutation in business letters.	—	—	C	I/P	P	M	R	R	R
hyphens . . .									
in syllabication.	—	C	I/P	P	M	R	R	R	R
in words that designate compound numbers, fractions.	—	C	I/P	P	M	R	R	R	R
in compound adjectives.	—	—	C	I/P	M	R	R	R	R
semicolons . . .									
in compound sentences.	—	—	—	—	C	I/P	M	R	R
in a series that is already punctuated.	—	—	—	—	—	C	I/P	M	R
joining closely associated sentences.	—	—	—	—	—	C	I/P	M	R

WRITING SCOPE AND SEQUENCE
Grade-Level Objectives

CODE
I/P: Introduce/Practice
P: Practice
M: Mastery
R: Review/Reinforce
C: Challenge

Sentence Construction with Vocabulary Development The student will . . .	K	1	2	3	4	5	6	7	8
explain the attributes of a *declarative* sentence.	I/P	**M**	R	R	R	R	R	R	R
compose *simple* declarative sentences that include . . .									
subject nouns with present tense regular action verbs.	I/P	P	**M**	R	R	R	R	R	R
subject pronouns, present tense regular action verbs.	I/P	P	**M**	R	R	R	R	R	R
subject noun plurals and action verbs.	I/P	P	**M**	R	R	R	R	R	R
adjectives, nouns, and present tense regular action verbs.	I/P	P	**M**	R	R	R	R	R	R
subject nouns/pronouns, linking verbs with adjectives.	I/P	P	**M**	R	R	R	R	R	R
subject nouns/pronouns, linking verbs with nouns.	I/P	P	**M**	R	R	R	R	R	R
subject nouns/pronouns with past tense regular verbs.	I/P	P	**M**	R	R	R	R	R	R
subject nouns/pronouns with past tense irregular verbs.	I/P	P	**M**	R	R	R	R	R	R
subject nouns/pronouns with main and helping verbs.	I/P	P	**M**	R	R	R	R	R	R
subject nouns/pronouns, action verbs, and object nouns.	I/P	P	**M**	R	R	R	R	R	R
subject nouns/pronouns, action verbs, and object pronouns.	I/P	P	**M**	R	R	R	R	R	R
subject nouns/pronouns, action verbs, and adverbs.	I/P	P	**M**	R	R	R	R	R	R
irregular noun plurals; action, linking, or helping verbs.	I/P	P	**M**	R	R	R	R	R	R
compound subjects, action/linking/helping verbs.	I/P	P	**M**	R	R	R	R	R	R
subject nouns/pronouns with compound action verbs.	I/P	P	**M**	R	R	R	R	R	R
subject nouns with action verbs and compound object nouns/pronouns.	C	I/P	**M**	R	R	R	R	R	R
subject nouns with action verbs with prepositional phrases.	I/P	P	**M**	R	R	R	R	R	R
compose declarative sentences that demonstrate meaning and usage of *synonyms, homophones, homographs,* and other *unfamiliar* spelling/vocabulary words.	I/P	**M**	R	R	R	R	R	R	R
explain the attributes of an *interrogative* sentence (question).	I/P	P	**M**	R	R	R	R	R	R
compose *interrogative* sentences that include subject nouns/pronouns with action/linking/helping verbs.	I/P	P	**M**	R	R	R	R	R	R
explain the attributes of an *exclamatory* sentence.	I/P	P	**M**	R	R	R	R	R	R
compose *exclamatory* sentences that include subject nouns/pronouns with action verbs.	I/P	P	**M**	R	R	R	R	R	R
explain the attributes of an *imperative* sentence (command).	I/P	P	**M**	R	R	R	R	R	R
compose *imperative* sentences that include subject nouns/pronouns with action/linking/helping verbs.	I/P	P	**M**	R	R	R	R	R	R
compose four types of simple sentences that demonstrate meaning and usage of *unfamiliar* spelling words.	I/P	P	**M**	R	R	R	R	R	R
explain the attributes of a *compound* sentence.	C	I/P	**M**	R	R	R	R	R	R

Sentence Construction with Vocabulary Development The student will . . .	K	1	2	3	4	5	6	7	8
compose *compound* sentences that include . . .									
subject nouns/pronouns and conjunctions *and, or, but.*	C	I/P	**M**	R	R	R	R	R	R
subject nouns/pronouns and conjunctions *for, nor, yet.*	—	C	I/P	**M**	R	R	R	R	R
explain the attributes of a *complex* sentence.	C	I/P	P	**M**	R	R	R	R	R
compose *complex* sentences that include . . .									
subject nouns/pronouns, conjunctions *if, after, when.*	C	I/P	P	P	**M**	R	R	R	R
subject nouns, conjunctions *than, unless, because, however.*	C	I/P	P	P	**M**	R	R	R	R
compose simple/compound/complex sentences that demonstrate meaning and usage of *unfamiliar* spelling words.	I/P	P	P	P	**M**	R	R	R	R

Morphology with Vocabulary Development The student will . . .									
explain the meaning of *syllable.*	I/P	P	**M**	R	R	R	R	R	R
explain the meaning of *vowel.*	I/P	P	**M**	R	R	R	R	R	R
explain the meaning of *consonant.*	I/P	P	**M**	R	R	R	R	R	R
identify vowels/consonants in spelling word syllables.	I/P	P	**M**	R	R	R	R	R	R
explain the meaning of *open* syllable.	I/P	P	P	**M**	R	R	R	R	R
explain the meaning of *closed* syllable.	I/P	P	P	**M**	R	R	R	R	R
explain the meaning of *consonant + le* syllable.	I/P	P	P	**M**	R	R	R	R	R
identify type of syllables in spelling words.	I/P	P	P	**M**	R	R	R	R	R
explain the meaning of *base word.*	—	I/P	P	P	**M**	R	R	R	R
identify base words in spelling words.	—	I/P	P	P	**M**	R	R	R	R
explain the meaning of *prefix.*	—	I/P	P	P	**M**	R	R	R	R
identify prefixes that express . . .									
number: e.g., *mono, uni, di, bi, tri, tetra, quad, hemi.*	—	C	I/P	P	**M**	R	R	R	R
time: e.g., *pre, post*	—	C	I/P	P	**M**	R	R	R	R
place: e.g., *sub, em, pro, ap, in, ar, at, tele, ex, dia.*	—	C	I/P	P	P	**M**	R	R	R
identify prefixes that add information: e.g., *re, be, al, en, con, com, para, e, super.*	—	C	I/P	P	**M**	R	R	R	R
identify prefixes that express negation/reversal: e.g., *un, a, re, im, de, an, dis, in, mis.*	—	—	I/P	P	**M**	R	R	R	R
explain the meaning of *suffix* (ending).	C	I/P	P	P	**M**	R	R	R	R
identify suffixes that add information to the meaning: e.g., *ful, ish, y, en, er, ance, ence.*	C	I/P	P	P	**M**	R	R	R	R
identify suffixes that indicate . . .									
number: e.g., *s, es, ren,*	I/P	P	**M**	R	R	R	R	R	R
time: e.g., *er, est, ed.*	I/P	P	**M**	R	R	R	R	R	R
part of speech: e.g., *er, tion, ion.*	—	C	I/P	**M**	R	R	R	R	R
tense: e.g., *ed, ing.*	C	I/P	**M**	R	R	R	R	R	R
explain the meaning of *word root.*	—	I/P	P	P	**M**	R	R	R	R
identify prefixes, suffixes, base or word roots in spelling words.	—	I/P	P	P	P	P	**M**	R	R

Parts of Speech with Vocabulary Development: Nouns The student will . . .	K	1	2	3	4	5	6	7	8
explain the meaning of *noun.*	I/P	**M**	R	R	R	R	R	R	R
identify nouns as persons, places, or things.	I/P	**M**	R	R	R	R	R	R	R
explain/identify nouns that are *concepts.*	I/P	P	**M**	R	R	R	R	R	R
explain the meaning of *plural* and *suffix* (ending).	I/P	**M**	R	R	R	R	R	R	R

WRITING SCOPE AND SEQUENCE
Grade-Level Objectives

CODE
I/P: Introduce/Practice
P: Practice
M: Mastery
R: Review/Reinforce
C: Challenge

Parts of Speech with Vocabulary Development: Nouns The student will . . .	K	1	2	3	4	5	6	7	8
use the suffix *s* or *es* to form noun plurals.	I/P	**M**	R	R	R	R	R	R	R
explain the meaning of *irregular* plural.	I/P	**M**	R	R	R	R	R	R	R
write irregular noun plurals.	I/P	**M**	R	R	R	R	R	R	R
identify suffixes that form nouns: *er, ren, ian, s, es, or, ar, ance, ment, ition, ive, ent, ation, ice, sion, age, ence, ison, edge, ist, ary, ness, ity, ing, ry, ial, al, y, ian, ful, ery, ate, ship, en, able, ual, tion, ible, dom, ency, atory, ard, ure, ety, ee, aire, itive, cy, ology.*	—	I/P	P	P	**M**	R	R	R	R
form nouns by adding suffixes.	—	I/P	P	P	**M**	R	R	R	R
explain the meaning of *subject* noun.	I/P	P	**M**	R	R	R	R	R	R
identify subject nouns in simple sentences.	I/P	P	**M**	R	R	R	R	R	R
After all parts of speech have been taught . . .									
explain the meaning of *object* noun.	I/P	P	**M**	R	R	R	R	R	R
identify object nouns in simple sentences.	I/P	P	**M**	R	R	R	R	R	R
explain the meaning of *common* and *proper* nouns.	I/P	P	**M**	R	R	R	R	R	R
identify common and proper nouns in sentences.	I/P	P	**M**	R	R	R	R	R	R
explain the meaning of *compound* noun.	C	I/P	**M**	R	R	R	R	R	R
identify compound nouns in simple sentences.	C	I/P	**M**	R	R	R	R	R	R
explain/ identify verbs used as nouns (verbals).	—	—	—	C	I/P	**M**	R	R	R
use nouns in sentences (see Sentence Construction).	I/P	**M**	R	R	R	R	R	R	R

Parts of Speech with Vocabulary Development: Verbs The student will . . .	K	1	2	3	4	5	6	7	8
explain the meaning of *action* verb.	I/P	**M**	R	R	R	R	R	R	R
identify action verbs in sentences.	I/P	**M**	R	R	R	R	R	R	R
add suffixes *s* or *es* to third-person singular action verbs.	I/P	P	**M**	R	R	R	R	R	R
explain the meaning of *linking* verb.	I/P	P	**M**	R	R	R	R	R	R
identify *linking* verbs in sentences.	I/P	P	**M**	R	R	R	R	R	R
explain the meaning of *tense* (time) . . .									
present tense.	I/P	P	**M**	R	R	R	R	R	R
past tense of *regular* verbs.	I/P	P	**M**	R	R	R	R	R	R
add the past tense suffix *ed* to regular action verbs.	I/P	P	**M**	R	R	R	R	R	R
explain the meaning of *irregular* verbs.	I/P	P	**M**	R	R	R	R	R	R
write the past tense of irregular verbs.	C	I/P	**M**	R	R	R	R	R	R
explain the meaning of *future* tense.	C	I/P	**M**	R	R	R	R	R	R
write verb phrases that express future action.	C	I/P	**M**	R	R	R	R	R	R
explain the meaning of *action happening now*.	I/P	P	**M**	R	R	R	R	R	R
write verb phrases to express action happening now.	C	I/P	**M**	R	R	R	R	R	R
explain the meaning of *principal parts* of verbs.	—	I/P	P	**M**	R	R	R	R	R
identify principal parts of verbs in sentences.	—	I/P	P	**M**	R	R	R	R	R
write verb phrases that use principal parts of verbs.	—	—	I/P	P	**M**	R	R	R	R
explain the meaning of *main* and *helping* verbs.	I/P	P	**M**	R	R	R	R	R	R

Parts of Speech with Vocabulary Development: Verbs The student will . . .	K	1	2	3	4	5	6	7	8
write main and helping verb phrases.	I/P	P	**M**	R	R	R	R	R	R
explain the meaning of *compound* verbs.	I/P	P	**M**	R	R	R	R	R	R
identify compound verbs in sentences.	I/P	P	**M**	R	R	R	R	R	R
identify suffixes that form verbs, e.g., *ing, en, ed, ate, er, fy, ish, ize, s, es, ade, age.*	C	I/P	P	P	**M**	R	R	R	R
form verbs by adding suffixes.	—	I/P	P	P	**M**	R	R	R	R
explain the meaning of *transitive* and *intransitive* verbs.	—	C	I/P	P	P	**M**	R	R	R
categorize transitive and intransitive verbs.	—	C	I/P	P	P	**M**	R	R	R
use verbs in sentences (see Sentence Construction).	I/P	**M**	R	R	R	R	R	R	R

Parts of Speech with Vocabulary Development: Pronouns The student will . . .	K	1	2	3	4	5	6	7	8
explain the meaning of *pronoun*.	I/P	P	**M**	R	R	R	R	R	R
explain the meaning of *subject pronoun*.	I/P	P	**M**	R	R	R	R	R	R
substitute subject pronouns for subject nouns: *she, he, we, you, it, I, they.*	I/P	P	**M**	R	R	R	R	R	R
After all parts of speech are introduced . . .									
explain the meaning of *object pronoun*.	I/P	P	**M**	R	R	R	R	R	R
substitute object pronouns for object nouns: *me, him, us, you, it, her, them.*	I/P	P	**M**	R	R	R	R	R	R
explain subject/pronoun agreement.	C	I/P	**M**	R	R	R	R	R	R
identify subject/pronoun agreement in sentences.	C	I/P	**M**	R	R	R	R	R	R
explain the meaning of *possession* (belonging to).	—	I/P	**M**	R	R	R	R	R	R
identify possessive pronouns in sentences: *my, mine, your, yours, her, hers, his, its, our, ours, their, theirs.*	—	I/P	**M**	R	R	R	R	R	R
explain the meaning of *interrogative pronoun*.	—	I/P	**M**	R	R	R	R	R	R
identify interrogative pronouns in sentences: *what, who, which, whose, whom.*	—	I/P	**M**	R	R	R	R	R	R
explain the meaning of *demonstrative pronoun*.	—	I/P	**M**	R	R	R	R	R	R
identify demonstrative pronouns in sentences: *this, that, these, those.*	—	I/P	**M**	R	R	R	R	R	R
explain the meaning of *reflexive pronoun*.	—	I/P	**M**	R	R	R	R	R	R
identify reflexive pronouns in sentences: *herself, myself, himself, itself, themselves.*	—	I/P	**M**	R	R	R	R	R	R
explain the meaning of *indefinite pronoun*.	—	I/P	P	**M**	R	R	R	R	R
identify indefinite pronouns in sentences:									
all, much, one, some, other, each, more, most.	—	I/P	P	**M**	R	R	R	R	R
any, many, anything, another, nothing, both.	—	I/P	P	**M**	R	R	R	R	R
few, something, everything, none, nobody, several.	—	I/P	P	P	**M**	R	R	R	R
either, neither, everybody, anyone, everyone.	—	I/P	P	P	**M**	R	R	R	R
use pronouns in sentences (see Sentence Construction).	—	I/P	**M**	R	R	R	R	R	R

Parts of Speech with Vocabulary Development: Adjectives The student will . . .	K	1	2	3	4	5	6	7	8
explain the meaning of *adjective*.	I/P	P	**M**	R	R	R	R	R	R
explain the meaning of *noun signal* (article).	I/P	P	**M**	R	R	R	R	R	R
use *a, the,* and *an* with *appropriate* nouns.	I/P	P	**M**	R	R	R	R	R	R
explain the purpose of using adjectives.	I/P	P	**M**	R	R	R	R	R	R
identify adjectives in sentences.	I/P	P	**M**	R	R	R	R	R	R
write *appropriate* adjectives with nouns.	C	I/P	**M**	R	R	R	R	R	R

WRITING SCOPE AND SEQUENCE
Grade-Level Objectives

CODE
I/P: Introduce/Practice
P: Practice
M: Mastery
R: Review/Reinforce
C: Challenge

Parts of Speech with Vocabulary Development: Adjectives The student will . . .	K	1	2	3	4	5	6	7	8
write phrases with multiple adjectives and commas.	C	I/P	P	**M**	R	R	R	R	R
explain the meaning of *comparative* adjectives.	C	I/P	**M**	R	R	R	R	R	R
add the suffix *er* to adjectives.	C	I/P	P	**M**	R	R	R	R	R
add the suffix *est* to adjectives.	C	I/P	P	**M**	R	R	R	R	R
use *more/most* with two- to three-syllable adjectives.	—	C	I/P	**M**	R	R	R	R	R
explain the meaning of *proper* adjective.	—	—	C	I/P	**M**	R	R	R	R
write phrases including proper adjectives.	—	—	C	I/P	**M**	R	R	R	R
identify suffixes that form adjectives: *ed, al, en, ish, ant, ent, ous, able, ible, ful, less, ern, ive.*	—	I/P	P	P	**M**	R	R	R	R
form adjectives by adding suffixes.	—	I/P	P	P	**M**	R	R	R	R
use adjectives and phrases in sentences (see Sentence Construction).	C	I/P	**M**	R	R	R	R	R	R

Parts of Speech with Vocabulary Development: Adverbs The student will . . .	K	1	2	3	4	5	6	7	8
explain the meaning of *adverb.*	I/P	P	**M**	R	R	R	R	R	R
explain the purpose of using adverbs.	I/P	P	**M**	R	R	R	R	R	R
identify adverbs in sentences.	I/P	P	**M**	R	R	R	R	R	R
write adverbs that express extent/when/where/how:									
so, no, now, up, not, ago, out, today, yes, just, too.	I/P	P	**M**	R	R	R	R	R	R
then, as, how, well, fast, north, back, away, soon, yet.	C	I/P	**M**	R	R	R	R	R	R
after, very, west, south, inside, outside, east, near.	C	I/P	**M**	R	R	R	R	R	R
down, why, still, never, here, most, more, when.	C	I/P	**M**	R	R	R	R	R	R
twice, where, first, even, behind, around, without.	C	I/P	**M**	R	R	R	R	R	R
maybe, tonight, indeed, ever, once, there, early.	C	I/P	**M**	R	R	R	R	R	R
close, alone, third, within, nothing, no, past, almost.	C	I/P	**M**	R	R	R	R	R	R
all, less, off, again, also, please, anyway, daily.	C	I/P	**M**	R	R	R	R	R	R
explain the meaning of *adverb phrases.*	C	I/P	P	**M**	R	R	R	R	R
write adverb phrases that express extent/when/where/how.	C	I/P	P	**M**	R	R	R	R	R
identify suffixes that form adverbs (*ily, ly*).	—	I/P	P	P	**M**	R	R	R	R
form adverbs by adding suffixes.	—	I/P	P	P	**M**	R	R	R	R
use adverbs/adverb phrases in sentences (see Sentence Construction).	I/P	P	**M**	R	R	R	R	R	R

Parts of Speech with Vocabulary Development: Conjunctions The student will . . .	K	1	2	3	4	5	6	7	8
explain the meaning of *conjunction.*	I/P	P	**M**	R	R	R	R	R	R
use *and/or* to join compound nouns.	I/P	P	**M**	R	R	R	R	R	R
use *and/or* to join compound verbs.	I/P	P	**M**	R	R	R	R	R	R
use *and/or* to join adjective phrases.	C	I/P	**M**	R	R	R	R	R	R
use *and/or* to join adverb phrases.	C	I/P	P	**M**	R	R	R	R	R

Parts of Speech with Vocabulary Development: Conjunctions The student will . . .	K	1	2	3	4	5	6	7	8
use *and/or* to join sentences.	I/P	P	**M**	R	R	R	R	R	R
use *but* to contrast nouns.	C	I/P	**M**	R	R	R	R	R	R
use *but* to contrast verbs.	C	I/P	**M**	R	R	R	R	R	R
use *but* to contrast sentences.	C	I/P	**M**	R	R	R	R	R	R
use conjunctions with complex sentences:									
if, as, after, than, when.	C	I/P	**M**	R	R	R	R	R	R
unless, because, however, while.	C	I/P	P	**M**	R	R	R	R	R
whether, though, since, although.	—	—	C	I/P	**M**	R	R	R	R
either . . . or, neither . . . nor.	—	—	C	I/P	**M**	R	R	R	R
use conjunctions in sentences (see Sentence Construction).	C	I/P	**M**	R	R	R	R	R	R

Parts of Speech with Vocabulary Development: Prepositions The student will . . .	K	1	2	3	4	5	6	7	8
explain the meaning of *preposition.*	I/P	P	**M**	R	R	R	R	R	R
use prepositions with nouns/pronouns (phrases):									
at, on, in, up, of, out, into, by, over, to, about, for.	I/P	P	**M**	R	R	R	R	R	R
after, inside, outside, near, down, under, from, along.	C	I/P	**M**	R	R	R	R	R	R
with, through, upon, between, without, behind, around, across.	C	I/P	**M**	R	R	R	R	R	R
by, above, before, within, beside, past.	C	I/P	P	**M**	R	R	R	R	R
except, among, aboard, during, until, since, toward.	—	C	I/P	P	**M**	R	R	R	R
against, beneath, beyond, throughout.	C	I/P	P	P	**M**	R	R	R	R
write adjective prepositional phrases.	C	I/P	**M**	R	R	R	R	R	R
write adverb prepositional phrases.	C	I/P	P	**M**	R	R	R	R	R
use prepositions in sentences (see Sentence Construction).	C	I/P	**M**	R	R	R	R	R	R

Related Sentences The student will . . .	K	1	2	3	4	5	6	7	8
explain the meaning of *topic.*	I/P	P	**M**	R	R	R	R	R	R
explain the meaning of *related sentences.*	I/P	P	**M**	R	R	R	R	R	R
distinguish between related and unrelated sentences.	I/P	P	**M**	R	R	R	R	R	R
compose two or three related sentences that include previously introduced language skills.	I/P	P	**M**	R	R	R	R	R	R

Paragraph Construction The student will . . .	K	1	2	3	4	5	6	7	8
explain attributes of paragraphs.	I/P	P	**M**	R	R	R	R	R	R
explain paragraph conventions (margins/indents).	I/P	P	**M**	R	R	R	R	R	R
explain stages in the writing process: *prewriting, composing, revising, editing, publishing* (by reading, speaking, media presentation).	I/P	P	P	P	**M**	R	R	R	R
use the writing process to compose . . .									
first-person informative-narratives.	I/P	P	**M**	R	R	R	R	R	R
third-person informative-narratives.	C	I/P	**M**	R	R	R	R	R	R
informative paragraphs.	I/P	P	**M**	R	R	R	R	R	R
first-person narrative paragraphs.	I/P	P	**M**	R	R	R	R	R	R
third-person narrative paragraphs.	C	I/P	**M**	R	R	R	R	R	R
summarize informative-narratives.	—	C	I/P	**M**	R	R	R	R	R
summarize informatives.	—	C	I/P	**M**	R	R	R	R	R
summarize narratives.	—	C	I/P	**M**	R	R	R	R	R

WRITING SCOPE AND SEQUENCE

Grade-Level Objectives

CODE
I/P: Introduce/Practice
P: Practice
M: Mastery
R: Review/Reinforce
C: Challenge

Composition The student will . . .	K	1	2	3	4	5	6	7	8
use the writing process to compose . . .									
first-person informative-narratives.	C	I/P	P	**M**	R	R	R	R	R
third-person informative-narratives.	C	I/P	P	**M**	R	R	R	R	R
informatives.	C	I/P	P	**M**	R	R	R	R	R
first-person narratives.	C	I/P	P	**M**	R	R	R	R	R
third-person narratives.	C	I/P	P	**M**	R	R	R	R	R
informal communications.	C	I/P	P	**M**	R	R	R	R	R
formal communications.	—	—	I/P	P	**M**	R	R	R	R
expository essays with references/bibliography.	—	—	—	—	I/P	P	**M**	R	R
persuasive essays.	—	—	—	C	I/P	P	**M**	R	R
summarize informative-narratives.	—	C	I/P	**M**	R	R	R	R	R
summarize informatives.	—	C	I/P	**M**	R	R	R	R	R
summarize narratives.	—	C	I/P	**M**	R	R	R	R	R

READING SCOPE AND SEQUENCE

Grade-Level Objectives

CODE
I/P: Introduce/Practice
P: Practice
M: Mastery
R: Review/Reinforce
C: Challenge

Literary Appreciation The student will . . .	K	1	2	3	4	5	6	7	8
explain the meaning of *attributes* of imaginative literature.	I/P	P	**M**	R	R	R	R	R	R
identify attributes in imaginative literature:									
precise language, emotional appeal.	.I/P	P	**M**	R	R	R	R	R	R
content, insight, and universality.	C	I/P	P	P	**M**	R	R	R	R
reflect on author's use of attributes:									
precise language, emotional appeal.	I/P	P	P	**M**	R	R	R	R	R
content, insight, and universality.	I/P	P	P	P	P	**M**	R	R	R
compare use of attributes across selections/cultures:									
precise language, emotional appeal.	C	I/P	P	**M**	R	R	R	R	R
content, insight, and universality.	C	I/P	P	P	P	**M**	R	R	R
identify elements in imaginative literature:									
characters (main and supporting) by: *their appearance, speech, actions/reactions, others' comments, author's comments*	I/P	P	P	**M**	R	R	R	R	R
settings (integral and backdrop).	I/P	P	**M**	R	R	R	R	R	R
plots (order, types of conflict, patterns of actions).	I/P	P	**M**	R	R	R	R	R	R
point of view (first and third person).	C	I/P	**M**	R	R	R	R	R	R
theme (main idea).	C	I/P	**M**	R	R	R	R	R	R
style :									
imagery, figurative language, hyperbole.	C	I/P	P	**M**	R	R	R	R	R
onomatopoeia, rhythm, alliteration.	C	I/P	P	**M**	R	R	R	R	R
allusion, symbolism, understatement.	—	—	—	—	—	C	I/P	P	**M**
connotation, denotation.	—	—	—	—	—	C	I/P	P	**M**
assonance, consonance.	—	—	—	—	—	C	I/P	P	**M**
tone.	—	—	—	—	—	C	I/P	P	**M**
reflect (evaluate) author's use of elements:									
characters, setting, plot.	C	I/P	**M**	R	R	R	R	R	R
point of view, theme (main idea).	C	I/P	**M**	R	R	R	R	R	R
style, tone.	—	—	—	—	—	C	I/P	R	R
compare elements across selections/cultures:									
characters, setting, plot.	C	I/P	**M**	R	R	R	R	R	R
point of view, theme (main idea).	C	I/P	P	P	**M**	R	R	R	R
style, tone.	—	—	—	C	I/P	P	P	P	**M**
explain elements of fluent, expressive reading.	C	I/P	**M**	R	R	R	R	R	R
read fluently and expressively.	C	I/P	**M**	R	R	R	R	R	R

Text Structure The student will . . .	K	1	2	3	4	5	6	7	8
explain the meaning of *author's purpose*.	I/P	P	**M**	R	R	R	R	R	R
explain/identify author's purpose in narratives.	I/P	P	**M**	R	R	R	R	R	R
explain the meaning of *narrative elements*.	I/P	P	**M**	R	R	R	R	R	R
identify narrative elements in paragraphs.	I/P	P	**M**	R	R	R	R	R	R
explain/identify author's purpose in informatives.	I/P	P	**M**	R	R	R	R	R	R
explain the meaning of *informative elements*.	I/P	P	**M**	R	R	R	R	R	R

READING SCOPE AND SEQUENCE

Grade-Level Objectives

CODE
I/P: Introduce/Practice
P: Practice
M: Mastery
R: Review/Reinforce
C: Challenge

Text Structure The student will . . .	K	1	2	3	4	5	6	7	8
identify informative elements in paragraphs.	I/P	P	**M**	R	R	R	R	R	R
explain/identify author's purpose in informative/narratives.	I/P	P	**M**	R	R	R	R	R	R
explain the meaning of *informative-narrative elements*.	I/P	P	**M**	R	R	R	R	R	R
identify both narrative and informative elements in paragraphs.	I/P	P	**M**	R	R	R	R	R	R
use elements to identify types of writing.	I/P	P	**M**	R	R	R	R	R	R
use elements to vary reading rate.	I/P	P	**M**	R	R	R	R	R	R

Mental Actions The student will . . .	K	1	2	3	4	5	6	7	8
explain the meaning of *mental actions* (metacognition).	I/P	P	**M**	R	R	R	R	R	R
explain the purpose of *consciously* using mental actions.	I/P	P	**M**	R	R	R	R	R	R
monitor comprehension of . . .									
words.	I/P	P	**M**	R	R	R	R	R	R
phrases.	I/P	P	**M**	R	R	R	R	R	R
sentences.	I/P	P	**M**	R	R	R	R	R	R
make connections with prior knowledge and text to . . .									
infer word meanings, topic, cause and effect.	I/P	P	**M**	R	R	R	R	R	R
elaborate on topic, main idea, outcomes.	I/P	P	**M**	R	R	R	R	R	R
make predictions of . . .									
type of writing, topic, topic sentence, main idea.	I/P	P	**M**	R	R	R	R	R	R
actions, events, behavior, outcomes.	I/P	P	**M**	R	R	R	R	R	R
reformat/categorize information to . . .									
identify essential and additional information.	I/P	P	**M**	R	R	R	R	R	R
identify elements of types of writing.	I/P	P	**M**	R	R	R	R	R	R
mentally summarize . . .									
retell narratives in correct sequence.	I/P	P	**M**	R	R	R	R	R	R
restate information in correct sequence.	I/P	P	**M**	R	R	R	R	R	R
identify stated main ideas in text.	I/P	P	**M**	R	R	R	R	R	R
derive implied main ideas in text.	I/P	P	**M**	R	R	R	R	R	R
use mental actions to comprehend print.	I/P	P	**M**	R	R	R	R	R	R

Resources

For the Teacher

Text and Grade-Level Teacher Guides
The Writing Road to Reading, Sixth Edition
Kindergarten Through Sixth-Grade Teacher's Guide (specify grade needed)*

Phonograms
70 Common Phonogram Cards, classroom set, 4¼ by 6 inches (10.8 by 15.2 cm); or individual student set, 3 by 4¼ inches (7.6 by 10.8 cm)
17 Additional Phonogram Cards, classroom set, 4¼ by 6 inches (10.8 by 15.2 cm)

CDs and DVDs
Phonogram sounds CD
Phonogram sounds DVD
Word analysis CD (sort words by alphabet, parts of speech, syllable division)
Kindergarten through sixth-grade language arts lessons DVDs (specify grade needed or complete set)*
Third-grade language arts DVD

Activity Materials
Word Builder Cards, individual, 4¾ by 2¾ inches (12.1 by 7 cm), all grades
Level 1 Word Builder Cards, 11 by 4.25 inches (27.9 by 10.8 cm), kindergarten–second grade
Level 2 Word Builder Cards, 11 by 4.25 inches (27.9 by 10.8 cm), third grade and above
Text Structure Cards, classroom set, 8½ by 11 inches (21.6 by 27.9 cm)
Mental Action Cards, classroom set, 8½ by 11 inches (21.6 by 27.9 cm)

*Contact SEI for product listing. To order resources, please use one of the following. Mail: Spalding Education International, 23335 N 18th Drive, Suite 102, Phoenix, AZ 85027. Phone: Metro Phoenix 623-434-1204; toll-free 1-877-866-7451. Fax: 623-434-1208.
Online: www.spalding.org.

The Comprehension Connection
User's Guide for McCall-Harby and *McCall-Crabbs Book A with Passage Analyses and Answer Keys* (kindergarten through second grade)
User's Guide for McCall-Crabbs Standard Test Lessons in Reading Books B–E with Passage Analyses and Answer Keys (third grade and above)

Strips and Posters
Manuscript Alphabet Strips, nine sections, 26 ¾ by 8 ¼ inches (68 by 21 cm)
Feature and Letter Formation Poster Set, class size, 18 by 24 inches (45.7 by 61 cm)
Feature and Letter Formation Poster Set for home use, 11½ by 15 inches (29.2 by 38.1 cm)
Primary Rule Pages 1, 3, 4 Posters, 18 by 30 inches (45.7 by 76.2 cm)
Rule Page 2 Poster, 27 by 30 inches (68.6 by 76.2 cm)
Parts of Speech Poster Set of 7, 24 by 18 inches (61 by 45.7 cm)
Text Structure Poster Set of 4, 18 by 24 inches (45.7 by 61 cm)
Text Structure Poster Set of 4, for home use, 12 by 16 inches (30.5 by 40.6 cm)
Mental Action Posters, Set of 2, class size, 18 by 24 inches (45.7 by 61 cm)
Attributes of Fine Literature Poster, class size, 18 by 24 inches (45.7 by 61 cm)

For Students

For Each Student in Kindergarten
One six-sided No. 2 pencil and ⅝-inch (1.6-cm) lined paper
One 6-inch (15.2-cm) ruler
One primary spelling/vocabulary notebook, ⅝-inch (1.6-cm) lines, 34 leaves
One *McCall-Harby Test Lessons in Primary Reading*
One set of *Learning to Read and Loving It, Series 1 Leveled Readers* (see lists of titles in "Children's Literature: Recommendations," page 199)
Children's books (see recommended titles in "Children's Literature: Recommendations")

For Each Student in First Grade
One six-sided No. 2 pencil and ⅝-inch (1.6-cm) lined paper
One 6-inch (15.2-cm) ruler
One primary spelling/vocabulary notebook, ⅝-inch (1.6-cm) lines, 34 leaves
One *McCall-Harby Test Lessons in Primary Reading*
One set of *Reading and Loving It, Series 2 Leveled Readers*
Children's books (see "Children's Literature: Recommendations")

For Each Student in Second Grade
One six-sided No. 2 pencil and ⅝-inch (1.6-cm) lined paper
One 6-inch (15.2-cm) ruler
One primary spelling/vocabulary notebook, ⅝-inch (1.6-cm) lines, 34 leaves

One *McCall-Crabbs Standard Test Lessons in Reading, Book A*
Children's books (see "Children's Literature: Recommendations")

For Each Student in Third Grade and Above
One six-sided No. 2 pencil, one red pencil, and one 6-inch (15.2-cm) ruler
One intermediate spelling/vocabulary notebook, ⅜-inch (1.0-cm) lines, 50 leaves
One *McCall-Crabbs Standard Test Lessons in Reading, Book B, C, D, or E*
Children's books (see "Children's Literature: Recommendations")

References

Adams, M. J. 1990. *Beginnning to read: Thinking and learning about print.* A summary prepared by S. A. Stahl, J. Osborn, and F. Lehr. Champaign, Ill.: Office of Public Affairs/Office of Publications for the Center for the Study of Reading.

Adams, M. J., and M. Bruck. 1995. Resolving the "great debate." *American Educator* 19:7, 10–20.

Anderson, R. C., E. H. Hiebert, J. A. Scott, and I. A. Wilkinson. 1985. *Becoming a nation of readers: The report of the Commission on Reading.* Contract No. 400-83-0057. Washington, D.C.: National Institute of Education.

Auckerman, R. C. 1984. *Approaches to beginning reading.* 2nd ed. New York: Wiley.

Ball, E. W., and B. A. Blachman. 1991. Does phoneme awareness training in kindergarten make a difference in early word recognition and developmental spelling? *Reading Research Quarterly* 26:49–66.

Beck, I. L., and C. Juel. 1995. The role of decoding in learning to read. *American Educator* 19:8, 21–25.

Biemiller, A. J. 1970. The development of the use of graphic and contextual information as children learn to read. *Reading Research Quarterly* 6:75–96.

Byrne, B., and R. Fielding-Barnsley. 1993. Evaluation of a program to teach phonemic awareness to young children: A one-year follow-up. *Journal of Educational Psychology* 85:104–111.

Byrne, B., and R. Fielding-Barnsley. 1995. Evaluation of a program to teach phonemic awareness to young children: A two- and three-year follow-up and a new preschool trial. *Journal of Educational Psychology* 87:488–503.

Chall, J. S. 1983a. *Stages of reading development.* New York: McGraw-Hill.

———. 1983b. *Learning to read: The great debate.* 2nd ed. New York: McGraw-Hill.

———. 1996a. *Learning to read: The great debate.* 3rd ed. New York: Harcourt Brace College.

———. 1996b. *Stages of reading development.* 2nd ed. New York: Harcourt Brace College.

Collins, A., J. S. Brown, and S. E. Newman. 1989. Cognitive apprenticeship: Teaching the crafts of reading, writing, and mathematics. In L. B. Resnick, ed., *Knowing, learning, and instruction: Essays in honor of Robert Glaser.* Hillsdale, N.J.: Lawrence Erlbaum Associates.

Cramer, R. L. 1998. The spelling connection: Integrating reading, writing, and spelling instruction. New York: Guilford.

Dehaene, S. 2009. *Reading in the brain.* New York: Viking Penguin.

Ehri, L. C., and L. S. Wilce. 1987. Does learning to spell help beginners learn to read words? *Reading Research Quarterly* 22:47–63.

Ehri, L. C. 1997. Learning to read and learning to spell are one and the same, almost. In C. Perfetti, L. Rieben, and M. Fayol, eds., *Learning to spell: Research, theory, and practice across languages.* Mahwah, N.J.: Lawrence Erlbaum Associates.

Ehri, L. C. 2000. Learning to read and learning to spell: Two sides of a coin. *Topics in Language Disorders* 20:19–36.

Farnham-Diggory, S. 1987. From theory to practice in reading. Paper presented at the annual meeting of the Reading Reform Foundation, San Francisco, Calif. (July).

———. 1990. *Schooling*. Cambridge, Mass.: Harvard University Press.

———. 1992. *Cognitive processes in education*. New York: HarperCollins.

Fletcher, J. M., and G. R. Lyon. 1998. Reading: A research-based approach. In W. M. Evers, ed., *What's gone wrong in America's classrooms?* Stanford, Calif.: Hoover Institution.

Foorman, B. R., D. F. Francis, S. E. Shaywitz, B. A. Shaywitz, and J. M. Fletcher. 1997. The case for early reading intervention. In B. A. Blachman, ed., *Foundations of reading acquisition and dyslexia: Implications for early intervention*. Mahwah, N.J.: Lawrence Erlbaum Associates.

Fuchs, D., L. S. Fuchs, A. Thompson, S. Al Otaiba, L. Yen, N. J. Yang, et al. 2001. Exploring the importance of reading programs for kindergartners with disabilities in mainstream classrooms. *Exceptional Children* 68:295–311.

Gentry, F. R., and S. Graham. 2010. *Creating better readers and writers*. Columbus, Ohio: Saperstein Associates.

Goodman, K. S., and Y. Goodman. 1979. Learning to read is natural. In L. B. Resnick and P. A. Weaver, eds., *Theory and practice of early reading*. Vol. 1. Hillsdale, N.J.: Lawrence Erlbaum Associates.

Graham, S. 2009–2010. Want to improve children's writing? Don't neglect their handwriting. *American Educator*. Winter: 20–23, 26–27, 40.

Groff, P. 1977. The new anti-phonics. *Elementary School Journal* (March).

Hatcher, P. J., C. Hulme, and A.W. Ellis. 1994. Ameliorating early reading failure by integrating the teaching of reading and phonological skills: The phonological linkage hypothesis. *Child Development* 65:41–57.

Hoerl, M. F., and D. Koons. 1995. Effect of Spalding multisensory phonics instruction on the literacy skills of high school special education students. In C. W. McIntyre and J. P. Pickering, eds., *Clinical studies of multisensory structured language education*. Salem, Ore.: International Multisensory Structured Language Education Council.

Hohn, W. E., and L. C. Ehri. 1983. Do alphabet letters help prereaders acquire phonemic segmentation skill? *Journal of Educational Psychology* 75:752–762.

IDEA Act of 2004 Regulations: Part 300, A, 300.9 c, 1, i.

Jenkins, J. R., P. F. Vadasy, J. A. Peyton, and E. A. Sanders, 2003. Decodable text—Where to find it. *Reading Teacher* 57:185–189.

Kosanovich, M., K. Ladinsky, L. Nelson, and J. Torgesen. 2006. Differentiated instruction: Small group alternative lesson structures for *all* students. Available at http://www.fcrr.org/assessment/pdf/smallgroupalternativelessonstructures.pdf.

Liberman, I. Y., and A. Liberman. 1992. Whole language versus code emphasis: Underlying assumptions and their implications for reading instruction. In P. B. Gough, L. C. Ehri, and R. Treiman, eds., *Reading acquisition*. Hillsdale, N.J.: Lawrence Erlbaum Associates.

Lukens, R. J. 2003. *A critical handbook of children's literature*. Boston, Mass.: Allyn and Bacon.

Lyon, G. R. 2001. Statement before the House Committee on Education and the Workforce. Available at www.house.gov/ed workforce/hearings/oeri5400/lyons.h+m.

Lyon, G. R., J. M. Fletcher, S. E. Shaywitz, B. A. Shaywitz, J. K. Torgesen, F. B. Wood, A. Schulte, and R. Olson. 2001. Rethinking learning disabilities. In C. E. Finn, Jr., A. J. Rotherham, and C. R. Hokanson, Jr., eds., *Rethinking special education for a new century*, Progressive Policy Institute and Thomas B. Fordham Foundation.

Mehta, P. D., B. R. Foorman, L. Branum-Martin, and P. Taylor. 2005. Literacy as an unidimensional multilevel construct: Validation, sources of influence, and implications in a longitudinal study in grades 1 to 4. *Scientific Studies of Reading* 9:85–116.

Mitchell, R. 1979. *Less than words can say*. Boston, Mass.: Little, Brown.

Moats, L. C. 2000. *Speech to print: Language essentials for teachers*. Baltimore, Md.: Paul H. Brooks.

———. 2005/2006. How spelling supports reading. In *American Educator* Winter/Spring: 12–16, 20–22, 42.

North, M. E. 1991. The writing road to reading: From theory to practice. *Annals of Dyslexia* 42:110–123.

———. 1995. The effects of Spalding instruction on special education students. In C. W. McIntyre and J. P. Pickering, eds., *Clinical studies of multisensory structured language education*. Salem, Ore.: International Multisensory Structured Language Education Council.

Pinker, S. 1999. Foreword. In D. McGuinness, *Why our children can't read and what we can do about it*. New York: Simon and Schuster.

Potter, B. *The Tale of Peter Rabbit*. New York: Penguin.

Report of the National Reading Panel. 2000. National Institute of Health Publication No. 00-4769 (April).

Report of the National Reading Panel. Reports of the Subgroups. 2000. National Institute of Health Publication No. 00-4754 (April).

Rieben, L., and C. A. Perfetti. 1991. *Learning to read: Basic research and its implications*. Hillsdale, N.J.: Lawrence Erlbaum Associates.

Russell, W. F. 1984. *Classics to read aloud to your children*. New York: Crown. (Quoting H. C. Andersen, *The ugly duckling*, 13–18.)

Shanahan, T., K. Callison, C. Carriere, N. K. Duke, P. D. Pearson, C. Schatschneider, and J. Torgesen. 2010-4038 (Sept. 2010) *Improving reading comprehension in kindergarten through 3rd grade*. Washington, D.C.: Institute of Education Sciences, National Center for Education Evaluation and Regional Assistance.

Share, D., and K. Stanovich, 1995. Cognitive processes in early reading development: Accommodating individual differences into a model of acquisition. In J. Carlson, ed., *Issues in education: Contributions from education psychology* 1:1–57.

Shaywitz, S. 2003. *Overcoming dyslexia*. New York: Knopf.

Smith, C. L., and H. Tager-Flusberg. 1982. Metalinguistic awareness and language development. *Journal of Experimental Child Psychology* 34: 449–468.

Smith, F. 1971. *Understanding reading*. New York: Holt, Rinehart and Winston.

Snow, E., M. S. Burns, and P. Griffin, eds., 1998. *Preventing reading difficulties in young children*. Washington, D.C.: National Academy Press.

Snow, E., P. Griffin, and M. S. Burns, eds. 2005. *Knowledge to support the teaching of reading: Preparing teachers for a changing world*. San Francisco, Calif: Jossey-Bass.

Stanovich, K. E. 1986. Mathew effects in reading: Some consequences of individual differences in the acquisition of literacy. *Reading Research Quarterly* 21:360–407.

———. 1993. Does reading make you smarter? Literacy and the development of verbal intelligence. In H. Reese, ed., *Advances in child development and behavior*. San Diego, Calif.: Academic.

———. 1994. Romance and reality. *Reading Teacher* 4:280–290.

Treiman, R. 1985. Phonemic awareness and spelling: Children's judgments do not always agree with adults'. *Journal of Experimental Child Psychology* 39:182–201.

———. 1992. The role of intrasyllabic units in learning to read and spell. In P. B. Gough, L. C. Ehri, and R. Treiman, eds., *Reading acquisition*. Hillsdale, N.J.: Lawrence Erlbaum Associates.

———. 1993. *Beginning to spell: A study of first-grade children*. New York: Oxford University Press.

Treiman, R., and J. Baron. 1983. Phonemic-analysis training helps children benefit from spelling-sound rules. *Memory and Cognition* 11:382–389.

Uhry, J. K., and M. J. Shepherd. 1993. Segmentation/spelling instruction as part of a first-grade reading program: Effects on several measures of reading. *Reading Research Quarterly* 28:218–233.

Vellutino, F. R., and D. M. Scanlon. 1991. The effects of instructional bias on word identification. In L. Rieben and C. A. Perfetti, eds., *Learning to read: Basic research and its implications*. Hillsdale, N.J.: Lawrence Erlbaum Associates.

Vellutino, F. R., D. M. Scanlon, and M. S. Tanzman. 1994. Components of reading ability: Issues and problems in operationalizing word identification, phonological coding, and orthographic coding. In G. R. Lyon, ed., *Frames of reference for the assessment of learning disabilities: New views on measurement issues*. Baltimore, Md.: Paul H. Brooks.

Index

Page numbers in *italics* refer to illustrations.

ABOUT THE AUTHOR:

Romalda Spalding, 1899–1994

Romalda Spalding was a remarkably gifted teacher; but more than that, she was a remarkable woman. Finding that professional preparation was not adequate to the task of helping all students learn to read and write, she embarked on a path that ultimately led to instructing teachers across the globe.

In New York City in 1938, her search for a better way to teach language led her to the eminent neurologist Dr. Samuel T. Orton. Under Orton's direction, she taught students who found reading and writing difficult, and at his invitation, she attended his course for pediatricians at Columbia's College of Physicians and Surgeons at the New York Academy of Medicine. For two and a half years, Orton taught Mrs. Spalding principles of learning and specific tutoring techniques for struggling students. She learned from Orton that the method of teaching determines which pathways develop in the brain, and that every phonetic language develops from speech to letters representing speech sounds and then to words and sentences. She soon realized that these techniques, which worked so well with children having difficulty, also often prevented reading problems—a concept that is now validated by research.

"With a good phonics system, the student says the sound he hears, writes the letter or letters which represent it, and sees this representation as he reads it," Mrs. Spalding said. She understood that *how* spelling is taught is of great importance and that it should be "taught as scientifically as possible," from the spoken word to the written form. Applying Dr. Orton's principles, she developed her multisensory method of language arts instruction. His direction to her, "When a problem is presented, divide it into its component parts, build them sequentially, and talk about each part," guided her every step.

Mrs. Spalding's formal work with Dr. Orton ended in 1941, with the advent of the war and her Navy commander husband's assignment to Boston. However, she continued to perfect and expand on Orton's method while teaching children with language problems, working with physicians at Harvard Children's Hospital, and later serving as a consultant in reading to the superintendent of the Catholic schools in Hawaii.

Recent medical studies into the way the brain works and reading research validate principles of learning and instruction used by Orton. These principles, enriched by Mrs. Spalding's classroom experience and her intense study of how children learn, were incorporated in The Spalding Method.

In 1957, with her husband's help and encouragement, she put her knowledge and experience into her book, *The Writing Road to Reading*. She devoted the rest of her life to teaching her method to teachers and parents and to tutoring students of all ages. Many honors were accorded her in recognition of her contributions to literacy. Among these, she was awarded an honorary doctor of humane letters by Chaminade University of Honolulu in 1975. She received commendations from the Hawaii house and senate in 1990 for her dedication to excellence as a teacher and a teacher of teachers, and for the special honors accorded her efforts to improve reading and writing. She served as adviser to the International Montessori Society and on the Council of Advisors, Orton Dyslexia Society (now International Dyslexia Association) until her death. Thousands of teachers and tens of thousands of children have benefited from Mrs. Spalding's tireless dedication to literacy. We at Spalding Education International take pride in carrying her legacy forward.